Sexual Desire and Romantic Love in Shakespeare

Sexual Desire and Romantic Love in Shakespeare

'Rich in Will'

Joan Lord Hall

EDINBURGH
University Press

Edinburgh University Press is one of the leading university presses in the UK. We publish academic books and journals in our selected subject areas across the humanities and social sciences, combining cutting-edge scholarship with high editorial and production values to produce academic works of lasting importance. For more information visit our website: edinburghuniversitypress.com

© Joan Lord Hall, 2021,2023

Edinburgh University Press Ltd
The Tun – Holyrood Road
12(2f) Jackson's Entry
Edinburgh EH8 8PJ

First published in hardback by Edinburgh University Press 2021

Typeset in 10.5/13 Adobe Sabon by
Servis Filmsetting Ltd, Stockport, Cheshire

A CIP record for this book is available from the British Library

ISBN 978 1 4744 8856 3 (hardback)
ISBN 978 1 4744 88570 (paperback)
ISBN 978 1 4744 8858 7 (webready PDF)
ISBN 978 1 4744 8859 4 (epub)

The right of Joan Lord Hall to be identified as the author of this work has been asserted in accordance with the Copyright, Designs and Patents Act 1988, and the Copyright and Related Rights Regulations 2003 (SI No. 2498).

Contents

Acknowledgements	vii
Introduction	1
1. 'Will' and the Dark Side of Sexual Desire	13
2. Male Lust, Power and Rape	38
3. Lustful Women and Male Fantasies of Female Desire	66
4. Romantic Love and Sexual Desire: The Fickleness of Fancy, Eyes and Love's Mind	97
5. The Petrarchan Love Convention: Romance at Odds with Sexual Desire	124
6. Sex, Love and Paradigms of Marriage	155
7. Homoerotic Desire and Same-Sex Bonding: Challenges to Heterosexual Partnership?	181
8. 'The Buildings of My Fancy': Family Ties and Sexual Desire	216
Works Cited	252
Index	266

To the memory of Robert Roth-Nelson

Acknowledgements

Although I have now retired after many years of teaching Shakespeare, several former colleagues (scholars in the field) urged me on as the study progressed. My thanks go to Richard Dutton and Richard Wilson in the UK for their encouragement, and to Professor Emeritus Reg Saner from the University of Colorado, Boulder, who provided some useful pointers on early chapter drafts. Editor Nancy Mann skilfully suggested ways of streamlining some of the material, and Commissioning Editor Michelle Houston at Edinburgh University Press was particularly helpful in steering the work toward publication.

I am grateful to Emily Weller for suggesting the subject in the first place. Her spontaneous question 'Why don't you write a book about Shakespeare and sex?' inspired me to delve more deeply into the topic to develop a fresh scholarly perspective on it. Last, but not least, I remain indebted to my late partner Robert Roth-Nelson for being an astute reader who could gauge whether the study, as it progressed, might also be of interest to non-specialists. It is to his memory that this book is dedicated.

Introduction

The early years of the twenty-first century have seen a spate of books on Shakespeare's treatment of love and sexuality. The topic remains perennially fascinating. What distinguishes this study from earlier ones? It emphasises differences, as well as commonalities, between Shakespeare's treatment of sexual desire and romantic love that builds toward marriage, and our own assumptions about these matters. Today we no longer tend to drive a wedge between them, or automatically privilege romantic love above sexual pleasure. But Shakespeare was composing his plays and poems within a Christian culture that often polarised love and lust, setting spiritual aspiration against physical appetite, and this is reflected in much of his early work. His narrative poem *The Rape of Lucrece* is a case in point, while in *Venus and Adonis* the celibate Adonis insists on distinguishing sexual desire from love. Shakespeare's early modern audience would have known St Paul's Epistle to the Romans, where Paul reinforces the moral distinctions (spirit as pure, flesh as prone to evil) when he ponders 'we know that the law is spiritual' but 'I am carnal, sold under sin' (7:14). Church weddings conducted in Shakespeare's time echo this. The 'Solemnization of Matrimony', recited from the *Book of Common Prayer* (1559), advised that the 'honourable estate' of marriage (St Paul's term) should not be undertaken 'to satisfy men's carnal lusts and appetites'.

In the discourse of many of Shakespeare's contemporaries, spiritual love and carnal lust remain opposed to one another, much as the binaries of reason and passion do – reason being regarded as a God-given higher faculty while passion, especially sexual passion, partakes of the bestial side of human nature. As Shakespeare's own dramatic vision grows more complex, however, his plays increasingly challenge the orthodox moral views of his age. In deconstructing binary oppositions, much of his drama no longer reinforces what is so often a premise of the earlier work: a clear dichotomy between sexual gratification and a higher form of love that aspires to an enduring relationship.[1]

Certainly Shakespeare's comedies celebrate romantic love leading into marriage. At the same time, though, in refusing to downplay the libido that fuels this quest for life partnership, these plays critique any high-flown romantic ideal that bypasses a lover's physical needs. Shakespeare's poetic drama is frank about sexual desire, its varieties and vagaries. But since neither the term 'sex', referring to sexual activity, nor the broader topic of sexuality was current in Shakespeare's time, this desire was of course expressed through different modalities. When the dramatist uses the word 'sex' it refers to biological difference.[2] Miranda, speaking from her place on the very sparsely populated island of *The Tempest*, illustrates this when she admits 'I do not know / One of my sex' (3. 1. 48–9). Similarly the label 'homosexual', identifying a male who favours erotic relations between men, wasn't formulated until the nineteenth century, and no one in Shakespeare's day would have used the word 'homoerotic' to describe male-to-male sexual attraction. Yet such attractions obviously existed.

As for treating sexuality as a social and 'historical construct',[3] not until the late twentieth century did the topic of sexuality – a concept that the structuralist Michel Foucault has shown changes over time and varies according to culture[4] – become an integral part of many literary disciplines. Gender studies, queer theory,[5] post-Freudian and feminist approaches are all concerned with sexuality. While my own study does not adopt any one methodology, it incorporates modern psychological theories, especially from feminist critics, that illuminate patterns of behaviour, based on anxiety and distrust, demonstrated by many of Shakespeare's male characters in response to women. It's also a given of recent presentist criticism that we interpret the past through the lens of the present moment. Because the 'contemporary discursive practices, ideologies, and events that constitute us' inevitably determine what we are looking for in early modern texts, no truly objective reconstruction of what they signify is feasible.[6] But as a counterbalance to presentism, this study also recognises the work of cultural materialists, respecting plays as texts belonging to a particular historical era, grounded in the social and ideological assumptions of late sixteenth- and early seventeenth-century England.

Not surprisingly, our postmodern understanding of sexual desire and romantic love that aspires to marriage connects in several ways with Shakespeare's presentation of these phenomena. But the differences in how Shakespeare and his society approach sexual issues are important too. Not only did certain terms that we now use in categorising sexual desire not exist in early modern English, but many key words in Shakespeare's work contain different shades of meaning from those now in play. Early modern signifiers and their denotations and connotations – semantic subtleties in the plays that readers in the twenty-first century might easily miss – are where this study begins. I chose the subtitle 'Rich in Will' (taken from Sonnet 135) because 'will' in Shakespearean contexts often denotes sex drive or passion, a meaning that has more or less disappeared in modern discourse. In Shakespeare's work this meaning rivals the sense of will as inclination or resolve that remains current today. Even though it is involuntary, sexual arousal is wilful; it defies resolution or traditional willpower.

Shakespeare's contemporary, the theologian Richard Hooker, is careful to distinguish rational 'Will' – the human faculty that allows 'Reason and Understanding' to prescribe 'the thing desired' – from 'that inferior desire which we call appetite'.[7] While Hooker doesn't overtly equate sexual desire with 'appetite' or involuntary will, he suggests as much when he notes that 'affections', the 'sundry forms and fashions of Appetite', cannot choose but 'rise at the sight of some things'.[8] Discussing involuntary sexual desire, St Augustine more explicitly notes that whereas other limbs 'obediently serve the will', the sex organs, 'excited by lust', 'resist' rational willpower.[9] Instead of separating out meanings, Shakespeare is content to employ the rich ambiguity of the word 'will'. Within its dramatic context, 'will' can signify determination, involuntary desire, or both. What sounds like tautology, Claudius's lament that he cannot pray 'Though inclination be as sharp as will' (*Hamlet*, 3. 3. 39), is actually an admission that he wouldn't be able to offer sincere prayers even if his 'inclination' were as urgent ('sharp') as sexual desire ('will'). Sonnet 135, 'Whoever hath her wish, thou hast thy Will', more clearly exploits the semantic wealth of the word. Through outrageous wordplay, the poet Will aims to satisfy with his own 'Will in over-plus' a promiscuous mistress whose sexual will is also 'large and spacious'.

'Affection' is another seemingly innocuous word that has different layers of meaning for Shakespeare's contemporaries. For us it signifies fondness between friends or family members rather than erotic interest. But in the passage quoted above, Hooker associates 'affections' with appetite. In Shakespearean contexts, too, 'affection' often denotes sexual desire or passion, as when Mardian in *Antony and Cleopatra* claims to feel 'fierce affections' when he thinks of Mars and Venus consorting together (1. 5. 17). In *The Merchant of Venice* Solanio draws on the less charged meaning of the word when he speculates that the 'better part of [his] affections' would be focused on his ships were he a merchant adventurer like Antonio (1. 1. 16). We might surmise that 'affection' is used similarly when Antonio, saying farewell to Bassanio, is described as gripping his friend's hand 'with affection wondrous sensible' (2. 8. 48). But given the intense love for Bassanio that Antonio expresses in the trial scene, the audience may wonder if 'affection' here has crossed over from the fondness of friendship into sexual passion.

Indeed the meaning of 'friend' is similarly indeterminate in early modern contexts. Friends (as is the case today) can refer to individuals who share a close emotional bond without sexual intimacy, but 'friend' in Shakespeare may also denote 'lover'.[10] When Claudio in *Measure for Measure* has impregnated his fiancée we're told that he has 'got his friend with child' (1. 4. 29). Iago, insinuating that Cassio has become Desdemona's sexual partner, invites Othello to imagine his wife 'naked with her friend in bed' (*Othello*, 4. 1. 3). Conversely, being 'lovers' in a same-sex relationship, a term Cassius applies to himself and Brutus (*Julius Caesar*, 5. 1. 94), implied devotion between male friends rather than sexual intimacy. This slippage between the two signifiers, 'friend' and 'lover', indicates that Shakespeare's early modern period didn't always make a sharp distinction between sexual and non-sexual close relationships. Nor would devoted male friendship and 'same-sex erotic acts and desires' necessarily be 'mutually exclusive'.[11] Semantic fluidity also adds to the complexity of Shakespeare's sonnets that centre on the 'fair friend'. The sonneteer shares with this young man both *amicitia* – the idealised 'classically based conception of male friendship'[12] – and a passionate, intimate relationship.

More often, though, we find that Shakespeare's early narrative poems and plays before 1600 (and some of his work beyond) draw firmer distinctions between love and lust, idealistic romantic aspiration and blatant desire. From the perspective of twenty-first-century Western culture, where 'hook-ups' for purely sexual purposes are no longer regarded as sinful, it's easy to forget that Shakespeare's society still condemned Lust as one of the Seven Deadly Sins. The 'Solemnization of Matrimony' itself envisages marriage more as a 'remedy against sin', a way of containing 'carnal' desire, than a celebration of intimate sexual union. Certainly by the time Shakespeare is composing *Antony and Cleopatra* (1606), his drama no longer sets sexual desire at odds with romantic or marital love. But the case is different in Shakespeare's dark comedies (*All's Well that Ends Well*, *Troilus and Cressida* and *Measure for Measure*), written between 1601 and 1604. These experimental, hard-to-categorise plays reinforce a troubling division between love and lust, exploring what happens when 'will' as sex drive displaces other kinds of love. They show how physical desire, divorced from romantic idealism, becomes socially disruptive, refusing to be contained within the confines of marriage. This is the main theme of Chapter 1, ' "Will" and the Dark Side of Sexual Desire'. Chapter 2, 'Male Lust, Power and Rape', continues to examine the dark side of Eros, first as Shakespeare represents it in the poem *The Rape of Lucrece* and then as he dramatises rape or threatened rape in plays across the canon. The physical violation of women, as our culture now acknowledges and as Shakespeare's treatment of rape demonstrates, is at least as much a misogynistic assertion of male power as the satisfaction of a physical urge. Also represented in Shakespeare's work is how male bonding or rivalry between men can drive this conquest of women.

Chapter 3, 'Lustful Women and Male Fantasies of Female Desire', explores how Shakespeare's work draws on the stereotypes of his age to depict female sexuality. In the early history plays and throughout the tragedies, powerful women are often demonised as unrestrained in their sexual needs; they defy the conventional image of females in the early modern period as discreet in their conduct, obedient to the male, and flawlessly chaste. As feminist critics have noted, the hidden nature of female erotic desire proves particularly threatening to a patriarchal society; it provokes male anxiety. Shakespeare's comedies are full of references to the cuckold and his horns (invisible only to him), branding him as a despised husband or lover whose partner has been unfaithful to him. Males' comic jests about cuckoldry deflect their fear of being degraded by rampant female sexuality or betrayed if they marry. For although a husband in Shakespeare's time can impose his authority in the household, even dominate his wife physically, he can never completely control the subtle power that she exerts through her sexual attractiveness. Consequently male fantasies of women's lust, developed in Shakespeare's tragedies and tragicomedies, tend to be grotesquely exaggerated.

Yet in many instances, as noted in Chapter 3, Shakespeare resists simplistic representations of women's sexuality. He creates a number of female characters – comic heroines such as Beatrice and Rosalind, or Juliet and Desdemona in the tragedies – who steer a middle course, mediating between the opposing stereotypes of lustful whore and icon of chastity. Moreover women in the underclass, such as the Hostess of the tavern-brothel in the *Henry IV* plays, are portrayed sympathetically. They make their living by contravening the double standard (chastity for women, sexual liberty for men) but do so without exploiting others or being licentious themselves. And Cleopatra, excoriated by the Romans as a 'whore' (*Antony and Cleopatra*, 3. 6. 67), succeeds in channelling her erotic power into a union with Antony that triumphantly combines 'will' (passion) with a romantic ideal. Through his representation of this extraordinary female, who envisages her sensual death as a gateway to eternal marriage with Antony, Shakespeare deconstructs the old binaries of lust and love.

Love, even if restricted to the category of romantic love, is notoriously difficult to define, much more so than physical lust. By the nineteenth century romantic love was often understood as a passionate desire for 'total merging between lover and beloved'.[13] The early modern period, though, in its literary treatment of romantic love, still drew on the chivalric code of courtly love established in the troubadour poetry of the Middle Ages,[14] paying almost religious homage to an idealised female who is desirable but (initially, at least) aloof. Renaissance romantic comedy follows a similar pattern: an aristocratic male reverentially courts a chaste female in the hope that she will return his love. This is the focus of Shakespeare's middle comedies, which dramatise the experience of falling in love followed by a testing of the suitor's devotion through various obstacles until he finally attains the intimacy of marriage with his beloved. Certainly the romantic lover's idealisation of his lady as both beautiful and chaste turns on its head the misogynist conviction that women secretly yearn to be sexually promiscuous. But once romantic love is positioned as the polar opposite of lust, how much sexual passion can it accommodate?[15] While Neo-Platonic and Petrarchan conventions of love don't entirely sublimate libido – the lover's appreciation of female beauty can become a refined form of Eros[16] – both downplay sexual desire or 'will'. The Petrarchan tradition in particular focuses on the emotional anguish of the courtly lover whose desire, at least temporarily, must be repressed.

Eyes and the phenomenon of love at first sight both feature prominently in courtly wooing. Chapter 4, 'Romantic Love and Sexual Desire: The Fickleness of Fancy, Eyes and Love's Mind', discusses Shakespeare's scepticism, in his early comedies, about fickle 'fancy': romantic infatuation based on a male's response to his lady's beautiful appearance. Because *A Midsummer Night's Dream* and *Love's Labour's Lost* move toward the commitment of marriage, they question whether physical attraction (what the eyes register) can lay the groundwork for a lasting relationship or, conversely, whether a love so idealised that it fails to acknowledge the realities of sexual desire can survive. The juice from the love-in-idleness flower in *A Midsummer Night's Dream* represents just how arbitrary desire can be. Placed on the eyes of the sleeping lovers, it explodes the whole notion of 'true love' at 'first sight'. Under the influence of the magic drug, Titania falls in love with the first creature she sees – Bottom in the guise of an ass – while Lysander and Demetrius switch their former allegiances as soon as they awake and see only the beauty of Helena. In *Love's Labour's Lost* Shakespeare critiques the main premise of Neo-Platonic love: the idea that aesthetic appreciation of the mistress's loveliness, especially her eyes, grants the lover access to a Platonic form not only of perfect beauty but of goodness and spiritual truth too. This ideal, pursued by the male aristocrats in the court of Navarre through courtly wooing and heightened rhetoric, fails to square with the urgency of sexual desire.

Taking a practical approach to love, Shakespeare mocks the idea, inherent in Petrarchism, that 'passion means suffering'.[17] Chapter 5, 'The Petrarchan Love Convention: Romance at Odds with Sexual Desire', analyses the playwright's ironic stance on excessive Petrarchan posturing and the pretentious, hyperbolic imagery in which it is usually couched. The plots of his romantic comedies feature high-born lovers, well versed in the rhetoric of desire. The diverse audience who came to see these plays at the Globe Theatre was not a predominantly courtly one, however. Catering to middle- and working-class spectators, down-to-earth and likely to shun extravagant courtship,[18] Shakespeare chose to scrutinise Petrarchan conventions in some detail. It is true that despite some undercutting of these conventions, as when Mercutio counterpoints Romeo's soaringly romantic poetry with bawdy wordplay, neither *Romeo and Juliet* nor Shakespeare's middle comedies fully demolish the ideal of the worshipful lover celebrating his lady's radiant beauty. Nor do they dismiss the role of the imagination in helping to create and sustain this love. They nevertheless question whether ungrounded adoration is compatible with a lasting day-to-day relationship, even while emphasising that sexual fulfilment cannot be endlessly deferred. Since during the early modern era most women needed to marry for economic reasons, we might expect Shakespeare's females to be fully invested in the goal of romantic love leading to monogamous marriage. In the middle comedies, though, it is usually the men who are infatuated romantics. The women they woo are more grounded, able to educate their suitors about the realities of love and the challenges of marriage. The cross-dressers Rosalind and Viola (in *As You Like It* and *Twelfth Night*) take on this role, puncturing Petrarchan illusions about how long the romance of love is likely to survive after the wedding.

Shakespeare, to be sure, concentrates more on the challenges of courtship than on whether idealised love can segue into the supposedly 'happy ever after' phase following the marriage ceremony. Several of his plays nevertheless project what post-wedding difficulties may ensue. Chapter 6, 'Sex, Love and Paradigms of Marriage', explores this. Even if the match is rooted in love and not mainly a family arrangement based on pragmatic considerations of property and dowry, 'infatuation' proves 'no basis for continued cohabitation'; inevitably the heady romance of courtship initiated by a male lover must give way to the 'discipline ... mutual respect and great forbearance' required of the marital tie.[19] In fact marriage in the early modern period projected a workable partnership based on friendship rather than romantic love or sexual passion.[20] At best a woman could aspire to the Protestant ideal of a 'companionate' marriage, a partnership in which spouses shared duties and welcomed sexual intimacy. Nevertheless this model, while promoting some equality between married partners, didn't truly displace the older patriarchal paradigm of marriage which ultimately granted a husband authority over his wife. No wonder, then, that Shakespeare presents challenges to marital happiness – whether they stem from the patriarchal assumption that a female should curb her own independence and remain subordinate to the male (as explored in *The Taming of the Shrew* and *A Comedy of Errors*), or from the anxious husband's fears over his wife's possible infidelity, which often leads to corrosive sexual jealousy. At the same time, Shakespeare offers an unusual solution. He posits that a union combining physical and spiritual love, the 'one flesh' of marriage that still upholds the individuality of both partners, might be viable; it emerges in the unconventional pairing of Antony and Cleopatra.

Antony and Cleopatra depicts a triumphant partnership that makes no attempt to disentangle love and lust; ironically, though, the lovers can celebrate their marriage only through death. And given how many of Shakespeare's plays explore the fracturing of heterosexual relationships through sexual jealousy, or shifting loyalties resulting from the fickleness of desire, they cannot be said to guarantee lasting happiness for lovers. Although Stanley Wells contends that Shakespeare is 'the greatest celebrant of heterosexual love',[21] this remains open to question. Rivalling the ideal of romantic love between a man and a woman, with its expectation of successful, happy marriage, are same-sex relations.

Chapter 7, 'Homoerotic Desire and Same-Sex Bonding: Challenges to Heterosexual Partnership?', covers this issue. With same-sex marriage now legalised in much of the Western world, our twenty-first century is culturally attuned to gay, bisexual and now transgender expressions of desire. Certainly the hetero-normative narrative is less dominant now than it was in Shakespeare's age. But Shakespeare's work also does much to complicate this narrative. His sonnets celebrate the narrator's love and erotic desire for his 'master-mistress', setting male-male passion alongside the poet's sexual entanglement with a 'dark' female. The dramatic content of Shakespeare's romantic comedies also sensitively draws on a spectrum of erotic desire that broadens beyond traditional male-female attraction. What's more, the theatre of the late Renaissance, with its all-male actors, provided an ideal forum in which to explore this. The convention by which boy actors represent young women (who then, as in *As You Like It* and *Twelfth Night*, re-adopt male personas) not only unfixes conventional gender distinctions but, as Jean E. Howard points out, generates 'conditions of erotic volatility in which desire' and sexual 'will' could 'flow in many and often contradictory directions'.[22] In Shakespeare's drama, too, there's a fine line between homosocial bonds – male camaraderie among soldiers, for instance – and homoerotic attraction, the kind of sexual 'will' that Antonio clearly feels for Sebastian in *Twelfth Night*. Strong, even passionate female friendships also emerge in Shakespeare's comedies. All this raises the question: can such intense same-sex relationships be compatible with the traditional marriages to which the genre of romantic comedy inexorably leads?

Even a family unit may be threatened from within by sexual desire. The firmly established boundaries that protect family members from complete intimacy become unstable when ties of love between parents and children or brothers and sisters turn romantic or sexual. Several of Shakespeare's plays touch on what Freud postulated as inevitable – erotic attraction between kin, even though this is usually repressed (both consciously and socially) as individuals move toward exogamous unions outside the family circle. In Shakespeare's plays such attraction remains latent. With the exception of reported forbidden love between father and daughter at the opening of *Pericles*, the 'will' of incestuous desire is neither directly voiced nor fully realised within the playwright's work. Nevertheless, such desire appears to be at the root of King Lear's need to keep Cordelia close to him, and Hamlet's anguish at his mother's remarriage; it forms part of the bond between Volumnia and her son Coriolanus. Erotic interest also colours several of the brother-sister relationships in Shakespeare's plays, especially those between Laertes and Ophelia in *Hamlet* and (more subtly) between Octavius and his sibling Octavia in *Antony and Cleopatra*. Such intense relationships rival exogamous ones. Finally, the late romances, in particular *The Tempest*, raise the spectre of father-daughter incest only to lay it to rest, as the action of these plays moves to restore family unity and succession through uniting royal children in wedlock. Shakespeare's nuanced dramatisation of the incest motif, and how desire generated within the family unit may block a child's progress toward conventional marriage, is the topic of the eighth and final chapter of this study, ' "The Buildings of My Fancy": Family Ties and Sexual Desire'.

Notes

1. Shakespeare's plays progressively challenge the opposition between sexual desire and a rarefied, at times spiritual response to female beauty, as his dramatic work moves toward integrating the two. This traditional schism is evident in the *Roman de la Rose* (1237–80), the fourteenth-century allegory that explores courtly love in two polarised sections. In the first part Guillaume de Lorris presents the Rose as 'love of the ideal woman', to be protected against defilement, while the second part, by Jean de Meung, 'looks upon the Rose as no more than sensual pleasure' (Denis de Rougement, *Love in the Western World*, p. 176).
2. Shakespeare uses the noun 'gender' three times in his plays but not in the sense that sociologists now use it – to refer to the culturally determined roles that males and females perform, as opposed to their biologically determined sexual difference. When Evans chastises Mistress Quickly for confusing the 'cases and numbers of the genders' (*The Merry Wives of Windsor*, 4. 1. 73), he is making a grammatical distinction. In other cases the noun 'gender' in Shakespeare refers to 'kind, sort, class' (sense 1 in the OED, now obsolete), as when Iago speaks of planting 'one gender of herbs' as opposed to 'many' (*Othello*, 1. 3. 323–4). All citations of Shakespeare's plays in this volume are from G. Blakemore Evans's *The Riverside Shakespeare* (1997).
3. See Michel Foucault, *The History of Sexuality: An Introduction*, vol. 1, p. 105. Post-Freudian feminists such as Ann Rosalind Jones, in 'Writing the Body: Toward an Understanding of *l'Écriture Féminine*', have disputed the idea that an individual possesses an 'essential stratum of sexuality'. Instead, they maintain, sexuality develops through early family interactions, as 'the sexed family imprints itself on the child's sense of herself as a sexed being' (pp. 367–8). Anthony Giddens, *The Transformation of Intimacy: Sexuality, Love and Eroticism in Modern Societies*, offers a less deterministic view. He contends that following the sexual revolution of the 1960s we understand 'sexuality' not simply as a social construct 'operating within fields of power' (p. 23) but as 'malleable, open to being shaped in diverse ways, and a potential "property" of the individual' (p. 27).
4. In *The History of Sexuality*, Foucault argues that whereas by the eighteenth century 'useful and public discourses' on sexual practices proliferated as a means of regulating sexual behaviour in Western society, the early seventeenth century (Shakespeare's era) maintained a certain 'frankness' about sexual practices and a 'tolerant familiarity with the illicit' (p. 3). As noted above, this was surely more evident within potentially subversive dramatic scripts than in the moral discourse of the time.
5. The 'main object of queer literary criticism' (relating to Shakespeare's work) has recently been described by Goran Stanivukovic, in the introduction to *Queer Shakespeare: Desire and Sexuality*, as 'the querying of the sexual binaries of homo- and heterosexuality' when it comes to defining desire and sexuality in the early modern period (p. 15).
6. Evelyn Gajowski, 'The Presence of the Past', p. 6. Recognising that we are living in a post-Freudian age and using some of Freud's theories to inter-

7. Richard Hooker, *Of the Laws of Ecclesiastical Polity* (1593), vol. 1, bk. 1, ch. 7, p. 170. Sir Philip Sidney, *The Defence of Poesy* (1595), likewise contrasts 'infected will' (base appetite) from 'erected wit': the rational power that strives toward 'perfection' (p. 109).
8. Hooker, *Of the Laws of Ecclesiastical Polity*, p. 170.
9. Augustine, *The City of God*, bk. 14, ch. 23, p. 471.
10. Paul Hammond, *Figuring Sex between Men from Shakespeare to Rochester*, explores how in this period the 'semantic field of the word "lover" overlaps to a considerable degree with that of "friend"' (pp. 18–21; p. 19). Jeffrey Masten, *Queer Philologies: Sex, Language, and Affect in Shakespeare's Time*, suggests 'one who loves' as the appropriate gloss for *friend* in early modern contexts (p. 226).
11. Marie H. Loughlin (ed.), *Same-Sex Desire in Early Modern England, 1550–1735*, p. 5.
12. Ibid. p. 4. The idea of perfect unity between two male friends was promoted by Cicero's *De Amicitia*, a text widely read in the Renaissance.
13. See Irving Singer, 'The Concept of Romantic Love', in *The Nature of Love, Vol. 2: Courtly and Romantic*, p. 290.
14. In *The Allegory of Love*, C. S. Lewis notes that the literature of courtly love, which first took shape in Provence at the end of the eleventh century, is characterised by 'Humility, Courtesy, Adultery, and the Religion of Love' (p. 2). Within this convention a knight sought to win favours from a married woman above him in rank. Because the plots of Shakespeare's romantic comedies drive toward marriage, adultery is not part of the mix. The other three components of courtly love do, however, become a staple of his plays.
15. Giddens, in *The Transformation of Intimacy*, ignores the subject matter of early modern sonnet sequences and Shakespeare's romantic comedies when he asserts that 'the rise of romantic love more or less coincided with the emergence of the novel'. Giddens finds within that nineteenth-century framework a tendency to separate romantic love 'quite sharply from the sexual/erotic component'. In fact his conclusion that in these 'romantic love attachments, the element of sublime love tends to predominate over that of sexual ardour' (p. 40) also applies to much Renaissance literature.
16. Jean H. Hagstrum, *Esteem Enlivened by Desire: The Couple from Homer to Shakespeare*, helpfully divides the 'complex, multilayered concept of love' into several categories. I follow the author in distinguishing libido (the sexual urge) from Eros, which Hagstrum defines as 'acculturated libido', or 'the absorption of sexual impulse into art and thought' (p. 10, p. 13).
17. Denis de Rougement, *Love in the Western World*, rather narrowly defines romance as 'suffering' that 'only truly flourishes where love is fatal' (p. 15).
18. Juliet Dusinberre, *Shakespeare and the Nature of Women*, notes how middle-class audiences in the public playhouses would be likely to endorse the Puritan ideal, which grants to 'chaste marriage' an 'equal spiritual prestige' to that of celibacy (p. 3). Presumably these audiences would be in tune with plays that moved toward this goal rather than with the promotion of

ideas, such as in the idealised Petrarchan treatment of love, that were more 'confined to the circle of the court' (p. 2).
19. Germaine Greer, 'The Middle-Class Myth of Love and Marriage', in *The Female Eunuch*, p. 209.
20. Hagstrum, *Esteem Enlivened by Desire*, concedes that '*Love vs. lust* was indeed a deep and wide obsession' during the Renaissance, but finds that 'the most persistent contrast may well be the one between friendship and love' (p. xiv). This is relevant both to how Shakespeare's age perceived marriage and to how several of Shakespeare's plays expose potential rivalry between male friendship and heterosexual love.
21. Stanley Wells, *Looking for Sex in Shakespeare*, p. 68. Wells nevertheless finds that both Shakespeare's homoerotic sonnets and his dramatic treatment of 'men loving men' (chapter 3) offer more interesting material for analysis than do the heterosexual relationships in Shakespeare's plays.
22. Jean E. Howard, 'Sex and Social Conflict: The Erotics of *The Roaring Girl*', p. 173.

Chapter 1

'Will' and the Dark Side of Sexual Desire

It is a given that Shakespeare's plays, the comedies at least, celebrate love and romance, but they do not ignore the dark side of sexual desire. This is where 'Rich in Will' begins. The term 'sexual desire' itself is relatively modern, for while the noun 'desire' crops up frequently in the lexicon of the plays, it is never explicitly paired with 'sexual'. In fact the use of the adjective 'sexual', as in 'sexual intercourse', dates only from the last two hundred years or so; the first instance cited by the *Oxford English Dictionary* (*OED*) comes in 1799.[1] And when Shakespeare uses the word 'sex' it refers not to the union of lovers but to the distinction between male and female. Thus Angelo in *Measure for Measure* nastily draws on the 'testimony' of Isabella's own 'sex' (that is, her biological difference) to urge her to 'be' a 'woman' by doing what he thinks a female is supposed to do: give her body sexually to a man (2. 4. 134–5).

Instead, words that in our own age are relatively free from sexual connotations – 'sense', 'blood', 'affection(s)' and, especially, 'will' – in Shakespeare's time contained a secondary meaning of sexual desire to which his audience would be attuned. We know that for Shakespeare's contemporaries the word 'blood' not only denoted a bodily fluid that carried 'vital spirits'[2] but often referred to sexual passion.[3] So when the poet defends his 'sportive blood' against the judgement of others in Sonnet 121 – ''Tis better to be vile than vile esteemed' – he is referring to sexual 'pleasure' (6, 3). In the twenty-first century the word 'affection' denotes 'fond or tender feeling' (*Webster's New World Dictionary*), much milder than what is cited by the *OED* as the now obsolete sense 3 of the noun: 'Feeling as opposed to reason; passion, lust.' When the Authorised Version of the King James Bible (1611) replaced the original phrase 'shameful lusts' in Romans 1: 26 with 'vile affections', the new version, which reads 'For this cause God gave them up to vile affections', would have conveyed to Shakespeare's contemporaries that meaning of lust or passion, in this case manifested through 'shameful' sexual practices. In the Trojan debate scene in *Troilus and Cressida*, Hector also uses 'affection' in a sexual sense. Privileging a husband's rights of ownership (which he calls a 'law / Of nature') above Paris's lustful theft of Helen, Hector argues that if a marriage is 'corrupted through affection' – threatened by sexual passion from the outside – then the adulterer's 'raging appetites' can be curbed and punished by social laws. Only impotent husbands, those with 'benumbed wills', would endorse a wife's straying (2. 2. 175–81).

Examples of the older meaning of affection/affections abound in *Much Ado about Nothing*. Benedict's friends trick him into thinking that Beatrice has fallen madly in love with him by making sure that he overhears the sexually charged word 'affection' three times within about twenty lines (2. 3. 100–1, 115, 123); meanwhile Leonato, collaborating with Don Pedro's plan to 'bring' the couple into 'a mountain of affection' with each other (2. 1. 367), underlines how his niece loves Benedict with an 'enraged affection' or 'passion' (2. 3. 100–1, 105). Duly primed to believe that Beatrice's 'affections have their full bent' (223), Benedict resolves in soliloquy to be 'horribly in love with her' (235). This is just before Beatrice herself enters to announce that dinner is served. Theatregoers would laugh when Benedict ponders Beatrice's insouciant words 'Against my will I am sent to bid you come into dinner'. The most obvious meaning is that Beatrice, indifferent to Benedict, can hardly be bothered to come and tell him that the meal is ready. But by interpreting 'against' in its secondary meaning of 'in expectation of'[4] rather than 'contrary to', Benedict can gleefully conclude that 'there's a double meaning in that' (257–9). He assumes, to his own advantage, that rather than being disinclined to call him in to dinner, Beatrice anticipates gratifying her 'will' or desire by enjoying his presence at table.

Readers of Shakespeare are most acquainted with sexual 'will' as it appears in Sonnet 135. Here Shakespeare expands the ribald meanings of the word while drawing on the abbreviation of his first name, italicised as *Will* in the 1609 Quarto:

Whoever hath her wish, thou hast thy *Will*,
And *Will* to boot, and *Will* in overplus;
More than enough am I that vex thee still,
To thy sweet will making addition thus.
Wilt thou, whose will is large and spacious,
Not once vouchsafe to hide my will in thine?
Shall will in others seem right gracious,
And in my will no fair acceptance shine?
The sea, all water, yet receives rain still,
And in abundance addeth to his store,
So thou being rich in *Will* add to thy *Will*

One will of thine to make thy large *Will* more.
Let no unkind, no fair beseechers kill;
Think all but one, and in me that one *Will*.

The poem, as Stanley Wells points out, is an outrageous piece of double entendre.[5] The speaker manages simultaneously to disparage the mistress's promiscuity (her will, including the sense of female genitalia as well as carnal desire, is 'large and spacious') and to suggest that he finds the 'abundance' of her promiscuous desire arousing.[6] As her lover, *Will* welcomes the way that this female is able to increase his sexual appetite and phallic power ('make thy large *Will* more') by simultaneously satisfying her own desires (becoming 'rich in *Will*/ will'). Shakespeare puns on 'will' in a similar way, as sexual desire and as his own name, in the more serious Sonnet 57, where he positions himself as his male friend's 'slave'. In the clinching couplet the speaker admits that 'So true a fool is love, that in your *Will*, / (Though you do anything), he thinks no ill'.

Sonnet 135 teasingly accepts, even celebrates, the sexual drive and its satisfactions. But in Shakespeare's plays the signifier 'will', though less foregrounded, is equally important in determining the range of meanings in the dramatic text. Often sexual 'will' or 'affection', what Thomas Wright in *The Passions of the Mind in General* (1601) calls 'Passions and Affections' that human beings have in common with 'beasts',[7] is set against 'grace', since our fallen nature cannot be transcended without divine help. As Berowne observes in *Love's Labour's Lost*:

> every man with his affects [passions] is born,
> Not by might mast'red, but by special grace. (1.1. 151–2)

Friar Lawrence in *Romeo and Juliet*, collecting herbs for medicinal purposes, points out a similar polarity – that the same flower can be both poisonous and beneficial. He applies this dictum to mankind: 'Two such opposed kings encamp them still / In man as well as herbs, grace and rude will' (2. 3. 27–8). With 'rude' the Friar clearly tilts the meaning of 'will' away from conscious intention and into unrestrained sexual desire. Angelo in *Measure for Measure*, who feels vanquished by the 'deed' of lust, laments that 'Alack, when once our grace we have forgot, / Nothing goes right—we would, and we would not' (4. 4. 33–4).

If not offset by 'grace', 'will' is frequently set against judgement or reason – the rational part of the soul that ideally counterbalances a person's animal nature.[8] As Sonnet 151 puts it, the body is always inclined to rebel against the 'nobler part' or soul. The poet confirms how, given permission by the soul to love, his 'gross' body and phallus comply;

'flesh stays no further reason' but moves into lustful mode, 'rising' at the very 'name' of his lover:

> I do betray
> My nobler part to my gross body's treason;
> My soul doth tell my body that he may
> Triumph in love; flesh stays no further reason,
> But rising at thy name doth point out thee
> As his triumphant prize ... (5–10)

The phonemic similarity between 'reason' and 'rising' (penile erection) reinforces the relentless displacing of rational judgement by sexual desire. Lust, like youthful rebellion, resembles 'oil and fire / Too strong for reason's force' (*All's Well that Ends Well*, 5. 3. 7). The Roman Antony, expected to exert self-control as a military leader, is rebuked by his comrade Enobarbus for making his 'will / Lord of his reason' by abjectly following his lover Cleopatra out of the Battle of Actium. To his shame, the 'itch of his affection' (sexual desire) has 'nick'd his captainship' (*Antony and Cleopatra*, 3. 13. 3–4, 7–8). Meanwhile Cleopatra, a female who embodies the sensuality of Egypt, wonders if the eunuch Mardian has 'affections' (1. 5. 12) and jokes that his 'will' comes up 'too short' (2. 5. 8).

Iago, too, has pertinent things to say about love and 'will' in *Othello*. Counselling the love-sick Roderigo, Iago insists that 'If the [beam] of our lives had not one scale of reason to poise against another of sensuality, the blood and baseness of our natures would conduct us to most prepost'rous conclusions' (1. 3. 326–9). On the face of it he is advocating rational self-determination, as he does in the gardening analogy that precedes this: 'Our bodies are our gardens, to the which our wills are gardeners' (320–1). And when he goes on to describe love as 'merely a lust of the blood and a permission of the will' (334–5), he could be using 'will' as conscious intention, emphasising that lustful impulses can be controlled by willpower. But the line also makes sense if 'blood' and 'will' are taken not as contrasts but as equivalent in meaning, in which case Iago (himself a victim of irrational feelings beyond his control) is actually undermining any assurance that passion can be deliberately chosen or consciously renounced. To the contrary, he is proposing that so-called 'love' is entirely dependent on sexual desire, since only desire or 'will' can permit or enable it.

Iago's cynical view, that the state of being in love represents nothing more than 'raging motions' and 'carnal stings' (330–1), is furthered by his observation, a few lines later, that Othello will tire of Desdemona sexually because 'These Moors are changeable in their wills' (346–7).

Later he suggests that Desdemona revealed a 'will most rank' in choosing to marry a black man (3. 3. 232). Infected by Iago, Othello is rapidly persuaded that Desdemona's deep attachment to him – a spiritual love, in which her 'heart's subdu'd / Even to the very quality of [her] lord' (1. 3. 250-1) – has been replaced by 'stol'n hours of lust' with Cassio (3. 3. 338). Ironically, Cassio is the one character in this play who, by virtue of holding polarised views of women, maintains a strict boundary between romantic adoration and crude desire. Refusing to take the bait when Iago comments that Othello's new wife is a woman 'full of game' whose eye 'sounds a parley to provocation', Cassio insists that Desdemona is perfectly chaste – a 'delicate creature' with 'right modest' eyes (2. 3. 19-25). While Desdemona is an object of worship for Cassio, 'a maid / That paragons description and wild fame' (2. 1. 61-2), he uses Bianca, a woman lower down the social scale, to satisfy his sexual needs, his 'will' and 'carnal stings'.

Shakespeare explores the seamier side of 'will', or what A. P. Rossiter calls 'lust', or a 'pointed absence of normal sexual love',[9] most fully in the problematic comedies *All's Well that Ends Well*, *Troilus and Cressida* and, especially, *Measure for Measure* – plays composed between 1601 and 1604, close in time to the creation of cynical Iago in *Othello*. In all three plays the reiteration of key signifiers, centring on 'will', alerts the audience to a major theme: how the male's urgent need for sexual gratification, impervious to moral and social restraints, displaces romantic attachment. Instead of being loved for their singular qualities, women are exploited for their erotic value. In *All's Well that Ends Well* Bertram is wedded to Helena, but his desire for the virgin Diana when he is soldiering in France overrides any commitment to forge a viable marriage with his wife. It prompts him to give away his heirloom ring to 'buy his will' (3. 7. 27), or to 'have his will' of the French maid, as a Victorian novel might put it. The Second Lord, unaware that Helena and not Diana is satisfying Bertram in bed, comments crudely on how the 'lascivious' youth Bertram 'fleshes his will' in the 'spoil' of Diana's 'honor' (4. 3. 300, 16-17). The deputy governor Angelo in *Measure for Measure* is so overwhelmed by sexual need for Isabella, his desire for this novitiate nun to yield her 'body' to his 'will', that he abandons his social duty to administer the law consistently (2. 4. 164).

On the face of it Troilus, unlike either Bertram or Angelo, appears to be a dedicated lover. But his romantic idealism is always shot through with sensuality. Troilus reveals the primacy of will as sexual desire not only in his love affair with Cressida but in the Trojans' intellectual debate on the true meaning of 'value'. In Act 2, where his compatriots discuss giving back tarnished Helen to the Greeks, Troilus stands against this strategy for ending the Trojan War, arguing for loyalty to what is actually a crime: Paris's theft of Menelaus's wife, Helen. The analogy that Troilus develops is telling. Although Hector has offered a warning – the 'will' that 'affects' something lacking true 'merit' simply 'dotes' (2. 2. 58–60) – Troilus makes it clear that his choice of a permanent partner would be determined by sexual interest ('will'), corroborated by his senses ('eyes and ears') rather than supported by reason or 'judgment':

> I take to-day a wife, and my election
> Is led on in the conduct of my will,
> My will enkindled by mine eyes and ears,
> Two traded pilots 'twixt the dangerous [shores]
> Of will and judgment: how may I avoid,
> (Although my will distastes what it elected)
> The wife I chose? (2. 2. 61–7)

The pairing of 'will' with 'enkindled' and 'distastes' propels the meaning of the word from conscious intention into sexual appetite. No wonder Hector asks Troilus whether his 'blood' (115) is

> So madly hot that no discourse of reason,
> Nor fear of bad success in a bad cause,
> Can qualify the same? (116–18)

He goes on to rebuke both Paris and Troilus for providing fallacious 'reasons' that owe more to 'the hot passion of distempered blood' than to objective judgement on the issue of 'right and wrong' (168–71). Ironically, it is Troilus's horrifying experience of seeing Cressida give herself to Diomedes in Act 5 that finally makes him distrust 'th' attest of eyes and ears' (5. 2. 122) – the physical senses that in the debate scene he relies on as 'pilots' to mediate between 'will' and 'judgment'. Incredulous at the infidelity he now witnesses, Troilus wonders if the 'organs' of sight and hearing in fact are deceptive, 'created only to calumniate' or defame Cressida (123–4).

In his dealings with Cressida, despite claiming that he possesses a 'winnowed purity in love' (3. 2. 167), Troilus again reveals an excess of sexual desire: the 'hot passion' that is fuelled by his senses. While he imagines taking a wife to prove a point in the debate scene, Troilus never suggests marriage to his lover. The satiric mode of *Troilus and Cressida* demolishes any naively high-flown or spiritual view of love, especially through the corrosive commentary of the cynic Thersites, who growls that nothing holds 'fashion' but 'wars and lechery' (5. 2. 195). Thersites is a constant reminder, too, of the darker consequences of lust when Greeks and Trojans 'war for a placket' (2. 3. 20) – 'placket' crudely envisages Helen as the slit in a petticoat – when he wishes venereal disease,

'Neapolitan bone-ache' (18–19) and 'rotten diseases of the south' (5. 1. 18), on anyone who crosses him. Meanwhile the bawd Pandarus, who plans to make his last 'will' (as testament) at the play's ending because he is suffering from terminal 'aching bones' (5. 10. 35), warbles to Paris and Helen about sexual union 'that tickles still the sore' (3. 1. 120). He proceeds to downgrade Cressida's budding love affair with a bowling metaphor when he brings her out as a prize to the panting Troilus: 'So, so, rub on and kiss the mistress' (3. 2. 49–50). Pandarus's advising the young lover Troilus to give his new mistress 'deeds' (55) – deeds referring to sexual acts here – picks up on Paris's pronouncement, as he toys with Helen in the previous scene, that 'hot blood begets hot thoughts, and hot thoughts beget hot deeds, and hot deeds is love' (3. 1. 129–30). In this play love is always envisaged as sexual desire in action.

Troilus apes the romantic Petrarchan lover when, mooning over Cressida in the opening scene, he hyperbolically praises his lady's hand as so exquisitely fair that in 'comparison . . . all whites are ink', so soft that it makes the young swan's 'down' feel 'harsh' (1. 1. 56–8). But his underlying motive of sexual pursuit becomes clear when he complains, in soliloquy, that Cressida's 'bed' is as far off as India while she remains 'stubborn-chaste, against all suit' (100, 97). His choice of simile, describing his love-sick self as 'less valiant than the virgin in the night' (11), also implies wishful thinking about sexually vanquishing a woman. Cressida is the object of Troilus's lust, and his persistent sensuality comes through in images of taste and food as he contemplates the 'imaginary relish' of the sweet 'nectar' of consummation (3. 2. 19, 22). He fears that he will swoon to death before enjoying this act or – perhaps a fate worse than death for this sybaritic lover – that he will 'lose distinction' in his 'joys' (27). Most of all he is anxious not to disappoint his lady in bed because he knows that the 'will', or rampant sexual urge, is 'infinite' while the 'execution is confin'd', just as 'the desire is boundless and the act a slave to limit' (82–3). Such technicality is not usually the primary concern of a courtly admirer. For her part, Cressida also focuses on sexual prowess, noting that 'all lovers swear more performance than they are able', to which the sensualist Troilus replies, 'Praise us as we are tested' (84–5, 90–1). He accepts, too, that sexual gratification is fleeting. Parting from Cressida, Troilus quickly resigns himself to the transience of consummated desire – the idea, as Sonnet 129 puts it, that 'expense of spirit' provoked by 'lust' is 'a joy propos'd' before the sexual act, but 'behind, a dream' (12). In images of appetite and taste, Troilus laments that Time 'scants us with a single famish'd kiss, / Distasted with the salt of broken tears' (4. 4. 47–8).

When Troilus, after just one night with his lover, is forced to hand her over to the Greeks, her new guardian Diomedes initially couches his desire for Cressida in the language of courtly love. Praising 'the lustre' in her 'eye' and 'heaven' in her 'cheek', he promises that she 'shall be [his] mistress, and command him wholly' (4. 4. 118–20). But after Troilus angrily registers the insult, Diomedes drops the role of worshipful Petrarchan lover, bluntly telling Troilus 'When I am hence, / I'll answer to my lust' (4. 4. 131–2). The ambiguous word 'lust', pairing with the 'lustre' in Cressida's eyes, could simply mean desire without an erotic edge, but in context it strongly implies that Diomedes intends to use Cressida for his sexual satisfaction. The audience already knows that the Greek is coldly cynical about women he considers sexually available. He has described Helen (even to her lover Paris) as a 'flat tamed piece' whose 'loins' are 'whorish' (4. 1. 63–4). In keeping with this dismissive attitude, Diomedes shows little respect for Cressida when he visits her at the Greek camp; confident of having her 'heart', he threatens to abandon her if she continues her prevarication ('fooling') over giving him Troilus's love-token (5. 2. 83, 101). Witnessing the scene along with Troilus, Thersites pruriently interprets Cressida's wavering as a way of further inflaming her keeper's lust ('Luxury'). His 'Fry, lechery fry' cynically reinforces the tenor of *Troilus and Cressida* – that sexual 'will' takes precedence over romantic love (55–7).

Troilus is established as a sensualist in the opening scene. Diomedes, representing the Greek youth who are 'swelling o'er with arts and exercise' (4. 4. 78), further downgrades the idea of love as anything more than transient physical desire. More surprising is when the 'strict' Angelo in *Measure for Measure*, whose 'blood' is reputed to be 'very snow-broth' (1. 4. 57–8), is overcome by 'sharp appetite' (2. 4. 161). Feeling the 'heat of blood' (5. 1. 472), he is prepared to violate the sanctity of his office as deputy duke in Vienna once he's aroused by Isabella, a virgin about to enter a convent. In propositioning her, Angelo offers to pardon her brother Claudio (ironically sentenced to death now that strict laws against fornication are being revived) if she will submit to his sexual will. Surprised by his sudden feelings of lust, Angelo nevertheless resigns himself to them. Ruefully he acknowledges 'Blood thou art blood' (2. 4. 15). Far from being a man who 'scarce confesses / That his blood flows' (1. 3. 51–2), he bears out Escalus's observation that at some point every male feels 'affections' or the 'resolute acting of blood' that might, if circumstances permit, achieve its sexual 'purpose' (2. 1. 10–13).

The drama doesn't shy away from this kind of insistent sexuality – the boundless nature of desire that society tries, often unsuccessfully, to contain. Composed early in the reign of King James, when the London suburbs had been described by Thomas Nashe as 'licensed Stewes'[10] (brothels) and law court records show an increase in the illegitimacy rate,[11] *Measure for Measure* explores what happens when state authorities try to clamp down on widespread sexual incontinence. Comments on such activity range from the libertine Lucio's seedy view of sex as a 'game of tick-tack' (1. 2. 190–1) or the 'rebellion of a cod-piece' (3. 2. 115) to the visible evidence of 'most mutual entertainment' in Julietta's pregnancy (1. 2. 154), which demonstrates the 'full tilth and husbandry' of her pre-contracted husband, Claudio (1. 4. 44). This is the only time in the play that sex is associated with a wholesome activity. More often it is viewed as socially disruptive 'license' (3. 2. 204), the by-product of 'too much liberty' (1. 2. 125). It's also assumed that pre-marital intercourse will result in pregnancy (as it has done with Juliet and the prostitute Kate Keepdown[12]), inevitably leading to more infants born out of wedlock. Lambasting such sexual activity as 'filthy vices', Angelo condemns the conceiving of illegitimate children as a form of counterfeiting, or 'coin[ing] God's image / In stamps that are forbid'. He even maintains that this fornication should be punished as severely as murder (2. 4. 42–6). Meanwhile Lucio scurrilously implies that since the Duke 'had some feeling of the sport' he would be more tolerant about extra-marital sex; never would he have ordered the execution of Claudio. Extravagantly, Lucio claims that rather than hanging 'a man for the getting a thousand bastards', the Duke 'would have paid for the nursing a thousand' (3. 2. 117–19).

None of the sexual relationships in the play are positioned as romantic, even the consensual coupling of Claudio and Juliet. When he is sentenced to death Claudio becomes jaundiced enough to agree that intercourse with his fiancée was 'lechery', even though their relationship qualifies as a valid marriage (1. 2. 139). In fact the 'true contract' by which Claudio gained access to Juliet's 'bed' (145–6) is a legally binding *per verba de praesenti* spousal: a promise made in the present tense between 'the two consenting parties, and by them alone'.[13] The new decree imposed by Angelo, however, punishes any sexual consummation that occurs before the validation of a church ceremony. In an image that mirrors Shakespeare's grimly pessimistic Sonnet 147, 'My love is as a fever, longing still / For that which longer nurseth the disease', Claudio generalises the poisonous result of indulging in sexual desire:

> Our natures do pursue,
> Like rats that ravin down their proper bane,
> A thirsty evil, and when we drink we die. (1. 2. 128–30)

Sonnet 147 posits that 'desire', because it feeds on what perpetuates its disease, 'is death' (8). Bitterly facing his own demise, Claudio also dismisses sexual longing as compulsive and damaging, a 'thirsty evil'. By assuaging it, like rats compelled to drink poison, lovers inevitably court their own destruction.

Pompey the pimp, part of the underclass that trades in prostitution, disparagingly refers to intercourse with women as 'groping for trouts in a peculiar river' (1. 2. 90). Pompey's approach to sex is pragmatic; he reckons that because men will always need sexual relief, he can make his living by enabling this. Threatened with loss of livelihood if the brothel where he works is closed down, Pompey asks the magistrate a commonsensical question: 'Does your worship mean to geld and spay all the youth of the city?' (2. 1. 230–1). Meanwhile the practical Provost concedes that 'All sects, all ages smack of this vice' (2. 2. 5) – as if fulfilling sexual needs must automatically be labelled as 'vice'. At the dark centre of sexual desire is Angelo, suddenly prey to the urgent 'will' he has repressed. Ashamed of his sexually arousing thoughts about Isabella, he also defines such desire as vicious, a 'strong and swelling evil' (2. 4. 6). As the disguised Duke points out in gnomic couplets, Angelo is particularly at fault because of his hypocrisy: 'Shame to him whose cruel striking / Kills for faults of his own liking!' (3. 2. 267–8). Angelo's 'affection' (lust) goads him into promising to release Isabella's brother if she consents to 'please' him by 'yielding up [her] body to [his] will' (2. 4. 168, 164). Outraged, Isabella picks up on this sexual meaning of 'will' when she laments that the deputy, despite pretending to be morally irreproachable, is typical of the corrupt ruling class: 'Bidding the law make curtsy to their will / Hooking both right and wrong to th' appetite' (175–6).

Whereas the Friar in *Romeo and Juliet* separates 'grace' from 'rude will', ironically it is Isabella's 'moving graces' (2. 2. 36) – her demonstration of virtue combined with pleasing comeliness – that contrives to 'soften' Angelo's 'strict' moral principles (1. 4. 70, 1. 2. 181). To his chagrin, Angelo's desire is provoked not by the wiles of the prostitute but by the innocence and graceful demeanour of a virgin planning to become a nun. Ruminating on the efficacy of his medicinal herbs, Friar Lawrence in *Romeo and Juliet* goes on to observe that 'Virtue turns vice, being misapplied' (2. 3. 21). The naive Isabella cannot see that she is facilitating this kind of reversal. Noting that she speaks 'Such sense that my sense breeds with it', Angelo soon discovers that his own 'sense' (sexual desire) is increasing in tandem with Isabella's good 'sense' – her rational arguments, intended to promote the virtuous action of mercy in Angelo (2. 2. 142). Oppositions dissolve here, as virtuous discourse provokes viciousness in Angelo. Feeling compelled to 'pitch' his 'evils' in the hallowed 'sanctuary' of Isabella's body (170–1), he allows himself to be swept along by desire, giving his 'sensual race the rein' (2. 4. 160).

In this sexually loaded play we find few instances of 'will' that simply mean intention, as when the Provost asks Angelo, 'Is it your will Claudio should die tomorrow?' (2. 2. 7). Even the opening scene, where the Duke hands off his authority, sets the tone for sexual innuendo with the connection between 'will and 'pleasure' (barely offset by 'your Grace') in Angelo's first words: 'Always obedient to your Grace's will, / I come to know your pleasure' (1. 1. 25–6). In Act 3, when the Duke disguised as a friar first asks for a 'word' with Isabella, she questions him with 'What is your will?'. Innocent enough, perhaps. But his reply, that he requires some 'satisfaction' that should ultimately 'benefit' Isabella (3. 1. 152–6), anticipates his offer to marry her at the end of the play – a union that would satisfy his desire or 'will'. A little later in the scene where he first accosts Isabella, we find the Duke using 'satisfaction' in a more overtly sexual sense. As part of arranging the substitution of Mariana's body for Isabella's, he directs Isabella to seem to comply with the deputy's wishes: 'if for this night he [Angelo] entreat you to his bed, give him promise of satisfaction' (262–3).

Attuned to these sexual undertones, the audience is prepared for what would otherwise be a very surprising proposal of marriage – after all, Isabella was headed for the convent! – in the play's finale. The first hint of the Duke's offer follows Isabella's apology for employing him when he was disguised as a friar. As well as pardoning her and promising still to be at her 'service', the Duke hopes that Isabella will now be 'free' to her benefactor: 'And now, dear maid, be you as free to us' (5. 1. 385–8). Leaving aside the possible sexual innuendo here on 'service' – Pompey has described Mistress Overdone, madam of the brothel, as 'one who has worn [her] eyes almost out in the service' (1. 2. 109–10) – to what kind of freedom is the Duke referring? Secondary meanings of 'free' in early seventeenth-century discourse include innocent and generous, but also liberal in the sexual sense. When Joan la Pucelle in *Henry VI, Part 1* claims she is pregnant, Warwick finds it a 'sign she has been liberal and free' with the French aristocrats (5. 4. 82). Othello, infected with suspicion that Desdemona has been sexually free with Cassio, indicts his wife's 'moist' hand as 'frank', suggesting too 'liberal' a heart (*Othello*, 3. 4. 39, 44, 46).

In *Measure for Measure*'s finale the Duke, having pardoned Claudio, urges the 'lovely' Isabella to 'Give me your hand, and say you will be mine' (5. 1. 492). He is now more openly inviting her to plight her troth to him – joining hands or 'handfasting' as part of the spousal contracts in Shakespeare's time that Ann Jenalie Cook covers in detail[14] – just as King Leontes in *The Winter's Tale* recalls how after a long courtship Hermione opened her 'white hand' to him to pronounce ' "I am yours for ever"' (1. 2. 103–5). Unlike Leontes, however, the Duke offers not one shred of prolonged and respectful courtship or the 'service' of a romantic lover. Isabella, who must be astounded at his words, remains silent. She may or may not give the Duke her hand in return, sealing the contract. Indeed the Duke's final offer to her, with its conditional 'if', seems less confident than pointedly practical:

> I have a motion much imports your good,
> Whereto if you'll a willing ear incline,
> What's mine is yours, and what is yours is mine. (5. 1. 536–8)

It is surely not too fanciful to discern further sexual implications here. Not only is the recipient of the Duke's proposal supposed to be 'willing', but the proposed free exchange of 'yours' with 'mine' is backed up by the secondary meaning of 'motion' as desire or appetite. It recalls how Angelo was reputed not to feel the 'wanton stings and motions of the sense' (1. 4. 59), just as Iago downgraded love to 'raging motions' and 'carnal stings' (*Othello*, 1. 3. 330–1).

All this points to the possibility that the Duke is a clandestine lecher who may, as Lucio has suggested, have 'some feeling of the sport' (3. 2. 119). At best Vincentio lacks the self-knowledge to recognise that he is not immune to 'the dribbling dart of love' or desire (1. 3. 2). The bawdy undertone in the word 'fit' (meaning sexually primed),[15] which the Duke uses in his plan to replace Isabella with Mariana in the tryst with Angelo, suggests a salacious interest: 'The maid will I frame, and make fit for his attempt' (3. 1. 255–6). The audience may hear an echo of the same innuendo when the Duke caps his first proposal to Isabella ('say you will be mine') with 'But fitter time for that' (5. 1. 493). By the play's end, we watch a man who seems as driven to have intimate relations with a would-be nun as Angelo has shown himself to be. In a play that deals in substitutions – Mariana for Isabella, the head of Ragozine (who replaces the reprobate Barnardine) for that of Claudio – Duke Vincentio appears to have taken over the 'vice' of Angelo, the man he terms his own 'substitute' (5. 1. 140). In a puzzling line from the series of gnomic couplets that conclude Act 3, the Duke laments 'Twice treble shame on Angelo, / To weed my vice and let his grow!' (3. 2. 269–70). While 'my vice' ostensibly refers to the licentiousness that flourished under the Duke's rule in Vienna, the noun phrase appears to apply to the Duke himself.

Just as Angelo urged Isabella to prove herself a female by submitting to him sexually (2. 4. 138), so the Duke pursues the same goal. Now, though, he does so by offering marriage as a sanctioned form of conjugation. Rather than honouring Isabella's choice to wear the habit of a chaste nun, he, like Angelo, promotes the idea that her inevitable role ('destined livery') is to be a sexualised female subject to men's desire.[16] As Jonathan Dollimore concludes, 'it is Isabella's fate to be coerced back into her socially and sexually subordinate position – at first illicitly by Angelo, then legitimately by the Duke who "takes" her in marriage'.[17] Actresses may play Isabella as shocked, backing away, or as reluctantly giving him her hand. Since she doesn't verbally consent to the Duke's proposition,[18] the text provides no decisive clues on whether or not she accepts it.

Granted, the audience may discern a dividedness in Isabella that could leave her open to the Duke's advances. When she first refers to her brother's pre-marital sex with his fiancée, Isabella confesses to Angelo that she is 'At war 'twixt will and will not' (2. 2. 33). She would like to save her brother's life, but the secondary meaning of 'will' indicates that she also remains conflicted on another level, reluctant to plead for remission of Claudio's sin (his unlicensed 'will') because the Church would view it as the deadly sin of lust. If 'will' signifies the claim of sexual desire, 'will not' represents its opposite: the choice to remain chaste. As a future nun, Isabella automatically sides with celibacy. The puritanical Angelo feels similarly divided when he later agonises over the consequences of his sexual act, feeling paralysed by moral conflict in 'we would, and we would not' (4. 4. 34). His strained pairing of opposites when he describes the 'sweet uncleanness' and 'saucy [lecherous] sweetness' of the act itself shows how torn he is between responding to sensual appeal and reviling what he believes to be the inherent sinfulness of capitulating to it (2. 4. 54, 45).

Critics have not been slow to detect this kind of Freudian conflict, a struggle to repress sexuality, in Isabella too; Ewan Fernie notes how Isabella's 'protestation of absolute chastity' turns into a 'sexual fantasy of her own martyrdom'.[19] When Isabella states that she would be willing to undergo flagellation or death rather than shamefully forfeit her virginity, it is the highly charged sexual terms in which she expresses this masochistic desire – Th' impression of keen whips I'd wear as rubies' and 'strip myself to death, as to a bed / That longing have been sick for' (2. 4. 101–3) – that make us wonder whether Isabella's horror at 'uncleanness' masks a subconscious attraction towards it. *Measure for Measure* goes beyond exploring the dark side of 'will' in a puritanical male; while Isabella's libido may be repressed by her fierce commitment to virginity, the implication is that both genders are driven by sexual desire. Just as Angelo, proud of his reputation for purity, tries unsuccessfully to deny his sensual nature, so Isabella's own sexuality appears to surface in her passionate determination to remain pure.

Yet it is a strange kind of dramatic resolution for a woman who has chosen the life of a nun to be expected to submit to the sexual desire of a ruler who wields state authority. This surely holds true even if that desire is contained in the 'sacrament' of Catholic marriage, which would apply to the city of Vienna.[20] The one relationship that actually seeks marriage, the love between Claudio and Juliet, is branded as 'sin' because it has already been consummated (2. 3. 28). In the finale the Duke further shames this union by ordering Claudio to 'restore' the reputation of 'wrong'd' Juliet by marrying her (5. 1. 525). The other characters whom the Duke pushes into marriage are deeply reluctant to form such lifelong commitments – Angelo to his former fiancée Mariana; Lucio to the prostitute Kate Keepdown, with whom he has fathered a child; and now presumably Isabella to the Duke himself. In the face of such reluctance, the Duke's apparently merciful solution begins to look more like punishment than mitigation, a way of trying to impose the restraint of social convention on sexual desires that do not lend themselves to strict regulation. Lucio certainly perceives it that way when he protests 'Marrying a punk . . . is pressing to death, whipping, and hanging' (5. 1. 522–3). Meanwhile Angelo, who previously proposed a 'devilish mercy' (deflowering a virgin in exchange for pardoning Claudio), now faces a parallel situation to the one he imposed on Isabella. As a condition of his own pardon, he must wed Mariana, the woman he rejected in the past despite being formally betrothed to her, and whom he presumably no longer desires.[21] No wonder this proud man, overcome with sexual shame, 'crave[s] death more willingly than mercy' (476). 'Morality and mercy', dispensed by the ruler or his surrogate in Vienna (1. 1. 44), have become all but indistinguishable in this tantalisingly paradoxical play.

Is marriage, the audience may wonder, really the best solution for sex offenders? The wedding ceremony in the 1559 Prayer Book, the 'Solemnization of Matrimony', states that the goal of marriage is to ward off the threat of 'carnal lusts and appetites' and 'avoid' the 'fornication' of extra-marital sex. Certainly the Duke's hastily organised nuptials seem to second that. While Francis Bacon reiterates in *New Atlantis* (1627) that 'marriage is ordained a remedy for unlawful concupiscence', he wryly notes the other side of the equation – that 'natural concupiscence' acts as a 'spur to marriage', especially if a chaste, virtuous society offers no 'dissolute houses' or 'courtesans' to satisfy men's 'corrupt will'.[22] Robert Burton in *The Anatomy of Melancholy* (1621) is more sceptical; he pronounces that 'immoderate, inordinate' love (or 'burning lust') will 'not contain itself within the union of marriage'.[23] Indeed the conclusion of *Measure for Measure* leaves open the question of whether the heralded sanctity of marriage can successfully contain the urgency of sexual will.[24] It seems more the case that enforcing such binding contracts through state power encourages a rift between 'marriage and desire'.²⁵ As Catherine Belsey comments about the eroticism so often dramatised in Renaissance plays, 'the Law-lessness of desire returns to destabilize the institutions set up to bring it under control'.²⁶

Angelo, in 'Bidding the law make curtsy to [his] will' (2. 4. 175), enacts the 'Lawlessness' or rapacity of male lust, impervious to social restraints and focused only on achieving its end. This is also the subject of Sonnet 129, which parallels Angelo's moral decline:

> Th'expense of spirit in a waste of shame
> Is lust in action, and till action, lust
> Is perjur'd, murd'rous, bloody, full of blame,
> Savage, extreme, rude, cruel, not to trust (1–4)

The opening line makes a metaphysical point in barely submerged physical terms, suggesting that lust is the wasteful ejaculation ('expense') of male semen ('spirit')²⁷ into the 'waste' of the female vagina. Admitting the 'strong and swelling evil / of his conception', Angelo similarly experiences the abstract idea (the 'conception') of sexual intercourse with Isabella as the 'strong and swelling evil' of physical arousal (2. 4. 6–7). Lines 3–4 of the sonnet characterise personified lust as morally corrupt – 'perjur'd', untrustworthy and 'cruel' in pursuing its goal. Exemplifying this, Angelo commits perjury – he breaks his pledge to pardon Claudio in return for sexual favours – and acts with cruelty when he threatens to impose on Claudio 'ling'ring sufferance' if Isabella doesn't submit to his will (2. 4. 167). The object of lust, according to Sonnet 129, is fiercely pursued ('Past reason hunted') and 'no sooner had' (possessed sexually) than she is

> Past reason hated as a swallowed bait
> On purpose laid to make the taker mad. (7–8)

Angelo too resents how lechery, like the devil, directs him to swallow the 'bait' by tempting his inherently angelic nature with the saint-like Isabella: 'O cunning enemy, that to catch a saint, / With saints doth bait thy hook! (2. 2. 179–80). Later, caught in a 'waste of shame' after gratifying his lust in the secret tryst, Angelo laments in soliloquy that 'This deed unshapes me quite'. He now views the bargain to release Claudio in exchange for taking Isabella's virginity as a 'ransom' full of 'shame' (4. 4. 20, 32).

'Lust in action', or what Isabella brands 'concupiscible intemperate lust' (5. 1. 98), is given particular emphasis in the 'bed trick', the substitution of one female for another (without the male recognising the exchange) that is featured in both *All's Well that Ends Well* and *Measure for Measure*. While this dramatic convention serves as a convenient plot device for getting the right partners together, it also emphasises how easily one female can replace another to satisfy the male's intemperate will. Women as objects of desire simply become interchangeable, robbed of 'distinctive subjectivity', as Maurice Charney puts it.[28] Because the love object is concealed in darkness, the wooer cannot see whether he is actually bedding the female he claims to love so uniquely. He certainly cannot 'feast upon her eyes', as Angelo, briefly using the language of the romantic lover, claims that he wishes to do with Isabella (2. 2. 178). If, as Shakespeare suggests, the object of this desire is a 'disembodied' fantasy rather than an actual woman, then the bed trick allows a man to indulge his lust indiscriminately – Angelo with Mariana, who has replaced his chosen object (Isabella), and Bertram with Helena instead of (as he supposes) Diana. When no particular female can be fully 'commensurate' with male 'desire', as Carol Cook notes in her discussion of *Troilus and Cressida*,[29] an anonymous sexual union in the dark, the premise of the bed trick, becomes grimly appropriate.

It is surely not the case that the female is the sexual aggressor here, as Stanley Wells wryly claims when he comments that this dramatic convention represents a kind of 'rape of the man by the woman'.[30] Rather than constituting female coercion, the bed exchange is all too easily achieved because of the male's indiscriminate need for sexual gratification. In *All's Well that Ends Well*, Helena wonders at the transferability of men's sexual desires. She has discovered that when a dark bedroom conceals the love object, Bertram can be 'wondrous kind' to the wife he has rejected (5. 3. 310). By demonstrating how 'lust doth play / With what it loathes for that which is away', men seem to Helena 'strange' indeed, since they 'can such sweet use make of what they hate' (4. 4. 24–5, 21–2).

While it reveals the promiscuous nature of male desire, the bed trick serves a more pragmatic purpose; it enables a legitimate marriage to be consummated. In this way it offers an outlandish, even fairy-tale solution to what remained a social problem of Shakespeare's time: breaches of the marriage contract, which had to be litigated in church courts.[31] In early modern society a woman could maintain her sexual honour only within a chaste marriage, so that if her male partner reneged on his nuptial vows, as Bertram does in abandoning Helena before their wedding night, the female might be driven to prove the legitimacy of the union by whatever means were available. Under early modern matrimonial law, as Subha Mukherji outlines in detail, physical consummation was the final stage in ratifying the contract. Therefore, to make the marriage fully legal, Helena must somehow fulfil the conditions that

Bertram coldly imposes on her in his farewell letter, in which he pledges to acknowledge her as his wife only if she can pry the heirloom ring off his finger and prove that he has conceived a child with her (3. 2. 57–9). She knows it is the act of consummation, the sexual 'deed' itself, that legally validates the marriage contract. Pandarus speaks in these coolly legalistic terms when, as 'witness' to a contractual 'bargain' sealed after he joins the hands of Troilus and Cressida (3. 2. 197–8), he urges the young man – not a bridegroom but an ardent lover – to move quickly from verbal promises to sexual consummation. Cynically Pandarus has already reminded the eager Troilus that since 'Words pay no debts, give her deeds' (55).

The fact that the marriage of Helena and Bertram is consummated by deceptive means – the entrapment of the bed trick – remains troubling. Bertram believes he is having sexual relations with Diana, satisfying his sexual 'will' (4. 3. 16) by taking to bed the desirable young woman he is so 'mad' for (5. 3. 260). Instead Helena uses the cover of darkness to put her own ring on Bertram's finger as proof that he has instead made love to his contracted bride. Proactive in arranging the substitution, she concedes that she is pulling off something morally shady – a sleight of hand through which a 'wicked meaning' (Bertram's immoral intention to seduce a virgin) or a 'sinful fact' (had he succeeded) technically becomes a 'lawful' deed, a husband's intercourse with his wedded wife (3. 7. 45, 38). For her part, Diana finds it 'no sin' to deceive or 'cozen' a man who planned to destroy her virtuous name (4. 2. 75–6). She is content to stay 'most chastely absent' from the sexual encounter (3. 7. 34).

Under Renaissance law Helena's device for consummating her marriage may actually be legally suspect. Swinburne's *Matrimony*, a document composed around 1600, contends that being 'seduced by Error' and 'mistaking one person for another' (as in the bed trick) fails to ratify a marriage, since it doesn't entail the 'true consent' of 'minds' essential to matrimony.[32] The trick nevertheless provides Helena with a way out of her dilemma; she can never fully be Bertram's wife until he has bedded her. But can such a coldly practical solution, in addition to exposing the promiscuity of Bertram's sexual desire, serve as the basis for a loving marriage? It adds to the uneasy sense, most pronounced in *Measure for Measure*, that marriage, as well as being an imperfect corrective for lust, often coerces the man into a union for which he is unsuited. Helena's reward for proving that she has outwitted Bertram is his promise to love her 'dearly, ever, ever dearly' (5. 3. 316). This husband, though, has just proved his callous indifference to women when he accuses Diana, the virgin he thought he had seduced, of 'infinite cunning' and 'Madding [his] eagerness with her restraint' (216, 213). Now he is forced to acknowledge Helena as his pregnant wife. While the couple's original contract is confirmed as a binding marriage, it's questionable whether Helena has actually brought Bertram to what Margaret Loftus Ranald calls a 'free, unforced consent to the consummated union' based on a 'new moral, emotional, and sexual maturity'.[33] Helena has pitted her strong will – her sexual feelings for Bertram as well as her firm intention to be acknowledged as his wife – against her husband's undisciplined libido. And she succeeds.

Helena, to be sure, is cunning in a good cause, and she compromises no one by substituting herself for Diana in Bertram's bed. Likewise the bed exchange in *Measure for Measure*, the means by which lustful Angelo actually consummates his pre-contracted marriage, does not injure Mariana. Instead, by granting her marital status it rescues her from the social isolation of being a jilted fiancée. Engineering the trick, though, may reflect poorly on both the Duke and Isabella. Chastising Pompey earlier as 'a bawd, a wicked bawd!' (3. 2. 19), the Duke in effect acts like a pimp himself. While he performs it less flagrantly, his role resembles that of Pandarus in *Troilus and Cressida*, who makes sure that his niece is 'tame' enough to receive her Trojan lover (3. 2. 44). Meanwhile Isabella is inconsistent when she condones, in Mariana, the fornication she condemned in Claudio. For although Claudio was pre-contracted to Juliet, just as Mariana was to Angelo, Isabella still sternly labels her brother's sexual act as 'vice' (2. 2. 29). Even the Duke, like Helena in *All's Well*, acknowledges 'deceit' in the bed trick, rationalising that because Mariana had a prenuptial agreement with Angelo (a contract *per verba de futuro*)[34] she deserves the recompense of a sexual union to legitimise it. Thus the end will justify the means, or 'flourish the deceit' (4. 1. 74). Meanwhile Isabella enters into the details of the bed exchange with some vicarious interest, carefully explaining how Mariana will need two keys to reach the secret garden where she will 'supply' Angelo in Isabella's place (5. 1. 212).

Just as Helena continues to value Bertram as her husband despite his callous treatment of her, so at the end of *Measure for Measure* Mariana stands by the male who has abused her. Loyally she insists she wants no 'better man' for a husband than the disgraced Angelo (5. 1. 426). Yet we learn that while she was betrothed to him years ago, 'affianc'd' by 'oath' (3. 1. 214), mercenary Angelo abandoned her when her dowry was lost in her brother's shipwreck. With supreme irony, not realising he has sealed their marriage by knowing Mariana in the biblical sense, Angelo concedes with disdain that he does 'know this woman' (5. 1. 216). He then coldly tries to dismiss her on a false pretext, claiming that he reneged on their former agreement to marry not because her dowry was compromised but because she was sexually lax, 'her reputation ... disvalued / In levity' (221–2). Once he is publicly shamed, despite going ahead with the Duke's order and marrying Mariana 'instantly', he begs the Duke for 'death' rather than life as a married man (377, 476). The bridegroom is nothing if not reluctant. Perhaps the 'quick'ning' in Angelo's eye that the Duke observes offers some hope that Angelo's feelings for Mariana can be rekindled (495). Otherwise Angelo's assertion stands: that the act of marrying his betrothed, the 'measure' he must pay for betraying and dishonouring her, seems to him a fate worse than death.

Can love and lust ever be reconciled? Not in these dark comedies. In Bertram and Angelo we find little capacity for warm emotional attachment or intimacy in the non-sexual sense. True, each man is pushed into wedlock, his conscious intention and sexual 'will' both diverted, and arranged marriages, where individuals are 'compelled'[35] to take partners they do not desire, are denigrated in both Shakespeare's *Romeo and Juliet* and *The Merry Wives of Windsor*. But in any case, Bertram and Angelo are not promising candidates for marriage. Each man has indulged his libido in a brief liaison rather than aspiring to a committed love relationship. Troilus may be an exception – he claims near the end of the play to love his lady with an 'eternal' and 'fixed' soul (5. 2. 166) – but it's also the case that he expresses his feelings in 'relentlessly physical terms',[36] and René Girard notes how his 'desire' to possess Cressida seems 'new', perversely reignited, once he sees her giving herself to Diomedes.[37] Parting with Troilus after one night together, Cressida ruefully complains 'I might have still held off, / And then you could have tarried' (*Troilus and Cressida*, 4. 2. 17–18). Her insight exactly matches the behaviour of Bertram and Angelo, men who quickly lose interest in their hard-to-win objects of desire, Diana and Isabella, as soon as they believe they have conquered these women sexually.[38]

What adds to the unsavoury side of sexual desire, certainly in *Measure for Measure*, is the focus on a governor turning predatory in his pursuit of a chaste woman. Here the male in a position of authority becomes, as Sonnet 129 puts it, 'in quest to have, extreme' (10). While Angelo doesn't physically force his chosen prey, as Tarquin does in *The Rape of Lucrece*, his offering Isabella the chance to trade her virginity for the life of her own brother is a particularly vile form of sexual harassment; Alan Sinfield goes as far as to equate it with the 'misogyny of the rapist who desires to spoil the pure, to violate ... hurt and degrade'.[39] Since Angelo has appropriated the power of the Duke, he assumes that his reputation for austerity and his respected 'place i' th' state' will work in his defence (2. 4. 156). No one, he is confident, will believe Isabella if she discloses Angelo's bribe – to gratify his 'sharp appetite' and 'will' (161, 164) in exchange for her brother's life. The Duke, too, is coercive. Having abdicated his secular authority (passing the burden of curbing secular licence in Vienna on to Angelo), Vincentio uses his disguise as a friar, the respect afforded to religion, to gain the women's confidence. As self-appointed agent of Providence who bears 'the sword of heaven' (3. 2. 261), he plays the puppet master in his role as 'meddling friar' (5. 1. 127), manipulating both Isabella and Mariana to further his scheme to expose Angelo's corruption. Too lax in controlling sexual 'licence' in the past, the Duke-friar can take credit for unmasking it now. And in a deeply ambivalent ending (should chastity give way to a charitable view of sexual desire, enabling Isabella to accept the overtures of the ruler?), the Duke's taking back political power from his 'substitute' enables him to use his office to try to bend the chaste Isabella to his will.

Ulysses's speech on 'degree' in *Troilus and Cressida* also comments on power and appetite as they operate in the social microcosm; it predicts universal, macrocosmic chaos when might or 'force' becomes 'right' and social 'order' crumbles (1. 3. 116). The Greek general paints a dark picture of what may happen once the status quo – in this case, the 'specialty of rule' in the Greek camp – breaks down (78). As brute force takes over, and 'every thing include[s] itself in power' (119), this sets in motion a relentless transformation downward:

> Power into will, will into appetite,
> And appetite, an universal wolf,
> (So doubly seconded with will and power),
> Must make perforce an universal prey
> And last eat up himself. (120–4)

Determined to uphold the orthodox Greek hierarchy, Ulysses projects how destructive 'appetite', backed up or 'seconded' by both 'power' and 'will' – additional sources of hungry desire – is like a wolf going on a 'universal' rampage. Devouring prey indiscriminately, rapacious appetite finally self-destructs by consuming itself.

Granted, Ulysses is not referring primarily to sexual will. He is giving a political speech, warning that aggressive will to power, or rebelling against one's place ('degree') within the ruling hierarchy, inevitably leads to social anarchy and self-defeating chaos in the war effort. But as the play's unfolding action demonstrates, the Trojan War itself is closely linked to sexual appetite. Paris, whose lust for Helen has precipitated the futile war in the first place, claims that if he possessed as much 'ample power' as he had 'will', he 'alone' would defend his theft of Helen (2. 2. 139–40). Meanwhile Troilus's sensual desire for Cressida finds an outlet in military aggression after she betrays him. Losing sight of Troilus trying to overtake his rival Diomedes on the battlefield, Thersites wonders if the two have 'swallow'd one another'. Like Ulysses predicting that uncontrolled appetite for power will finally 'eat up' itself, the cynical Thersites concludes that 'in a sort, lechery eats itself' (5. 4. 34–5).

While *Troilus and Cressida* links uncontrolled libido with destructiveness and social breakdown in Troy, *Measure for Measure* reveals how sexual desire both continually threatens the laws and institutions designed to maintain civilised behaviour in Vienna and undermines the integrity of the authority figure. In his moral and emotional confusion, Angelo complains that Isabella's sexual attractiveness 'subdues' and 'unshapes [him] quite' (*Measure for Measure*, 2. 2. 185, 4. 4. 20).[40] Ironically, the only leverage women in these problem plays possess is erotic power. Like Angelo unnerved by Isabella, Troilus confesses that desire for Cressida makes him 'weaker than a woman's tear' (*Troilus and Cressida*, 1. 1. 9); inflamed by Diana, Bertram in *All's Well* sacrifices his honour for one sexual encounter. Nevertheless males continue to exploit their power as authority figures. In the patriarchal Vienna of *Measure for Measure*, as Isabella recognises, supposedly upright rulers can bend the 'law' to their 'will', allowing crude 'appetite' to subsume both 'right and wrong' (2. 4. 175–6). In Troy Cressida becomes a pawn, forced to leave the city in exchange for Antenor and then crudely passed around the all-male Greek camp, a sex object kissed by the generals in turn. While Helena's cure of the French king in *All's Well that Ends Well* suggests her erotic power (afterwards the king is described as 'lustier' than a 'dolphin' (2. 3. 26)), as an abandoned wife she must resort to a humiliating bed trick to validate her marriage to Bertram. And to escape Angelo's sexual coercion, Isabella consents to the Duke's plan to substitute Mariana's body for her own. Clearly it is not only the brothel underworld of Vienna that deals in the trafficking of female bodies,[41] 'profiting' by women's vulnerability, as Isabella puts it (*Measure for Measure*, 2. 4. 128).

The males – Angelo in this play and Bertram in *All's Well that Ends Well* – nevertheless pay a high price for imposing their 'will' through 'lust in action'; they must accept as wives the women they were tricked into using sexually. Marriage under these circumstances promises neither romantic fulfilment nor a partnership based on mutual love and respect. *Measure for Measure* is relentless in turning matrimony into a practical legal arrangement, one that seems unlikely to stabilise, 'moralize and domesticate' unruly erotic desire,[42] or to serve as a 'remedy' against 'fornication', as the 'Solemnization of Matrimony' puts it. Composed just a few years after the comedies of love that celebrate successful courtship, *Measure for Measure* has appropriately been labelled a 'dark comedy'.[43] Certainly it is the play from Shakespeare's middle period that most centres on 'will' as the dark side of sexual desire.

Notes

1. Likewise the term 'sexuality', meaning 'recognition or preoccupation with what is sexual' (sense 2 of the *OED*), didn't enter the English language until the nineteenth century.
2. Gail Kern Paster, *The Body Embarrassed: Drama and the Disciplines of Shame in Early Modern England*, p. 72. Discussing Galen's theories, which remained current in Shakespeare's time, Paster finds that 'Galenic physiology proposed a body whose constituent fluids' – including milk, sweat, tears and semen – were 'all reducible to blood' and could turn into one another (p. 9).
3. Gordon Williams, *A Glossary of Shakespeare's Sexual Language*, glosses blood as the 'seat of appetite' (p. 44).
4. 'Against' is also used in this way by Oberon in *A Midsummer Night's Dream*, when he plans to make Demetrius fall in love with Helena: 'I'll charm his eyes against she do appear' (3. 2. 99).
5. In *Shakespeare, Sex, and Love*, Stanley Wells discerns that 'in lines 5–8 [of Sonnet 135] the senses successively of "penis" and "vagina" dominate' (p. 49); certainly 'hide my will in thine' (line 6) could refer to both male and female genitalia. Stressing how 'openly assertive' this 'Will' sonnet is in presenting sexuality, Joel Fineman, in *Shakespeare's Perjured Eye: The Invention of Poetic Subjectivity in the Sonnets*, finds that the poet's 'richly resonating name ... linguistically performs the copulation that the poet speaks about' (p. 293).
6. Helen Vendler, in *The Art of Shakespeare's Sonnets*, comments that in requesting the mistress to 'cram him in as well', the speaker of Sonnet 135 admits that he is 'aroused by participating vicariously' in her 'promiscuity' (p. 575).
7. Thomas Wright, *The Passions of the Mind in General*, bk. 1, ch. 2, p. 94.
8. Like Richard Hooker in *Of the Laws of Ecclesiastical Polity* (1593), Wright characterises the 'Will' as partly inclined to follow 'Reason', partly inclined to 'content the senses' (*The Passions of the Mind*, bk. 2, ch. 2, p. 133).
9. A. P. Rossiter, 'The Problem Plays', in *Angel with Horns*, p. 125.
10. Thomas Nashe, *Christs Teares over Jerusalem* (1593), p. 113.
11. Marilyn L. Williamson, 'The Problem Plays: Social Regulation of Desire', in *The Patriarchy of Shakespeare's Comedies*, pp. 55–110; p. 81.
12. Lisa Hopkins, *The Shakespearean Marriage*, comments on how in the 'teeming world' of this play even the wife of Elbow the constable is 'great with child' (pp. 78, 81).
13. B. J. Sokol and Mary Sokol, 'Making a Valid Marriage: The Consensual Model', in *Shakespeare, Law, and Marriage*, p. 14.
14. Ann Jenalie Cook, 'Formal Proposals, Public Contracts, and Proper

Weddings', in *Making a Match: Courtship in Shakespeare and his Society*, pp. 151–84.
15. It is used with this meaning in *Cymbeline*, when Cloten crudely expresses the wish that Imogen will be 'fit' for his planned rape, for 'a woman's fitness comes by fits' (4. 1. 4–6).
16. Alan Sinfield, 'Rape and Rights: *Measure for Measure* and the Limits of Cultural Imperialism', notes that 'the destined livery', or 'badge of the female', is 'sexual subjection to men' (p. 184).
17. Jonathan Dollimore, 'Transgression and Surveillance in *Measure for Measure*', p. 83.
18. Cook, *Making a Match*, notes that 'consent' ('required of both parents and children' when marriages were being arranged) formed 'the basis for all valid marriages' and spousal pacts (pp. 72, 155). The controlling Duke-friar, rather than proposing as an ardent lover, may be adopting a more paternal role in setting up marriage with Isabella, but she must still give her consent if the betrothal is to be valid.
19. Ewan Fernie, *Shame in Shakespeare*, p. 42. Brian Gibbons (ed.), *Measure for Measure*, focuses on the undercurrent of sexual 'longing' in his notes to this passage in 2. 4, while Kathleen McLuskie, 'The Patriarchal Bard: Feminist Criticism and Shakespeare: *King Lear* and *Measure for Measure*', comments that Isabella's 'single-minded protection of her sexual autonomy' is expressed through masochistic 'sexual imagery' (p. 93).
20. Margaret Loftus Ranald, *Shakespeare and his Social Context*, points out that the Anglican church 'rejected' the Catholic idea of marriage as a 'sacrament' and 'the Puritan wing . . . considered marriage as a civil contract' (p. 6).
21. Allan Bloom, *Shakespeare on Love and Friendship*, comments that at the end of *Measure for Measure* 'Shakespeare plays Jane Austen by giving everybody the kind of marriage he or she deserves' (p. 77). This may be true of Lucio and Angelo but applies less to Mariana, who may be condemned to a loveless marriage.
22. Francis Bacon, *New Atlantis*, pp. 173–4.
23. Robert Burton, *The Anatomy of Melancholy* (1621), vol. 3, sec. 2, p. 54.
24. Janet Adelman, *Suffocating Mothers: Fantasies of Maternal Origin in Shakespeare's Plays, Hamlet to The Tempest*, implies that the preference of Angelo and Bertram for illicit sex with unattainable virgins would make a long-term relationship problematic for them (p. 78). Richard P. Wheeler, *Shakespeare's Development and the Problem Comedies*, also finds that 'the marriages that conclude *All's Well* and *Measure for Measure* seem only superficially to resolve antagonisms that have developed between degraded sexual desire and the moralized social orders of these two plays' (p. 3).
25. Williamson, 'The Problem Plays: Social Regulation of Desire', notes in *Measure for Measure* a 'radical divorce of marriage from desire'; the Duke reinforces marriage as a 'contractual tie . . . to coerce men into social responsibility' (pp. 101–2). Jean H. Hagstrum, *Esteem Enlivened by Desire: The Couple from Homer to Shakespeare*, partly defends the marriages at the end of the play because they show 'it is better to honor sexuality of any kind than to ignore it or freeze it into the Puritan's rule book' (p. 378).

26. Belsey, 'Desire's Excess and the English Renaissance Theatre: *Edward II, Troilus and Cressida, Othello*', p. 99.
27. See Stephen Booth (ed.), *Shakespeare's Sonnets*, p. 441. In the OED sense 16 of the noun 'spirit' is 'certain subtle highly refined substances or fluids ... formerly supposed to permeate the blood'. While this meaning rarely occurs in Shakespeare's work, it does appear in Mercutio's prurient fantasy of how to 'raise a spirit in his mistress' circle' (*Romeo and Juliet*, 2. 1. 24). Less bawdily, it remains an undertone of Leontes's nostalgic memory of his innocent boyhood with Polixenes, when their 'weak spirits [had] ne'er been rear'd / With stronger blood' (*The Winter's Tale*, 1. 2. 72–3).
28. Maurice Charney, *Shakespeare on Love and Lust*, comments on the 'sexist assumptions' of the bed trick because it is 'founded on the idea that women' are indistinguishable 'sexual objects' (pp. 67–8).
29. Carol Cook, 'Unbodied Figures of Desire', 36, 38.
30. Wells, *Shakespeare, Sex, and Love*, p. 122. Marliss C. Desens, *The Bed-Trick in English Renaissance Drama*, also argues that 'rape' is 'at the heart of the bed-trick' (p. 142) but that when a female (such as Helena) arranges it, her 'humiliation', not her power, is emphasised (p. 66).
31. In 'Consummation, Custom and Law in *All's Well that Ends Well*', Subha Mukherji quotes from 'witness depositions' in contract suits that make 'copulation' or cohabitation factors that 'could make an otherwise uncertain match conclusive' (p. 119).
32. Quoted in Mukherji, 'Consummation, Custom and Law in *All's Well that Ends Well*', p. 134.
33. Ranald, *Shakespeare and his Social Context*, pp. 35, 49.
34. Mariana's statement to Angelo, 'This is the hand which, with a vowed contract, / Was fast belock'd in thine' (5. 1. 209–10), makes it clear that this was a binding *de futuro* spousal, as described in Cook, *Making a Match*, p. 213.
35. Williamson, 'The Problem Plays: Social Regulation of Desire', examines how *All's Well* treats the theme of 'enforced marriage' (pp. 59–61); she contends that 'wardship' often 'amounted to a system of forced marriages', and because Bertram is a ward of the king he is 'forced' to marry Helena, a poor physician's daughter (pp. 62–3).
36. Wells, *Shakespeare, Sex, and Love*, p. 186.
37. René Girard, 'The Politics of Desire in *Troilus and Cressida*', p. 197.
38. Sigmund Freud, 'The Most Prevalent Form of Degradation in Erotic Life' (1912), corroborates the idea that desire is increased by the difficulty of fulfilling it – that 'Some obstacle is necessary to swell the tide of libido to its height' (p. 67).
39. Sinfield, 'Rape and Rights: *Measure for Measure* and the Limits of Cultural Imperialism', p. 182.
40. Laura Lunger Knoppers, '(En)gendering Shame: *Measure for Measure* and the Spectacles of Power', discusses how the play 'presents Isabella's chastity' as sexually 'threatening' to Angelo (464).
41. Cook, *Making a Match*, comments on how 'the buying and selling of lives, wives, and female bodies stands at the core of *Measure for Measure*' (p. 144). Pompey's defiant refusal to be 'whipt out of his trade' (2. 1. 256)

suggests that trading in unlicensed sex will continue, despite the Duke's attempt to quell it through marriage.
42. Catherine Belsey, 'Marriage: Imogen's Bedchamber', in *Shakespeare and the Loss of Eden*, p. 81.
43. H. B. Charlton formalised the term in *The Dark Comedies*.

Chapter 2

Male Lust, Power and Rape

In *Measure for Measure*, Angelo exemplifies what Shakespeare's Sonnet 129 so painfully covers – the potential 'hell' of 'lust in action', with its savagery, tormented feelings of urgency, and subsequent shame:

> Th'expense of spirit in a waste of shame
> Is lust in action, and till action, lust
> Is perjur'd, mur'drous, bloody, full of blame,
> Savage, extreme, rude, cruel, not to trust,
> Enjoy'd no sooner but despised straight,
> Past reason hunted, and no sooner had,
> Past reason hated as a swallowed bait
> On purpose laid to make the taker mad:
> [Mad] in pursuit and in possession so,
> Had, having, and in quest to have, extreme,
> A bliss in proof, and prov'd, [a] very woe,
> Before, a joy propos'd, behind, a dream.
>   All this the world well knows, yet none knows well
>   To shun the heaven that leads men to this hell.

In Middle English, as in Chaucer's time, 'lust' could refer more broadly to pleasure or delight (*OED*, sense 1), or what we might now call 'lust for life'. And when Paulina in Shakespeare's *The Winter's Tale* describes the newborn Perdita as 'a goodly babe, / Lusty and like to live' (2. 2. 24–5), she is using the epithet 'lusty' to signify 'full of animal life and spirits'[1] – a meaning that endures. But by the late sixteenth century, some semantic indeterminacy notwithstanding,[2] the term 'lust' was more usually equated with lechery.

Indeed the Christian society within which Shakespeare's work is grounded tends to draw firm boundaries between virtuous love and sinful lust. The horror with which Shakespeare's age regarded sexual promiscuity is clear from the opening of *A Sermon Against Whoredom and Uncleanness*, contained in the *First Book of Homilies* (1547). The audience at church, since churchgoing was mandatory then, would hear how the 'outrageous sea of adultery ... whoredom, fornication and uncleanness, have not only [burst] in, but also overflowed almost the whole world'.[3] When Malcolm is testing Macduff's loyalty in *Macbeth*, he envisages 'boundless intemperance' in similar terms, painting it as a sin that will undermine the commonwealth. As part of his masquerade, he claims that were he to gain royal power he could never be sexually satisfied; all the women in Scotland, matrons and virgins alike, could not 'fill up / The cistern of [his] lust' (4. 3. 66, 62–3). In an image of overflowing that recalls the *Sermon*, Malcolm goes on to compare his lust to a torrent breaking through retaining walls:

> My desire
> All continent impediments would o'erbear
> That did oppose my will. (63–5)

After projecting an implacable sexual 'will', the 'voluptuousness' of an 'ill-composed affection' that is capable of confounding 'all unity on earth', he claims that this kind of tyranny will lead to worse crimes than 'black Macbeth' has committed (61, 77, 100, 52).

Of course Malcolm is fabricating this grim vision of himself as a future ruler. He goes on to affirm that he is sexually pure. But the extravagant vision of how a tyrant's unbridled lust would turn social 'concord' into 'hell' (98) indicates acute anxiety over the destructiveness of unrestrained sexuality. Our predominantly secular twenty-first century tends to view sexual desire – or 'lust in action' in its more benign form – as a welcome component in an adult love relationship. Or, judged by the contemporary hook-up culture, sexual intercourse between consenting partners is considered a pleasurable activity to be enjoyed for its own sake. For Shakespeare's contemporaries, however, lust as lechery was still condemned as one of the Seven Deadly Sins. St Paul, much preferring celibacy to monogamy, had only reluctantly conceded that 'to marry' was a 'better' alternative than 'to burn' in hell (1 Corinthians 7: 9). Moreover lust, or exercising sexual desire for its own sake, was not encouraged even if the partners were married. Nowadays, though, it's regarded as anomalous if married couples are not enjoying sexual intimacy together.[4] By 1980, the Anglican *Book of Common Prayer* was encouraging wedded couples to 'strengthen the union of their hearts and lives' through 'the joy of their bodily union'.[5] But in the late sixteenth century, marriage was celebrated not as a legal expression of sexual love as much as it was 'ordained', according to the ceremony outlined in the original 1559 *Book of Common Prayer* and carried through subsequent versions, for the 'procreation of children'. Just as importantly, being joined in matrimony was designated 'a remedy against sin and to avoid fornication [sex outside marriage]'.

This 'Solemnization of Matrimony' service goes on to make a point of distinguishing marriage as a sacred union entered into 'discreetly, advisedly, soberly, and in the fear of God' from one entered into 'lightly or wantonly, to satisfy man's [presumably woman's too] carnal lusts and appetites'. Certainly Shakespeare's contemporaries were likely to take a strong moral stand on 'carnal lusts and appetites' generated outside the bond of marriage. Writing in 1615, Alexander Niccholes reinforces the idea that 'lust' is the 'chief breaker' of marriages 'of all from eighteene to eight[y]'.[6] But even within the married state itself, as Stephen Greenblatt outlines,[7] excessive passion was frowned on, considered antipathetic to the sober 'mutual society, help, and comfort' which, according to the 'Solemnization', should obtain between wedded couples.

Shakespeare's drama, especially as it grows in complexity, avoids making such a firm distinction between strong sexual desire and a loving partnership. But during the 1590s, *The Rape of Lucrece*, as well as several of Shakespeare's early plays, was concerned to show how lust, or raging sexual 'will', differs from love. As a realist, the poet-dramatist doesn't shy away from exploring the dark side of male desire, the consequences of 'carnal lusts' within a patriarchal culture that had the power to subjugate women physically as well as socially. Shakespeare is clearly interested not just in presenting the phenomenon of rape but in analysing what fuels it. Several of his Roman and history plays present men's violent assaults on women as a combination of lustful desire, an urge to violate female chastity, and (in wartime especially) a brutal assertion of power over the relatively powerless. And at the end of his career, as part of a schematic contrast between innocent chastity and unregulated sexuality, Shakespeare's late romances return to the idea of how crude male lust may trigger attempted rape.

In *The Rape of Lucrece* Shakespeare explores a form of male lust close to that depicted in Sonnet 129, which excludes any mention of how sexual fulfilment may be part of a committed and loving relationship. Rather than forging an emotional or even a spiritual bond, violent 'lust in action' is sterile, an expenditure dissipated in a 'waste of shame'. Tarquin makes a quick concession to love when he considers asking Lucrece to take pity on his urgent desire: 'I'll beg her love', for 'there is no hate in loving' (240–1). But 'will', denoting sexual drive, appears fourteen times in the text, and 'lust' (and 'lustful'), used no fewer than twenty-five times, becomes the poem's dominant theme. The pinnacle of Tarquin's quest, the moment when 'pride' (sexual arousal) is at its height, packs the key words 'lust', 'will' and 'desire' into three lines:

> While Lust is in his pride, no exclamation
> Can curb his heat, or rein his rash desire,
> Till like a jade, Self-will himself doth tire. (705–7)

Nevertheless, Tarquin doesn't commit this atrocity without some prevarication. As well as depicting the war that Tarquin's 'hot' lust wages on Lucrece's chastity, *The Rape of Lucrece* debates at length whether moral considerations and honourable conduct should trump sexual desire. Tarquin's personal battle is between 'frozen conscience and hot-burning will' (247); his dilemma is whether he should be 'Pawning his honor to obtain his lust' (156).

For a time Tarquin's 'dread' of disastrous moral consequences (171) checks his 'reprobate desire' for Lucrece (300). The moral dilemma that Tarquin faces in many ways resembles what Shakespeare explores with greater poetic and psychological complexity in his later tragedy *Macbeth* (1606). *The Rape of Lucrece* links lust and murder as violent crimes through the description of 'dead of night' as a time when 'pure thoughts are dead and still, / While lust and murder wakes to stain and kill' (167–8). In *Macbeth*, too, the protagonist's murder of King Duncan is envisaged as a kind of monstrous sexual act, a rape on the sleeping king.[8] Like Macbeth, who becomes 'bound in / To saucy doubts and fears' (3. 4. 23–4) after committing his heinous crime, Tarquin understands in advance how 'The guilt being great, the fear doth still exceed' (229). Again resembling Macbeth, Tarquin rehearses the 'sundry dangers of his will's obtaining' (128), for he recognises that the transitory pleasure of conquering Lucrece will bring excessive shame and 'griefs' in its wake (139). Since Shakespeare takes at least seventeen stanzas to amplify this crisis of conscience, Tarquin appears sincere when he tells Lucrece 'I have debated even in my soul, / What wrong, what shame, what sorrow I shall breed' (498–9). Reinforcing the arguments against the base act of rape, Lucrece points out how Tarquin has a duty not to reward her hospitality and her husband's trusting friendship with the kind of 'black payment' (576) that runs counter to all norms of chivalry. But just as Macbeth, once he is resolute, identifies himself with 'wither'd murder' moving through the darkness 'with Tarquin's ravishing strides' – in other words, like the rapist striding purposefully towards his goal until he has accomplished ('done') the black 'deed' (*Macbeth*, 2. 1. 52–5, 2. 2. 14) – so in *The Rape of Lucrece* lustful Tarquin 'sets his foot upon the light' (673) and refuses to pity his victim.

As Tarquin ponders the downside of acting on lustful 'will' and then experiences revulsion after the rape itself, the poem's diction comes remarkably close to that of Sonnet 129. Debating his moral position beforehand, Tarquin anticipates the 'waste of shame' entailed by 'lust in action' in his apostrophe 'O shame to knighthood, and to shining arms!' (197). His 'will' is 'strong, past reason's weak removing' (243), just as 'lust' in Sonnet 129 hunts its prey 'past reason' (6); relentless sexual desire defies rational restraints. The sonnet's observation that lust is 'Enjoy'd no sooner but despised straight' (5) tallies with how Tarquin's 'hot desire converts to cold disdain' (691) when he 'chides his vanish'd loath'd delight' after the rape (742). He anticipates that what he seeks will turn out to be a 'dream, a breath, a froth of fleeting joy' (212), or what the sonnet depicts as 'Before, a joy proposed, behind a dream' (12).

Clearly Tarquin is trapped in a no-win situation. He knows that 'repentant tears ensue the deed' of rape (502) and yet he feels bound to continue his quest. Even at an early stage he is locked into a conundrum, debating 'The sundry dangers of his will's obtaining; / Yet ever to obtain his will resolving' (128–9). Tarquin's dilemma demonstrates how 'masculine desire' is what Mark Breitenberg calls a 'destabilizing if not self-destructive force':[9] a precariousness pointed up by the contradictory meanings within the signifier 'will' itself. For Tarquin's 'will' – insistent sexual desire as a force he is ultimately powerless to resist – overrides the other (primary) sense of 'will' as individual determination or resolve. Regrettably, positive willpower and rational choice are undercut by the relentless drive of masculine desire.[10]

Ironically Tarquin tries to marry these two meanings of 'will' when he forges ahead with the rape plan, declaring that 'my will is backed by resolution' (352). From this point on, however, he is driven solely by lustful desire, speciously rationalising that darkness will cover 'the shame that follows sweet delight' (357). Just as Sonnet 129 presents strong sexual desire as brutal in the act of 'having, and in quest to have', so Tarquin's lust becomes 'savage', 'extreme' and 'rude' indeed (10, 4). Once Tarquin is fully aroused, his hand 'Smoking with pride' (438), he pushes on like a remorseless warrior, finding that 'nothing can affection's course control, / Or stop the headlong fury of his speed' (500–1). He justifies his brutal action by envisaging lust as his military commander: 'Affection is my captain, and he leadeth' (271).[11] Anticipating the dark comedy that deals most bluntly with sexual desire, *Troilus and Cressida*, Tarquin's disdain for reason resembles that expressed by the sensualist Troilus. Trusting to the sensory 'pilots' of 'eyes and ears' to mediate between 'will and judgment', Troilus claims that 'reason and respect / Make livers pale and lustihood deject' (*Troilus and Cressida*, 2. 2. 63–5, 49–50). Likewise the charged-up Roman declares that 'Respect and reason' have no purchase on vigorous sexuality; instead they 'wait on wrinkled age' (275). Answering the prompting of his 'lustful eye' (179), Tarquin also resolves that 'desire' will be his 'pilot' (279).

Emphatically it is the 'eye', the visual impact of what Tarquin sees, that incites lustful desire instead of love. Conventional treatments of love in Shakespeare's time underline how the male's perception of the female's beauty, as well as the inspiration of her radiant eyes, moves his heart and sparks the phenomenon of love at first sight. For Neo-Platonic as well as Petrarchan lovers, the eye induces a sense of reverence, a perception of almost divine beauty that goes beyond sexual desire alone. But what Tarquin sees with 'greedy eyeballs' (368) simply drives his need to possess Lucrece sexually. In Shakespeare's slightly earlier erotic poem, *Venus and Adonis*, Venus reveres Adonis's physical beauty, cherishing and promising hourly to kiss the lovely 'purple flow'r' that springs from the blood of his death-wound (1168). But in *The Rape of Lucrece*, Tarquin's ocular attraction to Lucrece rapidly converts to aggressive lust rather than the 'admiration' (wonder) of love (418).

When he first sees her, Tarquin the warrior envisages the 'lilies' and 'roses' in Lucrece's face – the varying red and white of the lady's complexion conventionally celebrated in love poetry – as 'pure ranks' in a 'war' that he plans to win (71–3). Lucrece's eyes are later described by the poet, in traditional Petrarchan fashion, as 'two suns' (1224), and Lucrece herself dazzles her assailant with her 'greater light', even while she is sleeping (375–7). In her bedchamber, Tarquin's 'rage of lust' is briefly 'by gazing qualified' (424); that is, until Lucrece's chaste beauty ('alabaster skin') inflames his desire to violate her (419). Then his 'eye, which late this mutiny restrains, / Unto a greater uproar stirs his veins' (426–7). Now heart and eye work in tandem, but with brute physicality rather than emotional reverence, for 'his drumming heart cheers up his burning eye' (435). As soon as his 'eye commends the leading to his hand' (436), this hand becomes a means to lay siege to Lucrece's chastity. Tarquin's 'Will', his unrestrained sexual desire, is deaf to moral arguments, for having 'an eye to gaze on beauty', it simply 'dotes on what [it] looks, 'gainst law or duty' (495–7).

So far this analysis has centred on the presentation of lust: how Tarquin's overriding 'will' or sexual desire is fuelled by his 'lustful eye' as he gazes at Lucrece's body. But the act of rape in this poem does not take place in a social vacuum. The poem is situated in the patriarchal society of Rome, where men compete not only for military honour but for who owns the most beautiful and chaste wife. Such a male-dominated culture, not unlike that of Shakespeare in the early seventeenth century, tends to turn the female into what Nancy Vickers terms a 'commodity in the traffic between men'.[12] Tarquin's need to possess Lucrece is actually inspired by her husband Collatine, who rashly 'Unlock'd the treasure of his happy state' by boasting about his peerless wife to his fellow warriors (16). Collatine's *blason* on his wife's beauty – his conventional tribute to Lucrece's physical attractiveness, her 'red and white' complexion and eyes bright as heavenly stars (11–13) – inevitably fills Tarquin with 'envy' (39) as well as lust. As a 'play of power' between Tarquin and his comrade-in-arms, the 'boasting match' has disastrous consequences.[13] Even more than Lucrece's beauty, her chastity – the very 'name' of ' "chaste" ' – has 'set' a 'bateless edge' on Tarquin's 'keen appetite' (8–9). He resolves to steal the 'rich jewel' that belongs to a rival male (34).

Rape, as the forced sexual subjugation of a woman, is as much about the assertion of male power as about desire – often more so. Feminist commentators such as Anna Clark have observed that in male-dominated cultures, which of course includes Shakespeare's, 'sexual violence' can function 'as a means of patriarchal domination'.[14] The very opposite of a loving act, violent sexual assault implies hatred of women, for the misogynist 'rapist', in Alan Sinfield's words, 'desires to spoil the pure, to violate, to hurt and degrade'.[15] Shakespeare's poem portrays in considerable detail the dynamics of lust and the visual stimuli that excite males. But co-existing with Tarquin's physical response to Lucrece's beauty is his cruel urge to wield power over her – a fierce 'ambition' to dominate Lucrece sexually (411), to destroy what she and her husband Collatine most prize. Lucrece's vaunted chastity becomes a spur for Tarquin. As part of a culture that, like Shakespeare's, fails to respect women as men's equals but tends to view them more as valued possessions, he feels little compunction over degrading what is most precious to a married female. Moreover he can achieve his goal, violating Lucrece, through superior physical strength. When he confronts Lucrece in her bedroom Tarquin threateningly 'shakes aloft his Roman blade' (505), brandishing his sword as a phallic substitute before he takes her by force.

While exploring what drives Tarquin to conquer this female, *The Rape of Lucrece* does not bypass the victim herself. The poem's point of view is not restricted to that of the male rapist; more than half the narrative is devoted to showing how Lucrece, an icon of chastity, responds to being forced by a male aggressor. Although Lucrece attempts to resist Tarquin, through both her lengthy oratory (575–672) and her outcry as he rapes her (he has to use her nightdress to stifle the sound (681–2)), she is depicted, overall, as a victim who lacks the power to defeat her aggressor. While sleeping she is described as a 'virtuous monument', a passive female body 'To be admir'd of lewd unhallowed eyes' (391–2). Displaying Lucrece as the object of Tarquin's 'lustful' gaze, the narrator goes on to catalogue, voyeuristically, Lucrece's golden hair, 'alabaster skin' and 'coral lips' (419–20) before paying special attention to her breasts (407–8, 439–41). The dominant image of Lucrece is that of a helpless creature. She trembles like a 'new-kill'd bird' (457), as powerless as 'a white hind under the gripe's sharp claws' (543). In pleading with her attacker Lucrece refers to herself as a 'weakling' (584), while after the rape she indicts herself as a 'weak hive [belonging to her husband] in which a wand'ring wasp hath crept' (839). Tarquin's fierce overpowering of Lucrece is imaged as a wild animal claiming its victim: 'The wolf has seized his prey; the poor lamb cries' (677).

True, the victimised female is given a voice. But locked within the norms of her society, viewing herself as a devoted wife who, as the property of her husband, has disgraced him through her pollution, Lucrece cannot, as Coppélia Kahn points out, claim 'a vantage point distinct from the patriarchal ideology that generated Tarquin's act'.[16] Shakespeare's culture reiterates this idea that a woman's disgrace reflects badly on her husband. Thus William Gouge, in *Of Domesticall Duties* (1622), claims that '*a virtuous wife is a crown to her husband*' while '*an infamous wife is a shame to her husband*'.[17] Before he rapes her, Tarquin warns Lucrece that if she refuses to submit willingly he will tie her dead body to that of a servant. By making it appear that Lucrece has committed adultery with a 'worthless' slave (515), the rapist will ensure that her husband becomes 'The scornful mark of every open eye' (520).

The terrible act doesn't only imbue the victim with a sense of 'shame' (1202). It convinces her that the violation is her own 'trespass' (1070), a 'fault' that she has somehow committed herself (1073). While on one level she accepts that her rape was a forced 'offense', a 'compelled stain' on her honour (1701, 1708), she still torments herself for being too 'weak' to offer sufficient resistance to Tarquin. In her imagined dialogue with Collatine her verdict on herself is severe: 'Yet am I guilty of thy honor's wrack' (841). And although she expresses outrage when she tears with her nails the image of Sinon on the painting of the Fall of Troy because the traitor reminds her of Tarquin's deceiving appearance (1564), Lucrece tends to displace most of her anger elsewhere. She first turns her urge to retaliate into self-punishment, tearing her own flesh (739). Allying herself with the mythic figure of Philomel, who pricked her own breast to 'keep her sharp woes waking' after being raped (1136), Lucrece masochistically envisages placing a sword against her body for the same purpose.[18] To restore honour to the 'Dear lord' who owns the 'dear jewel' of married chastity that she has 'lost' (1191), Lucrece sees no other remedy than to shed her 'foul defiled blood' (1029).

Once she resolves to commit suicide, Lucrece becomes a more active agent, planning to restore her family's reputation even as she ensure the downfall of her rapist. Possibly, as Laura G. Bromley argues, she becomes heroic, turning herself from a victim into 'an individual capable of purposely creating a new integrated self to transcend her corruption'.[19] Lucrece is able to affirm 'I am the mistress of my fate' (1069). Yet her decision to destroy herself, courageous because suicide wasn't the 'culturally accepted thing' for wives to do in this society,[20] still works more to repair her husband's good name than her own. After revealing to her husband and father what has happened to her, this dutiful wife continues to feel her 'stain' more than they do. Collatine and Lucretius would willingly release her from any shame because, as she herself acknowledges, her mind remains 'immaculate and spotless' (1656). But having rebuked herself for having a 'spotted, spoil'd, corrupted' body (1172), which, when it was pure, served as a badge of honour for Collatine, she now plans to bequeath even her heroic 'resolution' to her husband (1200).[21]

This sense of women as the 'weak oppress'd sex' in *The Rape of Lucrece* is underlined by the narrator's maxim that 'men have marble, women waxen minds' (1240–2). This is how the patriarch Theseus in *A Midsummer Night's Dream* reminds Hermia of her obligation to her father – that she is 'but as a form in wax' to be 'imprinted' by him (1. 1. 49–50). When the narrator of *Lucrece* similarly asserts that an 'impression' may be 'form'd' in women by male 'force' (1242–3), he goes further, making physical domination of the female by the male seem almost inevitable. Even the female protagonist in *Measure for Measure*, Isabella, reinforces the conventional view that men exploit women's wax-like softness when she concedes to Angelo that women are 'ten times frail' and 'credulous to false prints' (2. 4. 128–30). Such orthodox thinking – that women's frailty and susceptibility encourage men to take advantage of them – tends to blame the female victim herself for being sexually violated.

Yet Lucrece, for all her subsequent self-flagellation, is in no way at fault. Building toward his act of rape, Tarquin is constantly portrayed as a sexual predator, Lucrece as the victim who has no choice but to resist. The poem's dominant trope of martial conquest reinforces the idea of male aggression. Equating his erotic quest with a military siege, Tarquin finds Lucrece's chaste body a 'never-conquered fort' to be scaled (481–482), just as her breasts are 'A pair of maiden worlds unconquered' (408).[22] The pure matron presents to him an irresistible challenge; soldier-like, his 'ambition' is to 'make the breach and enter the fort' (481). Like Richard III blaming Anne's 'beauty' and arresting gaze for driving him to kill her husband and father-in-law (*Richard III*), Tarquin impudently blames his victim for inflaming him to the point where he must violate her: 'Thy beauty hath ensnared thee to this night' (485). The 'fault', he claims, belongs to Lucrece, because her 'eyes' have lured him into a sinful assault on her chastity (482–3).

This military trope is so pervasive in the poem, so indicative of the dominant culture – men having authority through their physical and political power while women are subjugated and made to feel shame – that Lucrece herself employs it when she chastises her body as a 'blemish'd fort' (1175). She remains imprinted with the idea that her body is a shrine sacred to her husband, an edifice that must be fortified against attack by other men. Even in its poetic development, *The Rape of Lucrece* sets up a position of privilege for the male. Despite much of the narrative treating the aftermath of the rape – Lucrece's prolonged lamentation and her resolve to take her own life when her husband returns (747–1078) – it is the male subject who generates the most poetic power. Tarquin's conflict between hot lust and cool reason, along with his voyeuristic scanning of the female body as he moves toward his goal, is presented more arrestingly than are Lucrece's relatively conventional complaints. Whereas Lucrece is locked into what Coppélia Kahn calls 'a paradigm for all ages of the meaning of chastity in a patriarchy', the male aggressor gains traction as an 'inwardly divided, heroically torn subject'.[23]

How does this narrative depiction of sexual desire and conquest connect to references to rape elsewhere in Shakespeare's work? In his plays, sex is all too often equated with some form of male violence.[24] In *A Midsummer Night's Dream* Demetrius, full of loathing for discarded Helena, warns her that he may do her 'mischief' in the dark wood (2. 1. 237), advising her that she should not

> trust the opportunity of night,
> And the ill counsel of a desert place,
> With the rich worth of [her] virginity. (217–19)

Not above taking advantage of her masochistic, spaniel-like devotion, he makes raping her seem a distinct possibility.[25] This is a comedy that begins with Duke Theseus's description of winning Hippolita through phallic power – 'I woo'd thee with my sword' – and consolidating that power in a sadistic manner: 'And won thy love doing thee injuries' (1. 1. 16–17). When Laertes in *Hamlet* is warning Ophelia to guard her chastity, he uses a submerged military metaphor, 'keep you in the rear of your affection, / Out of the shot and danger of desire' (1. 3. 34–5), to suggest that women need to fight a rearguard action against men's aggressive sexual pursuit. Otherwise there's a strong chance that their own sexual nature ('affection') might be overcome by the fierce weapon, or 'shot', of male 'desire'.

Even *Romeo and Juliet*, which many readers view as the apotheosis of romantic tragedy, begins with 'phallic competitiveness',[26] as the Capulet servants depict sex in terms of violent male domination. Gregory remarks that women, as 'weaker vessels', are 'ever thrust against the wall', and he equates forced loss of virginity with decapitation when he casually speaks of cutting off 'the heads of the maids, or their maidenheads' (1. 1. 15–16, 25–6). Romeo is a little more refined when he complains, in the same scene, that Rosaline 'will not stay the siege of loving terms, / Nor bide th' encounter of assailing eyes' (1. 1. 212–13). But clearly he would like to conquer this female sexually. Metaphors of seducing women by laying 'siege' to them, which crop up in the comedies, signify that the male doesn't respect his quarry; the lustful Bertram in *All's Well that Ends Well* 'lays down his wanton siege' to seduce beautiful Diana (3. 7. 18), while *Cymbeline*'s Imogen finds the crude 'love-suit' of the bestial Cloten 'fearful as a siege' (3. 4. 133). Falstaff in *The Merry Wives of Windsor* turns into a more harmless version of Tarquin when he is thwarted from trying to 'lay an amiable siege to the honesty of Ford's wife' (2. 2. 234–5). Among verbs in Shakespeare that 'imply a man's deliberate siege of, and assault upon, a woman's power of sexual resistance', Eric Partridge lists 'assail', 'attempt', 'besiege', 'enforce', 'ransack', 'spoil' and 'wrack'.[27]

The Taming of the Shrew enacts male domination of a different kind, not through crude seduction or attempted rape but rather the reverse strategy; Petruchio's humiliating punishments include withholding marital rites from Kate. Treating her like a 'haggard', a hawk that resists being tamed, Petruchio sadistically plans to 'man [his] haggard' by keeping his new wife hungry ('passing empty') and sleep-deprived, just as 'we watch these kites / That bate and beat and will not be obedient' (4. 1. 190–6). Petruchio will also restrict her from any lovemaking, violent or tame. His resolve to treat this feisty woman as though she were a recalcitrant hawk mirrors Othello's use of the falconry metaphor. Determined to cast off Desdemona violently at the first whiff of marital disobedience, Othello also invokes male authority backed by force:

> If I do prove her haggard,
> Though that her jesses [straps] were my dear heart-strings,
> I'd whistle her off, and let her down the wind
> To prey at fortune. (*Othello*, 3. 3. 260–3)

Shakespeare's history play *Henry V*, which covers England's war to win France, returns to the idea of rape; it trades on the assumption that violating women is a way to solidify military conquest. In contrast to the earlier *Henry VI* trilogy, where Joan of Arc wins battles and Queen

Margaret organises the king's troops, women in the later play do not act as warriors. Instead they are envisaged as the spoils of war. The feminist critics Jean E. Howard and Phyllis Rackin point out how monarchs in the *Henry IV* and *Henry VI* plays, lacking a strong genealogical claim to the throne, need to dominate others through the 'ideology of masculine performance'. These critics go so far as to argue that such an ideology makes rape a 'necessary' crime.[28]

Although it never materialises on stage, Henry V's dark projection of what will happen if the Governor of Harfleur fails to surrender his city to the British forces may be even more horrifying, because so impersonal, than the description of Tarquin's assault on Lucrece. Tarquin is driven by the urgency of sexual desire as well as 'rage' to 'make the breach' and enter Lucrece's 'fair city' (468–9). When Henry first rouses his army to enter 'Once more into the breach' of Harfleur, he uses inflammatory rhetoric instead; his exhortation to 'stiffen the sinews', 'pry through' and let the brow 'o'erwhelm' (or cover) the eye (*Henry V*, 3. 1. 1–11) is a virtual 'invitation to gang rape'.[29] Sexual lust partners with male blood-lust. 'Disguis[ing] fair nature with hard-favor'd rage', Henry's soldiers are urged to prove their manhood by imitating the inhumane tiger (6–8). The king even hopes that English noblemen, by behaving savagely, will serve as role models to their social inferiors, becoming 'copy now to [men] of grosser blood' to 'teach them how to war' (24–5). Outside the walls of Harfleur Henry threatens the French ruthlessly, putting the blame on them if their virgins become the spoils of war:

> What is't to me, when you yourselves are cause,
> If your pure maidens fall into the hand
> Of hot and forcing violation? (3. 3. 19–21)

A specious justification becomes worse; Henry's vision turns more cruel. Along with 'headly murther' and 'spoil' (32), he promises rape by the 'flesh'd soldier' (11) as a direct consequence of the Governor's failing to beg for mercy. In a moment the French will see 'The blind and bloody soldier with foul hand / [Defile] the locks' of their 'shrill-shrieking daughters' (34–5).

Whether Henry fully intends to carry out this assault, or is adopting the callous persona of a military conqueror to intimidate his audience and claim the city, remains unclear. Kenneth Branagh's Henry, in the film production of *Henry V* (1989), showed distinct relief at not having to follow through on his threat. But the French princess, as Henry's 'capital demand' in the peace treaty forged at the end of the play (5. 2. 96), also represents French territory that the English king must conquer and appropriate. In the scene following Henry's horrific projection of what will happen to French virgins if Harfleur does not surrender, we are introduced to Princess Katherine, safe in her father's palace (3. 4). This juxtaposition of scenes has the effect of making the princess the 'potential rape victim we never actually saw at Harfleur'.[30] In coy fashion, Katherine's English lesson puts the female body on display and sexualises it; we know that once Henry is victorious in the war Katherine will have to submit to him, even though the king goes through the ritual of courting her. Certainly the king plays the crude soldier in his wooing game, wishing he could 'leap into a wife' as easily as he vaults on to his horse wearing full armour (5. 2. 137–9). When the French king compares cities to be conquered with virgins, by analogy his daughter Katherine becomes a city 'all girdled with maiden walls' (322). Despite his token courtship, Henry plans to wed Katherine as the 'way' to his 'will' (328) – a siege operation that echoes the warrior Tarquin's sexual assault on chaste Lucrece.

Henry's repeated premise, that battle will entail violent rape by the conquering soldiers, is canvassed in other plays that deal with warfare. Learning that Coriolanus is preparing to sack Rome with an army of Volscians, Cominius blames the Tribunes for what he imagines will inevitably happen to the Roman women. By banishing their own war hero, the Tribunes (charges Cominius) will have helped 'to ravish' their own daughters and must witness their wives 'dishonor'd' in front of them (*Coriolanus*, 4. 6. 81–3).[31] This vision of rape in war is amplified more brutally in the tragedy *Timon of Athens*, when hate-filled Timon hopes that the general Alcibiades will show no mercy when he invades the city. Earlier Timon savagely invokes 'confusion' on Athens by envisaging how raping virgins, submitting them to disease, would be a vile way of tearing down the moral norms of civilised society: 'To general filths / Convert o' th' instant, green virginity!' (4. 1. 21, 6–7). Now he begs Alcibiades, 'Put armor on thine ears and on thine eyes / Whose proof nor yells of mothers, maids, nor babes, / . . . Shall pierce a jot' (4. 3. 124–7). Timon pledges to show no pity if, when the warrior sacks the city, he gives 'holy virgins to the stain / Of contumelious, beastly, mad-brained war' (5. 1. 173–4).

Such projections of rape are part of the brutality of war that Shakespeare depicts. But the early tragedy *Titus Andronicus* (1592–4), which Shakespeare composed in collaboration with George Peele,[32] is the only one of his plays in which lust leads to actual rape. Mercifully – and for practical reasons – the act itself, the rape of Titus's daughter Lavinia, takes place offstage.[33] Though unseen, it forms part of a series of horrific acts, including mutilation and cannibalism as well as sexual assault, that turn this Senecan revenge play into an odd mixture of realism and literary stylisation. Set in ancient Rome, *Titus Andronicus* places rape within the context of Roman history. Since Shakespeare was composing the play about the same time that he worked on *The Rape of Lucrece*, it's not surprising that the script (which contains fifteen of the twenty instances of the word 'rape' found in the whole of Shakespeare's work) refers more frequently to Tarquin and Lucrece than does any other play in the canon. Titus wonders whether it's the cruel Roman emperor Saturninus who has raped his daughter, just as Tarquin 'left the camp to sin in Lucrece' bed' (4. 1. 64). Titus goes on to compare himself to Junius Brutus, who urged Lucrece's father and husband to take revenge 'for Lucrece's rape' (91). Meanwhile the iconic Lucrece herself has been dubbed 'not more chaste / Than this Lavinia' (2. 1. 108–9).[34] One effect of these classical allusions might be to cushion the Elizabethan audience from making connections between rape that happened centuries ago and sexual violence within their own culture. It's been convincingly argued by Catherine R. Stimpson, however, that introducing this historical parallel has the opposite effect; it underscores the contemporary relevance of rape by giving 'weight' to the idea that this brutal act has happened before and 'will occur again'.[35]

As is the case with Tarquin's violation of Lucrece, the rape of Lavinia combines sexual voracity with an insistence on male power. Aaron, the recipient of Tamora's 'burning lust' (5. 1. 43), is a caricature of the 'lusty Moor' – Iago's spiteful label for Othello (*Othello*, 2. 1. 295). But despite his boast, near the play's end, that almost every day he would 'Ravish a maid or plot the way to do it' (5. 1. 129), Aaron is not the play's sexual predator. Instead he hands off that role to Chiron and Demetrius, Tamora's sons, by encouraging them to rape Lavinia. In Act 2 they not only violate her but chop off her hands and cut out her tongue to prevent her from revealing their crime. After taking 'turns' to serve their 'lust' (2. 1. 129–30), they deny their victim any 'means of self-expression'.[36] By Act 5, the young men are reduced to their symbolic roles in the action, representing Rape and Murder when they accompany Tamora in her guise as Revenge, planning to hoodwink Titus into believing they will aid his own revenge mission.

The crudity of the young men's lust is highlighted with some realism at the beginning of Act 2. Chiron and Demetrius, described by Leslie A. Fiedler as 'more like walking phalluses than complete men',[37] enter the stage fighting over which one should win Lavinia. Although Chiron blithely asserts 'I love Lavinia more than all the world' (2. 1. 72), within less than thirty lines Aaron has convinced him to take advantage of the 'unfrequented' forest walks that are 'Fitted by kind for rape and villainy' (115–16). Protestations of love are quickly forgotten; 'shadowed from

Heaven's eye', both brothers feel entitled to 'revel in Lavinia's treasury' (130–1). The sexual rivalry between these males has quickly turned into camaraderie, what Eve Kosofsky Sedgwick calls the 'traffic in women' that forms a bond 'between men'.[38]

While the siblings are driven by sexual urgency, raping Lavinia is also an assertion of power, personal as well as political. Like their mother, Chiron and Demetrius hope to triumph over the hated Andronici family, and raping Titus's daughter is one way to achieve that. Notwithstanding their mother's new status, promoted from the Queen of the Goths to the Empress of Rome once she marries Saturninus, the brothers are part of the Goth nation that has been subjugated by the Romans in the recent war. Sexual conquest, combined with their murder of Lavinia's Roman husband, can assuage their sense of having been dominated by the enemy. This one-upmanship through rape is what also motivates Jack Cade, the working man aspiring to be ruler of England in *Henry VI, Part 2*. In his rise to power he imagines taking on the *droit de seigneur* (the landlord's aristocratic right to enjoy his female tenants before their husbands do) when he boasts, 'There shall not be a maid be married, but she shall pay to me her maidenhead ere they have it' (4. 7. 121–3). The irony is that by doing so Cade would become as depraved as those he indicts. His imagined violence mimics the brutality of the noblemen who (he claims) 'ravish' the commoners' 'wives and daughters' before the men's very 'faces' (4. 8. 30–1).

Chiron and Demetrius, comrades in barbarism, don't rape Lavinia in front of her husband Bassianus; they kill him first, provoked by Tamora's false claim that the married couple have threatened to kill her. Lavinia's insistence on her 'chastity' – her female badge of honour – only provides further incentive for them to violate her with 'worse than killing lust' (2. 3. 124, 175). Their plot to compound the outrage on Lavinia by raping her over the body of her dead husband, making 'his dead trunk pillow' to their 'lust' (130), might initially seem too gross to be Shakespeare's invention. While it's tempting to blame Peele, this is not one of the scenes attributed to him; what's more, Shakespeare introduces a similar motif in his late play *Cymbeline* (1610). There the brutish Cloten, angry that Imogen could consider the 'very garment' of her husband Posthumus more worthy than his own self-styled 'noble' person, resolves to kill Posthumus 'in her eyes' and then dress up in her dead husband's clothes before he rapes her (3. 5. 135–8). Like Tarquin competing with Collatine in *The Rape of Lucrece*, or Tamora's sons triumphing over Lavinia's husband by killing him before raping his wife, that would be Cloten's way of besting Posthumus. Forcibly possessing Posthumus's chaste wife would, he believes, be a way to appropriate his rival's identity and status. Cloten fantasises that when his 'lust hath din'd', he will cut his rival's garments in pieces and brutally kick Imogen all the way back home (141–4).

In its treatment of attempted rape *Cymbeline*, though to a much lesser extent than *Titus Andronicus*, also echoes *The Rape of Lucrece*. Italianate Iachimo, considerably subtler in his tactics than Cloten is, manipulates the suspicious husband Posthumus into believing that his wife is seducible by aping the role of romantic lover; he creates a *blason* that pays tribute to the particularity of Imogen's body. Stealthily emerging from the trunk in Imogen's bedchamber to gather evidence, Iachimo compares himself to Tarquin, who 'thus / Did softly press the rushes ere he waken'd / The chastity he wounded' (2. 2. 12–14). Just as Tarquin is spurred to rape after Lucrece's husband Collatine describes his wife as both beautiful and chaste – 'that name of "chaste" unhapp'ly set / The bateless edge on his keen appetite' (*The Rape of Lucrece*, 8–9) – so Iachimo salaciously confesses that he was provoked to test Imogen's fidelity by hearing Posthumus praise her amazing purity: 'He spake of her as Dian had hot dreams, / And she alone were cold' (*Cymbeline*, 5. 5. 180–1). A boasting match results in a crude bet. As the rival male, Iachimo competes to possess Posthumus's chaste wife sexually. If he fails, he can at least convince the husband that he has done so, and thus assert his superiority over a man who believes he has been shamefully cuckolded.

Several of the details through which Iachimo objectifies the sleeping female body parallel those in *The Rape of Lucrece*. Imogen's 'white and azure-lac'd' eyelids (2. 2. 22), for instance, recall Tarquin's gloating over the 'azure veins' on Lucrece's breasts, visualised as 'ivory globes circled with blue' (419, 407). It's as if Iachimo, unable to conquer Imogen's body, nevertheless succeeds in violating her with his male gaze. The physical detail he observes most closely is the 'mole cinque-spotted' (2. 2. 38) on her left breast. To convince Posthumus that he has 'tasted' Imogen in bed (2. 4. 57) Iachimo describes kissing that mole, which, he claims, 'gave [him] present hunger / To feed again, though full' (137–8). As with the lustful eye of Tarquin, which offers its owner such satisfaction that 'cloy'd with much, he pineth still for more' (*The Rape of Lucrece*, 98), Iachimo's sexual appetite is envisaged as both insatiable and self-perpetuating.

A parallel story to that of Lucrece and Tarquin is elaborated in Ovid's *Metamorphoses* – the poetic text, translated into English by Arthur Golding in 1567, that so sparked Shakespeare's imagination in his early work. Significantly it is Ovid's dark myth that the playwright draws on: the tale of how Philomel, raped by her brother-in-law Tereus, is eventually transformed into a nightingale. In Shakespeare's poem, violated Lucrece finds consolation in how her predicament mirrors that of 'lamenting Philomele' (1079). Distraught with grief, she begs '"Come, Philomele, that sing'st of ravishment, / Make thy sad grove in my dishevell'd hair"' (1128–9), and, identifying with the self-lacerating anguish of the mythological bird, imagines pricking her breast to remind herself of her 'sharp woes' (1136). *Cymbeline* offers just one allusion to the Philomel myth when Iachimo, enjoying his vicarious assault on a passive woman, notes that before she fell asleep Imogen was reading the tale of Tereus. Fittingly, she turned down the page where 'Philomele gave up' (2. 2. 46).

In *Titus Andronicus* Shakespeare further draws on this mythic prototype of rape, referring to Philomel/Philomela no fewer than six times. Aaron alludes to the second part of the classical story – the cutting out of Philomel's tongue to prevent her from revealing the identity of her ravisher – when he cruelly resolves that Lavinia 'must lose her tongue to-day' (2. 3. 43). Whereas 'Fair Philomela' retained her fingers and 'in a tedious sampler sew'd her mind', Lavinia has been doubly silenced, deprived of the ability to speak or to write (2. 4. 38–9). After the rape it is Titus who insists on the parallel. Elevating his daughter's violation to the status of classical myth, making her a pattern of wronged chastity, enables Titus, at least to some degree, to mitigate his sense of outrage and family shame. Seeing mutilated Lavinia struggling to turn the pages of 'Ovid's Metamorphosis' and point to the lines on Tereus's 'rape' confirms for him that she has been 'Ravish'd and wrong'd as Philomela was' (4. 1. 42–8, 52). As Titus goes on to trap and kill the rapists Chiron and Demetrius, baking their remains in a pie for their mother to eat, Titus feels confident that he will be revenged 'worse' (more fully) than was Progne – Tereus's wife, who murdered her husband for raping her sister Philomel (5. 2. 195).

It is Lavinia's uncle Marcus who makes the stark fact of Lavinia's violation even more grotesque by prettifying it. He elaborates on it in a lyrical style that, as Lynn Enterline notes, ironically resembles the worshipful language of a Petrarchan lover itemising, or rhetorically 'dismembering', his mistress's body parts.[39] Marcus's verse, at odds with the horrifying spectacle of Lavinia present on stage, envisages a raped and mutilated woman as both beautiful and erotically appealing. Describing her arms as 'circling shadows kings have sought to sleep in' (2. 4. 19), Marcus particularises Lavinia's lost loveliness even while he distances her as a mythological figure; he notes how her 'lily hands', now hacked off, would 'Tremble like aspen leaves upon a lute' before her rapist, a 'craftier Tereus', cut 'those pretty fingers off, / That could have better sew'd than Philomel' (44–5, 41–3). Incongruously, he images the 'crimson river of warm blood' between her 'rosed lips' as a 'bubbling fountain stirred with the wind' (22–4). Shakespeare uses the same technique, couching a brutal crime in a decorative language, when Quintus Andronicus discovers the 'blood-stained hole' into which his brother has fallen – the 'dark' pit where Chiron and Demetrius have thrown the body of Bassianus before they rape Lavinia (2. 3. 210, 224). David Willbern points out how, in the description that follows, the 'image of a violated vagina' becomes a 'symbolic substitute' for the offstage rape:[40]

> What subtile hole is this,
> Whose mouth is covered with rude-growing briers,
> Upon whose leaves are drops of new-shed blood
> As fresh as morning dew distill'd on flowers? (198–201)

The grotesquely incongruous simile, comparing 'new-shed' vaginal 'blood' to morning dew on flowers, compounds rather than assuages the horror of the unseen rape.

Shakespeare's comedies, while they explore the connection (or disjunction) between sexual desire and romantic love, shun the full force of 'lust in action'. One partial exception comes in the early comedy *Two Gentlemen of Verona*. Near the end of the play Proteus threatens to 'force' Silvia to 'yield' to his impetuous 'desire'. Improbably this Petrarchan lover suddenly transforms into a conquering Tarquin figure when he abandons courtly rhetoric and resolves 'I'll woo you like a soldier, at arms' end, / And love you 'gainst the nature of love – force ye' (5. 4. 57–8). In theatrical terms his threat of sexual attack may be a crisis manufactured to bring about a hasty denouement. If the moment offers a deeper message, it is to underline how easily infatuation can shift from a promise of eternal devotion to predatory lust. As David Schalkwyk points out in his study on *Shakespeare: Love and Language*, it represents the tipping point at which aggressive sexual desire (will) finally breaks through the fantasy image of the idealised mistress.[41] To the relief of the audience, Proteus (prompted by Valentine's generous offer to relinquish Silvia) quickly switches back to his former love Julia. Sexual violence, along with this lover's dangerous instability, is deflected into the comic resolution of a double marriage.

The Merry Wives of Windsor, Shakespeare's only foray into city comedy, centres on the comedy of attempted seduction – Falstaff's appetite for sexual adventure with Mistress Ford and Mistress Page – and not on brutal coercion. In *Henry IV, Part 1* Prince Hal has mocked Falstaff as a 'bolting-hutch of beastliness' (2. 4. 450), while in *Part 2* Mistress Quickly indignantly claims that 'if his weapon be out' he 'will foin [fornicate] like any devil, he will spare neither man, woman, nor child' (2. 1. 15–17).[42] Now, in *Merry Wives*, Falstaff's lechery is comically defused through a series of tricks that prevent the would-be seducer from attaining his goal. The wives' plan to chastise him until 'the wicked fire of lust' has 'melted him in his own grease' (2. 1. 67–8) reaches its climax in the Herne the Hunter episode in the forest. Wearing horns that represent not only the mythological creature but also a disgraced would-be lover, Falstaff is punished for his transgressive desires by being pinched by children dressed as fairies. In this fantastic scenario, the pretend fairies' song is simply melodramatic. It gives a comic spin to the 'fire' of 'lust' that could, in other circumstances, have serious consequences:

Fie on sinful fantasy!
Fie on lust and luxury!
Lust is but a bloody fire,
Kindled with unchaste desire . . . (5. 5. 93–6)

It is late in his career, through the tragicomic romances, that Shakespeare returns to a primary concern of his early work: how far love and lust remain distinct from one another. *Cymbeline* in particular, but also *Pericles*, *The Tempest* and (to a lesser extent) *The Winter's Tale*, consider violent sexuality as an underlying menace, one that threatens to end in rape. Shakespeare's dark comedies, as discussed in Chapter 1, confront this troubling aspect of sexuality head on. The romances, though, are much more optimistic overall. Schematic in their presentation of good versus evil, they show chastity winning the battle against crude sexual 'will', while offering hope that institutions set up to maintain civilised society – marriage between loving couples and the bonded family unit – will succeed in banishing or at least containing unruly erotic desire.

Pericles begins with 'monstrous lust': the incestuous relationship between the King of Antiochus and his daughter (5. 3. 86).[43] In Act 4, before Pericles discovers that his daughter Marina and wife Thaisa are alive after many years of separation, high romance turns to realism as the play again confronts the grim side of uncontrolled sexuality. After escaping a murderous plot, virginal Marina, a '[master] piece of virtue' (4. 6. 111), is sold into the dangerously 'unwholesome' world of the brothel at Mytilene (4. 2. 21).[44] Mytilene is a decadent city where the mere description of Marina's beauty in the marketplace 'stirs up the lewdly inclin'd' (142–3). When this young woman proves able to 'freeze the god Priapus' through her powerful moral sermons in the whore-house (4. 6. 3–4), the Bawd consigns the corrupt pandar Boult to 'crack the glass of her virginity' (142); if necessary Boult will acclimatise Marina to prostitution by raping her. Marina's purity, however, turns into a magical deterrent. First she resists Lysimachus, governor of Mytilene, who had planned to enjoy her as a 'creature of sale' (78). Then she convinces Boult to abandon his profession of a 'damned doorkeeper' and no longer exploit women as commodities to satisfy men's lust (165). In accordance with romance conventions *Pericles*, the improbable 'old tale', allows Marina to escape from this den of vice unscathed.

In *Cymbeline* both Iachimo and Cloten launch assaults on Imogen's chastity. After fabricating tales of Posthumus as an insatiable lecher, 'vaulting variable ramps' in Rome, Iachimo offers his sexual services to Imogen to avenge her husband's infidelity (1. 6. 134). But when she indignantly rejects him, unmasking his 'beastly mind' (153), he is content to play the voyeur in her bedchamber while she sleeps. He alludes to Tarquin's stealth, but quickly foregoes the rapist's sexual aggression. Having taken on the challenge of trying to prove Imogen false but failing to compromise her sexual honour, he settles instead for inflaming her husband's jealousy.

Instead of Iachimo, the boorish Cloten is cast in the role of sexual predator. Although he claims noble birth, he resembles his evil mother, the Queen, a 'most delicate fiend' who married King Cymbeline only to acquire royalty (5. 5. 47). The choric Second Lord appropriately describes Cloten as a 'crafty devil' (2. 1. 52), while Imogen brands her coarse pursuer as both 'base' (2. 3. 126) and an 'irregulous devil' (4. 2. 315). Trading on his position at court, Cloten insists he is a worthy replacement for Imogen's husband. In fact he is the antithesis of Posthumus. Until maddened by jealousy, Posthumus is tenderly respectful toward Imogen, and, despite not being born into nobility, he is lauded by Iachimo as sitting among the Romans 'like a [descended] god' (1. 6. 169). Cloten, though, is nothing if not crude in his sexual pursuit. Three times he exploits the double entendre 'penetrate' when he encourages the dawn musicians to impress Imogen through their musical instruments, to 'penetrate her with [their] fingering' (2. 3. 12–14, 27). He even plans to bribe one of Imogen's women to admit him to her bedchamber, bawdily commenting, with a pun on 'stand' as phallic erection, that gold can make the most chaste of Diana's rangers 'yield up / Their deer to th' stand o' th' stealer' (69–70). Incensed by rejection, planning to pursue his prey to Milford Haven and rape Imogen after killing her husband and dressing in his clothes, Cloten crudely fantasises that she will be 'fit' (sexually primed) for the enterprise (4. 1. 4). This 'double villain' is thwarted from his attempt to commit rape only by being beheaded by the rustic Guiderus (Cymbeline's lost son), whom Cloten has ironically insulted as 'villain base' (4. 2. 89).

In a grotesque mistaking, Imogen awakes to find Cloten's headless body. Immediately she concludes that not only the courtly clothes but the limbs that she is seeing belong to her divinely formed lord, Posthumus; extravagantly she praises his 'foot Mercurial, his Martial thigh, / The brawns of Hercules' (4. 2. 310–11). Verging on black comedy, this painful sequence with the headless body, in which Imogen thinks that she recognises her husband's superior form, reinforces the idea that external appearances, male bodies, closely resemble one another. Which man is the beast, which one is god-like? If Cloten's dead carcass can easily be mistaken for that of Posthumus, Shakespeare seems, in Fiedler's words, 'to be on the verge of suggesting that in terms of their sexuality, *all men are Clotens*'.[45] Comparing himself favourably to the rival husband, Cloten has already boasted that 'the lines of my body are as well drawn as his' (4. 1. 9–10). Then, after beheading him, Guiderus confirms that 'Thersites' body is as good as Ajax', / When neither are alive' (4. 2. 252–3). The implication is clear. Without their heads, male bodies, as the source of potentially rapacious sexual desire, may be indistinguishable from one another. The head alone is the seat of reason and true mark of distinction.

For both Plato, who elevated the mind or psyche, and Christian thinkers such as Richard Hooker,[46] reason was the highest human attribute. 'Man', as Hamlet observes wonderingly, is 'noble in reason' (*Hamlet*, 2. 2. 304). Lamenting his mother's quick recovery from the death of his father, the prince observes that 'a beast, that wants discourse of reason, / Would have mourn'd longer' (1. 2. 150–1). Animals, lower than humans on the great Chain of Being, were defined as both lacking in reason – as when the circumspect Second Lord designates the 'ass' Cloten as a 'fool' (*Cymbeline*, 1. 2. 37, 24) – and sexually unrestrained, prone to follow their baser instincts. When the Friar in *Romeo and Juliet* warns Romeo, distraught at being banished, that his 'wild acts' denote 'The unreasonable fury of a beast' (3. 3. 110–11), he is drawing on the association of beasts with irrationality, suggesting that the young lover's wild behaviour has transformed him into an animal. When Dromio of Syracuse is sexually propositioned by the kitchen maid Luce in Ephesus, he plays on the secondary connection between animals and lust. Drolly he narrates how Luce, 'being a very beastly creature', would 'have [him] as a beast' (*The Comedy of Errors*, 3. 2. 86–8). Similarly Falstaff, bent on seduction in *The Merry Wives of Windsor*, concedes that 'powerful love . . . in some respects makes . . . a man a beast' (5. 5. 4–6).

The highest intellect reputedly belonged to angels. But human beings, as the Neo-Platonist Pico della Mirandola notes, are privileged in being able to transform themselves into different modes of being. They can cultivate their rational natures, climbing upward by the 'soul's judgment' to be 'reborn into the higher forms, which are divine', or they can degenerate 'into the lower forms of life, which are brutish'.[47] Cloten illustrates this, just as Lucrece experiences to her cost how readily lustful men forfeit their 'gentle minds' when they 'prove beasts' (*The Rape of Lucrece*, 1148). In his chapter in *The French Academie* entitled 'Of Intemperance, and of Stupidity or Blockishness', the Christian writer de La Primaudaye emphasises that the 'beast *Lust*' is the enemy of both reason and virtue.[48] He might well be describing Cloten. The violent severing of Cloten's head from his body, which reduces him to common flesh, underlines how this clotpoll (blockhead) is the antithesis of judgement and moral discrimination. Just as Sonnet 151 laments how the poet feels enslaved by his 'gross body's treason' (6), so Cloten's 'nobler part' has been displaced by raw sexual desire.

The Winter's Tale also progresses through stark contrasts. The play's bifurcated action offsets the base side of sexuality – King Leontes's lurid fantasies in the wintry Sicilian court – with the renewal of the spirit through 'great creating Nature' in pastoral Bohemia (4. 4. 88). The emotional warmth and untainted sexuality of Perdita (the princess raised as a shepherdess) serve as antidotes to Leontes's gross imaginings of a lustful affair between his queen, Hermione, and Polixenes, King of Bohemia, sixteen years earlier: the dark musings that give rise to his conviction that female lust affords 'No barricado for a belly' (1. 2. 204). Perdita's spontaneous passion, as she imagines her suitor Florizel not 'dead' but buried 'quick, and in [her] arms' (4. 4. 131–2), is mirrored in the response of the Bohemian prince. Plighting his troth to her, Florizel dismisses the other possibility, the aggressive side of passion, when he promises her that his 'lusts' will never 'burn hotter than [his] faith' (4. 4. 33–4). The dance of the twelve satyrs, an antimasque that precedes the pair's informal betrothal (342), acts as a reminder that sexual desire may indeed turn bestial. Perdita in her role as Flora has already evoked the shadow of rape, recalling how Proserpina was snatched into 'Dis's wagon' (abducted by Pluto) while she was gathering spring flowers (116–18). And before Florizel pledges chastity, his examples of how deities in love 'have taken / The shapes of beasts upon them' – Jupiter 'became a bull and bellow'd' (in this disguise he ravished Europa) while Neptune metamorphosed into a bleating ram (27–9) – reinforce the idea that even gods may resort to coercion to satisfy their sexual needs. The mortal Florizel remains chaste, however. His dedication of everything he possesses to the 'service' of his lady elicits from Perdita an assurance that she matches the 'purity' of her beloved's thoughts with the 'pattern' of her own (377, 382–3).

Similarly Ferdinand, wooing Miranda in *The Tempest*, reassures Prospero that his intentions are honourable. His imagination briefly skips to the dark side, fantasising rape when he pledges that no time or place, not even the 'murkiest den' (resembling the shadowy 'detested vale' where rape and murder are committed in *Titus Andronicus* (2. 3. 93)), will ever 'melt [his] honor into lust' (4. 1. 27–8). For his part Prospero, whose experience has shown him the rapacity of human ambition and desire, remains obsessed with maintaining his daughter's sexual purity. He threatens future misery, 'barren hate' and 'discord', if Ferdinand dares to coerce Miranda sexually, 'break her virgin knot', before their wedding day (15–20). Warning against too much prenuptial 'dalliance', he observes that even 'the strongest oaths are straw / To th' fire i' th' blood' (51–3). Prospero's masque, conjuring up goddesses to celebrate a 'contract of true love', must exclude unruly sexual desire or 'will', the aspect of love that Venus and her mischievous son Cupid encourage. Accordingly Ceres, goddess of fruitfulness, declares that she has 'forsworn' the company of this wayward pair (91). And the divine messenger Iris assures Ceres that the plan of Venus and Cupid to put a 'wanton' charm on the human couple, which would cause them to break their vow of pre-marital chastity, has been foiled (95).

At the opposite pole from the royal couple's chaste love is the open lust of Caliban. Before the play's action this 'abhorred slave' has tried to rape Miranda, betraying his master's trust by seeking 'to violate / The honor' of Prospero's only child (1. 2. 351, 347–8). Shakespeare again suggests that rape is a power game: Caliban's motive for violent assault on Miranda is as much to assert authority as to satisfy sexual needs. Because Prospero has usurped Caliban's place as lord of the island, his idea of revenge is to lay claim to the territory by ravishing Prospero's pure daughter. Mating with Miranda, he speculates, would allow him to realise his own colonial dream; he imagines 'peopl[ing] / This isle with Calibans' (350–1).

In the play's allegorical scheme (which is not kind to the 'monster'), Caliban represents base flesh. In showing no remorse for his brutal attempt on Miranda's chastity, he symbolises degenerate sexuality,[49] body without spirit, and 'earth' (as Prospero calls him) residing below the element of air (1. 2. 314). Despite his promise to sue for 'grace' at the end of the play (5. 1. 296), Caliban appears immune to it. Deemed a 'demi-devil' (272), he resembles *Cymbeline*'s Cloten, except that he is beastly not merely in mind but in appearance, and not only metaphorically devilish but reportedly conceived by the devil himself. As a prototype of base instinct, 'earth' Caliban (1. 2. 314) is automatically associated with sin, just as Sonnet 146 ruefully acknowledges that the poet's 'Poor soul' must reside at the 'centre of [his] sinful earth' (1). Lowest on the chain of being, animalistic in his lust, Caliban emerges as the monstrous 'thing of darkness' – the dark side of sexuality – that Prospero is most reluctant to 'acknowledge' as his own (5. 1. 275–6).

In this romance, as in the other plays celebrating chaste royal unions, love wins out over lust. Overweening sexual 'will' in males proves self-defeating; rapists and would-be rapists do not fare well in Shakespeare's plays. This is the case whether they are satisfying crude sexual desire (the 'hell' of uncontrolled lust described in Sonnet 129) or combining it with a brutal show of control, asserting male power over a chaste female who represents a social prize – a pattern enacted in *The Rape of Lucrece* and echoed in the violation of Lavinia in *Titus Andronicus* and Cloten's quest to rape Imogen in *Cymbeline*. Only the ideology of warfare tacitly accepts that women will become collateral damage. As represented in *Henry V*, war gives military leaders, through their soldiers, a pass for rape and pillage.[50] Because one measure of appropriating desirable new territory is to dominate sexually the females who reside there, women in regions under attack are especially vulnerable; they are treated as 'legitimate booty', a means to humiliate the 'defeated nation'.[51] A royal few, such as Princess Katherine, a 'maid' worth many French 'maiden cities' to Henry, may be co-opted into the world of the conqueror through marriage (*Henry V*, 5. 2. 326–7). Mainly, though, women trapped in the culture of war remain as shadows in Shakespeare's history plays, potential victims of the warriors' aggressive will to power.

Notes

1. Alexander Schmidt, *Shakespeare Lexicon and Quotation Dictionary*, vol. 1, p. 677.
2. Most illuminating here is Catherine Belsey, 'Love as Trompe-l'oeil: Taxonomies of Desire in *Venus and Adonis*', which contends that both '*love* and *lust*' in the early modern period are often used as 'synonyms for desire' (266).
3. *A Sermon Against Whoredom and Uncleanness*, in Gerald Bray (ed.), *The Book of Homilies*, p. 96. Bray notes that the 1559 version replaces 'adultery' with 'breaking of wedlock'.
4. David R. Shumway, *Modern Love: Romance, Intimacy, and the Marriage Crisis*, traces the discussion of intimacy – communication on the emotional level as well as sexual fulfilment – as a 'newly emerging discourse' in the late twentieth century that 'has come to complement and compete with the older discourse of romance' (p. 133). He considers this new discourse a response to the modern marriage crisis (the rise in divorce, the decline in couples getting married) – a crisis that clearly contrasts with the more sacramental,

Christian view of marriage that was current during Shakespeare's early modern era.
5. Noted by Jean H. Hagstrum, *Esteem Enlivened by Desire: The Couple from Homer to Shakespeare*, p. 4.
6. Alexander Niccholes, *A Discourse, of Marriage and Wiving*, pp. 31–2.
7. Stephen Greenblatt, 'The Improvisation of Power', in *Renaissance Self-Fashioning: From More to Shakespeare*, notes how the church father St Jerome cites Seneca: 'A man ought to love his wife with judgment, not affection' (pp. 247–8).
8. James L. Calderwood, *If It Were Done: Macbeth and Tragic Action*, stresses Shakespeare's exploitation of the sexual sense of 'done' and 'deed' in Macbeth's laconic 'I have done the deed', arguing that the brutal 'deed' of killing Duncan is envisaged as 'both a murder and a sexual act' (pp. 42–6).
9. Mark Breitenberg, 'Publishing Chastity: Shakespeare's "The Rape of Lucrece"', in *Anxious Masculinity in Early Modern England*, p. 30. Breitenberg notes how in the poem 'masculine desire appears as the supreme example of self-assertive will *and* as the agent of a complete loss of self-control' (p. 99).
10. Complicating the situation is Tarquin's brief disgust that a 'martial man' could be 'soft fancy's slave' (200). As Stephen Orgel explores in 'Nobody's Perfect: or Why Did the English Stage Take Boys for Women?', the idea was a common one in Shakespeare's time: that 'sexual passion for women renders men effeminate ... the love of a woman threatens the integrity of the perilously achieved male identity' (14–15).
11. Katharine Eisaman Maus, 'Taking Tropes Seriously: Language and Violence in Shakespeare's *Rape of Lucrece*', notes how Tarquin allows the military trope to guide his actions at the expense of his 'judgment' (79).
12. Nancy J. Vickers, '"The blazon of sweet beauty's best": Shakespeare's *Lucrece*', p. 97.
13. Ibid. pp. 102, 106.
14. Anna Clark, *Women's Silence, Men's Violence*, p. 2. Catherine R. Stimpson, 'Shakespeare and the Soil of Rape', extends the way that Lucrece is victimised by 'patriarchal authority' to restrictions on women's sexuality in the early modern period. Stimpson finds that 'the rape victim may be painfully emblematic of the plight of women' during that era (p. 62).
15. Alan Sinfield, 'Rape and Rights: *Measure for Measure* and the Limits of Cultural Imperialism', p. 182.
16. Coppélia Kahn, '*Lucrece*: The Sexual Politics of Subjectivity', p. 152.
17. William Gouge, *Of Domesticall Duties*, p. 411 (spelling modernised).
18. 'Introduction: Re-reading Rape', in Lynn A. Higgins and Brenda R. Silver (eds), *Rape and Representation*, finds that a rape myth such as that of Philomel tends to position women as '"essentially" vulnerable and mute' (p. 5). This is one way in which the allusion may work in *The Rape of Lucrece*.
19. Laura G. Bromley, 'Lucrece's Re-Creation', 201.
20. Maus, 'Taking Tropes Seriously', 69.
21. Coppélia Kahn, 'The Rape in Shakespeare's *Lucrece*', points out that 'once a man assumed guardianship of a woman in marriage, the chastity of his wife became a primary component of his honour' (61). As Lucrece,

'the perfect patriarchal woman', is 'content to be but an accessory to the passage of property and family honor from father to son', she has 'no sense of herself as an independent moral being apart from this role' (60).
22. Margaret Loftus Ranald, 'The Siege of Lucrece', in *Shakespeare and his Social Context*, notes how Shakespeare incorporates the stages of contemporary siege warfare into the structure of *The Rape of Lucrece*. The poem shows Tarquin's preparatory siege; his initial assault on the fortress of Lucrece's body; and Lucrece's defence as 'captain' of this fort when Tarquin briefly invites a 'truce parley' before forcing a final surrender (pp. 158–9, 163).
23. Kahn, '*Lucrece*: The Sexual Politics of Subjectivity', pp. 142, 148.
24. Michael Hattaway, 'Male Sexuality and Misogyny', considers this violence a disastrous corollary of male 'chivalry'. He speculates that 'warlike aims ... disguised as service to the female' turned into 'a hunt for prizes and maidenheads' (p. 108).
25. Laura Levine, 'Rape, Repetition, and the Politics of Closure in *A Midsummer Night's Dream*', finds the play full of 'sexual coercion' (p. 215). Levine notes how Demetrius's threat to leave Helena 'to the mercy of wild beasts' in the forest (2. 1. 228) makes a 'tacit analogy between the impulse to rape and the wild beasts that men evoke to represent that impulse' (p. 218).
26. Coppélia Kahn, 'Coming of Age: Marriage and Manhood in *Romeo and Juliet* and *The Taming of the Shrew*', in *Man's Estate: Masculine Identity in Shakespeare*, p. 87.
27. Eric Partridge, *Shakespeare's Bawdy*, pp. 30–1.
28. Jean E. Howard and Phyllis Rackin, *Engendering a Nation: A Feminist Account of Shakespeare's English Histories*, p. 196.
29. C. L. Barber and Richard P. Wheeler, *The Whole Journey: Shakespeare's Power of Development*, p. 220.
30. Howard and Rackin, *Engendering a Nation*, p. 8. The authors point out in detail how in a war situation 'the sexualized bodies of women become a crucial terrain where ... battle is played out' (p. 5). Kahn, ' "The Shadow of the Male": Masculine Identity in the History Plays', in *Man's Estate*, also discusses how male sexuality in *Henry V* takes the form of 'collective violence against women' (p. 81). Joane Nagel, *Race, Ethnicity, and Sexuality: Intimate Intersections, Forbidden Frontiers*, explores in both historical and contemporary contexts how 'strategies of competition and domination include the sexual control of ethnic Others' bodies and territories' (p. 10).
31. Richard III uses similar rhetoric, this time threatening that if his soldiers allow themselves to be conquered by Richmond's troops, those 'bastard Britains' will 'lie with our wives' and 'ravish our daughters' (*Richard III*, 5. 4. 336–7).
32. John Dover Wilson (ed.), *Titus Andronicus*, surmises that Shakespeare was called in at short notice 'to help Peele expand the play' (p. xxxvii).
33. In *Eroticism on the Renaissance Stage*, Celia R. Daileader points out that 'offstage sex' in early modern drama is a practical condition of 'male/female erotic representation on an all-male stage' (p. 19).
34. Admittedly these references come from two scenes – Act 2, scene 1 and Act 4, scene 1 – now usually attributed to Peele. Brian Vickers, *Shakespeare*,

Co-Author: A Historical Study of Five Collaborative Plays, reviews the linguistic and metrical evidence to make a convincing case for Peele as the author of Act 1, as well as 2. 1, 4. 1 and possibly 2. 2 (pp. 219–39, 243). But since Shakespeare was composing *The Rape of Lucrece* around the same time that he worked on *Titus Andronicus*, he could well have prompted these additions.

35. Stimpson, 'Shakespeare and the Soil of Rape', p. 57. Kathleen McLuskie, '"Lawless desires well tempered"', also finds connections between the way that 'frequent instances of rape or attempted rape' were graphically detailed in church depositions of the time, and the erotic representation of 'sexuality on the contemporary stage' (pp. 104, 122).

36. Marion Wynne-Davis, '"The Swallowing Womb": Consumed and Consuming Women in *Titus Andronicus*', finds that by participating in revenge against the perpetrators of her rape, Lavinia lays 'claim' to 'an independent self' and thus becomes more than a victim (p. 133). Wynne-Davis links this to an Elizabethan act of 1597 that acknowledges raped women as violated individuals. Instead of considering rape as 'theft' of property belonging to the woman's family, this act legislates it as a sin against the 'corporal person of the woman'; it also decrees execution for 'misdoers' who force females against their will (pp. 131, 140).

37. This is how Leslie A. Fiedler, 'The New World Savage as Stranger: or, "'Tis new to thee"', in *The Stranger in Shakespeare*, categorises these inarticulate rapists, along with the would-be rapist Cloten in *Cymbeline* and Caliban in *The Tempest* (p. 203).

38. Eve Kosofsky Sedgwick, *Between Men: English Literature and Male Homosocial Desire*, p. 16.

39. Lynn Enterline, *The Rhetoric of the Body from Ovid to Shakespeare*, comments on how Lavinia is addressed 'as if she were an aesthetic beauty best understood in terms of the dismembering rhetoric' of the Petrarchan '*blason*' (p. 8).

40. David Willbern, 'Rape and Revenge in *Titus Andronicus*', 170.

41. David Schalkwyk, *Shakespeare: Love and Language*, analyses Proteus's action in psychological terms, as 'the Imaginary' reaching toward 'the Lacanian Real' (p. 46).

42. The unusual word 'foin' clearly denotes fornication when Doll Tearsheet wonders when ageing Falstaff will leave off 'fighting o'days and foining o'nights' (*Henry IV, Part 2*, 2. 4. 232).

43. Walter Cohen, in *The Norton Shakespeare*, states the scholarly consensus – that the first two Acts of *Pericles*, or most of the 'first nine scenes', were composed by George Wilkins (p. 2710).

44. Stanley Wells, *Shakespeare, Sex, and Love*, notes that Shakespeare's co-author (George Wilkins) kept an inn on Turnbull Street that doubled as a brothel (p. 74). Whether or not Shakespeare frequented the place, the sordid brothel scenes presented in Act 4 are presumed to be his work alone.

45. Fiedler, 'The New World Savage as Stranger', in *The Stranger in Shakespeare*, p. 204.

46. In *Of the Laws of Ecclesiastical Polity* (1593), the Anglican Richard Hooker defends the Law of Reason as established through the God-given Law of Nature. It is through the 'light of their natural understanding' (reason) that

human beings are able to judge what is 'virtuous or vicious, good or evil, for them to do' (bk. 1, ch. 9, p. 182).
47. Giovanni Pico della Mirandola, 'Oration on the Dignity of Man', p. 225.
48. Pierre de La Primaudaye, *The French Academie*, pp. 189–90 (spelling modernised).
49. Madhavi Menon, 'Encore! Allegory, *Volpone*, *The Tempest*', in *Wanton Words: Rhetoric and Sexuality in English Renaissance Drama*, finds Caliban an emblem of 'uncontrolled sexual desire' (p. 155).
50. Unfortunately, in many parts of the world this has not changed. Aryn Baker, 'War and Rape', focusing on the atrocities in South Sudan, notes that while international tribunals can now prosecute rape as a war crime or a crime against humanity, 'rape in war' still results from 'a masculine culture rooted in violence that has devalued women' (41).
51. See Susan Brownmiller, 'War', in *Against Our Will: Men, Women and Rape*, pp. 33, 36.

Chapter 3

Lustful Women and Male Fantasies of Female Desire

So far the portrayals of lust examined in Shakespeare's work have centred on males. What about female sexual desire? In the early modern period, a woman's erotic drive was inevitably judged from a masculine perspective, and this is where the male's fear of betrayal manifests itself. Twentieth-century Freudian and post-Freudian psychoanalytic theory has stressed the role of the mother in moulding a male's deepest attitudes toward women, positing various stages of early childhood development. Most relevant in feminist theory is the pre-Oedipal phase,[1] in which the child's pleasurable fantasy of symbiosis with a nurturing mother may produce both separation anxiety and fears of maternal engulfment, even annihilation or castration.[2] Ultimately the mother-infant dyad breaks down, as the male child needs to differentiate himself from his mother and establish his own autonomy and agency.[3]

This psychological model of ambivalent responses toward the mother figure, extending into how men respond to lovers and wives, illuminates several of the adult sexual relationships explored in Shakespeare's plays. After witnessing Cressida giving herself to Diomedes, the idealistic Troilus hesitates to acknowledge what he most fears is true – that his lover's infidelity has confirmed how all women, mothers not excepted, are capable of betrayal. Desperately he begs 'Let it not be believed for womanhood! / Think we had mothers' (*Troilus and Cressida*, 5. 2. 129–30). *Hamlet* offers the clearest example of how the protagonist's fraught relations with his mother, Gertrude – whether the result of pre-Oedipal anxieties or thwarted Oedipal desire – contaminate his view of all women to the point that he sees even Ophelia as sexually fickle and conniving. It's well known that early modern society, which privileged males in terms of power and agency, tended to demean and distrust females as 'Other'.[4] All too often in Shakespeare's tragedies, as in his culture, a male's sexual desire co-exists with anxiety not only that the female will prove treacherous but that her erotic power will debilitate him.[5] Even the devoted Romeo, once his refusal to fight Tybalt leads to Mercutio's death, laments that his love for Juliet's 'beauty' has made him 'effeminate' (*Romeo and Juliet*, 3. 1. 114).

One way to combat this fear is to deprive the female of her autonomy, just as Hamlet seeks to disempower and silence Ophelia by banishing her to 'a nunnery', out of the arena of desire. The signs of an ideal woman, underlined in handbooks of this era, are 'the enclosed body, the closed mouth, the locked house'.[6] In *The Excellencie of Good Women* (1613), Barnabe Rich affirms that the laudable woman 'openeth not her mouth but with discretion',[7] just as she keeps her body chaste. To jaundiced male eyes, as Peter Stallybrass outlines, the reproductive, maternal female body, with its emphasis on large belly and opened apertures, might appear 'grotesque'.[8] Such a defiantly carnal body – a challenge to the idealised, sanitised female form of the romantic Petrarchan convention – could trigger male fears about a woman's uncontrolled libido. The opening of *The Winter's Tale* confirms this; Leontes's suspicions over his wife's fidelity seem prompted by his awareness of her heavily pregnant body.

Even if a woman's fertile body didn't provoke anxiety, her sexual appetite was often considered bestial or 'monstrous' in its voraciousness.[9] The Scholastic tradition, inherited from the Middle Ages, positioned women as more lecherous and sinful (like Eve, the 'tempter' of Adam)[10] than resembling the Virgin Mary in being pure and virtuous. Early modern medical literature also promoted the idea, expressed by Jacques Ferrand in 1623, that 'a woman is in her Loves more Passionate, and more furious in her follies than a man is'.[11] Aristotle and Galen, whose theories were still followed in the early seventeenth century, actually offered a spurious physiological grounding for this – that women's 'cold and moist dominant humours' made them desire 'completion' through extra heat from 'intercourse with the male'.[12] And because females were thought to be less reasonable and more instinctual than males, they were viewed as particularly susceptible to sexual temptation.

This meant that a woman's sexuality, more dangerous because it remains physically hidden, had to be curbed and contained. Conduct books of the time emphasised the patriarchal ideals of female chastity and modest submission to male authority. While Phyllis Rackin argues that 'repressive prescriptions' in this period 'should not be regarded as descriptions' of women's 'actual behavior',[13] the sheer number of prescriptive handbooks published in the sixteenth and early seventeenth centuries[14] indicates how strongly Shakespeare's society wished to reinforce traditional standards of female behaviour. True, some Reformation humanists promoted wider opportunities for women,[15] but scholars such as Sir Thomas Elyot, in *The Defence of Good Women* (1545), still linked women's education to 'their social function as wives and mothers',[16] while Juan Luis Vives, despite his humanist agenda in *The Instruction of a Christian Woman* (1523), continues to advocate modest and submissive behaviour in women. Although exceptions had to be made for a female ruler such as Elizabeth I, the established paradigms of women as more frail and less rational than men held their ground. Above all, a woman's sexual purity was regarded as the index of her honour. A single woman should stay virginal, a wife or widow chaste. Occupying no middle ground, no shades of grey between the polarities of chaste and unchaste, a woman who exhibited her sensual nature (outside and possibly even within marriage) was likely to be stigmatised as whorish.[17] In literary contexts too, men are stern critics of immodest female demeanour. Ulysses in *Troilus and Cressida* is quick to categorise Cressida as a 'daughter of the game' because she exhibits strong sex appeal in the Greek camp; scathingly he remarks that 'Her wanton spirits look out / At every joint and motive of her body' (4. 5. 56–7).

Marriage provided one context in which a woman's libido might be contained. Even within the newer Puritan model of 'companionate' marriage in the early seventeenth century,[18] the wife remained legally the property of her husband and subordinate to him. That also meant he could control her sexuality. Montaigne, not virulently anti-feminist, sensibly derides anxious husbands for their excessive efforts to curb their wives' liberty. He nevertheless takes for granted the 'appetite and lust' of women in general and the 'naturall violence of their desires'.[19] A husband must find a way, as Edmund Tilney advises in his handbook on marriage, *The Flower of Friendship*, to negotiate a wife's erotic drive so that her 'private will' and 'appetite' is subsumed within his own.[20] The fear remains, however, that even a habitually chaste woman may suddenly turn promiscuous. By focusing on husbands who doubt their wives' fidelity – often without any justification – several of Shakespeare's plays contribute significantly to the theme of how male jealousy is sparked by anxiety over females' rampant sex drive.

In analysing how late Renaissance drama portrays erotic desire in females, it's sometimes difficult to distinguish between male-imposed categories – the tendency in the early modern period to stereotype women as chaste or whorish[21] – and what a dramatic character represents in her own right. Shakespeare often deconstructs these polarities. The virginal heroines of the comedies, in particular, look forward to sexual union with the men they love. They are presented as desiring subjects, their virtue not undercut by expressing their sexuality. Rosalind, who cannot wrestle with her 'affections' for Orlando (*As You Like It*,

1. 3. 21), and Viola, who is 'almost sick' for bearded Orsino (*Twelfth Night*, 3. 1. 46), are cases in point. Organising the bed trick, Helena in *All's Well that Ends Well* becomes an active agent in working to possess Bertram physically, while Perdita, longing for Florizel to be 'buried ... quick and in [her] arms' (*The Winter's Tale*, 4. 4. 131–2), is forthright about her erotic feelings. In *The Tempest* Miranda, too, discards 'bashful cunning' when she impulsively tells Ferdinand 'I am your wife, if you will marry me' (3. 1. 81–3). Tragic heroine Juliet, even younger than Miranda, expresses frank desire for Romeo. Her 'Gallop apace, you fiery-footed steeds' speech conveys her longing for the cover of 'love-performing night' in which 'true love acted' – she means sexual consummation – can become 'simple modesty' (*Romeo and Juliet*, 3. 2. 1, 5, 16).[22] Discarding maidenly modesty in the balcony scene, Juliet is the one who proposes marriage to fulfil the lovers' urgent 'truelove passion' (2. 2. 104). Likewise Desdemona, acting as 'half the wooer' in *Othello* (1. 3. 176), shows a healthy combination of 'sensuality and affection',[23] a sexual as well as a spiritual commitment to her husband when she refuses to sacrifice 'the rites for why I love him' by staying in Venice while he travels to Cyprus (257).

What these characters from Shakespeare's romantic comedies and tragedies have in common is that they are deeply in love; as such their sexual desire can be celebrated rather than decried. Shakespeare's early work, though, often focuses on lustful rather than loving women. Tapping into male fears over women's sexuality as 'grotesque, and unsettling',[24] the *Henry VI* trilogy and *Titus Andronicus* present female desire as dangerously subversive, flouting patriarchal norms – a pattern that is reworked in *King Lear*, where Goneril and Regan combine rapacious lust with ruthless immorality. Cleopatra is unusual in defying this stereotype of the lustful, immoral woman; she is shown as both fierce in her desire and tenderly loving, sometimes duplicitous but never flagrantly evil. She transforms frank lust for Antony – while he is away she muses 'O happy horse, to bear the weight of Antony!' (1. 5. 21) – into a love that attains mythological proportions. To most Romans she is a 'whore' (3. 6. 67). Enobarbus, however, thinks she outshines even the most imaginative depictions of the goddess of love, 'O'erpicturing that Venus, where we see / The fancy outwork nature' (*Antony and Cleopatra*, 2. 2. 200–1).

In Shakespeare's narrative poem *Venus and Adonis* (1593) the goddess herself, frank in her desire for youthful Adonis, is also treated sympathetically, caught in a titillating display of frustrated female passion. Whereas male lust in *The Rape of Lucrece* (1594) is shown to be hateful and destructive, female desire, while powerful, is less threatening; it cannot physically escalate into violent rape. What's more, in Venus's response to the beautiful Adonis Shakespeare blurs the distinction between love and lust to suggest that Venus is not simply driven by sexual 'will'. Although Adonis's arguments in favour of chastity polarise lust and love, Venus's passion foreshadows the dynamic of *Antony and Cleopatra*, in which sexual desire is welcomed as an integral part of romantic love.

The poem begins by defying standard male-female roles. Venus, a 'bold-fac'd suitor' (6), takes over the traditional masculine role of the wooer, pursuing a narcissistic youth whose sole desire, paralleling that of the aloof Petrarchan mistress, is to 'grow unto himself' (1180).[25] Adonis's virginal coldness is set in witty contrast to the 'hot desire' not only of Venus (1074) but of his horse, a stallion that curvets and leaps with 'ears up-prick'd' and 'crest' standing on end when he sees a mare in heat (271–2). Shunning this phallic passion, Adonis fails to respond to the embraces of the lubricious goddess, despite all her efforts: 'The warm effects which she in him finds missing / She seeks to kindle with continual kissing' (605–6).

Much of the poem's comic appeal lies in this role reversal, through which female sexuality is made to seem powerfully masculine. Determined to consummate her passion despite Adonis's need to abstain, the goddess's craving turns reckless; she fears she will 'die by drops of hot desire' (1074). Her 'affection' (sexual desire) is a 'coal that must be cool'd' as the combat between 'willful' Venus and her 'unwilling' prey continues (387, 365). Salaciously she invites Adonis to treat her body as a park, where he may 'graze' on her lips or 'Stray lower, where the pleasant fountains lie' (233–4). 'Forgetting shame's pure blush' (the modesty traditionally expected of a woman) and instead inviting 'honor's wrack' (558), she is almost overcome with animal lust:

> With blindfold fury she begins to forage;
> Her face doth reek and smoke, her blood doth boil,
> And careless lust stirs up a desperate courage,
> Planting oblivion, beating reason back ... (554–7)

This comes after her 'goodnight' kiss turns ravenous: 'Now quick desire hath caught the yielding prey, / And glutton-like she feasts, yet never filleth' (547–8). Like 'surfeit-taking' Tarquin, who 'Devours his will' but whose sexual desire is never satisfied (*The Rape of Lucrece*, 698–700), Venus plays the merciless aggressor, impervious to reason or shame as she tries to fulfil her 'careless lust'. Lacking male strength, the goddess cannot overpower or actually ravish Adonis. Still, she does everything but.

Yet neither Venus nor the poet framing her story consistently separates this 'hot' sexual 'desire' from a fuller response of 'love'. At the very height of her passion Venus uses a physical image to push Adonis to reciprocate her feelings. She asks him to imagine sexual arousal – how, when a man's eyes feast on the naked white body of his 'true-love', his 'other agents' (genitals) crave similar satisfaction, so that 'when his glutton eye so full hath fed, / His other agents aim at like delight' (399–400). This sexual invitation, which equates the object of a man's erotic desire with his 'true-love', culminates in Venus's exhortation to Adonis, 'O learn to love' (407). The narrative also conflates love and lust when Adonis inadvertently falls on top of Venus, who, in 'the very lists of love', tries to make him comply:

> Now is she in the very lists of love,
> Her champion mounted for the hot encounter . . . (595–6)

Despite being the aggressor Venus, goddess of romantic love, is also a victim of unrequited love: 'She's Love, she loves, and yet she is not lov'd' (610). Earlier Venus envisages love as a transcendent, even spiritual force – a 'spirit all compact of fire' (149). And while her eyes ('Love's eyes'), like those of an adoring Petrarchan lover, 'pay tributary gazes' to Adonis's face (632), she claims that her love isn't simply based on the visual; her 'ears would love' the 'inward beauty' of Adonis's mellifluous voice even if she couldn't see his physical loveliness (433–4).

Discussing the signifiers 'love' and 'lust', Catherine Belsey points out that they were often 'synonyms for desire' in the early modern period. Only by the end of the sixteenth century, she claims, were the terms more 'consistently used as antitheses', driven by the Reformists' belief that a loving companionate marriage could include 'properly regulated' desire as opposed to lust. While it's difficult to pin down precisely when this shift occurred – medieval discourse frequently contrasts lust of the flesh with spiritual love of God – Belsey's point about the semantic 'indeterminacy'[26] of the two terms before 1600 is well taken when it comes to Venus's response to Adonis. In Venus physical desire merges with reverential adoration. Just as the ancient Greek signifier Eros 'does not differentiate between love and desire',[27] so the goddess experiences 'love' primarily as sexual passion but also as an emotionally intense, even transcendent experience. For her 'desire' can be both painful and 'sweet' (386), and when Adonis leaves to go hunting, she sings traditionally of the woes of love (836–40). Distraught after Adonis is killed by the boar, Venus anticipates the 'sorrow' attendant on love (1136).

It is Adonis, determined not to lose himself in sexual passion – he pleads 'Before I know myself, ask not to know me' (525) – who takes a puritanical stand in trying to reinstate the distinction between love and lust. Over four stanzas he moralistically chides the goddess for confusing the two in her efforts to seduce him, twisting logic to make 'reason' a 'bawd to lust's abuse' (792). Adonis claims not to reject love itself but only to hate Venus's grossly earthy version of it. Personifying lust as a 'hot tyrant' that feeds on fresh beauty, he trades on stock images of the natural world, gentle versus harsh, to reinforce his case in a series of binaries:

> Love comforteth like sunshine after rain,
> But lust's effect is tempest after sun;
> Love's gentle spring doth always fresh remain,
> Lust's winter comes ere summer half be done. (799–802)

He concludes by reviling the rapacity and deception inherent in lust: 'Love surfeits not, Lust like a glutton dies; / Love is all truth, Lust full of forged lies' (803–4). Young Adonis of course is hardly an expert in Eros; we learn at the opening of the poem that 'Hunting he lov'd, but love he laugh'd to scorn' (14). Characterised by 'bashful shame' (the traditional female response) rather than sexual desire, he fears damaging his budding phallic power by being too 'early pluck'd' (528): 'If springing things be any jot diminish'd, / They wither in their prime' (417–18).

This virginal youth pits cold restraint against the warmth of experienced passion; while Venus is 'red and hot as coals of glowing fire', the young man remains 'Red for shame, but frosty in desire' (35–6). By showing how she embraces the demands of sexual desire along with the emotional pain of disappointed love, Shakespeare turns passionate Venus into the more sympathetic figure. Her yearning for Adonis combines an aesthetic, even a spiritual appreciation of his beauty – the basis of Neo-Platonic love – with healthy desire to possess him physically. Finally her desire is sublimated in grief once Adonis, having avoided sex with a goddess, loses his life to the fierce boar. The poem ends with Venus in love, not in lust. Transforming from sexual aggressor to heartbroken mother, she cherishes in her bosom the purple flower of Adonis's wound, resolving 'My throbbing heart shall rock thee day and night' (1186).[28]

Venus is the only sexualised female in Shakespeare's early work who is presented sympathetically. In the *Henry VI* trilogy (1590–2)[29] Joan la Pucelle and Queen Margaret are powerful women, feared by the English warriors, and both are taunted for their sexual freedom in defying the patriarchal image of the modest, sexually bashful woman. The character of Joan la Pucelle in *Henry VI, Part 1* is broadly sketched from two completely opposite viewpoints – that of the French and that of the English military. The French quickly accept her as a saviour figure, a 'holy maid' (1. 2. 51) and 'holy prophetess' (1. 4. 102) who has been granted divine power to conquer the English troops. Rather than deriding her as a lustful woman, they respect her for combining chastity with the bold persona of an 'Amazon' (1. 2. 104). Charles the Dauphin praises her as such after she proves her martial prowess – a masculine attribute – by defeating him in personal combat, making good her claim to exceed her 'sex' through physical 'courage' (89–90). Although the besotted Dauphin offers to be her loving servant, Joan vows to remain chaste, to avoid the 'rites of love' until she has driven the English out of France (1. 2. 113–15).

The English nobility, however, abhor this powerful female. Mirroring the likely response of the Elizabethan audience, they find Joan's warrior role unnatural, a flouting of traditional gender roles as she dresses in masculine attire and competes in the male domain of the battlefield.[30] Fighting for England's stake in France, unsettled by her transgressive behaviour and seemingly supernatural power in battle, they defensively brand Joan as both a witch and a whore. The scapegoating of anti-social, sexually unconventional women as witches in the early modern period – females who supposedly increased their evil power through sexual intercourse with demons (familiars) and possibly with the devil himself – is well documented.[31] By exploiting the phonetic similarity between 'pucelle' (French for 'maid') and 'puzzel', English slang for 'slut', the play-script presents Joan as a combination of devilish power and sexual promiscuity. The British use both terms, 'witch' and 'whore', to denounce her as a lustful woman. Incensed by Joan's martial prowess at Orleans, the warrior Talbot not only derides her as a 'witch' (1. 5. 6, 21) and a 'damn'd sorceress' (3. 2. 38) but accuses her of being a 'high-minded strumpet' (1. 5. 12). He calls her a 'foul fiend' who, not satisfied with being mistress to the Dauphin, is 'Encompass'd' with 'lustful paramours!' (3. 2. 52–3). Burgundy (after he deserts to the English side) conflates the two terms by calling Joan 'vile fiend and shameless courtesan' (45), and when York captures her, he berates her as 'ugly witch' and 'hag' – a whore (5. 3. 34, 42). Countering expectations about appropriate female behaviour by playing an unorthodox, masculine role, Joan becomes what Coppélia Kahn calls 'a composite portrait of the ways women are dangerous to men'.[32]

The portrayal of Joan la Pucelle turns to caricature in Act 5, where scenes now believed to be composed by Marlowe, Shakespeare's co-author of *Henry VI, Part 1*,[33] reinforce the stereotype of her as a lustful sorceress. Up to this point the audience has been given no real evidence, other than English prejudice, that Joan is either a witch or a sexually promiscuous woman. Suddenly, in Act 5, scene 3, she is literally demonised. Joan invokes Fiends, who actually appear on stage as she bribes these 'familiar spirits' (10) with the prospect of 'blood-sacrifice'; she reminds them they have fed on her blood in the past and offers them her body and even her soul (20–2). She lies to her captors about her commerce with 'wicked spirits' (5. 4. 42) and describes the English warriors (not herself) as 'polluted' with 'lusts' (43). Even Joan's father, a poor shepherd, denounces his daughter as a whore, a 'cursed drab' (32). Joan's claim to be pregnant by one of the French royals (possibly Alencon or even Reignier) in order to save her life is designed to make her appear both lustful and craven (72–8). Thus the play-script reduces Joan to ashes even before she is burned at the stake. York's final label of her as he leads her away is 'foul accursed minister of hell!' (93).

In a more nuanced portrayal of the lustful woman in the *Henry VI* trilogy, Shakespeare develops Queen Margaret as a virago whose strong sex drive – feared as unruly in women – is part of her masculine, warrior-like spirit. Shakespeare followed his main source, Hall's Lancaster-York Chronicle (1550), in characterising Margaret, the Princess of Naples, 'more like a man than a woman' in 'stomach and courage';[34] as such she continually defies the stereotype of female modesty and reticence. Because she first enters the stage immediately after York leads off the tarnished 'enchantress' Joan la Pucelle (*Part 1*, 5. 3. 42), the audience is invited to find parallels between the two women. Just as Joan wins the Dauphin with her 'courage' and her erotic power, so Suffolk, impressed with Margaret's independence, echoes Hall's Chronicle when he promotes her to Henry for her 'valiant courage and undaunted spirit / (More than in women commonly is seen)' (5. 5. 70–1). Margaret's unabashed sexual nature first comes to the fore near the end of *Henry VI, Part 1*, when she returns the kiss that Suffolk (wooing her as the king's surrogate) gives her, boldly declaring 'That for thyself' (5. 3. 185).

After her royal marriage Queen Margaret builds on her persona as a boldly sexual woman by taking Suffolk as her lover; early in *Part 2* she complains that her saintly husband Henry lacks Suffolk's 'courage, courtship, and proportion' (1. 3. 54). Again, though, she assumes a masculine role with her lover, deriding him as a 'coward woman', too 'soft-hearted' in failing to stand up to his enemies (3. 2. 307). Once Suffolk is dead, by *Henry VI, Part 3*, Margaret channels her sex drive into fiercely protecting the Lancastrian succession to the throne from the rival claims of the Duke of York and his sons. While Joan was castigated as a witch and a whore, the Yorkists slander Margaret for being too tough – too unfeminine – and for being sexually bold; they call her both a 'shameless callet', or strumpet (2. 2. 145), and 'Iron of Naples' (2. 2. 139). When Margaret orchestrates the death of York, he combines the two charges in the pejorative phrase 'Amazonian trull' (1. 4. 114), a warrior-like lewd woman.[35]

In Margaret's astounding theatrical performance, when she ties York to a stake and sadistically invites him to wipe away his tears with a napkin soaked in his son Rutland's blood, Shakespeare fully displays the queen's courage and tough brazenness. It is Margaret's defiance of traditional feminine behaviour that York focuses on in his shocked outburst 'O tiger's heart wrapp'd in a woman's hide!' (1. 4. 137). Reproaching her for her ruthlessness, 'more inhuman, more inexorable' than 'tigers of Hyrcania' (154–5), he condemns her all the more severely because he finds her actions 'ill-beseeming' to her gender (113). York reminds her (and the audience) that females are expected to be nurturing, subordinate and passive:

> Women are soft, mild, pitiful, and flexible,
> Thou stern, obdurate, flinty, rough, remorseless. (141–2)

Finally Shakespeare complicates the portrait of Margaret by counterpointing her 'flinty' and 'remorseless' traits with maternal tenderness. When the York brothers avenge the murder of their father and young Rutland by stabbing to death Prince Edward, it is Margaret's turn to suffer as an anguished parent watching her son die. Certain that her heart 'will burst', this mother curses the sons of York as 'bloody cannibals' (5. 5. 59, 61) – a role she goes on to adopt in *Richard III*, where she is no longer a proactive woman who threatens men with her political and sexual power, but a diminished figure, railing at the new king from the sidelines.

While Shakespeare's presentation of subversive Queen Margaret is relatively complex, Tamora, the 'lascivious Goth' of *Titus Andronicus* (2. 3. 110), confirms a slightly different assumption – that female lust often pairs with evil. Since females are viewed as particularly susceptible to lust, they are assumed to be prone to other Deadly Sins too. In the opening scene Tamora asks Titus to show compassion – 'Sweet Mercy is nobility's true badge' (1. 1. 119) – by sparing her son Alarbus. When Titus refuses, she too renounces all feminine tenderness, committing instead to an evil course of revenge; in an aside she pledges to 'find a day to massacre' the whole Andronicus family (450). Progressively she takes on the masculine role of villain, framing Titus's sons for the murder of Bassianus and callously encouraging her sons Chiron and Demetrius to rape Titus's daughter Lavinia.

By Act 2 the portrait of Tamora as lecherous as well as evil is defined more sharply. She brazenly continues her affair with Aaron even after her political marriage to the Roman emperor Saturninus. Her lustful relationship with the Moor seems to be common knowledge; Bassianus (who pays for the insult with his life) derides Tamora's 'honor' as 'spotted' and 'detestable', tainted with 'foul desire', while his wife Lavinia tauntingly suggests that the empress and the Moor are 'singled forth to try experiments' while the rest of the court party is out hunting (2. 3. 74–5, 79, 69). When instead of a white heir for the emperor Tamora produces a black baby – the 'fruit of her burning lust' (5. 1. 43) – she callously sends word that Aaron should kill their child. Fearing social disgrace, she abandons maternal protectiveness to plan infanticide. Ironically, in Act 5 this monstrous woman, emblem of the 'malevolence' of a 'dreaded devouring mother',[36] must literally consume the remains of her two adult sons in Titus's grotesque banquet of revenge.

Tamora's fierce ruthlessness, the absence of pity that is viewed by Shakespeare's society as such an important attribute in women, is crystallised in the image of her as a tiger – violent and animalistic. When Henry V exhorts his soldiers to 'imitate the action of the tiger' by going 'Once more into the breach' at Harfleur, his speech evokes both the violent 'rage' of killing and the bestiality of an aggressive sexual attack (*Henry V*, 3. 1. 6–8). His urging his men to 'Stiffen the sinews' and 'bend up every spirit / To his full height' (16–17) is almost an invitation to rape. When Lavinia begs Tamora to prevent her sons from raping her, she also associates Tamora with this cruellest of animals, just as York rebukes Queen Margaret for her 'tiger's heart' (*Henry VI, Part 3*, 1. 4. 137). It is wholly unnatural, argues Lavinia, for the 'tiger's young ones', Tamora's barbaric sons, to teach their 'dam' to be ruthless rather than tender (2. 3. 142). Again like York, amazed that fierce Margaret can still 'bear a woman's face', Lavinia cannot believe that Tamora, with her 'woman's' features (136), would refuse to rescue her from the males' 'worse than killing lust' (175). But Tamora shows vicarious pleasure in egging on her sons, displaying neither 'grace' nor 'womanhood'. Instead she has become a 'beastly creature' (182). Titus's grandson Lucius reinforces this bestial image of Tamora in the play's epilogue, when he calls her a 'ravenous tiger' whose 'life was beastly and devoid of pity' (5. 3. 195, 199).

This 'beastly creature' designation, the belief that women, like animals, are governed by base appetite, is further developed in the characters of Goneril and Regan in *King Lear* (1605–6), composed a dozen years after *Titus Andronicus*. Arguably, Shakespeare's exaggerated portrait of female wickedness draws on the era's most misogynistic assumptions about women; certainly Lear's older daughters are portrayed as monstrous in their defiance of patriarchal authority.[37] But their heartlessness goes beyond the subversiveness of Joan la Pucelle or Queen Margaret to represent a self-centred evil that offers a stark contrast to Cordelia's selfless goodness. It is after they strip their father of his retinue and fail to rescue him from the storm that they are equated, like Margaret and Tamora, with tigers. Shocked that a 'woman's shape' hides the fiend-like nature of his wife Goneril, and appalled at the sisters' callousness, Albany is finally driven to wonder 'Tigers, not daughters, what have you perform'd?' (4. 2. 67, 40).

While Tamora is quickly established as both heartless and lecherous, Goneril and Regan reveal their sexual rapacity, in their aggressive pursuit of Edmund in Act 4, only after demonstrating their hard-heartedness in the first two Acts. Goneril, the bolder of the two sisters, sanctimoniously accuses the king's retinue of 'riotous' knights of being sexually decadent, practising 'Epicurism and lust' at her residence (1. 3. 6, 1. 4. 244). Yet she is the first to show strong sensual interest in the social climber Edmund, self-described as 'rough and lecherous' (1. 2. 131), when she senses he will prove a more satisfying sexual partner than her 'milk-liver'd' husband Albany (4. 2. 50). After she and Edmund collude in the heartless blinding of Gloucester, Goneril is eager to impose a 'mistress's command' on him (21). Boldly embracing him, she trusts that her kiss will 'stretch' his 'spirits' into the air' (23) – excite him sexually.

Once she is widowed, Regan joins in the fierce hunt for Edmund. Opportunistic Edmund not only reciprocates the women's lust – he boasts that 'To both these sisters have I sworn my love' (5. 1. 55) – but exploits each woman's desire to possess him as a husband. Only one of the rival sisters can succeed, however. In the letter that Edgar intercepts, Goneril proposes that her lover find a way to 'cut off' her husband Albany – in effect castration by murder – so that she and Edmund can rule the kingdom together (4. 6. 263–4). It is telling that Edgar feels more disgust at discovering this female's boundless sexual desire ('will') than horror at her murderous intention. 'O indistinguish'd space of woman's will!' he exclaims (271). Indeed by Act 5 each sister privileges erotic possession of Edmund's body above anything else, including the fate of the body politic.[38] Fulfilling Albany's prediction that bestial humans will prey on themselves, like vile 'monsters of the deep' (4. 2. 50), Goneril first poisons her sister and then desperately commits suicide. As Albany notes, the violent deaths of Goneril and Regan create no 'pity' in the audience (5. 3. 233); unlike Edmund, the play's Machiavel who belatedly tries to save Cordelia, neither sister has displayed any hint of 'good' in her 'nature' (5. 3. 244–5). Rather, both are moulded into types of 'sterile' lechery[39] in the service of evil.

Significantly it is a disillusioned male, Edgar, who brands women's sexual 'will' as infinite, an 'indistinguish'd space'. Depictions of lecherous women, with the aggression and cruelty that traditionally accompanies this stereotype, are relatively scarce in the canon; indeed two of the more caricatured portrayals (Joan la Pucelle and Tamora) appear in plays that Shakespeare co-authored – *Henry VI, Part 1* with Marlowe and *Titus Andronicus* with Peele. More often in Shakespearean drama the lustful female appears as a figment of the male imagination. Once a husband's suspicion that his partner is being sexually unfaithful triggers fantasies of female promiscuity, he readily assumes that female desire – hidden but insatiable – will turn a formerly chaste wife into a whore. Phyllis Rackin has pointed out that Shakespeare's 'representations of male sexual jealousy'[40] are more prevalent than in other drama of the period. It's true that the playwright, while tapping into the strong distrust of females shared by his culture, is particularly interested in delving further into it. Male anxiety over being made a cuckold – that is, wearing horns visible to everyone but himself because his wife has cheated on him – percolates through Shakespeare's comedy as well as tragedy. In *As You Like It* the wise fool Touchstone, about to get married, opines that 'As horns are odious, they are necessary' (3. 3. 51–2). Cynically he resigns himself to the idea that his wife, oversexed like all women, will violate the boundaries of marriage. More usually, though, Shakespeare's male characters shun the idea of wearing a cuckold's horns as painfully humiliating, since horns signify to the world at large that a husband has become a neutered animal (an ox) who can no longer control or satisfy his wife's desire. In almost every instance of male jealousy in Shakespeare's plays, men lash out with violence against such a stigma. Their paranoid assumption, the sense that women are lustful 'betrayers and men are their victims',[41] underlies the marital crises that develop in several of Shakespeare's tragedies and tragicomedies.

As a dramatic character, Queen Gertrude in *Hamlet* is enigmatic. Certainly she is presented very differently from the wilful, immoral women of Shakespeare's early plays: Queen Margaret or evil Tamora. While she appears to be sensual (Hamlet reports her 'appetite' for her husband King Hamlet, in 1. 2. 144) and sexually compliant (she partners quickly with Claudius), it's not clear that she is aggressively lustful. When the Ghost laments Gertrude's sexual 'falling-off' with the 'incestuous . . . adulterate beast' Claudius, he defends his wife as a helpless victim of sexual passion (1. 5. 47, 42). Personifying 'lust' as an unstoppable force, he laments that even if linked to a 'radiant angel' such as Gertrude, strong desire will eventually 'prey on garbage' (55–7). It is Hamlet, furious that his mother has betrayed her son as well as, in effect, cuckolded her first husband, who verbally lashes Gertrude for her unbridled desire, the 'heyday' in her 'blood' not yet tamed by age (3. 4. 69). Through the lens of his disgust he sees her as a woman so swept away by passion for a 'satyr' that she has abdicated any responsibility for her actions. Sexual desire has co-opted judgement: 'Reason panders will' (88). Hamlet's salacious vision of Gertrude's bedroom activities – 'Stew'd in corruption / honeying and making love over the nasty sty!' (93–4) – is, of course, one he conjures up alone. The text provides no means of testing his vision against the reality of Gertrude's relationship with Claudius. Freudian feminist critics such as Janet Adelman have convincingly attributed Hamlet's animus against Gertrude to unresolved pre-Oedipal conflicts – a sense of primal betrayal resulting from the infant's painful discovery that he cannot merge with his mother.[42] Certainly Hamlet's obsession with his mother's sexuality goes far beyond a young man's distaste for middle-aged passion.

This combination – denouncing a mature woman's sexual behaviour while being fascinated by it – surfaces in the Romans who respond to Cleopatra. Philo opens *Antony and Cleopatra* by denigrating the Queen of Egypt, pointing to how Antony simultaneously stirs up and cools down her 'gypsy's lust' (1. 1. 10). Pompey makes the standard pejorative link between female desire and witches when he prays that Cleopatra's 'witchcraft' will 'join with beauty, lust with both' to bring about Antony's political downfall (2. 1. 22). The puritanical Octavius Caesar, who may be playing on the sense of 'quean' as sluttish woman[43] when he asks Cleopatra's ladies 'Which is the Queen of Egypt?' (5. 2. 112), dismisses the offspring of the famous couple as the fruits of 'lust' (3. 6. 7). For his part, Antony charges Cleopatra with promiscuity only when he suspects her of sexual betrayal. Finding her kissing the hand of Octavius's messenger, he furiously castigates her for 'hotter hours' unknown to him, bitterly recalling how he found her as a 'morsel' left over by Julius Caesar (3. 13. 116–18). After she enrages him by fleeing from the second naval battle, seeming to side with the enemy, he denounces her as 'triple-turn'd whore' and treacherous 'witch' (4. 12. 13, 47). In their defensive dismissal of Cleopatra as whorish, however, Antony's fellow Romans seem more unnerved by her erotic magnetism, or possibly envious at not winning her favours, than repelled by her lust. This is how Ulysses in *Troilus and Cressida* reacts when Cressida, handed round among the Greek generals, makes him 'beg' for a kiss. Offended by the slight, he quickly brands her as a 'sluttish' camp follower, a daughter of 'the game' (4. 5. 48, 62–3).

Admittedly Cressida is the one female in Shakespeare's plays who, trusted by her lover, does prove unfaithful during the dramatic action. At first, though, the playwright presents her as vulnerable and sexually susceptible rather than fickle or simply lustful. She has played hard to get with Troilus less to arouse him than to defend herself against the cooling of male ardour. Because she recognises that 'Men prize the thing ungain'd more than it is' (1. 2. 289), she fears being abandoned if she gives herself completely to a lover. Confessing that a key part of her nature is self-protective, Cressida describes as 'unkind' the 'self' that 'itself would leave to be another's fool' (3. 2. 149–50). From this it's a short step to discarding an absent lover and settling for whatever is offered in the present. While 'one eye' looks back regretfully on Troilus, she admits 'But with my heart my other eye doth see' (5. 2. 107–8); she feels driven both by her emotions ('heart') and by sexual impulse (the pull of her 'other eye'[44]) into accepting Diomedes's overtures. Lacking self-esteem, tending to base 'her identity on male desires and definitions',[45] she replaces Troilus with a man who can instantly 'prize' her as a lover.

Meanwhile Troilus, destined forever to be known as a 'true' lover (3. 2. 182), bucks the trend of the anxious male quick to suspect the chastity of his lady. Desperately wanting to believe in her fidelity, Troilus wonders if his eyes are deceiving him as he watches Cressida sign herself over to Diomedes. He clings to the hope that 'eyes and ears' have both become unreliable witnesses, 'Created only to calumniate', smearing Cressida with the appearance of corruption (5. 2. 122–4). For all his acute disillusionment, however, Troilus himself may have set up Cressida for this betrayal. Before they consummate their affair, Troilus doubts that any female could be perfectly constant in love:

> O that I thought it could be in a woman –
> As if it can, I will presume in you –
> To feed for [aye] her lamp and flames of love,
> To keep her constancy in plight and youth . . . (3. 2. 158–61)

This underlying assumption that women are fickle becomes a self-fulfilling prophecy. Cressida herself buys into the stereotype of the treacherous woman by pledging that she will become the epitome of falsehood (' "As false as Cressid" ') if ever she 'swerve[s] a hair from truth' (196, 184). And with his nervous exhortations 'Be thou but true of heart' and 'But yet be true' (4. 4. 58, 74) – the conditions he sets for visiting Cressida in the Greek camp – Troilus himself projects uncertainty over whether she can remain faithful.

Troilus displaces anger about his mistress's betrayal on to the male who has seduced her, resolving, 'As much [as] I do Cressid love, / So much by weight hate I her Diomed' (5. 2. 167–8). More often Shakespeare shows a male character who is tortured by sexual suspicion reacting explosively, completely reversing his earlier perception of his beloved.

In *Much Ado about Nothing*, Claudio's unleashing of vitriol against his bride is disturbingly intense. Convinced on misleading visual evidence that Hero has been sexually intimate with another man, Claudio waits until the wedding ceremony to cast her off publicly. Previously he has revered Hero as the 'sweetest lady' (1. 1. 187); now he accuses her of seeming as chaste as 'Dian in her orb' but actually more 'intemperate' in her 'blood' than Venus.[46] His overheated imagination brands her as bestial in lust, like 'those pamp'red animals / That rage in savage sensuality' (4. 1. 57–61).

Comparing Desdemona's fair appearance with what he thinks is her true foulness, Othello also references Diana, goddess of chastity. As he responds to Iago's insinuations, Othello switches with alarming speed from perceiving his bride as 'honest' (chaste) and her 'name' as 'fresh / As Dian's visage' to considering her reputation as 'begrim'd and black' as his own face (*Othello*, 3. 3. 386–8). Drawing on misogynistic assumptions about women's voracious 'appetites', he laments how often and how easily wives stray, duping their husbands:

> O curse of marriage!
> That we may call these delicate creatures ours,
> And not their appetites! (3. 3. 268–70)

In a patriarchal society where men could 'call' their wives their exclusive property – as is the case in *The Rape of Lucrece* – it was especially important for that possession to remain pure. Should a woman indulge her sexual desires with any other man, her value would be 'diminished immeasurably', as Keith Thomas points out.[47] Othello quickly progresses from brooding over Desdemona's 'stol'n hours of lust' (3. 3. 338) with just one man, Cassio, to fantasising that the 'general camp', every soldier down to the lowest rank, might have 'tasted her sweet body' (345–6). Inflamed by Iago's word-painting of Cassio and Desdemona together as rutting animals, as 'prime [lustful, sexually aroused] as goats' and 'hot as monkeys' (403), Othello loses all rational control. His conviction that he is a cuckold, scorned as a strange animal because 'A horned man's a monster and a beast' (4. 1. 62), unleashes such distorted imaginings that he brands Desdemona as a 'cunning whore' (89) and publicly denounces her as 'devil' (244).

Ironically Desdemona has welcomed the 'rites' of marriage in front of the Venetian Senate (1. 3. 257). She shows none of the 'fear' and disgust that her father, racially stereotyping Othello as a black alien, expects the Moor to provoke in a modest white woman (71). Othello himself projects soberness and sexual restraint. He distances himself from the 'heat' of youthful 'appetite' (262–3), and what Iago later refers to as the 'unbitted lusts' of a sensual nature (331), when he claims that 'young affects' (sexual impulses) are 'defunct' in him (263–4). He is not, surely, claiming impotence through the word 'defunct'. Still, Othello is a middle-aged warrior unversed in Venice's sophisticated art of lovemaking and therefore prone to social and sexual insecurity. He proves vulnerable to Iago's suggestion that lustful, promiscuous Venetian wives routinely inflict on their husbands the 'forked plague' of cuckoldry (3. 3. 276).

Leontes, who also exhibits extreme sexual jealousy in *The Winter's Tale*, creates his own paranoid fantasy that his wife is having a 'hot' affair with his childhood companion Polixenes. In contrast to newlywed Othello, Leontes (whose son Mamillius must be at least seven years old) has been married to Hermione for close to a decade. Yet he idealises the 'innocence' of his prepubescent relationship with Polixenes above the 'guilty' sexual desire between married couples following the Fall (1. 2. 69, 74).[48] He is all too ready to find sexual undertones in Hermione's hope that Polixenes will remain 'for some while' her 'friend' (108), which – like Iago musing that Desdemona might 'mean no harm' by lying 'naked with her friend in bed' (*Othello*, 4. 1. 3) – he wilfully takes in its possible sense of lover. Still, after Hermione's courtly persuasion, cajoling Polixenes to stay longer in the Sicilian court, it is jolting when Leontes speculates on his wife's 'liberty' and 'fertile bosom' (112–13), luridly translating Hermione's cordial gestures into 'paddling palms' and 'practic'd smiles' (115–16). Soon he is imagining the sensuality of 'kissing with inside lip' as an index of Hermione's 'breaking honesty' (286–8).

Prey to dark fantasy, Leontes persuades himself in tortured verse ('Affection! thy intention stabs the centre') that his wife's sexual passion ('affection') is leading him to the heart of truth, even while he subliminally acknowledges that his own passionate response may be deluded because it joins with what is 'unreal' (1. 1. 138–41). Convinced that Hermione's lust has transformed him into a cuckold wearing degrading horns – he refers to the 'hard'ning of [his] brows' and 'infection' of his 'brains' (145–6) – Leontes fails to perceive that his mind has been infected with unwarranted suspicion. From here it is a small step to his belief that pregnant Hermione is carrying the child of Polixenes.

It's true that in an age before paternity tests, let alone reliable contraception, the jealous husband could never be sure that his wife's child had been conceived by him. He must trust the word of the mother. This specific male anxiety emerges in several of Shakespeare's plays.[49] Even the magus Prospero says he believes that Miranda is his daughter only because his now deceased wife was a 'piece of virtue' (*The Tempest*, 1. 2.

56). Queen Margaret's love affair with Suffolk in *Henry VI, Part 2* could have destabilised the whole basis of patriarchal authority – legitimate succession – had doubt been publicly cast on whether King Henry was the father of Prince Edward. Since the 'dissemination of property and status'[50] in a patrilineal society requires a chaste wife giving birth to an heir, the onus was on a husband to regulate his wife's sexuality to achieve that end. Presumably because it was impossible to establish paternity definitively, early modern law made some allowance for a wife's straying in deciding the legitimacy of an heir. Because a wife was regarded as her husband's property, any offspring she produced from an adulterous liaison could be claimed by her spouse – assuming he knew he was not the biological father but still chose to keep the child. This becomes clear in the debate that opens *King John*. Philip the Bastard is granted the right to his inheritance as the oldest son in his family, even though his mother, Lady Faulconbridge, confesses that he was conceived by Richard I, the Lionheart. Using a barnyard analogy, King John himself confirms that a husband is entitled to keep any 'calf' bred from his 'cow' (1. 1. 124). If the Bastard's mother 'did play false', explains John, the 'fault was hers' and need not affect the status of the child. Again trading on the male assumption that women, weak and lecherous, are likely to cuckold their husbands, he emphasises how all married men shoulder this risk (that a woman will prove unfaithful) as one of the 'hazards' of taking a wife (118–19).

What is pragmatically, even cynically, accepted by King John – a woman's lustful 'fault' in cheating on her husband and the expectation that he will raise the child as his own – repels Leontes. Once his daughter is born, Leontes is adamant about not keeping the baby: 'Nay, I'll not rear / Another's issue' (*The Winter's Tale*, 2. 3. 192–3). Although father and son are 'as like as eggs', the king's misogynistic delusion extends to wondering whether Mamillius, born years earlier, is not his own child (1. 2. 130). Physical resemblance certainly provides the acid test in *King John*. The Bastard Philip is certain that his massive 'limbs' could not spring from Faulconbridge's puny 'shape' (1. 1. 239, 138), while Elinor, mother to King John, confirms that Philip resembles his father, King Richard; he has 'a trick of Cordelion's face' (85).

The Bastard's mother, who eventually admits her marital infidelity, is careful to defend herself from any charge of sexual laxity. After all, her seducer was King Richard himself, who 'strongly urg'd' her through a 'long and vehement suit' when her husband was abroad (1. 1. 254–8). Still, the more common belief was that a woman's uncontrollable desire would quickly lead to promiscuity if she played 'false' to her husband with any other man. Like Othello envisaging the 'whole camp' enjoying

Desdemona, Leontes is quick to fantasise about women's indiscriminate lustfulness, progressing from the wife who has been 'sluic'd by her neighbor' to the grotesque idea that a woman's 'belly' will 'let in and out the enemy / With bag and baggage' (204–6). Convinced that Hermione is an 'adult'ress' (*The Winter's Tale*, 2. 3. 4), Leontes repeatedly calls his newborn daughter a 'bastard' (74, 140, 155, 175). It is unfortunate that Polixenes has been staying in Sicily for the whole nine months of Hermione's pregnancy, despite the sheer improbability, except to a deeply prejudiced mind, that Hermione would begin an affair with Polixenes the moment he arrived. Hermione's pregnant body seems to trigger in Leontes old pre-Oedipal anxieties – the syndrome in which the infant, yearning for union with his mother, fears abandonment,[51] while the adult fears that his wife has betrayed him sexually.

Cymbeline reverts to the pattern of *Othello*; now it is the husband Posthumus who is tricked by an Italianate villain into believing that his wife Imogen is unchaste. Seemingly eager to believe the worst – like Othello, who doesn't really need the 'ocular proof' of Desdemona's handkerchief to confirm his fears – Posthumus has to be reminded that a 'corporal sign' (an intimate detail) would provide more conclusive evidence of Imogen's lust than the mere sight of her stolen bracelet (2. 4. 119–20). Once Posthumus hears Iachimo describe the distinctive mole under Imogen's breast (135) he is readily convinced that Imogen has made love to this stranger. Thus Shakespeare captures in Posthumus's reaction one of the darker psychological facets of jealousy: its wilfully induced masochism. This husband apparently yearns for the humiliation of being cuckolded, fiercely rejecting any benign explanation that Iachimo might offer:

> If you will swear you have not done't, you lie,
> And I will kill thee if thou dost deny
> Thou'st made me cuckold. (2. 4. 144–6)

Again like Othello, who masochistically allows himself to visualise Desdemona in bed with Cassio (*Othello*, 3. 3. 397–405), Posthumus falls prey to self-lacerating voyeurism. Iachimo himself claims that he 'proceeded' to seduce Imogen 'By both your wills' (2. 4. 55–6), managing to gratify the husband sexually as well as the wife. Almost instantly repudiating the belief that his wife is 'chaste as unsunn'd snow', Posthumus titilatingly imagines Iachimo mounting Imogen 'like a full-acorn'd boar', encountering no opposition (2. 5. 13, 16).

In the unbalanced anti-feminist rant that follows, Posthumus wishes he could banish any trace of the 'woman's part' from his physical make-up (2. 5. 20). When he speculates that the 'venerable' man he called his father was absent when he was conceived ('stamp'd'), Posthumus conflates the male's ingrained fear of being illegitimate ('counterfeit'), a victim of female infidelity, with the broader idea that all men are 'bastards' simply because they have been contaminated by their mothers (2–6). Disgusted that women must be 'half-workers' in the act of procreation, he builds his paranoid catalogue of female 'faults' into the hysterical climax of 'Lust and rank thoughts, hers, hers; revenges, hers' (2, 24). To ensure a comic resolution, however, Shakespeare shifts the dramatic momentum of *Cymbeline* away from potential violence; instead of 'revenges', Posthumus ends his diatribe with melodramatic bluster, resolving to 'write' satires against women. He consoles himself with the idea that their own notorious 'will' – voracious sexual appetite – can 'plague' or punish women: 'Detest them, curse them; yet 'tis a greater skill / In a true hate, to pray they have their will' (32–5).

The audience senses that this husband's delusion will not lead to a tragic outcome; Posthumus must eventually realise that his faithful wife has been defamed. At this point he most resembles Ford, the jealous husband in Shakespeare's comedy *The Merry Wives of Windsor*. Convinced that he's being cuckolded by Falstaff, anxious Ford lacks any faith in his wife's 'honesty'. He compulsively obsesses over 'the hell of having a false woman' (2. 2. 291–2) and curses 'all Eve's daughters' as lustful (4. 2. 24). But since his jealousy is partly presented as a 'humor' – a physiological and psychological imbalance resulting in 'fantastical humors and jealousies' (3. 3. 170–1) – it can be comically exploded. Once Mistress Ford explains the wives' plan to shame Falstaff, Ford assures her that he would rather 'suspect the sun with [cold]' than his wife 'with wantonness' (4. 4. 7–8). Posthumus, too, is ready to renew trust in his wife. By Act 5 he can even forgive what he still imagines to be Imogen's adulterous lapse; he calls it 'wrying [deviating] but a little' (*Cymbeline*, 5. 1. 5). While this late play moves toward romantic reconciliation, Shakespeare has reiterated a troubling pattern: jealous husbands become deeply misogynistic, automatically branding all women as whores once they wrongly suspect their chaste wives of infidelity.

King Lear is a widower, no longer a husband. His rants against women are nevertheless horrifyingly intense. It is after he has been cast out by Goneril and Regan – those 'pelican daughters' his 'flesh' is ashamed to have 'begot' (*King Lear*, 3. 4. 74–5) – that he becomes obsessed with women's treachery. Just as the jealous delusion of Leontes seems prompted by pre-Oedipal anxieties over maternal betrayal, so Lear's angry rejection of female sexuality suggests a similar regression. From the start Lear expects his daughters to nurture him, but when, as the Fool points out, he makes his two older 'daughters' his 'mothers' by

empowering them (1. 4. 173), he finds himself subject to their cruelty.⁵²
It's no coincidence that Lear's form of retaliation against Goneril, after
she breaks her promise to house both him and his hundred knights, is to
try to blight her sexual nature, to prevent her from becoming a mother;
he delivers a chilling curse on her fertility when he prays to the goddess
Nature: 'Into her womb convey sterility, / Dry up in her the organs of
increase' (278–9). And when Regan greets her father soon afterwards,
Lear is ready to assume a terrible blot on his dead wife's chastity – the
notion that Regan is not his daughter but was conceived with a man
other than her husband – if Regan is not truly 'glad' to see him. His
vindictive response demonstrates both paternal insecurity and the dark
suspicion that all women are pernicious, innately untrustworthy:

> If thou shouldst not be glad,
> I would divorce me from thy [mother's] tomb,
> Sepulchring an adult'ress. (2. 4. 130–2)

Lear's distrust of female sexuality peaks in his mad rant on 'luxury'
(lust) in Act 4. The verse fragments as he struggles to contain his nau-
seating vision of female lust, choking on the hypocrisy of the 'simp'ring
dame' who pretends to be sexually modest. Such a woman, he contends,
shakes her head 'to hear of pleasure's name' while longing to engage
in sex; he fantasises that neither 'The fitchew nor the soil'd horse goes
to't / With a more riotous appetite' (4. 6. 118–23). The king now views
all females as satyrs (a male image of lust) or centaurs 'down from
the waist', bestial in their sexuality. He further demonises women by
characterising their genitalia, likely to be infected with venereal disease,
as a horrific 'sulphurous pit', or hell itself:

> But to the girdle do the gods inherit,
> Beneath is all the fiend's: there's hell, there's darkness,
> There is the sulphurous pit, burning, scalding
> Stench, corruption . . . (126–9)

Poor Tom, the persona that Edgar creates to disguise himself in *King
Lear*, is also obsessed with sexual debauchery. As a mad, demonically
possessed outcast, Tom feels guilt-ridden, tormented by the 'foul fiend'
as punishment for a former life in which he 'out-paramour'd the Turk'.
At court he was a serving-man 'proud in heart' (sexually bold), who
'slept in the contriving of lust, and wak'd to do it'. But as a kept man
who 'serv'd the lust of [his] mistress' heart', he also positions himself as
a victim of female lechery (3. 4. 85–92); his warning 'Let not the creak-
ing of shoes nor the rustling of silks betray thy poor heart to woman'
(94–6) implies that women are the sexual tempters. Just as Edgar's

impersonation of a bedlam beggar catalyses Lear's madness, so Poor Tom's outpourings on clandestine sex with wealthy females at court serve to unleash the king's pent-up disgust at female desire.

In his own person, too, Edgar envisages females as sexually depraved. After mortally wounding his half-brother, he judges that it was the sin of Edmund's conception that ultimately led to his father Gloucester's blinding. Moralising on how Gloucester was justly punished for adulterous sex, he opines that 'The dark and vicious place where thee he got / Cost him his eyes' (5. 3. 173–4).[53] If the phrase is taken literally as the 'place' where male seed is planted – rather than glossed as 'the adulterous bed and so the act of adultery'[54] – then Edgar, like Lear gagging at the 'hell' and 'darkness' of the vagina, is envisaging female genitalia, and by extension lustful women, as the ultimate site of corruption.

Timon of Athens provides the most savage denunciation of lust in the whole canon.[55] Once philanthropic Timon is deserted by his flattering friends, his invective goes beyond lambasting female corruption[56] to invoke a total 'confusion' of values (4. 1. 21), transforming 'virtue' into the unrestrained sexuality of 'riot'. He prays that 'Lust' and 'liberty' will

> Creep in the minds and marrows of our youth,
> That 'gainst the stream of virtue they may strive
> And drown themselves in riot! (25–8)

While Timon excoriates women's hidden sexual desire – he urges Alcibiades the warrior to strike down the counterfeit 'matron' who is 'honest' (chaste) only in her outward appearance (4. 3. 113–14) – he is presented as misanthropic rather than misogynist. In fact Timon elicits women's help in his fervent wish that 'Destruction fang mankind' (4. 3. 23). He encourages the camp followers of Alcibiades to 'be whores still' (140), bribing them with gold to seek out male clients and 'Give them diseases' in return for 'their lust' (85). While King Lear prays in the storm that the gods' ferocious thunderbolts will let loose orgasmic destruction on human life – 'all germains spill at once / That makes ungrateful man!' (*King Lear*, 3. 2. 8–9) – Timon is more specific in hoping that the prostitutes' activity, spreading painful venereal disease by exploiting men's desire for sex, will 'defeat and quell / The source of all erection' (4. 3. 163–4).

Timon is promoting the idea, current in Shakespeare's time, that women were responsible for transmitting venereal disease while remaining relatively immune to it themselves.[57] In an age when syphilis was spreading rapidly, men tended to view themselves as the victims of unchaste women who deceive men by concealing that they themselves are infected. Thus Falstaff, a patron of the Boar's Head (a tavern doubling as a bawdy-house), assumes that prostitutes there are spreading the 'pox' by providing sexual services; the old knight laments to Doll Tearsheet that 'we catch of you Doll, we catch of you' (*Henry IV, Part 2*, 2. 4. 45–6).

But in this history play Shakespeare defies any preconceived notion that prostitutes and 'bawds' (brothel managers) are immoral women who derive satisfaction from exploiting men's need for sex. Certainly Doll Tearsheet and Mistress Quickly flout the demand that respectable females adhere to the standards outlined by the Puritan William Gouge – 'sobrietie, mildnesse' and of course chaste 'modestie'.[58] Instead the playwright presents them sympathetically as part of the vulnerable underclass. True, they support themselves through a trade that makes use of women, but in catering to men's desire for illicit sex, these 'sisters of the hold-[door trade]', as the pimp Pandarus calls them in *Troilus and Cressida* (5. 10. 51), are scraping together a living rather than gratifying their own sexual needs. Whereas Pandarus takes a sleazy interest in Troilus's sexual initiation of his niece, urging the couple to 'press' their bed 'to death' with 'pretty encounters' (3. 2. 208–9), Doll and Mistress Quickly in the *Henry IV* plays appear to take little vicarious pleasure in the sexual activity they facilitate. Rather, they are practical realists, bent on survival and less obsessed with sex than are many women slightly above them in social rank, such as Juliet's prurient Nurse. For although she is not a professional 'bawd', the Nurse is immediately branded as such by Mercutio (*Romeo and Juliet*, 2. 4. 130).

Closing *Troilus and Cressida* with his cynical epilogue, Pandarus acknowledges that his syphilitic 'aching bones' will soon kill him. In *Henry V* we gather that Doll has also succumbed to venereal disease, dead of a 'malady of France' (5. 1. 81–2).[59] Nevertheless *Henry IV, Part 2* presents both Doll and Nell Quickly as much more likeable than the jaded and conniving Pandarus. Feisty in refusing to be bested by an obnoxious male – she derides the braggart Pistol as a 'bottle-ale rascal' and 'an abominable damn'd cheater' (2. 4. 131, 140) – Doll remains loyal to the ageing Falstaff, whom she prefers over her younger clients, 'scurvy' boys all (272–3). Affectionately she calls him a 'sweet little rogue', and at the end of the tavern scene she runs to join him in the back chamber, even though she must know, as young Poins comments, that 'desire' has long outlived 'performance' in the old libertine (260–1). And despite Falstaff's hollow promise to buy her a new skirt and cap when he acquires some money (274–5), Doll is unlikely ever to be paid for her services. The Hostess is equally kind to Falstaff, despite his having broken his promise to do the respectable thing and marry her (2. 1. 91–3) and his failure to pay back the money (at least 100 marks) that he owes her. Movingly describing his death in *Henry V*, she loyally defends Falstaff from the charge of being a lecher, admitting that he begged for alcohol but denying that he 'cried out' for 'women' (2. 3. 29–30).

Without patronising them, Shakespeare portrays both females as spirited and generous, lacking in malice or guile. The drama is also realistic about how the underground profession of prostitution – providing sexual services that upper-class men readily pay for – ironically makes these women particularly vulnerable to prosecution by male authorities. Both are treated as criminals at the end of *Henry IV, Part 2*, sent off to be whipped because, as the Beadle tells Quickly, 'the man is dead that you and Pistol beat amongst you' (5. 4. 16–17). Why are the officers not arresting Pistol? Instead it's the females who become scapegoats when they, and not the men, are accused of turning their milieu, the tavern/brothel, into a place of murderous riot.[60] Branded as disorderly, they are automatically banished from the new male order established in the scene that immediately follows – Hal's coronation as Henry V.

Like the Hostess in the Henriad, Mistress Overdone in *Measure for Measure* is an enterprising woman from the underclass who is trying to maintain some appearance of respectability. Married no fewer than nine times, this bawd[61] is now running what the constable calls a 'very ill house' (2. 1. 67) where her male customers blame her for spreading venereal disease – the 'hollow' bones and the 'sciatica' from which she herself suffers (1. 2. 56, 59). Understandably, because she depends on servicing men's sexual needs for her income and is already 'custom-shrunk' (84), she fears losing her living entirely when she hears that all brothels in the city suburbs must be demolished. 'What shall become of me?' she wonders (105). While hard-headed about keeping her profession, Mistress Overdone is tender-hearted. She is concerned that worthy Claudio has been sentenced to death simply for getting his fiancée pregnant, and later we learn that she has 'kept' and is raising the illegitimate child that the libertine Lucio fathered with the prostitute Kate Keepdown (3. 2. 202). As with the women from the Eastcheap brothel, again it is the female Overdone, and not her male associates, who suffers punishment for her trade. The Duke censors the tapster Pompey for being a 'wicked bawd', a pimp making his living off 'filthy vice' (19–23); nevertheless Pompey avoids a prison sentence by changing his trade ('mystery') to that of hangman's assistant (4. 2. 39). His assurance to Mistress Overdone that the authorities will take 'pity' on her if she practises her trade elsewhere is too carelessly given (1. 2. 108–9). In fact the magistrate Escalus orders her arrest after Lucio callously informs on her (3. 2. 190, 198).

The one exception to Shakespeare's sympathetic presentation of prostitutes and madams comes in *Pericles*.[62] In this play that deals in stark contrasts, the female Bawd, who is not individualised with a name, appears particularly callous. Like Mistress Overdone, she claims to have brought up bastard children, 'some eleven' of them, but her associate Boult points out that after the girls reach the age of eleven she has 'brought them down again', presumably turning them into prostitutes (4. 2. 14–16). Showing no sympathy after Marina is forced into the brothel, the Bawd crudely plots to turn the young woman's virginity into a valuable commodity: ' "He that will give most shall have her first" ' (4. 2. 59–60). When Marina resists, the Bawd conspires with the pandar Boult to try to 'Crack the glass of her virginity' (4. 6. 142). Like Lavinia in *Titus Andronicus*, shocked that Tamora defies compassionate 'womanhood' by refusing to save her from rape, Marina incredulously asks the Bawd, 'Are you a woman?' (4. 2. 82). This hardened female's determination to corrupt chaste Marina, knowing that her pox-ridden brothel is a place where 'Diseases have been sold dearer than physic' (4. 6. 98), does constitute a form of wickedness. In this tragicomic romance, however, any catastrophic outcome must be averted. And despite her sordid vicarious enjoyment of how Marina will 'taste gentlemen of all fashions' (4. 2. 78–9), the Bawd never considers murder. Instead it is the jealous husbands, Othello, Posthumus and Leontes, who do so, determined to destroy their wives for what they fantasise to be marital betrayal.

The wives who are maligned for lust, while refusing passively to accept being wrongly accused,[63] nevertheless remain remarkably loyal to their husbands even before these men, recognising their errors, become contrite. Othello's epiphany comes only after he has murdered Desdemona. Perceiving that his wife's 'chastity' has always been as 'cold' as her dead body is now, Othello melodramatically relegates himself to hell, begging 'roast me in sulphur!' for his crime (5. 2. 275–6, 279). Leontes practises penance for a 'wide gap' of time, believing that he has, as Paulina insists, 'kill'd' his faithful paragon of a wife (*The Winter's Tale*, 4. 1. 7, 5. 1. 15). Remorseful in prison, Posthumus begs the gods 'For Imogen's dear life take mine' (*Cymbeline*, 5. 4. 22). The two tragicomedies end happily, with husband and wife reconciling. And since Hermione takes on the role of caring mother to Perdita as well as loving wife to Leontes[64] at the end of *The Winter's Tale* (5. 3. 123), there's hope that Leontes's fractured trust in women will be restored. Nothing, though, can completely erase the harshness of the husbands' unwarranted rejection of their partners, a chilling reminder of how readily men in Shakespeare's plays both fear and demonise female sexuality.

Notes

1. This is part of 'object relations' theory. Anthony Elliott, 'The Making of the Self', in *Psychoanalytic Theory: An Introduction*, discusses how conflicts in the pre-Oedipal stage lead to a 'splitting' of 'the pre-Oedipal mother into good and bad objects' (p. 30).
2. Janet Adelman, *Suffocating Mothers: Fantasies of Maternal Origin in Shakespeare's Plays, Hamlet to The Tempest*, observes that for the male infant, 'the mother's separateness constitutes the first betrayal; insofar as she is not his, she is promiscuously Other' (p. 264, n. 23).
3. Coppélia Kahn, *Man's Estate: Masculine Identity in Shakespeare*, explores the young male's need to assert his 'sense of masculinity' through separation from his mother (p. 10). The premise in Adelman's *Suffocating Mothers* is that adult males must try to escape the 'suffocating maternal matrix' with its fantasies of 'maternal malevolence' ('Introduction', p. 3).
4. Stephen Greenblatt, *Renaissance Self-Fashioning: From More to Shakespeare*, contends that the socially constructed (masculine) self in the Renaissance is 'achieved in relation to something perceived as alien, strange, or hostile', which may be female – a 'witch' or an 'adulteress' (p. 9). The work of psychologist Jacques Lacan, positioning females as 'Other', has proved particularly influential in feminist criticism. Supplementing Freud's theories, Lacan postulates that masculinity is constructed around the sign of the phallus (representing the father), from which women, as Other, are automatically excluded.
5. Madelon Gohlke (Sprengnether), '"I wooed thee with my sword": Shakespeare's Tragic Paradigms', analyses how in these plays 'structures of male dominance . . . conceal deeper structures of fear, in which women are perceived as powerful' (p. 153).
6. Peter Stallybrass, 'Patriarchal Territories: The Body Enclosed', p. 127.
7. Barnabe Rich, *The Excellencie of Good Women*, p. 24.
8. Stallybrass, 'Patriarchal Territories' (pp. 123–4), emphasising the socially subversive nature of the female grotesque, draws on the definition of the grotesque body given by M. Bakhtin, *Rabelais and His World*. Gail Kern Paster, *The Body Embarrassed: Drama and the Disciplines of Shame in Early Modern England*, analyses how medical treatises of the time 'construct the female body as effluent, overproductive, out of control' (p. 21).
9. Ian Maclean, 'Theology, Mystical and Occult Writings', in *The Renaissance Notion of Woman*, covers some of the theological debates in which woman was considered to be less than human (pp. 12–13), or even 'a monstrous creation' (p. 30).
10. Thus Angelo, desiring the chaste Isabella, wonders if this female deserves blame for stirring his lust; he ponders 'Is this her fault or mine? / The tempter, or the tempted, who sins most, ha?' (*Measure for Measure*, 2. 2. 62–3).
11. Jacques Ferrand, *Erotomania*, p. 214.
12. Maclean, 'Medicine, Anatomy, Physiology', in *The Renaissance Notion of Woman*, p. 30. Galen's model also implied that women, with their inverted male genitalia, were inferior or unfinished versions of men. See

Thomas Laqueur, *Making Sex: Body and Gender from the Greeks to Freud*, pp. 63–148.
13. Phyllis Rackin, 'Dated and Outdated: The Present Tense of Feminist Criticism', p. 58.
14. See Suzanne W. Hull, *Chaste, Silent and Obedient: English Books for Women, 1475–1640*. Hull, pp. 141–2, cites as typical the prescription of Pierre de La Primaudaye, in *The French Academie* (1586), that 'Wives must be modest, wise, chaste, keepers at home, lovers of their husbands, and subject unto them'.
15. Juliet Dusinberre, 'Femininity and Masculinity', in *Shakespeare and the Nature of Women*, outlines Thomas More's efforts to make sure that women could be educated beyond the arts of music, dancing and needlework, in order 'to challenge the male idea of femininity' (p. 225).
16. Hilda L. Smith, *Reason's Disciples*, p. 40. Smith points out that during this period 'educational and public service opportunities ... remained closed to women' (pp. 40–1). When women offered a counter-defence during this period, it was usually in reaction to misogynistic tracts; Esther Sowernam's 'Esther hath hang'd Haman' (1617), for example, is written in response to Joseph Swetman's irate 'Arraignment of Lewd, Idle, and Inconstant Women' (1615). Natalie Davis, 'Sexual Inversion and Political Disorder in Early Modern Europe', concedes that images of the 'disorderly woman' in festive inversions could work as a form of 'resistance' to women's subjection but mainly as temporary subversion (pp. 183, 154).
17. Valerie Traub, 'Jewels, Statues and Corpses: Containment of Female Erotic Desire (*Hamlet, Othello, The Winter's Tale*)', in *Desire and Anxiety: Circulations of Sexuality in Shakespearean Drama*, contextualises 'Shakespeare's preoccupation with the uncontrollability of women's sexuality' as a 'shared vulnerability of men in his intensely patriarchal and patrilineal society' (p. 27).
18. See Mary Beth Rose, *The Expense of Spirit: Love and Sexuality in English Renaissance Drama*, on how Puritans in the early modern period argued that 'companionship between man and woman' was 'fundamental to marriage' (p. 126).
19. Montaigne, 'Upon Some Verses of *Virgil*', in *Essays*, vol. 3, ch. 5, pp. 79, 81.
20. Edmund Tilney, *The Flower of Friendship* (1571), p. 112.
21. This connects with Freud's premise, in 'The Most Prevalent Form of Degradation in Erotic Life', that an 'incestuous fixation of childhood' can cause men to divide females into two categories: the 'lower type of sexual object' with whom they can have satisfying sexual relations, and the woman who should remain, on the model of the mother, idealised and pure (pp. 64–5).
22. Marjorie Garber, *Coming of Age in Shakespeare*, comments on Juliet's 'remarkable forthrightness and self-knowledgeability in sexual desire' (p. 165).
23. Arthur Kirsch, *Shakespeare and the Experience of Love*, p. 14.
24. Laura Gowing, 'Consent and Desire', in *Common Bodies: Women, Touch and Power in Seventeenth-Century England*, pp. 101–2.
25. Michael Keevak, *Sexual Shakespeare*, notes how *Venus and Adonis* is

unusual in presenting a '"masculine" female wooer and a "feminized" male object of desire' (p. 60).

26. Catherine Belsey, 'Love as Trompe-l'oeil: Taxonomies of Desire in *Venus and Adonis*', 266, 275.
27. David Schalkwyk points this out in *Shakespeare: Love and Language*, p. 2.
28. Kahn, *Man's Estate: Masculine Identity in Shakespeare*, comments on how Venus changes from a would-be seducer and a 'devouring mother' with 'oral demands' to a 'nurturant mother' who can cosset Adonis as a flower at the end (p. 45).
29. As reported in October 2016, the New Oxford Shakespeare will now list Christopher Marlowe as co-author, with Shakespeare, of the three parts of *Henry VI*. I have continued to refer to 'the playwright' (Shakespeare) in discussing the plays, while acknowledging scenes 3 and 4 of Act 5 in *Part 1* as the work of Marlowe.
30. Jean E. Howard and Phyllis Rackin, '*Henry VI, Part 1*', in *Engendering a Nation: A Feminist Account of Shakespeare's English Histories*, deduce that Shakespeare's audience would regard Joan's transvestite appearance, taking on masculine dress, as flouting male authority (p. 51). Leslie A. Fiedler, 'The Woman as Stranger; or, "None but women left. . . ."', in *The Stranger in Shakespeare*, also notes how Joan's 'battlefield transvestism' is presented as a 'final horror' (p. 66), part of how Shakespeare succeeds in 'disfiguring, lasciviously defiling, riddling and shredding the Maid' of Orleans (p. 51).
31. Keith Thomas, *Religion and the Decline of Magic*, contends that 'the mythology of witchcraft was at its height when women were generally believed to be more sexually voracious than men' (p. 679).
32. Kahn, '"The Shadow of the Male": Masculine Identity in the History Plays', in *Man's Estate*, p. 55. Howard and Rackin, in '*Henry VI, Part 1*', comment on how Joan manifests the 'illicit supernatural power of a disorderly woman' (p. 45).
33. In 'Marlowe finally credited among cast of Bard's co-writers', *The Guardian*, 24 October 2016, Gary Taylor (one of the Oxford Shakespeare editors) confirms that specialists agree that 'Shakespeare did not write the passage where Joan of Arc pleads for help from demonic spirits and then is captured by the English' (p. 9). Marlowe's *Doctor Faustus* (1592), first performed at the same time as *Henry VI, Part 1*, depicts necromancy in a similar way.
34. Edward Hall, *The Union of the Two Noble and Illustre Families of Lancaster and York* (1548), p. 169.
35. Simon Shepherd, *Amazons and Warrior Women: Varieties of Feminism in Seventeenth-Century Drama*, points out that there is a 'long history' of connecting Amazons with lust (p. 16). Whereas in the eyes of the French Joan is an admirable Amazonian warrior, and Hippolita in *A Midsummer Night's Dream* is respected as Queen of the Amazons, the term is pejorative when applied to Queen Margaret by the opposition.
36. David Willbern, 'Rape and Revenge in *Titus Andronicus*', 166.
37. Kathleen McLuskie, 'The Patriarchal Bard: Feminist Criticism and Shakespeare: *King Lear* and *Measure for Measure*', argues that Goneril and Regan are misogynistically presented as 'evil' because they are disrupters of patriarchy (p. 102).
38. Paul Kahn, *Law and Love: The Trials of King Lear*, makes a similar point

in discussing the 'politicized body' versus the 'eroticized body' in the play (p. 147).
39. Paula S. Berggren, 'The Woman's Part: Female Sexuality as Power in Shakespeare's Plays', discusses how 'When female lechery is not actually sterile' in Shakespeare's plays, 'its progeny [such as Tamora's children] is malignant' (p. 24).
40. Phyllis Rackin, *Shakespeare and Women*, p. 25. Rackin goes further in contending that Shakespeare's 'representations' of male jealousy do not express a 'normative view' (p. 25).
41. Kahn, '"The Savage Yoke": Cuckoldry and Marriage', in *Man's Estate*, p. 119. Kahn explores in detail the implications of male anxiety over cuckoldry.
42. Janet Adelman, '*Hamlet* and the Confrontation with the Maternal Body', in *Suffocating Mothers*, p. 30.
43. As when the jealous husband Ford in *The Merry Wives of Windsor* refers to the old woman of Brainford as 'A witch . . . an old cozening quean' (4. 2. 172).
44. Gordon Williams, *A Glossary of Shakespeare's Sexual Language*, cites the bawdy meaning of 'eye' as vagina.
45. Gayle Greene, 'Shakespeare's Cressida: "A Kind of Self"', p. 146. Greene finds that Cressida, objectified by men, lacks any true agency or autonomous self.
46. Carol Cook, '"The Sign and Semblance of Her Honor": Reading Gender Difference in *Much Ado about Nothing*', notes the 'sexual dualism' in Claudio's attitude toward Hero (197).
47. Keith Thomas, 'The Double Standard', 203–4.
48. Catherine Belsey, *Shakespeare and the Loss of Eden*, points out that marriage in Paradise, originally envisaged as innocent, also led to the 'loss of innocence', just as Eve was considered both a 'blessing and a curse' (pp. 75, 77).
49. Even Isabella in *Measure for Measure*, angry that her brother Claudio finds his life more valuable than her virginity, casts doubts on Claudio's legitimate descent from their father: 'Heaven shield my mother play'd my father fair!' (3. 1. 140).
50. Mark Breitenberg, *Anxious Masculinity in Early Modern England*, p. 17. Howard and Rackin, '*Henry VI, Part 1*', in *Engendering a Nation*, make the point that the 'transmission of patrilineal authority', which 'could take place only through the bodies of women', could be subverted by 'female sexual transgression' (p. 26). Marion Wynne-Davis, '"The Swallowing Womb": Consumed and Consuming Women in *Titus Andronicus*', also emphasises that 'control of the womb was paramount in determining a direct patrilineal descent' (p. 136).
51. Murray M. Schwartz, 'Leontes' Jealousy in *The Winter's Tale*', discusses the roots of Leontes's jealousy stemming from his sense of maternal 'malevolence' (273).
52. Adelman, 'The Absent Mother in *King Lear*', in *Suffocating Mothers*, argues that 'Lear re-enacts a childlike rage against the absent or rejecting mother as figured in his daughters' (p. 100).
53. Admittedly the 'dark and vicious place' might refer to Gloucester's geni-

tals when he 'got' (conceived) his son Edmund. But William C. Carroll, 'Language and Sexuality in Shakespeare', notes how in Shakespeare's plays female sex organs are routinely associated with images of 'absence, emptiness' and 'darkness' (p. 18).
54. This is how Kenneth Muir glosses the line in the Arden edition of *King Lear*.
55. It is now accepted, as laid out in detail by Brian Vickers, *Shakespeare, Co-Author: A Historical Study of Five Collaborative Plays*, pp. 244–90, that *Timon of Athens* is a collaboration between Shakespeare and Thomas Middleton. Vickers presents prosodic and stylistic evidence that Middleton is responsible for Act 3 of the play as well as Act 1, scene 2 (the first banquet scene) and the final part of Act 4, scene 3. As my comments on Timon's developing misanthropy apply to the whole play, I have not separated out the sections composed by Middleton from those written by Shakespeare.
56. Because he is single and apparently childless, actors have sometimes played Timon as gay (he is, after all, an Athenian who could be practising the model of same-gender love endorsed by ancient Greek culture). Timon addresses men as 'friends' or 'friend' twelve times in the feasting scene (Act 1, scene 2), though not necessarily emphasising its secondary meaning of 'lover'.
57. Traub, 'Invading Bodies/Bawdy Exchanges: Disease, Desire and Representation', in *Desire and Anxiety*, argues that 'women were uniquely figured as carriers of the disease, perhaps because of their perceived immunity' in that their symptoms were often less obvious (p. 76).
58. This is how William Gouge characterises appropriate wifely behaviour in *Of Domesticall Duties*, p. 279.
59. Some editors conjecture a confusion here of 'my Doll' with Nell (Quickly), who is, perhaps surprisingly, married to Pistol by the opening of *Henry V*. Possibly both women have died of venereal disease, whereas opportunistic Pistol lives on, resolving 'bawd I'll turn' (5. 1. 85).
60. Barbara Hodgson, *The End Crowns All: Closure and Contradiction in Shakespeare's History*, comments on how eventually Doll and Mistress Quickly are 'demonized as corrupt' when the threat of a disorderly Carnival spirit is 'displaced' on to them (p. 172). Howard and Rackin, 'The *Henry IV* Plays', in *Engendering a Nation*, deduce that for Shakespeare's audience 'Doll, the sexually independent woman, and Quickly, the economically independent woman, form a threatening combination' (p. 179).
61. There's convincing evidence that Thomas Middleton revised the play before its inclusion in the 1623 Folio, and that he supplied the name 'Mistress Overdone' for the woman who originally appears as Bawd in Act 1, scene 2 (see *Thomas Middleton: The Collected Works*, p. 1543). Middleton's additions at the opening of this scene do not substantially change Shakespeare's characterisation of this female, however.
62. As noted by Stanley Wells, *Shakespeare, Sex, and Love*, Shakespeare's collaborator in *Pericles*, George Wilkins, kept an inn on Turnbull Street that doubled as a brothel (p. 74). Although the brothel scenes presented in Act 4 are presumed to be Shakespeare's work alone, one wonders if Wilkins had a hand in the creation of the scabrous Bawd.
63. Jane Adamson, *Othello as Tragedy: Some Problems of Judgment and*

Feeling, complains of Desdemona's 'apathetic submission' towards the end of the play (p. 220). But Desdemona flashes out with 'By Heaven, you do me wrong!' when Othello demonises her as lustful (*Othello*, 4. 2. 81) and fights to save her life even as she refuses to blame her husband for her death (5. 2. 80). Likewise Hermione magnanimously waives any wish for 'revenge' on Leontes (*The Winter's Tale*, 3. 2. 123) but passionately defends her 'honor' in her trial (108). Imogen staunchly defends Posthumus as 'A very valiant Briton and a good' (*Cymbeline*, 4. 2. 369) but understandably reacts with anger – 'False to his bed?' – when she first hears that her husband is accusing her of infidelity (3. 4. 40).

64. Peter Erickson, 'Reformed Masculinity', in *Patriarchal Structures in Shakespeare's Drama*, stresses Hermione's 'maternal standing' in the final scene and how 'Leontes's capacity to reevaluate Hermione's nurturant presence leads to the reformation of his male identity' (p. 169).

Chapter 4

Romantic Love and Sexual Desire: The Fickleness of Fancy, Eyes and Love's Mind

It is in the late romances, *Cymbeline* and *The Winter's Tale*, that husbands most distrust the sexual 'will' of wives and their capacity for betrayal. Shakespeare's early romantic comedies offer a contrast; they focus instead on aristocratic courtship leading to marriage. And while these plays do not ignore the reality of erotic desire underlying the mating game, they usually minimise the darker side of libido in favour of courtly wooing. Questing for life partners, the male characters regard females as desirable love objects, not to be reviled but to be wooed in extravagantly romantic fashion.

Yet the early comedies *A Midsummer Night's Dream* and *Love's Labour's Lost* are ambivalent in celebrating the dance toward partnership; Shakespeare offers a counterbalancing critique of romantic love. These plays explore how easily idealised romantic love may turn out to be shallow infatuation – sexual desire or 'will' prompted by visual attraction. Eyes have always played a key role in the notion of falling in love at first sight,[1] a convention rooted in Neo-Platonism that Shakespeare follows in plays such as *Romeo and Juliet, As You Like It* and *Twelfth Night*. In his *Commentary on Plato's Symposium* (1484), the Neo-Platonist Ficino[2] writes that love, which stems from the divine, 'takes its origin from sight'. In the Greek ideal of love between two males, love 'shines out' from the body of the younger man, 'especially through the eyes, the purest windows of the soul'. This 'ray of light',[3] carried to the eye from the heart by a 'spiritual vapor',[4] 'flies through the air' and, 'penetrating the eyes of an older man, pierces his soul' and 'kindles his appetite'.[5]

Shakespeare's romantic drama applies this idea – the heart smitten through the eyes – to love generated between males and females. Such falling in love is reciprocal and instantaneous in *The Tempest*, where Prospero rejoices that Miranda and Ferdinand 'At the first sight / . . . have chang'd eyes' (1. 2. 441–2). But usually within the Petrarchan convention, as shown in *Love's Labour's Lost*, the woman is not equally smitten. Traditionally it is the female's beauty, centred in her dazzling eyes, that sparks desire in the male who looks at and into those eyes, while the mistress's heart too often remains unaffected. The comedies go further in questioning how trustworthy eyes are as a guide to love, how prone to shift their preference. Explored in Shakespeare's sonnets too, the male's visual assessment of his beloved tends to remain incurably subjective, just as it often fails to penetrate more deeply beneath appearances to perceive the loved one's true worth.

In Neo-Platonic philosophy, an aesthetic response to the female's lovely form can ignite a spiritual form of love – a perception of moral beauty (virtue) and even a pathway to the divine. But the reality is different in Shakespeare's romantic comedies, in which love based on ocular appeal alone is usually a matter of sexual attraction. As such it remains a fickle and shifting 'fancy' rather than the uplifting discovery of a true soul-mate, or the kind of epiphany celebrated in Romeo's almost instantaneous intuition, 'It is my soul that calls upon my name', when he hears Juliet's voice on the balcony (*Romeo and Juliet*, 2. 2. 164). Romeo has already fallen in love at first sight with what he discerns as Juliet's 'true beauty' (1. 5. 53).

Love at first sight, based on the mistress's physical 'beauty', doesn't always prove this 'true' in Shakespeare's early comedies. A key to understanding how unreliable the eyes are in forming a grounded attachment that goes beyond transient 'fancy' comes in the casket scene in *The Merchant of Venice*:

> Tell me where is fancy bred,
> In the heart or in the head?
> How begot, how nourished?
> . . .
> It is engend'red in the eyes,
> With gazing fed, and fancy dies
> In the cradle where it lies. (3. 2. 63–9)

In this song 'fancy' is characterised as a relatively fleeting attraction, driven by sexual will. It is a whim of the 'heart', the seat of the affections, rather than based on judgement (the 'head'). Because it is fuelled by the eye – the lover feeds his infatuation by 'gazing' on physical beauty – such mesmerising attraction appears doomed to early extinction, dying in the 'cradle' of the eyes soon after birth. In its dramatic context, such superficial 'fancy' contrasts with the deeper passion that, as the unassuming lead casket makes clear, requires the lover, in this case Bassanio, to 'give and hazard all he hath' (2. 7. 16). It is by rejecting mere fancy, risking everything for his love, that Bassanio wins the right to marry Portia.

Like 'will', 'fancy' is a polysemous signifier in Shakespeare's lexicon. Sometimes it substitutes for the word 'love', as in *The Winter's Tale*, where Prince Florizel vows to be guided by his 'fancy', not as a passing whim but as deep love for Perdita (4. 4. 482). More often the word connotes what the casket ditty, warning of superficial appearances, declares that it is – a shallow, ephemeral affection, 'engendered' in the gazing eye. *Twelfth Night* contains many such instances, as when Orsino, who troublingly refers to Viola in the finale as his new mistress and 'fancy's queen', earlier admits that men's 'fancies are more giddy and unfirm' than those of women (5. 1. 388, 2. 4. 33). Hermia in *A Midsummer Night's Dream* notes how followers of 'poor' fancy are giddy too; she labels them 'thoughts and dreams and sighs' (1. 1. 154–5).

The reference to 'dreams' is significant, for 'fancy' here is closely allied to the word 'fantasy'. Alison Thorne has discussed how fantasy ('fantasie') in early modern discourse often refers to creative, transformative imagination,[6] as in Theseus's speech on how the 'shaping fantasies' of madmen, lovers and poets distort reality (*A Midsummer Night's Dream*, 5. 1. 5). Likewise 'fancy' may sometimes be used positively to denote creative imagination. When Cleopatra, expounding on her 'dream' of 'Emperor Antony', declares that 'nature wants stuff / To vie strange forms with fancy', she is privileging the products of the imagination ('fancy') above the material ('stuff') of the real world. Although she concludes that Antony was a wonderful creation in himself – 'nature's piece 'gainst fancy / Condemning shadows quite' – she first magnifies his uniqueness through her idealising imagination, envisaging how 'His face was as the heav'ns' while 'his rear'd arm / Crested the world' (*Antony and Cleopatra*, 5. 2. 76–100).

More often 'fancy' retains its connotations of giddiness and instability. In *The Winter's Tale*, practical Paulina derides as 'weak-hing'd fancy' Leontes's lurid and unfounded speculation that Hermione is adulterous (2. 3. 119). Meanwhile love-sick Orsino verges on tautology when he claims that 'fancy' is so 'full of shapes' that 'it alone is high fantastical' (*Twelfth Night*, 1. 1. 14–15). In keeping with the association of fancy/fantasy with idle dreaming, Mercutio in *Romeo and Juliet* ends his Queen Mab extravaganza by dismissing such 'vain fantasy' (often glossed as 'fancy') as the ephemeral stuff of dreams. It is 'thin of substance' and 'more inconstant than the wind' (1. 4. 98–100). Egeus, the angry father in *A Midsummer Night's Dream*, complains that the romantic suitor Lysander has 'stol'n the impression' of Hermia's 'fantasy', pushing her into loving (or fancying) him by giving her all kinds of trivial knick-knacks – 'bracelets', 'gawds' and 'nosegays' – that are simply pleasing to her eye (*A Midsummer Night's Dream*, 1. 1. 32–4).

Shakespeare's early comedy *Two Gentlemen of Verona* (c. 1593) is all about the inconstancy of fancy and how it is based on ocular appeal. Described as a 'votary to fond desire' (1. 1. 52), young Proteus is indeed a chameleon, shifting his sexual fancy from Julia to Silvia as soon as his 'former love / Is by a newer object quite forgotten' (2. 4. 194–5). It is the painted portrait of Silvia, a mere shadow of her beauty, that feeds his eye and, as he confesses, 'hath dazzled [his] reason's light' (210). In other words, a purely visual representation confuses his better judgement. He breaks his engagement to Julia because he is swayed by the sight of new loveliness, susceptible to what Claudio, the impulsive young lover in *Much Ado about Nothing*, observes: that 'beauty is a witch / Against whose charms faith melteth into blood' (2. 1. 179–80). Only at the play's conclusion does Proteus, aiming to be a faithful romantic lover, resolve to rein in his all too fickle eyesight. He reasons that if he observes beauty objectively, 'What is in Silvia's face, but I may spy / More fresh in Julia's with a constant eye?' (5. 4. 114–15).

Hermia, pushed by her father to accept Demetrius over Lysander, comments that it is 'hell' to 'choose love by another's eye' (1. 1. 140). But the aristocratic male in Shakespeare's comedies usually has the power to make his own choice; he singles out for his loved one a woman whom he finds beautiful and desirable. Claudio in *Much Ado about Nothing*, who judges his bride-to-be by appearances only – he's easily deceived by a visual trick into thinking that Hero is unfaithful to him – insists that in romantic courtship 'Let every eye negotiate for itself' (2. 1. 178). Likewise Bertram in *All's Well that Ends Well* protests that he should be allowed to use the 'help of [his] own eyes' in choosing a wife (2. 3. 108) before he reluctantly 'submit[s]' his 'fancy' to the 'eyes' of the French king by entering into marriage with Helena (167–8). Benvolio in *Romeo and Juliet* urges Romeo to get over his infatuation for Rosaline by using the 'liberty' of his 'eyes' to 'examine other beauties' (1. 1. 227–8). Since Romeo has pledged the 'devout religion' of his 'eye' to Rosaline (1. 2. 88), sceptics might question whether his sudden switch to Juliet signals romantic love at its finest or simply lust at first sight. Indeed the Friar, shocked at the fickleness of Romeo's desires, worries that 'Young men's love then lies / Not truly in their hearts, but in their eyes' (2. 3. 67–8). It is nevertheless the deepening of the poetry, the freshness of Romeo's images when he responds visually to Juliet – 'O, she doth teach the torches to burn bright!' (1. 5. 44) leading into the powerful metaphor 'It is the East, and Juliet is the sun' (2. 2. 2) – that convinces the audience he is experiencing more than simply sexual attraction. His response of wonder, expressed so authentically, bodes well for constant 'loving' rather than what the sceptical Friar calls 'doting' (2. 3. 82). Significantly, *Romeo and Juliet*, which celebrates romantic passion even as it turns tragic, never uses the term 'fancy'.

The question remains: how reliable is the visual perception of the would-be romantic lover who is mesmerised by the object of his desire? Shakespeare's sonnets, mainly composed in the 1590s, when Shakespeare was also exploring the nature of love and lust in dramatic terms, offer some illumination here. Sonnet 46 describes a 'war' between the poet's 'eye' and his 'heart' over which of these two can truly possess the 'fair' youth. There is no question about the desirability of the loved one; this is the young man whose lovely appearance 'steals men's eyes and woman's souls amazeth' (Sonnet 20, 8). In its concluding couplet Sonnet 46 reconciles the rival demands of eye and heart by declaring that the poet's eye is entitled to enjoy the 'outward part' of his beloved while the poet's heart can claim the youth's own 'inward love of heart':

> As thus – mine eye's due is thy outward part,
> And my heart's right thy inward love of heart. (13–14)

Eyes can be pernicious, however. Lovers may not be quite as fickle as Cupid, the god of love who is often represented as 'blind', but their vision is distorted. Sonnet 114 describes the 'alchemy' of the poet's eye and how, under the influence of his beloved, this eye can falsely change 'monsters' into 'cherubins' that resemble youth's 'sweet' self. The biased eye transforms what is objectively corrupt into something speciously good, 'Creating every bad a perfect best / As fast as objects to his beams assemble' (5–8). The poet knows that this delusion, guided (in Helen Vendler's words) by 'slavish visual worship',[7] is a form of moral turpitude, and yet his 'eye loves it' and drinks up the 'flatt'ry' of this aberrant 'seeing' (14, 9).

It is toward the end of the sonnet sequence, where the speaker is addressing the dark mistress,[8] that he most laments the gap between erotic desire, fed by visual stimuli, and a more reasoned evaluation of the loved one.[9] While the similes of Sonnet 147 – 'black as hell, as dark as night' (14) – are explicit about the mistress's moral degradation, the poet expresses deep chagrin at being so drawn toward this promiscuous woman that he cannot view or judge her appearance or character objectively. In Sonnet 137 he laments how, overpowered by 'blind fool' love, 'the judgment of [his] heart is tied' to 'eyes' falsehood' (1, 7–8). The same tension between correct evaluation and the eye of the besotted lover emerges in Sonnet 148:

> O me, what eyes hath love put in my head
> Which have no correspondence with true sight (1–2)

More troublingly, the poet acknowledges that the source of his desire (his 'heart'), at odds with what he actually sees, has subdued his rational faculties, even though he feels compelled to go on loving or lusting in spite of that. This is also the theme of Sonnet 141. The poet's 'eyes' objectively see and 'despise' a 'thousand errors' in the mistress, but his 'heart' nevertheless remains 'pleased to dote' on her (1–4). The poet's harshest self-indictment comes in Sonnet 152. The poem ends with the admission that the speaker's 'eye' (with pun on first person 'I') is 'perjured' because it has confirmed the opposite of what he really sees. His very eyesight has becomes complicit in the 'foul' lie that the mistress is physically 'fair', just as the poet has sworn, falsely, that she is morally true and sexually constant: 'For I have sworn thee fair; more perjur'd eye, / To swear against the truth so foul a lie' (13–14).

A Midsummer Night's Dream is far-reaching in exploring whether attraction is based on any kind of sound judgement, or whether the vision of the lover is inevitably distorted by sexual desire.[10] The opening scene, in which Egeus demands that his daughter marries Demetrius (his suitor of choice), underscores the gap between the eye of the lover and the judgement of the patriarch who wields authority. When Hermia pleads 'I would my father look'd but with my eyes', Duke Theseus responds with his firm 'Rather your eyes must with his judgment look' (1. 1. 56–7). She is expected to fit her 'fancies' to her father's firm resolve or 'will' (118).

Eyes play a key role in the dynamics of desire and romance because what stimulates the male lover is gazing at and registering the compelling attractiveness of the beloved's eyes. These female eyes reputedly have the power to vanquish the lover's heart, binding him to her in devoted adoration. Destructively, they may smite him like 'lightning' (*Love's Labour's Lost*, 4. 2. 115) or 'wound' to the point of seeming to murder him, as the romantic swain Silvius who is love-sick for black-eyed Phoebe in *As You Like It* contends (3. 5. 16). Similarly Venus complains to the cool Adonis, 'Thine eye darts forth the fire that burneth me' (*Venus and Adonis*, 196). Betrayed by Demetrius, Helena ponders on how her former suitor broke his vow to her as soon as he 'looked on Hermia's eyne' (*A Midsummer Night's Dream*, 1. 1. 242). Because she lacks confidence, Helena meekly concedes the superior power of Hermia's 'blessed and attractive eyes' (2. 2. 91) while exaggeratedly downplaying her own:

> What wicked and dissembling glass of mine
> Made me compare with Hermia's sphery eyne! (98–9)

This makes even more comic, though painful to the disbelieving Helena, the turnaround of Demetrius once his eyes have been anointed by the magical juice of the love-in-idleness flower. Seeing Helena anew, he greets her with the hyperbolic 'To what, my love, shall I compare thine eyne? / Crystal is muddy' (3. 2. 138–9). The potent juice precipitates, as it symbolises, the giddiness and unpredictability of sudden visual attraction. Besotted under its influence, as soon as he transfers his affections to 'transparent' Helena (2. 2. 104) Lysander switches from seeing dark, petite Hermia as beautiful to deriding her as 'tawny Tartar' (3. 2. 263) and 'dwarf' (328). Lysander now calls Helena's eyes, not Hermia's, 'Love's richest book' (2. 2. 122).

In fact it is Helena who earlier discounts the importance of sight – or at least the eyes of the lover, when she deems them incapable of assessing beauty objectively or grounding love on balanced judgement. Love, like its personification Cupid, appears to be blind. And the vision of the lover cannot be trusted because, Helena reflects, 'Love looks not with the eyes but with the mind' (1. 1. 234). At first this is puzzling, if we take 'mind' in its traditional sense as denoting intellect or rational faculties – found, for example, when Olivia in *Twelfth Night* is falling in love with Viola disguised as Cesario. Sensing how the youth's attractions 'creep in' at 'her eyes' (1. 5. 298), Olivia fears that his visual appeal has clouded her judgement. Perplexed, she confesses in an aside: 'I do I know not what, and fear to find / Mine eye too great a flatterer for my mind (308–9). Clearly Helena, in contrast to Olivia, is not referring to 'mind' in this way, just as she is not suggesting how a lover, in accordance with Plato's theory of forms, can aspire to an intellectual idea of his beloved that transcends physical sight. The more likely meaning of Helena's 'Love looks not with the eyes but with the mind' emerges when she goes on to explain, two lines later, 'Nor hath love's mind of any judgment taste' (*A Midsummer Night's Dream*, 1. 1. 236). In the comic dance toward romantic fulfilment, love's 'mind' can prove as unreasonable as 'fancy'. Instead of rational discrimination it suggests subjective awareness, often slanted toward desire or strong inclination. The *OED* gives as sense 10 of the noun *mind* 'purpose, intention, desire or wish', close to how *will* in early modern contexts refers to sexual desire as well as to intention.[11] In the context of Helena's speech, love's mind has become virtually synonymous with irrational desire.

Helena points out that in Athens she is judged to be just as beautiful as Hermia. But Demetrius, 'doting on Hermia's eyes' (1. 1. 230), is so infatuated with his new love that he can no longer view beauty objectively. 'He will not know what all but he do know,' complains Helena bitterly (229). All-engulfing 'fancy', taking over the lover's 'mind' as a form of wayward sexual desire, simply lacks perspective. For her part, Helena 'Devoutly dotes, dotes in idolatry' (109) on a man who apparently hates and rejects her, so that she masochistically fawns over Demetrius like an abused 'spaniel' (2. 1. 204–5).[12]

This idea of being solely focused on one's beloved and blind to any other external phenomenon or visual stimulus – whether a delightful landscape or 'deformed'st creature' (10) – is explored less negatively in Shakespeare's Sonnet 113. There the poet declares that 'Since I left you, mine eye is in my mind' (1); not only is he oblivious to the reality of 'bird', 'flow'r' or any actual 'form' around him, but his mind 'shapes' or transforms ugly as well as beautiful forms ('crow' or 'dove', 12) into the 'feature' of his beloved (5–6, 12). Thus he concludes:

> Incapable of more, replete with you,
> My most true mind thus maketh mine [eye] untrue. (13–14)

Fixated on his absent lover, the poet prefers the image of his fair friend, filling his mind's eye, to any objective visual evidence. Since his mind is 'true' or constant in love, it must be superior to his disabled eyes. Or so he believes, and with less self-recrimination than he voices in Sonnet 114, where he admits that his 'mind' relishes the deceiving 'alchemy' of the eye (1, 4).

'Mind' is also used in this sense, as strong inclination that has no 'taste' of 'judgment', in *Troilus and Cressida*. Pledging his vows to Cressida, Troilus, who often couches sensual desire in the language of idealism, seems to be aspiring toward an almost Platonic ideal, an intellectual apprehension of romantic love that isn't merely dependent on an attractive physical appearance but is capable of

> Outliving beauties outward, with a mind
> That doth renew swifter than blood decays! (3. 2. 162–3)

Troilus's appeal to 'mind' at first appears similar to Othello's explanation for wanting Desdemona to accompany him to Cyprus. Prepared to forfeit 'young affects' (youthful passion) in favour of love as the marriage of compatible souls, Othello resolves to be 'free and bounteous' to his wife's 'mind' (*Othello*, 1. 3. 263–5); he reveres her as his 'soul's joy' (2. 1. 184). Moreover Desdemona, who 'saw Othello's visage in his mind' (1. 3. 252), also claims a spiritual and not primarily a physical attraction to her husband. But because Troilus's reference to 'mind' is followed closely by the signifier 'blood' (referring to sexual passion), 'mind' in his speech shades into its meaning of powerful inclination or desire. Such a 'mind' wishes constantly to feed and 'renew' the 'will' of sexual passion rather than balancing it with reason.

Troilus's hope for an endless perpetuation of love is short-lived; unfortunately for him, Cressida turns out to be like Demetrius in having an erring or wandering eye. Once she is forced to leave Troy Cressida quickly trades Troilus for the available Greek lover Diomedes, conceding that for many women (stereotyped as the more fickle gender) 'The error of our eye directs our mind' (5. 2. 110).[13] In other words, fleeting visual attraction fuels a woman's sexual desire for a man. In a play concerned with transience, Cressida powerfully exemplifies what Ulysses points out to the warrior Achilles, that 'the present eye praises the present object' (3. 3. 180). Concluding her speech on the 'error of our eye' by acknowledging that 'Minds sway'd by eyes are full of turpitude' (5. 2. 112), Cressida suggests that if individuals shift quickly from one love object to another based on a pleasing appearance, then their minds – intentions and desires – are likely to become depraved. She goes on to express the dividedness of her feelings in terms of double vision. Her immediate affections, like her eyes, are now drawn to Diomedes, the new suitor who claims that she has already given him her 'heart' (83). Split between past and present desire, she must regretfully abandon the absent Troilus: 'Troilus, farewell! One eye looks on thee, / But with my heart the other eye doth see' (107–8).

Since love's 'mind' is often interchangeable with 'heart', which is directed by passionate emotion rather than by stable judgement, it might have been less puzzling for a modern audience had Shakespeare also chosen the noun 'heart' instead of 'mind' in Helena's couplet on love's mind, which reads in full:

> Love looks not with the eyes but with the mind;
> And therefore is wing'd Cupid painted blind.
>   (*A Midsummer Night's Dream*, 1. 1. 234–5)

Shakespeare forges this connection in Sonnet 137, where he laments that the 'judgment' of his 'heart' (rather than his rational mind) favours 'corrupt' vision (8, 5). While 'mind' pairs nicely with 'blind', Helena's rhyming couplet could have substituted 'heart' for 'mind' without eliminating the idea that love is as blind as the god Cupid. One possible variation to get this idea across would be 'Love looks not with the eyes but with the heart, / And there blind Cupid plays his wanton part'. Alternatively, Helena's line might have replaced mind with 'will' (or sexual desire), a word with which it often overlaps in meaning. Thus

Romeo, urgently wanting to possess Rosaline physically, laments that 'love, whose view is muffled still / Should, without eyes, see pathways to his will' (*Romeo and Juliet*, 1. 1. 171–2). But *A Midsummer Night's Dream* is only partly concerned with lust or sexual 'will'; it also concentrates on the vagaries of romantic love – all that love's 'mind' or the heart desires.

What the action of *A Midsummer Night's Dream* makes clear is that neither the heart (as emotional centre) nor the 'mind' of love is compatible with reason. Attraction is whimsical. Its arbitrary nature is symbolised by the love-in-idleness flower, where a secondary meaning of 'idle' for Shakespeare's audience is 'foolish or baseless' (*OED, sb.* 2). When Puck places the juice of this magical flower on the sleeping eyes of the male lovers, both men 'madly dote' (2. 1. 171) on the first person they see when they awake, who happens to be Helena.[14] Lysander speciously makes the claim to Helena that 'The will of man is by his reason sway'd, / And reason says you are the worthier maid' (2. 2. 115–16). We know that will as sexual desire runs counter to judgement, but Lysander tries to justify rationally why his sudden, inexplicable attraction to Helena has made him desert Hermia, the woman to whom he has romantically sworn eternal 'loyalty' (2. 2. 63). A submerged pun – the phonemic similarity between 'reason' and 'rising' (penile erection) – further suggests how Lysander is confusing sexual attraction with judgement.[15] He compounds his delusion by telling Helena that 'Reason becomes the marshall of my will / And leads me to your eyes' (120–1). Troilus speaks truer when he says that his 'will' (sexual appetite rather than intention) is kindled by his 'eyes' (*Troilus and Cressida*, 2. 2. 63). Infatuated under the spell of the magic juice, Lysander insists that he had no 'judgment' when he swore devotion to Hermia (*A Midsummer Night's Dream*, 3. 2. 134).

'Cupid's flower', love-in-idleness, also causes the fairy queen Titania to fall for Bottom transformed into an ass – a union through which Shakespeare showcases the grotesque side of erotic desire. Titania's eye is taken with an ass, literally 'enthralled to [his] shape' (3. 1. 139). Oberon's trick is sadistic in that he hopes the juice will make Titania 'full of hateful fantasies' (2. 1. 258) – fantasy here denotes fancy, or strong attraction – if she wakes up when 'some vile thing is near' (2. 2. 34). His motive is to lure her changeling boy away from her, and it is a mark of her powerful desire for Bottom that she gives up this boy quite easily, despite earlier vowing that she would not do so for her whole 'fairy kingdom' (2. 1. 144). As Bottom sagely puts it, wondering why this beautiful fairy is instantly attracted to him, 'reason and love keep little company together now-a-days' (3. 1. 143–4). Irrational love is indeed akin to madness. It is a theme echoed in many of the comedies – that 'to be wise and love / Exceeds man's might' (*Troilus and Cressida*, 3. 2. 158). But *A Midsummer Night's Dream* enacts, more graphically, the illogicality of passion, when Titania commands her gossamer attendants to serve gross Bottom and even claims, in a parody of Neo-Platonic doctrine, that the ass's 'fair virtue's force' is what has moved her instantly to swear 'I love thee' (3. 1. 140–1). The audience is left to imagine any sexual union between these stark opposites, ethereal Titania and bestial Bottom; Jan Kott reminds us that for Shakespeare's contemporaries the ass was 'credited with the strongest sexual potency' and the largest phallus.[16] We witness how sensually and visually enchanted Titania's eye is with her new lover's ass-like qualities as she strokes his 'amiable cheeks', admiring his 'sleek smooth head' and 'fair large ears' (4. 1. 2–4).

Oberon restores the status quo when he undoes the 'hateful imperfection' of Titania's 'eyes' by applying Dian's bud to her sleeping eyelids (4. 1. 63). This antidote is powerful, cancelling out the effects of Cupid's flower by taking 'all error' (or fickleness) 'from the eye'. As a result the fairy king and queen renew their 'amity' (87), just as Theseus predicts that his marriage to Hippolita will create an 'everlasting bond of fellowship' (1. 1. 85). Mindful of the past affairs that Oberon and Titania have reputedly enjoyed – among others, with Hippolita and Theseus (2. 1. 71–6) – the audience may be dubious. Rather than 'everlasting' love, might the union of the Athenian duke with the Amazonian queen herald a quarrelsome relationship like that of their fairy counterparts? Even more, we are invited to question the permanence of any partnership, whether lasting passion or firm 'amity', between Demetrius and Helena, Lysander and Hermia. Since Puck binds the original couples to each other by magical means, the audience must take on faith that 'Nought shall go ill' for them (3. 2. 462).

True, Lysander's fierce 'fancy' for Helena is obliterated by Dian's bud, so that he can, as Puck predicts, find 'True delight / In the sight / Of [his] former lady's eye' (455–7). With its connotations of chastity (by association with the goddess Diana), Dian's bud restores Lysander to his true love now that any magically induced illusion melts away. But what about Demetrius? He stays, presumably for life, under the spell of the magic juice. The most favourable interpretation is that love-in-idleness works paradoxically but beneficially for Demetrius, having the opposite effect from 'madly' doting in that it restores his original bond with Helena. No antidote is applied to his eyes; he discovers, under the influence of the magic juice, that his 'heart' stayed with Hermia only 'guestwise', like a transient visitor, so that 'now to Helen is it home return'd' (3. 2. 171–2). To the royal hunting party in Act 4, Demetrius reaffirms his passion for Hermia as a temporary aberration, like an 'idle gaud, / Which in my childhood I did dote upon' (4. 1. 167–8). Once Helena again is the 'object and the pleasure of his eye', his 'heart' is now faithful and true, no longer subject to fickle sexual desire:

> And all the faith, the virtue of my heart,
> The object and the pleasure of mine eye,
> Is only Helena. (169–71)

The less favourable implication, however, is that Demetrius remains under a delusion, permanently besotted, his love based on an idle 'fancy' that might again shift its love object if the spell wears off. Adding to its arbitrary nature, 'true love' appears to be a gift bestowed by the fairies, whose wantonness is exemplified in the hobgoblin Puck. When the fairy king and queen bless the house after the newlyweds have retired to bed, Oberon pledges 'So shall all the couples three / Ever true in loving be' (5. 1. 407–8). Yet watching this magical play, we are encouraged to take this on faith – to submit willingly to the illusion of 'happily ever after' rather than simply dismissing the action as a fanciful dream about the vagaries of love.

Acts 2 and 3 take spectators through the shifting nature of sexual desire in the dark forest of the id. But in drawing them back to Athens for the final act of the play, *A Midsummer Night's Dream* offers a more optimistic vision of the relationship between fancy and romantic love – one that celebrates the ability of love to re-form reality, to view the loved one in the best possible light and to trust in the constancy of affectionate regard. Just as Bottom's 'most rare vision' (4. 1. 204–5) has been fully realised, acquiring a local habitation and a name when Titania takes him into her love bower, so Hippolita discerns that the 'strange' narratives the lovers recount in the full light of day all cohere. Their 'story' moves beyond mere illusion, the potential superficiality of 'fancy's images', to create a consistent though marvellous ('admirable') reality. Hippolita discovers, wonderingly, how

> all the story of the night told over,
> And all their minds transfigur'd so together,
> More witnesseth than fancy's images,
> And grows to something of great constancy;
> But howsoever, strange and admirable. (5. 1. 23–7)

The lovers share a mutual, transformative vision, 'something of great constancy'. Love's mind, or in this case their 'minds transfigur'd so together', now corresponds to the creative imagination, capable of reconciling opposites and apparent incongruities.

This brings us back to Helena's important perception about the nature of love in that early speech. Before pronouncing that 'Love looks not with the eyes but with the mind' or heart, she observes that 'Things base and vile, holding no quantity, / Love can transpose to form and dignity' (1. 1. 232–3). In its best sense, love's 'mind', though irrational even to the point of becoming 'lunatic' (as Theseus notes in his speech on imagination), also partakes of the poetic imagination. If it creates an illusion, it can be a life-affirming one. It allows 'airy' Titania to transfigure the earth-bound Bottom, finding splendour in the ass. It enables Lysander, like the inspired 'lover' who can see fair Helen of Troy's beauty in a 'brow of Egypt' (5. 1. 10–11), again to revere the dark-complexioned Hermia, whom he briefly reviled as 'Ethiop' (3. 2. 257). Rather than being equivalent to the biased heart or the desiring will, love's mind now allies itself with the synthesising and 'transfigurative'[17] power of the imagination.

Expounding on how the 'lunatic, the lover, and the poet / Are of imagination all compact' (5. 1. 7–8), Theseus has moved beyond his role, at the start of *A Midsummer Night's Dream*, as an authority figure who sternly advises Hermia to follow her father's judgement. The duke is now advocating imagination, and the edifying power of illusion, to make 'concord' out of 'discord' (60). The decision to have the actor of Theseus double as Oberon – a trend begun by Peter Brook's landmark 1969 production for the Royal Shakespeare Company – brilliantly suggests how the Athenian duke, through his alter ego as the fairy king, must work through tensions in his own romantic relationship with Hippolita, who of course doubles as Titania. And Oberon's use of the magical juice, which has the effect of transforming Demetrius into a faithful lover again, might serve as proxy for the 'private schooling' that Theseus promises to Demetrius, as well as to Hermia's father, in the daylight world of Athens (1. 1. 116). As it turns out, both Egeus and Demetrius have been misguided in trying to push Hermia into the wrong love match; not she but they require some imaginative correction.

By the end of the play, when the Mechanicals perform 'Pyramus and Thisbe', Theseus encourages the small audience of newlyweds to accept in good faith this botched dramatic production. Even the best actors, he explains, are 'shadows', and the 'worst are no worse, if imagination amend them' (5. 1. 211–12). In his epilogue Puck, as surrogate for the playwright, entreats the larger audience attending Shakespeare's play to show a similar generosity in order to redeem the 'weak and idle' theme of the play (427). With this kind of faith and imagination, the dream of love will no longer remain a nightmare of confusions and 'hateful fantasies' in the forest – an interlude that might have turned, like 'Pyramus and Thisbe', from 'mirth' to 'tragical' (57). Instead the erotic dream will segue into what Theseus wishes for the newlyweds: 'joy and fresh days of love' (29). Thus the play celebrates Keats's tribute to the 'holiness of the heart's affections and the truth of the imagination'[18] not only as all-important but as interlinked, for the renewal of the 'heart's affections' depends on creatively reimagining the loved one.

At the end of *A Midsummer Night's Dream* two visions of romantic love remain in balance. As well as sceptically exploring how sexual desire can masquerade as true love – the absurdity of Lysander's sudden conviction, once he is under the spell of instant attraction, that Helena and not his beloved Hermia is 'My love, my life, my soul' (3. 2. 246) – Shakespeare embeds a romantic ideal in this fairy-tale drama. On one level 'fancy' is a fleeting attraction fed by the eye. But such desire may spark, through the lover's imagination, what David Schalkwyk calls a 'projective vision'[19] that has the power not only to redeem mundane reality but to transfigure and to bestow lasting value on the loved one, just as Cleopatra elevates Antony in her creative dream of him after his death. If the audience trust, with Puck, that 'Jack shall have Jill, / Nought shalt go ill' (3. 2. 461–2), they can believe that for the lovers in *A Midsummer Night's Dream* romantic love, which begins with sexual desire based on visual attraction, may continue to be transformed, through idealising imagination, into a relationship of 'great constancy'.

Love's Labour's Lost was probably composed around 1594, a little earlier than *A Midsummer Night's Dream*. The play also offers two opposing versions of romantic love. On the one hand sexual desire, or fickle infatuation based on physical attractiveness, may masquerade as romantic aspiration, but in its ideal form the love of a woman can become a moral and even a spiritual inspiration. Freud defines these opposing versions as 'sensual, earthly love' versus 'unsensual, heavenly love', noting how a maturing individual strives to find 'a synthesis' between the two. The bridge that links them, he explains, is affection or tenderness, for a successful 'passionate love marriage' depends on transforming 'sexual impulsions' into a 'lasting and ... affectionate tie'.[20] The spokesman for love in Shakespeare's play, Berowne, uses a simile from the natural world to evoke this kind of delicate sensibility: 'Love's feeling is more soft and sensible / Than are the tender horns of cockled snails' (4. 3. 334–5).

Love's Labour's Lost envisages the idealised, 'heavenly' version of love as a form of intellectual aspiration and access to divine beauty. In his treatise expounding love, Neo-Platonist Ficino calls this the 'higher beauty of the soul, the mind, and God'.[21] If the premise expounded at length in Act 4, scene 3 of the play is sound – that love is 'first learned in a lady's eyes' – then the 'heavenly rhetoric' of these female eyes can be a source of true enlightenment (4. 3. 324, 58). Infused with 'Promethean fire' (300), her eyes transmit to the adoring lover a higher knowledge, more powerful than anything acquired through book learning. And over time desire, generated by the sparkling eyes of the mistress, may also become a pathway to greater understanding and appreciation of the loved one's true being, transforming the male's aesthetic response to a beautiful exterior into an enduring love relationship. Such a relationship would be grounded in moral worth – love as 'a seamless unit joining the inner virtue with the outward sign of its presence'.[22] This ideal remains frustrated and unfulfilled in the play, however. In contrast to *A Midsummer Night's Dream*, where 'Jack shall have Jill' (3. 2. 461), *Love's Labour's Lost* does not end 'like an old play' in a celebration of love and marriage (5. 2. 874).

Berowne becomes the play's advocate for this higher form of love communicated through female beauty. At the play's opening, he and his fellow aristocrats, Longaville and Dumaine, have pledged to join the King of Navarre in forming an academy, vowing to spend three years in the pursuit of learning, cloistered away from distracting females. Berowne is nevertheless reluctant to sign on as a scholar. While the king urges the lords to win glory by waging 'war' against their 'affections' (1. 1. 9), Berowne recognises the importance of sexual passion – that 'every man with his affects is born' (151). He has already argued that the 'fairer eye' of the female can provide more access to the 'light of truth' than can great books:

Study me how to please the eye indeed
By fixing it upon a fairer eye,
Who dazzling so, that eye shall be his heed,
And give him light that it was blinded by. (80–3)

This idea of a reciprocal exchange of 'light', vision transmitted from eye to eye, is also touched on in *Two Gentlemen of Verona*. The song 'Who is Silvia?' speculates that the god of love, blind Cupid, will be cured when he seeks out the lady's dazzling eyes to 'help' or supplement his own sight: 'Love doth to her eyes repair, / To help him of his blindness' (4. 2. 46–7). But in Act 1 of *Love's Labour's Lost* the purveyor of Neo-Platonic wisdom is Berowne, who is still practising his rhetorical skills. A self-confessed 'love's whip' and enemy to Cupid (3. 1. 174), he expands this persuasive image about the illuminating effect of the lady's 'fairer eye' more as a way of framing a clever argument than as offering a serious proposition.

Indeed *Love's Labour's Lost* tends to philosophise about romantic love rather than showing it in action. Whereas the fast-moving plot of *A Midsummer Night's Dream* uses the dramatic device of love-in-idleness juice placed on the male lovers' eyes to create instant and bewildering attraction, the earlier play offers a more leisurely disquisition on the role of the eyes in fostering romantic love. Attracted to Rosaline despite his initial determination 'I will not love', Berowne exclaims, 'Oh but her eye – by this light, but for her eye I would not love her' (4. 3. 9–10). The lords tend to blame the ladies for enslaving them through ocular power, as when Longaville declares that only the 'heavenly rhetoric' of Maria's eye has persuaded his 'heart' to the 'false perjury' (58–60) of abandoning his original plan to be cloistered in study. Just as the 'fair sun' evaporates vapours, so his shining beloved has extinguished the 'breath' of his vow to forego the company of women (66–8). Meanwhile the King of Navarre expresses his passion for the Princess through the conventional motifs of a Petrarchan sonnet. To Navarre the lady's 'eye-beams' are brighter than the sun's rays; her face, shining 'light' through his tears, offers more radiance than the moon (25–31). Berowne remains hidden, smugly observing his love-sick companions from above like a 'demigod' (77). But the satirist is unmasked when Jaquenetta produces Berowne's own love letter. Exposed as one of the smitten, Berowne is not to be outdone in expounding the dazzling effect of his 'heavenly' Rosaline's beauty (217).

Berowne's lengthy defence of love that follows (4. 3. 286–362) is based on his confident question: 'For where is any author in the world / Teaches such beauty as a woman's eye?' (308–9). While it is more secular in its application, his exposition echoes the Neo-Platonic concept that physical beauty – in this case, a woman's face and eyes – can lead to higher knowledge in the beholder, even a perception of divine truth. Dante's *Vita Nuova* (1295) had first described the lover's 'progress toward the divine as beginning with his first intuition of the ideal in the eyes of his beloved' Beatrice.[23] And in Castiglione's influential *The Book of the Courtier* (first published in Thomas Hoby's translation in 1561), the speaker Peter Bembo, also following Neo-Platonic philosophy, expands on the idea of aristocratic passion as a 'coveting to enjoy beautie'. Whereas 'sensuall love',[24] the kind evoked in Shakespeare's *Venus and Adonis* (1593),[25] often remains obsessed with a beautiful exterior (the 'thinne shadowes of beautie'), Bembo argues that physical or sexual attraction can provide a pathway to virtue, a stepping stone whereby the soul, through reason, may grasp the 'unitie of the heavenly beautie, goodnesse and wisdom'.[26] Because 'Beautie commeth of God', it must possess goodness. It serves to channel the 'most holy fire of true heavenly love'.[27] Unlike Bembo's, Berowne's speech does not lead toward the Christian God but couches in classical terms the conviction that

> when love speaks, the voice of all the gods
> Makes heaven drowsy with the harmony. (4. 3. 341–2)

Berowne nevertheless concludes his peroration by arguing that 'religion' is what requires the men to break their old bond, their original vow to live a celibate life, in order to follow 'charity' instead (360–2). 'Charity' is how *agape* (the highest form of love) is translated in the Authorised Version of the King James Bible (1611), where Paul's First Epistle to the Corinthians underlines a key message of the New Testament – that if I 'have not charity, it profiteth me nothing' (1 Corinthians 13: 2).

Berowne also argues, in pragmatic fashion, that women's eyes offer greater reward than traditional book learning does. Over and above the 'leaden contemplation' that can destroy physical vigour, women's eyes supply knowledge as the true 'ground, the books, the academes' (4. 3. 318, 299). The sentiment here is that of Demetrius in *A Midsummer Night's Dream*, who swears that Helena's eyes are 'Love's richest book' (2. 2. 122). Shakespeare's Sonnet 14, too, expresses the same idealistic notion that the eyes of the loved one convey 'knowledge':

> But from thine eyes my knowledge I derive,
> And, constant stars, in them I read such art
> As truth and beauty shall together thrive. (9–11)

At first Berowne's speech depicts the male spectator as simply overwhelmed by the beauty of his mistress:

> What peremptory eagle-sighted eye
> Dares look upon the heaven of her brow,
> That is not blinded by her majesty? (4. 3. 222–4)

Just as Tarquin's eyes are 'blinded with a greater light' when he draws the curtain to view Lucrece's loveliness (*The Rape of Lucrece*, 375), so Berowne argues that even an 'eagle-sighted eye' would be blinded by the 'majesty' of his mistress's face. But he then returns to the earlier idea he proposed in Act 1 – that the 'fairer eye' of the female, which initially dazzles the sight of the male lover, can actually enlighten him, literally 'give him light' (1. 1. 81–3). Looking into and receiving the 'Promethean fire' sparkling in a woman's eyes can elevate the gaze of the lover himself. Male lovers need no longer be enslaved by female eyes; instead they become energised by a passion that, as Berowne hyperbolically projects, could shake fifty years off a 'wither'd hermit' who is fully a hundred years old (4. 3. 300, 238). For love, claims the newly converted

Berowne, is exponentially powerful; it 'Courses as swift as thought in every power, / And gives to every power a double power' (327–8). Just as Theseus in *A Midsummer Night's Dream* reminds his audience of how the lover's imaginative gaze can transform the loved one, like the poet's 'eye' rolling in a 'fine frenzy' from 'earth to heaven' (5. 1. 12–13), so, contends Berowne, love 'adds a precious seeing to the eye' (*Love's Labour's Lost*, 4. 3. 330). The tables are turned; instead of being overwhelmed by the female's sparkling eyes, the male lover can receive their power. Reversing the extravagant image of the 'eagle-sighted eye' blinded by such beauty, Berowne now promises that 'A lover's eyes will gaze an eagle blind' (331). This is the ocular power also attributed to the subject of Sonnet 20, the 'master-mistress' of the poet's passion. Not only does the fair youth possess amazing physical beauty, but his 'eye', which the poet claims is 'more bright' than any woman's, is capable of 'Gilding the object whereupon it gazeth' (5–6). It can transfigure, even improve, what it beholds.

The poetry soars in Berowne's long speech on love. The whole purpose of his elaborate defence of love's power is to render the lords' original vow invalid because it's akin to political treachery, 'Flat treason 'gainst the kingly state of youth' (4. 3. 289). Berowne must demonstrate that the young men have chosen well, gaining enlightenment from beautiful female eyes instead of from books. Overlapping passages (the content of lines 292–314 appears to be reworked later in the speech) suggest that the printer retained Shakespeare's original draft, lines that the dramatist might have 'blotted' in favour of his revised version. But repetition with variation, as the speech stands, does serve to hammer home Berowne's message. For *Love's Labour's Lost* is as much about the art of rhetoric, the use and abuse of persuasive language, as it is about the visual impact of the loved one's beauty. In fact four of the six instances of the word 'rhetoric' in Shakespeare's whole canon occur in this play.

In a play about linguistic cleverness, where speech is often tortured to further the cause of romantic love, the main function of the schoolmaster Holofernes is to parody excessively pedantic rhetoric. Displaying a weakness for Latinate neologisms, he praises Ovid for 'smelling out the odoriferous flowers of fancy, the jerks of invention' (4. 2. 124–5). Rivalling absurd Holofernes in his verbal shenanigans is the Spaniard Armado, described by the king as a 'child of fancy' with 'a mint of phrases in his brain' (1. 1. 165–70). As such Armado, who becomes infatuated with the wench Jaquenetta and woos her in grandiose language, forges an important link between 'fancy' – immediate physical attraction based on visual appeal – and the fanciful, frivolous use of language.

Berowne presents a more sophisticated version of Armado's fantastical speech; as a would-be master of language, Berowne is often overmastered by what he terms 'painted rhetoric' (4. 3. 235). As soon as she hears that he is part of the male academy, the sceptical Rosaline brands Berowne an opportunist, one whose 'eye begets occasions for his wit' (2. 1. 69). Indeed he demonstrates this linguistic facility in Act 4's long third scene, when he defends Rosaline's unconventional dusky beauty through a series of witty paradoxes. He manages this in a fanciful but less inspired way than Theseus's imaginative 'lover', who can transform a dark gypsy 'brow' into the beauty of Helen of Troy (*A Midsummer Night's Dream*, 5. 1. 11). By insisting to his companions that 'No face is fair that is not full so black' (4. 3. 249) and 'Therefore is she born to make black fair' (257), Berowne cleverly inverts the conventional Elizabethan preference for pale skin and golden hair.

Granted, in such a sophisticated milieu as Navarre's enclave there's an expectation that even 'natural desires' must be articulated with rhetorical finesse.[28] But silence, or fewer verbal flourishes, can nevertheless serve the cause of romantic love more adeptly. As the narrator of *The Rape of Lucrece* observes, 'Beauty itself doth of itself persuade / The eyes of men without an orator' (29–30). Initially Navarre's gazing in admiration at the Princess – what the servant Boyet calls 'the heart's still rhetoric, disclosed with eyes' (2. 1. 229) – demonstrates this kind of mute wonder at a woman's beauty. But resorting to elaborate rhetorical tropes muddies the purity of the response. As Richard Meek explores in *Narrating the Visual in Shakespeare*, 'language can obscure rather than enable vision'.[29] It is when Navarre rushes ahead to verbalise his feelings, making 'a mouth of his eye / By adding a tongue' (251–2), that the result is a shallow, botched response that runs counter to his quest:

> His tongue, all impatient to speak and not see,
> Did stumble with haste in his eyesight to be. (238–9)

Praising female beauty with much more flourish, Berowne finds it impossible to keep his voice 'still' and muted. Eager to impress his listeners, he over-embellishes his insights by making a mouth of his eye. Thus he shows himself incapable of heeding the sage advice of Theseus in *A Midsummer Night's Dream*, that 'Love . . . and tongue-tied simplicity / In least speak most' (5. 1. 104–5). Aspiring to high-flown romantic love, Berowne must eventually learn to control the rhetorical excess of his discourse.[30]

In fact Berowne's exaggerated art of persuasion, like his lovemaking, is doomed to failure. At the very least it must be put on hold at the end of the play. Ultimately none of the women – Rosaline, Maria, Katherine and the princess of Navarre – is convinced that the men's declaration of romantic love is more than a rhetorical game. From the start the Princess is suspicious of the 'painted flourish' of elaborate compliment (2. 1. 14), rejecting Boyet's fulsome praise of her with the admonition that 'Beauty is born by judgment of the eye, / Not altered by base sale of chapmen's tongue' (15–16). Excessive verbal praise, she contends, cheapens beauty by turning it into an object for sale when instead it should be evaluated by 'judgment of the eye'. As Alison Thorne explains, this is a term current among sixteenth-century Italian theorists such as Vasari and Lomazzo, who advocated 'judgment of the eye' (*giudizio dell' occhio*), supplemented by the 'arte' of 'Perspective',[31] as the means to evaluate proportion and beauty in visual art. While it allows for some variation, 'judgment of the eye' guarantees a more objective aesthetic evaluation than does the biased vision of the adoring lover. For, as Sonnet 148 makes clear, the lover's besotted eye is almost never an index of true 'judgment' (3).

Like the sonneteer whose biased eye can make 'every bad a perfect best' (Sonnet 114, 5), a skilful lover such as Dumaine in *Love's Labour's Lost* has the 'wit to make an ill shape good' (2. 1. 60). But this is wit in the service of sexual desire or fancy – what Bembo in *The Book of the Courtier* warns against as 'sensuall love' – rather than adherence to the 'divine' love that Berowne promotes. Despite initially finding in Navarre's commendable verbal reticence 'love's still rhetoric', the 'old love-monger' Boyet (253) finally registers in the adoring gaze of the king little more than infatuation ('sensuall love'); he observes that all Navarre's 'behaviors did make their retire / To the court of his eye, peeping through desire' (234–5). Fostering erotic desire, 'all his senses were lock'd in his eye' (242).

The relative superficiality of the lords' attraction, not tested by time or adequate knowledge of the loved one, is foregrounded in the trick the ladies play on their male counterparts. When the suitors come disguised as Russians in an elaborate game of courtship, the women in turn wear masks. This means that each lord ends up swearing his devotion to the wrong lady – the King to Rosaline, Berowne to the Princess, Dumaine and Longaville to Maria and Katherine respectively. By engineering 'mock for mock' (5. 2. 140), deliberately confusing their identities, the ladies reveal each man as 'wit turn'd fool' (70). Their successful ruse suggests again the easy interchangeability of love objects.[32] Wooing the wrong female, merely 'the sign of she' (469), obviously casts doubt on the authenticity of the male's original declaration of love, supposedly based on perceiving the uniqueness of his loved one. The men are all guilty of projecting an 'idealized object of desire' upon an actual woman.³³ What's more, the fact that each woman's eyes are at least partially concealed, and certainly unrecognised by her ardent lover, undercuts Berowne's whole case that 'love is first learned in a lady's eyes'.

Predictably Berowne is the man most disoriented by the trick. After masochistically presenting himself as the victim, inviting Rosaline to 'Bruise me with scorn . . . / Cut me to pieces with thy keen conceit' (5. 1. 397–9), he appears to be truly humbled as a romantic lover. Accordingly he vows to renounce both actual vizards (masks) and the misleading arts of courtly language, with its elaborate 'taffeta phrases, silken terms precise' and 'three-piled hyberboles' (406–7), and instead express himself in the plain language of 'russet yeas' and 'honest kersey noes' (413). Rather than broadcasting his falling in love with such linguistic flair, he will communicate his 'wooing mind' with frank sincerity (412–13). Still, it proves hard for him to keep this promise. A 'trick / Of the old rage' (416–17), his enjoyment of rhetorical sallies, stays in force. It appears as difficult for Berowne to control the proliferation of rhetorical tropes – what George Puttenham in *The Arte of English Poesie* terms 'ornament' that should not be 'used in excess', since it comes at the expense of 'plainness' and 'simplicity'³⁴ – as it is for him to act with decorum in his pursuit of romantic love. Suggesting that women's beauty is responsible for the men's mistakes, he resorts to the conventional conceit that the suitors have 'caught' the 'plague' from women's 'eyes' (421). Yet Berowne himself has rushed headlong into the trap set by the masked women, failing to recognise the one pair of eyes, Rosaline's, that supposedly inspired in him such soaring passion.

The play's denouement comes quickly after the Nine Worthies playlet, another opportunity for Berowne and his companions to showcase their sharp, even cruel wit. The messenger Marcade's interruption of the entertainment does not favour the cause of the suitors. After Marcade confirms the death of the Princess's father, the King of France, the stricken daughter cuts through Navarre's tactless insistence on pursuing 'love's argument' (5. 2. 747) with her curt 'I understand you not, my griefs are double' (752). Berowne nevertheless continues to play the rhetorician. To please his sombre audience he reneges on the idea of love as a divine power kindled in a woman's eyes. In extraordinary fashion, he now expands on romantic love as mere fancy, a 'wanton' sport that devolves into ridiculous behaviour. He characterises this emotion, fed by the eyes alone, as superficial and mutable:

As love is full of unbefitting strains,
All wanton as a child, skipping and vain,
Formed by the eye and therefore like the eye,
Full of straying shapes, of habits, and of forms,

Varying in subjects as the eye doth roll
To every varied object in his glance (760–5)

Why this shocking turnaround, from advocating love as an authentic response to 'heavenly beauty' to deriding it as 'vain' sexual attraction, prompted by a fickle eye? Again Berowne is using a rhetorical strategy; he concedes some frivolity in order to strengthen his main argument: that the lords' offer should now be taken seriously. After apologising for the 'loose love' adopted by all the suitors (766), he once again transfers blame on to the women by proposing a new syllogism: 'Our love being yours, the error that love makes / Is likewise yours' (771–2). Paradoxically, the 'heavenly eyes' of the ladies are no longer a source of inspiration but are responsible for the 'faults' of the men (769). It is therefore up to the ladies to turn 'sin' into 'grace' by forgiving the men and accepting their avowals of lasting devotion (775–6).

The Princess remains unconvinced, however, that the lords' hasty proposals are sincere. Quite simply, she rates their romantic courtship as mere game-playing – 'pleasant jest' and rhetorical 'bombast' (780–1). She therefore decrees that the suitors must spend a full year of penance to prove their constancy, if they are to make the serious 'world-without-end bargain' of marriage (789). When courtly lover Berowne asks his lady to 'impose some service' on him (840), Rosaline decides to punish him for that tendency to be flippant she remarked on earlier – his facility in using his 'fair tongue' and 'gracious words' to crack jokes that keep his audience spellbound (2. 1. 72–3). As a corrective for his hurtful 'wounding flouts', this man 'replete with mocks' must visit the 'speechless sick' in hospital and test his witticisms on a group of 'groaning wretches'. Exerting his rhetorical skill to try to impress the terminally ill must surely prove sobering, curing him of the 'fault' of taking too much pride in his levity (5. 2. 843–4, 851–2, 866); it should also tame his indecorous desire to win his lady through 'taffeta phrases' and clever word games. In view of Navarre's original edict forbidding a woman to come within a mile of his court 'on pain of losing her tongue' (1. 1. 123–4), it is pleasingly ironic that the females refuse to be silenced. Their final role is to curb the ostentatious, fanciful oratory that overlays the men's heady romantic aspirations.

The play ends on a questioning note. Unlike *A Midsummer Night's Dream*, it doesn't suggest that creative imagination can transform transitory desire or 'will' into the 'constancy' of love. Might the men's erotic desire become an inspirational force of 'double power' and 'wonder' (4. 2. 328, 113) which, combined with tenderness and respect, could integrate sexual desire into the loving commitment of marriage? Or will sexual attraction remain shallow, a matter of ephemeral 'revels, dancing, masks, and merry hours' (4. 3. 376)? To Navarre's optimistic hope that a year's trial will bring about the desired end, Berowne offers the blunt rejoinder 'And that's too long for a play' (5. 1. 878). Although it remains within the genre of comedy, *Love's Labour's Lost* is remarkable in setting forth an ideal Neo-Platonic love – what Freud terms the 'unsensual' and 'heavenly' variety of love that informs both Dante's *Vita Nuova* and Petrarch's sonnets – and countering it with scepticism over whether that higher form can ever be achieved in a young, impatient lover. Even the ideal itself is likely to undermine an actual relationship. Viewing the mistress as an embodiment of a Neo-Platonic idea (earthly beauty as an index of divine goodness) surely works against a lover's appreciation of the female as a singular as well as a desirable being. The danger is that what Ficino calls *amore divino* cannot be reconciled with the physical drive he denigrates as *amore bestiale*.[35]

The mistress's eyes may be like the sun in their splendour and power, but there is no guarantee that the men can receive and reciprocate that power within a long-term relationship based on more than sensual desire toying with an abstract ideal. In *Apolonius and Silla* (1581), Barnabe Rich is careful to distinguish stable and 'reasonable love', based on 'desert', from the 'foolishness' of transient 'fancies'. He concludes that 'if the bare show of beauty, or the comeliness of personage might be sufficient to confirm us in our love, those that be accustomed to go to fairs and markets might sometimes fall in love with twenty in a day'.[36] The aristocrats in *Love's Labour's Lost*, locked in a more circumscribed environment, appear similarly vulnerable. Rather than discovering what Pierre de La Primaudaye in *The French Academie* calls 'true and good love' that is 'grounded upon virtue' and goodness, they seem ready to make a final commitment, pledging themselves to marriage, merely through 'lust' of the 'eyes'.[37]

Castiglione's Bembo likewise warns of too much haste in falling in love, for when the young courtier sees the face of a beautiful woman, 'his eyes snatch that image and carrie it to the hart'. In his tribute to women's eyes as the source of 'true Promethean fire', Berowne testifies to what the love-struck aristocrat in *The Courtier* also discovers – that 'those lively spirits, that twinckle out through the eyes, put continuall fresh nourishment to the fire'.[38] But Bembo, who ends his discourse by attributing to God and not to beautiful women the 'shining beames' of true 'light', soberly advises the romantic lover to 'raise up reason' to counteract attraction based merely on 'sense and appetites'.[39] Ficino, too, makes it clear that it is through God's 'divine' light that the soul recognises what is 'heavenly',[40] rather than (as Berowne reiterates) through the 'heavenly eyes' of the mistress (5. 2. 767–9).

While they outwardly aspire to a higher spiritual love, the infatuated lords in *Love's Labour's Lost* fail to apprehend the uniqueness of their chosen ladies or to reconcile urgent desire, or 'heat of blood' (5. 2. 800), with any Neo-Platonic ideal. They remain as vulnerable to superficial fancy and the vagaries of sexual attraction ('will') as they are enchanted by their own rhetorical frivolity, as likely to display 'wantonesse' in their behaviour as in their language.[41] Possibly the trials of absence and service will encourage a fuller, more grounded love that might mature into the union of marriage. Abandoning conventional worship of the female's 'heavenly' beauty, integrating 'esteem'[42] with desire, could enable each man to recognise his loved one's singularity as well as her moral worth.[43] Can the lords achieve this deeper bond of mutual understanding and love with the ladies they desire?[44] We are left uncertain.

Notes

1. Maurice Charney, *Shakespeare on Love and Lust*, also notes that 'Eyes are at the center of the love discourse in Shakespeare' (p. 15) in that most frequently 'Love enters through the eyes and it is spontaneous, irresistible, and absolute' (p. 9).
2. The writings of Ficino and Plato were available in Latin and Tuscan Italian during the sixteenth century; Shakespeare's contemporaries might have accessed the ideas of Plato's *Symposium* through Geoffrey Fenton's *Monophylo* (1572), written in English. In Marsilio Ficino, *Commentary on Plato's Symposium on Love*, translator and editor Sears Reynolds Jayne also notes that Ficino's *De Amore* (1484), translated into French by Guy Le Fevre de la Broderie, formed part of the 1581 English court entertainment *The Fortress of Perfect Beauty* – a text that was subsequently used by both Chapman and Spenser between 1590 and 1596 (*Commentary*, p. 22). These dates are close to the composition of *Love's Labour's Lost* (c. 1594).
3. *Commentary on Plato's Symposium on Love*, speech VI, ch. 10, pp. 125, 126.
4. Ibid. speech VII, ch. 4, p. 160.
5. Ibid. speech VI, ch. 10, p. 126.
6. Alison Thorne, '*Antony and Cleopatra* and the Art of Dislimning', in *Vision and Rhetoric in Shakespeare: Looking through Language*, notes that in Renaissance aesthetic theory *fantasie* (powerful creative imagination in art as well as poetry) counters Aristotle's view of the imagination as 'reproductive', simply forming 'likenesses of external objects from the sensory data it receives' (pp. 168–9).
7. Helen Vendler, *The Art of Shakespeare's Sonnets*, p. 482.
8. Joel Fineman, *Shakespeare's Perjured Eye: The Invention of Poetic*

Subjectivity in the Sonnets, finds that overall the poet connects 'true vision' with 'ideal desire' in the sonnets addressed to the young man (p. 179). It is the sonnets addressed to the dark mistress that replace the 'poetics of a unified and unifying eye' with the 'poetics of a double tongue' (p. 15), reflecting 'divided desire' (p. 84).

9. Judith Dundas, ' "To See Feelingly": The Language of the Senses and the Language of the Heart', comments that in such a case *seeing can no longer be relied upon to reflect the radiance of true beauty*' because the eye 'sees in accordance with the heart, whether or not that heart is on the side of virtue' (51).
10. Lisa Hopkins, *The Shakespearean Marriage*, also notes that for the young lovers in *A Midsummer Night's Dream* 'love is figured essentially as an attribute of the ocular nerve, dangerously susceptible to external manipulation' (p. 59).
11. The *OED*'s definition coincides with Alexander Schmidt's *Shakespeare Lexicon and Quotation Dictionary*, which places this meaning of 'mind' under category 6: 'will, desire, intention, purpose' (vol. 1, p. 772).
12. Jillian Keenan, '*A Midsummer Night's Dream*: Stand and Unfold', in *Sex with Shakespeare*, makes Helena's response the springboard for her book's exploration of the 'Spanking Thing', a fetish within a sadomasochistic relationship (p. 22).
13. John D. Cox, ' "The Error of our Eye" in *Troilus and Cressida*', finds this line symptomatic of the whole play, 'since everyone makes decisions as Cressida does, judging by appearances rather than reality' (150). Rather than focusing on Cressida's confusion of appearance with reality, as Cox does, my emphasis is on how love's 'mind' is directed by sexual 'will'.
14. Commenting on the easy circulation of desire in the play, which is prompted by the eyes, Valerie Traub, *Desire and Anxiety: Circulations of Sexuality in Shakespearean Drama*, notes that the 'desires' of the characters 'are passed from one erotic subject to the next, as their gazes converge first on this, and then on that potential lover' (p. 6).
15. As noted in Chapter 1, the same connection between 'reason' and 'rising' is made in Sonnet 151.
16. Jan Kott, *Shakespeare Our Contemporary*, further contends that 'The slender, tender and lyrical Titania longs for animal love' (p. 82).
17. Thorne, *Vision and Rhetoric in Shakespeare*, p. 168. Thorne also finds that here 'imagination' positively transfigures 'the lover's vision of things', just as it helps to create the 'mythological identities' of Antony and Cleopatra (p. 167).
18. To Benjamin Bailey, 22 November 1817, in *Letters of John Keats*, selected by Frederick Page, p. 48.
19. David Schalkwyk, *Shakespeare: Love and Language*, p. 25. Schalkwyk, however, finds a gap between the 'constancy of love' and the 'shaping "fantasies" of desire' in this play (p. 32).
20. Sigmund Freud, 'Group Psychology and the Analysis of the Ego' (1921), in *The Standard Edition of the Complete Psychological Works of Sigmund Freud*, vol. 18, pp. 143, 112, 139.
21. *Commentary on Plato's Symposium on Love*, speech II, ch. 7, p. 54.

22. This is how C. Stephen Jaeger defines the aristocratic 'culture of love and friendship' in medieval and Renaissance Europe, in *Ennobling Love*, pp. x, 19.
23. Paul E. Memmo, Jr, 'The Poetry of the *Stilnovisti* and *Love's Labour's Lost*', 2. Philippa Berry, 'Introduction', in *Of Chastity and Power: Elizabethan Literature and the Unmarried Queen,* also discusses how Dante's vision precedes the Petrarchan and Neo-Platonic traditions, in which the chaste woman is seen as a bridge 'between heaven and earth'. She may become a 'passive mediator of (self-) knowledge to man', capable of reconciling 'the opposition of spirit and matter within her person' (pp. 3–4).
24. Baldassare Castiglione, *The Book of the Courtier*, trans. Thomas Hoby, bk. 4, pp. 303, 306.
25. In this poem designed to 'captivate the eye' (281), Venus frequently focuses on Adonis's physical appeal.
26. Castiglione, *The Book of the Courtier*, bk. 4, pp. 320, 321.
27. Ibid. bk. 4, pp. 308–9, 319. Ficino's *Commentary on Plato's Symposium on Love* also posits that desire, first attaching to the 'body of the beloved', moves 'second to the Soul, third, to the Angel, and finally to God, the first origin of this splendor' (speech VI, ch. 10, p. 126).
28. Donatella Baldini, 'The Play of the Courtier: Correspondence between Castiglione's *Il libro del Cortegiano* and Shakespeare's *Love's Labour's Lost*', 10. Baldini emphasises the courtly codes that influence the men's behaviour in Shakespeare's play.
29. Richard Meek, ' "To See Sad Sights": Reading and Ekphrasis in *The Rape of Lucrece*', in *Narrating the Visual in Shakespeare*, p. 62.
30. In *Wanton Words: Rhetoric and Sexuality in English Renaissance Drama,* Madhavi Menon explores the 'insistent link between rhetorical language and figural sexuality' in several of Shakespeare's plays, briefly including *Love's Labour's Lost* (p. 4).
31. Quoted from Gian Paolo Lomazzo, in Alison Thorne, '*Ut Pictura Poesis* and the Rhetoric of Perspective', in *Vision and Rhetoric in Shakespeare*, p. 89. Lomazzo's work (1584) was translated into English by Richard Haydocke as *A Tracte containing the Artes of Curious Paintinge, Carvinge, and Buildinge* in 1598. Thorne, pp. 89–102, discusses Renaissance Italian commentary on art as reflected in *Arte of Limning* (c. 1600) by the English miniaturist Nicholas Hilliard, and in George Puttenham, *The Arte of English Poesie* (1589).
32. Katharine Eisaman Maus, 'Transfer of Title in *Love's Labor's Lost*', comments that through this trick 'The ladies in *Love's Labor's Lost* perform the equivalent of a bed-trick on the level of the signifier' (p. 218).
33. Thomas MacCary, *Friends and Lovers: The Phenomenology of Desire in Shakespearean Comedy,* characterises this as the 'idolatry of love' manifested by the play's immature men (p. 112).
34. George Puttenham, *The Arte of English Poesie*, 'Of Ornament Poetical', bk. 3, ch. 1, p. 150; 'Of Figures and Figurative Speeches', bk. 3, ch. 7, p. 166 (spelling modernised). Castiglione, through the voice of Count Lewis, also recommends that the courtier should use words that are 'apt, chosen, cleare, and well applied, and (above all) in use also among the people' (*The Book of the Courtier*, bk. 1, p. 56).

35. See Irving Singer, 'Neoplatonism and the Renaissance', in *The Nature of Love, Vol. 2: Courtly and Romantic*, p. 171.
36. *Apolonius and Silla*, in Barnabe Rich, *His Farewell to Military Profession* (1581), p. 181. The story parallels, and may be a source for, *Twelfth Night*. When Silla disguises herself as a male servant (Silvio) to be close to Apollonius, the lady Julina falls in love with her.
37. Pierre de La Primaudaye, 'Of a House and Family' and 'Of Voluptuousness and Lechery', in *The French Academie*, pp. 239, 494 (spelling modernised).
38. Castiglione, *The Book of the Courtier*, bk. 4, p. 313.
39. Ibid. pp. 322, 313. In another verbal parallel to Shakespeare's play, the speaker Lord Cesar in Hoby's translation of Castiglione's work notes how even when young men offer 'tokens, sutes, teares', their courtship may turn out to be 'but lost labour' (*The Book of the Courtier*, bk. 3, p. 223).
40. Ficino, *Commentary on Plato's Symposium on Love*, p. 158.
41. Ben Jonson, in *Timber, or Discoveries*, comments that 'wantonnesee of language' denotes a 'sicke mind' (p. 593).
42. The ending of *Love's Labour's Lost* fully raises the issue that Jean H. Hagstrum explores in *Esteem Enlivened by Desire: The Couple from Homer to Shakespeare*: the idea that 'pair bonding that leads to a long-term relationship ... not only permits but requires the reciprocal enlivening of desire and esteem' (p. 17), or a 'friendly esteem impregnated with eros' (p. 378).
43. In *Sexual Desire: A Moral Philosophy of the Erotic*, the philosopher Roger Scruton speculates, less idealistically, that desire itself is what underlies the Neo-Platonic link between physical beauty and moral beauty (virtue). He posits that since 'Desire obliges you to find value in its object', you will perceive the loved one as an 'embodiment of virtue' (p. 237).
44. Memmo, 'The Poetry of the *Stilnovisti* and *Love's Labour's Lost*', more optimistically finds in the lords' year of penance a progress toward 'humility and grace' (12). Memmo argues that rather than renouncing erotic desire in favour of heavenly love, a state achieved by Dante and Petrarch through the deaths of Beatrice and Laura, the lords will apprehend the 'synthesis of both earthly and celestial beauty' that Spenser's sonnet sequence *Amoretti* finally celebrates (7).

Chapter 5

The Petrarchan Love Convention: Romance at Odds with Sexual Desire

Shakespeare notoriously debunks traditional romantic expectations in his anti-Petrarchan Sonnet 130, 'My mistress' eyes are nothing like the sun'. His lady's eyes match her hair, unconventionally 'black' instead of golden; her cheeks fail to resemble roses; and 'Coral is far more red than her lips' red'. Instead of smelling like perfume, her breath 'reeks'.[1] Olivia in *Twelfth Night* also parodies, though less outrageously, the Petrarchan lover's *blason* of his mistress's lovely physical attributes.[2] After Viola/Cesario admires the lady's 'truly blent' beauty – the traditional 'red' of her lips offsetting the 'white' of her skin (1. 5. 247–8, 239) – Olivia drily offers to record for posterity her very ordinary features: '*item*, two lips indifferent red; *item*, two grey eyes with lids to them'. Meanwhile Jaques's 'All the world's a stage' speech in *As You Like It* pokes fun at the young male sonneteer who, 'sighing like a furnace', composes a 'woeful ballad' not to his mistress's eye but, more absurdly, to her 'eyebrow' (2. 7. 148–9).[3] Just as Shakespeare's drama scrutinises the stereotype of women as lecherous betrayers of men, so his plays remain sceptical about the polar opposite – excessive idealisation of females as chaste, unattainable beauties. Granted, the playwright doesn't always mock standard Petrarchan notions of love; *Romeo and Juliet* celebrates not only the authenticity of love at first sight but the creative energy of a worshipful lover. But Shakespeare's romantic comedies, as well as this early love tragedy, counterbalance idealised approaches with stringent realism;[4] they explore how the role adopted by the Petrarchan lover fails to mesh with the realities of sexual desire.

Shakespeare employs several strategies to point up the absurdity of exaggerated Petrarchan poses. First, he uses the male lovers' own heightened language to parody certain stylistic devices of the poetic convention: in particular, the hyperbole and oxymoron woven around the motif of the lover's suffering once he is smitten by his lady's sun-like, dazzling eyes. Whether it's the males in *Love's Labour's Lost* writing sonnets engorged with overworked Petrarchan conceits, or Romeo whipping up oxymorons to express his frustrated desire before he meets his true love Juliet, the effect of these inflated figures of speech is to expose the pretentiousness of romantic lovers when they strike attitudes rather than speaking from the heart. Shakespeare often uses a satiric voice from outside the main action to mock the standard Petrarchan figure. Or he introduces several key dramatic characters, such as Mercutio in *Romeo and Juliet* or the worldly Fool Touchstone in *As You Like It*, whose frankly sexual perspective undercuts the Neo-Platonic and Petrarchan notion that the lady is to be revered as a beautiful, etherealised object of desire.

Shakespeare's comedies focus on the wooing of royal or well-born lovers. But in the public theatre Shakespeare was catering to a predominantly middle- and working-class audience, citizens and artisans who were unlikely to identify with a courtly, 'literary culture' that deified females.[5] No wonder, then, that several of these plays burlesque aristocratic courtly wooing through the earthy sexual chase that goes on further down the social scale. Members of the down-to-earth servant class, or the rustics Touchstone refers to as 'country copulatives', are more honest than their social superiors about the demands of the flesh. Finally, the bawdy wordplay in these comedies provides another means of demystifying the civilities of romance, challenging the emphasis of Petrarchism on idealised rather than physical love. Courtly women who engage in verbal sparring and sexual repartee with their suitors use wit as a barricade, but they also reveal a certain knowingness about the erotic side of the romantic quest. Racy banter between Shakespeare's couples, whether aristocrats or wealthy citizens, serves as a reminder of the insistent desire that always threatens to break through Petrarchan posturing.

The source of what turned into a highly conventional treatment of love was of course both fresh and complex – Petrarch's own poetry. Composed in the mid-fourteenth century, Petrarch's *Canzoniere* built on the medieval tradition of the French troubadours, in which the unattainable 'sovereign mistress' is revered by the 'abject lover'.[6] It is Petrarch who most encapsulates the ideal nature of the mistress and the conflicting emotions, often painful or melancholy,[7] that she inspires in the lover. In Petrarch's case it was Laura – more a type of female beauty than a fully realised person – who served as a springboard for the poet to explore his varying responses to her. The reverential poet-lover eventually channels sexual passion into spiritual aspiration.[8] And by the time the Petrarchan convention takes hold in English Renaissance literature, nearly two centuries after the poet lived, it's assumed that such worship of the female will never turn into a consummated love affair. The lady must remain on a pedestal, idolised and unattainable,[9] to spark and refuel the lover's desire. Thus Troilus, emulating a Petrarchan lover, fears that achieving sexual consummation will destroy him, proving 'a joy too fine, / . . . For the capacity of [his] ruder powers' (*Troilus and Cressida*, 3. 2. 23–5). And in John Lyly's earlier play *Endimion* (c. 1590), the lover Eumenides actually hopes that his lady 'will practice her accustomed coyness, that I may diet myself on my desires: otherwise the fullness of my joys will diminish the sweetness' (3. 4).[10]

By the mid-sixteenth century in England several of Petrarch's sonnets[11] had been translated, with slight adaptations, by Sir Thomas Wyatt, who retained Petrarch's poetic form of octave followed by sestet.[12] It was the Earl of Surrey's poems, also popularised in Tottel's collection of *Songes and Sonnettes* (1557), which introduced the form that Shakespeare adopts for his sonnets – three quatrains with alternating rhymes and a concluding couplet. Although oxymoronic conceits are not the staple of Petrarch's best poetry, Wyatt's translation of Canzone 134 helped to perpetuate the image of the lover tormented by antithetical feelings: 'I fear and hope, I burn and freeze like ice'; 'I desire to perish and yet I ask for health'.[13] Drawing on the Tuscan poet's early recollection of falling in love with Laura on Good Friday of 1327, when her 'beautiful eyes "bound" him in love' ('*chè i be' vostr'occi, Donna, mi legaro*'),[14] Petrarch's imitators also elaborated the topic of the mistress's radiant eyes. By the 1590s, however, Petrarchism had become an outmoded convention, ripe for parody. In his sonnet sequence *Astrophil and Stella*, Philip Sidney retreats from 'poor Petrarch's long-deceased woes' (Sonnet 15) to urge a more personal response to love: 'Look in thy heart and write' (Sonnet 1).

Shakespeare's early play *Love's Labour's Lost*, as noted in the previous chapter, is indebted to the Neo-Platonic notion of love expounded by Bembo in Castiglione's *The Courtier*. It is this historical character, Pietro Bembo (1490–1547), who forged links between Neo-Platonism and Petrarchism. A scholar and writer who lived a century and a half after Petrarch, Bembo promoted the work of the Tuscan poet as a model for Italian poetic expression. Neo-Platonism and Petrarchism are alike in foregrounding the importance of eyes in transmitting love – the mistress's eyes as a source of inspiration while the eyes of the male lover, receiving and apprehending this almost divine beauty, connect directly to his heart. *The Courtier* emphasises how when the susceptible male (even an older man, like Bembo) sees the face of a 'beautifull woman', his eyes 'snatch that image' and carry it to his heart; then the 'lively spirits' that 'twinkle out through [her] eyes' will fan the fires of love.[15]

Similarly Petrarch celebrates how love opened his heart though Laura's beautiful eyes ('*begli occhi*', Canzone 126, 11) while an early sonnet explains how love found an easy conduit through his own eyes to his heart ('*et aperta la vie per gli occhi al core*') when he first beheld Laura (Canzone 3, 10).

In *Love's Labour's Lost* the lords write their tributes to the ladies as elaborate sonnets, trading on Petrarchan images too overworked to communicate genuine emotion. In his sonnet justifying the breaking of his oath to remain celibate, Longaville calls his lady a 'goddess' and 'a fair sun' (4. 3. 63, 67); Petrarch's original sonnet (Canzone 90) had extolled Laura as a heavenly spirit and a living sun ('*uno spirito celeste, un vivo sole*', 12). Meanwhile Navarre claims that the face of the Princess, reflected in every tear he weeps, shines brighter than the sun. Four references to his own tears – each drop on his cheeks absurdly equated to a 'coach' that carries the image of this lady who rides 'triumphing' over his 'woe' – perpetuate the stereotype of the self-absorbed Petrarchan lover, continually sighing and weeping (33–4). In a late sonnet Petrarch explains that after enduring twenty-one years of unrequited love for Laura he wept for ten years after her death (Canzone 364, 1–4). But the lords in *Love's Labour's Lost*, untested in fidelity and more concerned with romantic love than with spiritual progress, trivialise Petrarch's motifs – eyes like the sun and copious tears – in a way that reflects their own narcissism rather than an appreciation of the mistress beyond physical attraction.[16]

Berowne, at least, conveys the idea of love in a fresher way. Although he builds on traditional Neo-Platonic and Petrarchan comparisons – he likens Rosaline's eyes to 'Jove's lightning' and finds her 'celestial' – he argues with more originality that true learning must be acquired through the mesmerising beauty of the mistress: 'All ignorant that soul that sees' her 'without wonder' (4. 2. 115–17, 113). His longer oration in Act 4 explores more fully how love, 'first learned in a lady's eyes', both adds 'a precious seeing to the eye' and is as 'musical / As bright Apollo's lute, strung with his hair' (4. 3. 324, 330, 340). Moreover, once he is chastened by his mistress, Berowne vows to reject Petrarchan rhetoric altogether! As in Shakespeare's Sonnet 21, which foregoes the stock 'ornament' of comparisons to 'sun and moon' and resolves 'let me, true in love, but truly write' (3, 7, 9), Berowne pledges to abandon 'three-pil'd hyberboles'. Instead he will express his love in plain, 'russet' language (5. 2. 407, 413).

Two Gentlemen of Verona, composed by the early 1590s, echoes the world of *The Courtier*. 'Grounded in the courtly assumptions of the game', it also contains 'a good deal of parody' of romance conventions.[17]

Young Valentine is a classic case of biter bit. First he mocks the dire emotional state of the typical Petrarchan lover who suffers from unrequited love:

> To be in love – where scorn is bought with groans;
> Coy looks with heart-sore sighs, one fading moment's mirth
> With twenty watchful, weary, tedious nights (1. 1. 29–31)

Nevertheless, a few scenes later he has fallen in love with the 'divine' Silvia (2. 4. 147) and become as abject as his besotted friend Proteus. Because he mocked love, Valentine is now plagued with all the clichéd symptoms of Petrarchan misery: 'penitential groans', 'nightly tears' and 'daily heart-sore sighs'. Taking its revenge, romantic love has chased sleep from Valentine's 'enthralled eyes', making them 'watchers' of his own 'heart's sorrow' (131–5).

Duke Orsino in *Twelfth Night* (1601) represents a more sophisticated portrait of the Petrarchan lover. Though not outright parody, Orsino's character emphasises self-absorption and cultivation of love-sickness above authentic feeling, despite the Duke's boast that his heart alone can endure the 'beating of so strong a passion' (2. 4. 94). The object of his boundless desire is Olivia, whom he scarcely knows but who conveniently feeds his fantasies. Matching Lacan's theory that desire feeds on lack, absence and fantasy,[18] Orsino's yearning illustrates, too, the stasis at the heart of Petrarchism: the reality, as Mark Breitenberg puts it, that 'consummation' with the idolised chaste female must be 'deferred' if she is to 'retain [her] value for the desiring male subject'.[19] Accordingly the Duke positions Olivia as a 'sovereign cruelty' to be adored from afar, a woman who actually rekindles his desire by being unattainable (2. 4. 80). Because music answers to his self-induced melancholy, gratifying his notion of being 'slain by a fair cruel maid' (54), he calls for Feste's song 'Come away death'. Masochistically Orsino feeds his 'appetite' for such plangent offerings rather than truly wanting his sexual craving to 'sicken, and so die' (1. 1. 3).

In the play it is Viola, disguised as Cesario, who offers a counterbalance to Orsino's Petrarchan infatuation. Viola distances herself from her master's hackneyed address to Olivia as 'Most radiant, exquisite, and unmatchable beauty' by branding it 'poetical' (1. 5. 170–1, 195). When she expresses a more individualised passion in her 'Make me a willow cabin at your gate' speech, the verse catches fire. Bypassing the trite description of how Orsino loves his chosen lady with 'adorations, fertile tears, / With groans that thunder love, with sighs of fire' (255–6), Viola breaks through the 'loyal cantons of contemned love' – the conventional verses (canzoniere) of Petrarchan imitators – with the simpler urgency of how she would 'call upon [her] soul within the house' and halloo Olivia's 'name' to 'the reverberate hills' in 'the dead of night' (269–72). Later, back with her master, she underlines the depth of her feeling for him by inventing a surrogate sister who, instead of ostentatiously verbalising her unrequited love, pined like 'Patience on a monument, / Smiling at grief' (2. 4. 114–15). Excessively romantic Orsino has earlier resorted to a stock Petrarchan metaphor by comparing his heart, wracked by desires, to a deer (or 'hart') pursued by 'fell and cruel hounds' (1. 1. 20–1).[20] But it is Viola who must endure a silent emotional death if she can never reveal her deep love for the Duke.

Romeo and Juliet is the only play of Shakespeare's that actually refers to Petrarch. The context is clearly one of mockery. Mercutio, taunting his friend for being love-sick, not knowing that Romeo has fallen deeply in love with Juliet, declares 'Now is he for the numbers that Petrarch flow'd in. Laura to his lady was a kitchen wench (marry, she had a better love to berhyme her)' (2. 4. 39–41).[21] Mercutio has creatively derided Romeo's masochism in love when he refers to his friend as 'already dead, stabb'd with a white wench's black eye; run through the ear with a love-song' (13–15). Indeed the play begins by parodying the posturing figure of the Petrarchan lover before Romeo and Juliet transform standard poetic devices into a vehicle that can express their energising passion; the freshness of their celestial imagery injects emotional life into what had become a stale convention.[22]

It is in the play's opening scene that Romeo, introduced as 'the topos of the languishing lover',[23] appears merely to be cultivating sexual longing. His cousin Benvolio sets the tone. Aping the love-sick persona of Petrarch's sonnet (Canzone 35), who wishes to be 'concealed from other men' ('*celata altrui*', 11), Benvolio seeks solitude in the 'covert of the wood' (1. 1. 125). Romeo's father, Montague, intensifies this image of the melancholy lover by recounting how his son, adding his tears to the morning dew, 'steals home' at dawn and 'Shuts up his windows, locks fair daylight out' (137–9) – a clear echo of Petrarch's sestina (Canzone 22), where the poet walks 'still weeping' ('*vo lagrimando*', 12) at night, cursing the time when first he 'saw the sun' (17). Not until Romeo breaks down in the Friar's cell (Act 3, scene 3), bitterly weeping because banishment from Verona will permanently separate him from Juliet, is the audience convinced that this lover is able to feel grief keenly.

Challenged by Benvolio to confide the cause of his sadness in the play's opening scene, Romeo resorts to amplifying love in a medley of oxymorons – 'heavy lightness, serious vanity', a 'Feather of lead, bright smoke, cold fire, sick health' (1. 1. 178, 180). Although he claims to 'feel' this love, Romeo seems detached, fancifully portraying love as an external phenomenon by spinning ingenious variations on the paradoxical style. The effect is humorous, signalled by Romeo's question to his friend: 'Dost thou not laugh?' Benvolio's rejoinder, 'No coz, I rather weep' (183) parodies the way that the Petrarchan lover feels skewered by conflicting emotions; 'I feed me in sorrow, and laugh in all my pain' is how Wyatt translates line 12 of Petrarch's famous Canzone 134 ('*Pascomi di dolor, piagendo rido*').

Where Romeo surprisingly departs from typical Petrarchan behaviour is in his frank expression of lust for Rosaline. Unlike the courtly lover, who may desire his mistress but respects her cool reserve, early in the play Romeo focuses on physical gratification. Pursuing Rosaline aggressively, he is disappointed that the object of his desire is so 'well arm'd' with chastity that she cannot be bribed to 'ope her lap to saint-seducing gold' (1. 1. 210–14). Romeo's determination to conquer Rosaline sexually contrasts sharply with Petrarch's sonnet (Canzone 140), translated by Wyatt as 'The long love that in my thought doth harbor'.[24] Here, although the poet-lover's sexual desire 'presseth with bold pretence' (3–4), he retreats when his beloved 'With [his] hardiness takes displeasure'. He switches from sexual frustration to 'reason, shame, and reverence' after his mistress rebukes him (line 7 of Wyatt's version).[25]

Romeo's coarseness changes to reverence, however, when he falls deeply in love with Juliet at first sight. He still feels sexual desire. But the exchange he initiates when he dances with Juliet at the Capulets' ball testifies to his humble adoration; it combines sensuality with delicate feeling. In a clever interweaving of religious conceits – standard Petrarchan fare – with reminders of the lover's body (hands and lips), Romeo envisages Juliet's hand as a 'holy shrine' that his pilgrim's rough fingers may profane or, if she accepts his 'mannerly devotion', that his lips may kiss (1. 5. 94–8): 'O then, dear saint, let lips do what hands do!' (103). Juliet offers no bashful resistance; this young woman is no Laura. Instead she's content to grant Romeo's prayer and take the 'sin' from his lips (107), a sin he then contrives to steal back in a second kiss. Their developing attraction is negotiated within the formal constraints of a sonnet; the lovers exchange lines in the third quatrain and split the couplet between them before Romeo concocts an extra quatrain as an opportunity to kiss his beloved again. Whereas the Petrarchan sonnet is frequently a 'testament to the separation of lovers' or to male desire that must be deferred, the sonnet embedded in this ritual of courtship celebrates reciprocal desire. As Roger Stilling notes, it fosters 'mutuality and exchange of emotion'[26] between the lovers.

Romeo has already taken Petrarchan imagery to new heights with his spontaneous response to first glimpsing Juliet: 'O she doth teach the torches to burn bright!' (44). In herself she represents more than light; she creates radiance around her. In the balcony scene Romeo's expression of romantic adoration intensifies when simile is absorbed into metaphor. Juliet is not just like the sun, she *is* the sun, as in Petrarch's sonnet, Canzone 248, where Laura alone is a sun (*'ch'è sola un sol'*, 3). And if it is still night, then Juliet's sparkling eyes and even the 'brightness of her cheek' will shame the stars and fool the birds into thinking that dawn has already broken (2. 2. 2, 19). Celebrated as 'dear saint' and 'bright angel' by Romeo (55, 26), Juliet is equally reverential towards her beloved, almost to the point of blasphemy when she calls Romeo the 'god' of her 'idolatry' (114). Moreover she continues to defy the stereotype of an aloof Petrarchan mistress. Dismissing conventional 'compliment', she readily admits to Romeo that she is 'too fond' (2. 2. 89, 98)[27] and offers 'all' of herself to him even before he requests her 'faithful vow' (50, 127). As Romeo explains to the Friar in the following scene, Juliet fully reciprocates his love and 'Doth grace for grace and love for love allow' (2. 3. 86).

Juliet's invocation to night, as she waits impatiently to consummate her marriage, also breaks with stereotype; she becomes less the reluctant bride than the eager lover. Traditionally the thwarted male longs for an eternal night in the arms of his mistress, the *'sol una notte'* that Petrarch briefly imagines in his sestina (Canzone 22, 33). In Juliet's speech it is the female who takes on that role when she calls on 'civil night', a 'sober-suited matron all in black', to

> Hood my unmann'd blood, bating in my cheeks,
> With thy black mantle . . .
> Come, gentle night; come, loving, black-brow'd night;
> Give me my Romeo . . . (3. 2. 10–21)

Juliet is both 'modest and desirous'.[28] While she personifies dark night as sheltering her maidenly modesty (like a 'sober-suited matron' or a falconer covering her 'unmann'd blood'), she trusts that protective night will become an enabler of passion, 'loving' and 'love-performing' (20, 5). From there Juliet segues into a heightened tribute to her lover that surprises with its originality. Romeo, more conventionally, has imagined that his mistress's sun-like brightness can shame the stars and dispel night's darkness. Juliet's fantasy, though, extends beyond her lover's mortal existence[29] to invite night, when Romeo dies, to take him and 'cut him out in little stars'. Fashioned into a dazzling constellation,[30] Romeo would 'make the face of heaven so fine' that no one would pay attention to the 'garish sun' during the day but would opt for starlight instead. As a result, 'all the world will be in love with night' (22–5).

Overall Juliet is the one who renounces hackneyed Petrarchan conceits. Whereas Romeo, playing the traditional lover, opens the balcony scene by idealising her physical beauty, Juliet expresses in simpler language the generous abundance of her love: 'the more I give to thee, / The more I have' (2. 2. 133–4). Only when she briefly reacts in horror to the news that Romeo has killed her cousin Tybalt does Juliet resort to the kind of tortured oxymorons through which Romeo earlier conveyed his adolescent pining for love. After denouncing Romeo as 'fiend angelical', Juliet moves into the awkward wordplay of raven/ravening in 'Dove-feather'd raven! wolvish-ravening lamb' (3. 2. 75–6). These static antitheses are an aberration, however; Juliet's rejection of her husband lacks emotional authenticity. As soon as the Nurse concurs with 'Shame come to Romeo!' (90), Juliet quickly defends him again. The play's action, too, foregoes stasis as it rushes ahead into tragedy. The Petrarchan convention of languishing in love becomes (in Rosalie Colie's phrase) 'unmetaphored by action'[31] as the lovers leap from romantic longing into fully consummated desire. Jolted by the discovery that Romeo is a Montague – 'My only love sprung from my only hate!' (1. 5. 138) – Juliet experiences firsthand the painful paradoxes within which the conventional Petrarchan lover often remains trapped.

In the early comedies, composed before 1600, Shakespeare often uses a different device; he punctures the stereotype of the romantic lover through the jests of a Clown or an ironic commentator. Speed, the 'clownish servant' of Valentine in *Two Gentlemen of Verona*, satirises the 'marks' that show his master is in love: 'to sigh, like a schoolboy that had lost his A B C; to weep, like a young wench that had buried her grandam ... to speak puling, like a beggar at Hallowmas' (2. 1. 19–26). Matching the lover's habits of sighing, weeping and whimpering with the more commonplace practices of schoolboys, wenches and beggars helps to demystify the esoteric behaviour of those who purport to be in love. Meanwhile Launce, Proteus's servant, mocks the Petrarchan lover's penchant for tears. He first chastises his dog, Crab, for failing to weep (the 'cruel-hearted cur' did not 'shed one tear' at parting from Launce's family (2. 3. 9–10)) and then claims, with excessive Petrarchan hyperbole, that 'if the river were dry, I am able to fill it with my tears; if the wind were down, I could drive the boat with my sighs' (51–4). In *Love's Labour's Lost* Moth, servant to the grandiose Armado, also deflates the affected posturing of the romantic lover through homely comparisons ('a rabbit on a spit' or a man depicted in an everyday pose) when he advises his master to 'sigh a note and sing a note ... with your arms crossed on your thin[-bellied] doublet like a rabbit on a spit; or your hands in your pocket like a man after the old painting' (3. 1. 13–14, 18–21).

As You Like It, which ultimately celebrates romance, features several characters who seize the opportunity to satirise conventional approaches to love. The court jester Touchstone, who knows that 'all nature in love [is] mortal in folly' (2. 4. 55–6), brings the romantic lovers Rosalind and Orlando down to earth while also deflating the passion of Silvius, the besotted shepherd from pastoral convention. As libertine turned cynic, Jaques is not to be outdone; he mocks the hackneyed sentiments in which Orlando clothes his beloved when he enquires 'have you not been acquainted with goldsmiths' wives, and conn'd them out of rings?' (3. 2. 270–2). In an amusing case of biter bit, the disdainful shepherdess Phoebe mercilessly taunts her devoted swain Silvius just before she herself falls in love with Rosalind as Ganymede. Her satire draws on the Petrarchan idea that women's eyes have the power to devastate, even kill their admirers:

> Now I do frown on thee with all my heart,
> And if mine eyes can wound, now let them kill thee . . .
> Or if thou canst not, O, for shame, for shame,
> Lie not, to say mine eyes are mur[d]erers! (3. 5. 15–19)

The same extravagant courtly conceit, that the lady with her beautiful eyes can be an 'executioner', is exploited by the cynical Bastard in *King John*. Riffing off Lewis's adulation of Lady Blanch's 'eye', the Bastard uses a grisly metaphor to underscore the absurdity of claiming that a lover can be hung, drawn and quartered by his mistress's physical beauty:

> Drawn in the flattering table of her eye!
> Hang'd in the frowning wrinkle of her brow!
> And quartered in her heart! (2. 1. 504–6)

In *As You Like It* the most serious and sustained critique of the Petrarchan love convention comes from the heroine Rosalind herself when she undertakes to educate the love-sick Orlando. Disguised as Ganymede she explains that the 'marks' of a 'man in love' are a 'lean cheek' and a 'beard neglected' (3. 2. 369–75) – signs she fails to see in Orlando. In a mounting series of parallel adjectival structures she tells him 'your hose should be <u>un</u>garter'd, your bonnet <u>un</u>banded, your sleeves <u>un</u>button'd, your shoe <u>un</u>tied, and every thing about you demonstrating a careless desolation' (378–81). While seeming to advise Orlando to cultivate this Petrarchan persona – flaunting how hopelessly in love he is by looking so dishevelled – Rosalind succeeds in exposing the inauthenticity of such posturing.

More often, Rosalind as Ganymede counters Orlando's heady

romanticism with heavy doses of realism. Her impersonation of a worldly wise young male frees her to express down-to-earth, even cynical views on love that would be difficult to convey were she speaking in her own character as Orlando's revered mistress.[32] It enables her to introduce bawdy humour to deflate his Petrarchan seriousness, as when she puns on the spurned lover being put out – not 'out of his apparel' (as he might wish) but 'out of his [love] suit' (4. 1. 86–7). Using her persona as a misogynistic youth to project the 'giddy offenses' of a contrary mistress (3. 2. 349) – dual gender roles that the boy actor playing Rosalind can negotiate – Rosalind/Ganymede demolishes Orlando's 'hopelessly romantic notion of wooing'.[33] Inoculating her admirer against unrealistic expectations about love and the female he desires, she warns him that women can be 'changeable . . . shallow, inconstant' creatures, not celestial goddesses (3. 4. 411–12). When Orlando melodramatically says he will 'die' if rejected by his Rosalind (4. 1. 93), she is quick to debunk the idea. Not even 'patterns of love' like Troilus or Leander have ever done so, for 'men have died from time to time, and worms have eaten them, but not for love' (100, 106–8). Disillusioning this Petrarchan idealist about marriage, the end point of courtship, Rosalind reminds him that married love is just as likely to last 'a day' as forever: 'maids are May when they are maids, but the sky changes when they are wives' (146–9). When Orlando protests that a married Rosalind would not be fickle or shrewish, she counters that he might find his wife's 'wit' going to his neighbour's bed (168–9). Rather than marrying 'a remote Petrarchan beauty'[34] he will be taking on a flesh-and-blood woman whose mercurial temperament and sexual needs must be respected. Living in a romantic bubble, she warns love-struck Orlando, will not prepare him for the challenges of marriage.

    Rosalind the realist takes on the role of satirist to educate her lover. In *Love's Labour's Lost* Berowne, who has boasted about being 'love's whip' in the past, continues to draw on his gift for satirical mockery even after he falls prey to desire. Lambasting 'Dan Cupid' as 'Regent of love-rhymes' and 'Th' anointed sovereign of sighs and groans' (3. 1. 181–2), the 'critic' Berowne understands well that the condition of love is as urgently sexual as it is spiritual; he hails the god of love as 'Dread prince of plackets, king of codpieces' (184). Yet in pursuing Rosaline he resigns himself to the conventional role of Petrarchan lover, forced to 'love, write, sigh, pray, sue, groan' as Cupid's revenge for his disparagement of love in the past (204). His character foreshadows that of another confirmed bachelor turned lover: Benedict in *Much Ado about Nothing*. A 'profess'd tyrant' toward the female sex (1. 1. 169), Benedict has railed against romantic coupling. He cultivates this witty, anti-Petrarchan stance until he falls in love with Beatrice and then must extricate himself from his earlier resolve to remain a bachelor; amusingly he rationalises that 'When I said I would die a bachelor, I did not think I should live till I were married'. Moreover he justifies his new position, his retreat from being love's critic, by reminding the audience of what underpins the conventions of courtship – the mating urge. He should marry, he argues, because 'the world must be peopled' (2. 3. 242–4).

None of Shakespeare's romantic comedies debunk the Petrarchan convention as thoroughly as does *Troilus and Cressida*. The play goes beyond incidental satire, or the ironic commentary of self-aware lovers such as Berowne or Rosalind, to demolish romance on a broader scale by collapsing love into sex. In the opening scene Pandarus devalues Troilus's high-flown discourse on the 'cruel battle' of Petrarchan torment (1. 1. 3) by equating seduction with preparing and baking a 'cake' (23–6). Scurrilous Thersites likewise reduces to sexual fetishism Troilus's passionate vow to strike down Diomedes for wearing on his helmet the glove Troilus gave as a love-token to Cressida: 'He'll tickle it for his concupy' (5. 2. 177).

In *Romeo and Juliet* Shakespeare provides a more sustained structural counterpoint to Petrarchan idealism. He creates two comic characters, the Nurse and Mercutio, whose function is to offer salient reminders – to the main protagonists as well as to the wider audience – about the sex drive, the urgent 'will', that underlies romantic aspirations. The first words of the Nurse, entering with Juliet, are 'Now by my maidenhead at twelve year old' (1. 3. 2). Focused on sex, she garrulously relates the story of Juliet's tumble as an infant, which ends with the bawdy punchline 'Thou wilt fall backward when thou hast more wit', capped by Juliet's apparent agreement, 'Ay' (42–4). Since women 'grow by men' (95), the Nurse is eager to recommend as husband for Juliet whichever male is at hand. Paris is a 'very flower' (78) until Romeo emerges as the favoured suitor. Then Romeo is the one who can boast a 'body . . . past compare' as the Nurse catalogues Romeo's physical attributes – his face, leg, hand and foot (2. 5. 40–3) – in a parody of the Petrarchan lover's *blason*. She relishes the idea that the newly married Juliet will 'Bear the bur[d]en soon at night' (76). And when she visits the Friar's cell and urges dejected Romeo to 'stand, and you be a man', she cannot help piling on phallic suggestiveness with 'For Juliet's sake . . . rise and stand!', followed by a double entendre on vaginal penetration: 'Why should you fall into so deep an O?' (3. 3. 88–90). Since she believes one male body can simply replace another, the Nurse switches back to favouring Juliet's first suitor as soon as Capulet insists that his daughter wed Paris. 'O he's a lovely gentleman!' proclaims the Nurse; 'Romeo's a dishclout to him' (3. 5. 218–19). If Juliet can have no sexual 'use' of Romeo, it is better, argues the Nurse, for her to be 'happy' in a 'second match' (222).

The Nurse's comic role in underlining the sexual component of love, deflating the pretensions of romance, becomes less relevant as the tragedy progresses. Juliet's 'Gallop apace, you fiery-footed steeds' speech (3. 2. 1–31) shows how the young wife needs no reminding that physical consummation is the capstone of love. Juliet's passion for Romeo has moved her far beyond the Nurse's coarsely pragmatic advice to jettison the banished husband and take a new sexual partner. It is the Nurse's failure to apprehend Juliet's unwavering emotional and spiritual commitment to Romeo that propels the young woman into maturity. Rejecting her shallow companion as 'wicked fiend' (3. 5. 235), Juliet boldly adopts the Friar's bold plan to fake her death and thereby avoid marriage to Paris.

Adolescent Romeo may initially need more grounding than Juliet does. His close friend Mercutio serves as the opposing voice to bring Romeo down to earth, to shake him out of his affectation. Despite his tribute to romantic imagination in the early Queen Mab speech, Mercutio's dramatic function is to inject earthy realism into the whole business of romantic love through bawdy wit. The irony is that once Romeo has acknowledged Juliet, not Rosaline, as his beloved with 'Did my heart love till now?' (1. 5. 52), he no longer needs Mercutio's ribbing; by the end of Act 1 Romeo has already dropped his Petrarchan posturing. Still, Mercutio continues to mock romantic aspiration until his death in Act 3. While his irreverent, frankly sexual approach to love, unlike the corrosive voices in *Troilus and Cressida*, never seriously undermines the lovers' passionate idealism, it provides an important counterweight to it.[35]

When Mercutio first enters in Act 1, scene 4 it is not only to mock the self-indulgent Romeo but to spoof the whole notion of suffering for love. He would like his friend to 'dance' (13). But Romeo, even more crippled than the lover in Petrarch's Sonnet 134 – the third line of which Wyatt translates as 'I fly above the wind, yet can I not arise' – claims that he cannot 'soar' with Cupid's 'light feathers' or 'bound a pitch above dull woe' (20–1). To Romeo's masochistic 'Love pricks like thorn' Mercutio retorts, with bawdy innuendo, 'Prick love for pricking, and you beat love down' (25, 28). Pursuing Romeo after the ball, he caricatures his friend as 'humors! madman! passion! lover!' (2. 1. 7) and then, mistakenly believing that Rosaline is still the object of Romeo's desire, he imagines conjuring her up. In a lewd parody of the Petrarchan sonneteer who anatomises his mistress in a *blason* of his lady's physical attributes (centring on her eyes, lips, complexion and hair), Mercutio progresses from Rosaline's 'bright eyes' and 'scarlet lip' to praising her 'fine foot, straight leg, and quivering thigh, / And the demesnes that there adjacent lie' (17–20). Even more grossly, punning on 'spirit' as erection or semen, and 'circle' as vagina, he conjectures how Romeo could

> raise a spirit in his mistress' circle,
> Of some strange nature, letting it there stand
> Till she had laid it and conjur'd it down (2. 1. 24–6)

He follows this with an even more explicit reference to love hitting 'the mark', if Rosaline were 'an open[-arse]'[36] and Romeo a 'pop'rin pear' (32–8). While Mercutio's ribaldry answers to Romeo's earlier crude wish for Rosaline to 'ope her lap' for him, it is completely at odds with the worshipful love sonnet Romeo has created with Juliet in the previous scene.

Mercutio is off-track again when he encounters Romeo in Act 2, scene 4. Finding him ripe for the 'numbers that Petrarch flow'd in', he mocks his friend not only for being 'stabb'd with a white wench's black eye' but for being sexually tormented too: 'O flesh, flesh, how art thou fishified' (37–9). When Romeo joins in his friend's word games, indulging in some 'broad' humour on 'goose' as prostitute (76–87), Mercutio thinks he has succeeded in jolting Romeo out of his love-sickness: 'Why, is not this better now than groaning for love? Now art thou sociable, now art thou Romeo' (88–90). For Mercutio, being 'sociable' means being jovial in the company of male friends rather than pursuing a degrading romantic attachment. Maddened by desire, preoccupied merely with sexual conquest, 'this driveling love', says the cynical Mercutio, 'is like a great natural [fool] that runs lolling up and down to hide his ba[u]ble in a hole' (91–3). One sex-obsessed character responds to another as Mercutio, identifying the Nurse as a 'bawd', bids her good afternoon with the ribald greeting 'the bawdy hand of the dial is now on the prick of noon' (130, 112–13).

Just as Juliet grows to despise the Nurse's crude equation of love with lust, so Mercutio's coarse satire on Petrarchan love becomes irrelevant to Romeo as soon as he is committed to Juliet. Once the hero is no longer an adolescent who wants to joke about sexual desire, the tone of the play shifts accordingly. And when Mercutio's sexual aggression finds an outlet not in outrageous wordplay but in fatal swordplay against Tybalt in Act 3, his death propels the play into tragedy, away from any possibility of a romantic outcome for the 'death-mark'd' lovers.

In the first half of *Romeo and Juliet*, at least, the Nurse and Mercutio provide salutary reminders of the sexual impulse that underlies romance. Several of Shakespeare's early comedies offer a similar emphasis by counterpointing aristocratic couples with lovers lower down the social scale, characters who foreground the earthy side of desire.³⁷ *The Comedy of Errors* establishes this pattern when the servant Dromio of Syracuse, mistaken for his twin brother from Ephesus, is pursued by the obese kitchen maid Luce. Ironically, this happens shortly after the Syracusan Antipholus addresses Luce's upper-class counterpart, Luciana, as 'more than earth divine' and his 'sole earth's heaven' (3. 2. 32, 64). If Luciana is spiritual essence, Luce is all flesh. The astounded Dromio marvels at her 'very reverend body', which is 'all grease', and bawdily finds out 'countries' in her 'globe' that include the 'low' Netherlands (90, 96, 114–15, 139). While Luce seems to him a 'beastly creature' in her overt sexuality, or a 'witch' because she can identify hidden marks on his body (88, 144), Dromio's master Antipholus remains incorrigibly romantic. Despite his 'earthy gross' apprehension, Antipholus is compelled to wonder, like the conventional Petrarchan lover, if Luciana is a 'god' (34, 39).

In *Two Gentlemen of Verona* the comic servant Launce, not to be left out of the love fest, confesses that he is in love with a 'milkmaid'. While admitting she may not actually be a virgin (maid), he finds in her 'more qualities than a water spaniel' and judges her superior to a horse because she can both 'fetch' and 'carry' (3. 1. 272–5). These bestial comparisons are a far cry from Launce's master Proteus envisaging Silvia, in Petrarchan fashion, as a 'celestial sun' (2. 6. 10). Suitors, it appears, tailor their expressions of desire to a female's social status. While sexually available kitchen hands and milkmaids in the comedies are often demeaned as animals, aristocratic lovers revere their mistresses as angels or goddesses.

One important role of Armado in *Love's Labour's Lost* is to parody the lords' linguistic excess with his own muddled 'Sweet smoke of rhetoric' (3. 1. 63). But this 'fantastical' Spanish braggart is also a 'child of fancy' (1. 1. 170); he falls as readily into sexual infatuation, or what he calls 'the humor of affection' (1. 2. 60), as he does into affectation. After Armado sees the clown Costard wooing the country wench Jaquenetta, she becomes the object of his desire – a pursuit in which Armado becomes the ridiculous counterpart of the lords who are busy courting aristocratic ladies. Puffed up with his own self-image, Armado justifies his decline into 'love' for a low-born woman with a pompous syllogism: 'as it is base for a soldier to love, so am I in love with a base wench' (1. 2. 58–9). If 'Cupid's buttshaft is too hard for Hercules' club', reasons Armado in a strained analogy, then a 'Spaniard's rapier' will not make a dent in it (175–7). Pedantically he goes on to grade Jaquenetta's lowliness by absurdly building up, through grammatical comparative and superlative, to the supreme baseness of his mistress's foot: 'I do affect the very ground (which is base) where she (which is baser) guided by her foot (which is basest) doth tread' (167–9).

In choosing to idolise a woman who is the very opposite of the remote Petrarchan lady, Armado turns the whole convention upside down. Resolving to play the romantic lover by cultivating melancholy and praising his beloved's complexion as 'most immaculate red and white' (1. 2. 90–1), he nevertheless treats Jaquenetta as a social inferior to be conquered sexually. Despite claiming to be the 'heroical vassal' of a woman who is hyperbolically and tautologically a 'More fairer than fair' woman (4. 1. 64, 62), Armado the *miles gloriosus* presents himself as an aggressive warrior rather than a Petrarchan devotee. The tone of his letter to her is far from reverential. Modelling his courtship on a garbled version of Caesar's famous *veni, vidi, vici*, he uses the formal technique of catechism to reply, pretentiously, to his own questions:

> Shall I command thy love? I may. Shall I enforce thy love? I could. Shall I entreat thy love? I will. What shalt thou exchange for rags? robes; for tittles? titles; for thyself? me. (80–3)

In view of his threat to 'enforce' love, it's not surprising to learn (from Costard in Act 5) that Jaquenetta is 'two months' pregnant with Armado's child (5. 2. 672–3) – an earthy reminder of the end result of desire. Aping the lords and going one better in the play's finale, this would-be romantic lover vows to be put on trial. Rather than confining himself for a year to a remote hermitage, as the king will do, the Spaniard plans to labour in a rural setting, where he will serve Jaquenetta and (with a double entendre) 'hold the plough for her sweet love three year' (883–4). Armado's planned service to his beloved – one that does not ignore sex – counters, even calls into question, the lords' more rarefied quest.

Touchstone, the jester of *As You Like It*, also shows a preference for country wenches. Like Armado chasing Jaquenetta, Touchstone promotes love in a lower key – lust rather than aspirational romantic love – when he pursues the goat-herder Audrey in the Forest of Arden. Wiser and wittier than Armado, his role is to remind other lovers in the forest that they cannot ignore the realities of sexual desire. Even before he pairs off with Audrey, Touchstone reminisces on how he once courted the milkmaid Jane Smile and, in a take-off of the delicate white hand of the Petrarchan mistress, how he kissed 'the cow's dugs that her pretty chopp'd hands had milked'. He recalls, with a pun on cods as testicles, that he once took two peapods (called peascods or 'cods') and pretended to woo Jane by asking her to wear them for him (2. 4. 49–52). Touchstone's parody is prompted by Silvius, the pastoral lover who boasts of feeling more 'passion' than down-to-earth shepherd Corin ever did (41). More pointedly, Touchstone deflates Orlando's romantic pretensions when he parodies verses celebrating the 'fair, the chaste, and unexpressive she' that Orlando, turned Petrarchan sonneteer, has pinned on forest trees (3. 2. 10). Touchstone jabs back at this lover's conventional couplet, 'All the pictures fairest lin'd / Are but black to Rosalind' (92–3), by underscoring the sexual motive behind any romantic quest: 'He that sweetest rose will find, / Must find love's prick and Rosalind' (111–12). His blunt 'Then to cart with Rosalind' (108), implying that Rosalind should be paraded around as a whore, debunks Orlando's over-the-top portrait of his beloved as 'the quintessence of every sprite', a perfect female 'devis'd' by 'heavenly synod' (3. 2. 139, 150).

Touchstone is refreshingly frank about his own sexual attraction, neither romantic nor intellectual, to Audrey. No conventional beauty, she's an 'ill-favor'd thing', though one he can claim as his 'own' (5. 4. 58). When she admits to being 'foul' (homely looking) but insists she is not a 'slut', he candidly hopes, lacking the Petrarchan lover's respect for chastity, that 'sluttishness may come hereafter' (3. 3. 41). Audrey rhymes with bawdry, and Touchstone's practical approach to the demands of sexual desire comes through in his couplet 'Come sweet Audrey, / We must be married, or we must live in bawdry', where the second 'we must' gains special emphasis by adding two extra syllables to the regular pentameter (96–7). Driven by the demands of the flesh, Touchstone would be happy to bypass a formal wedding ceremony in favour of speedy gratification. Yet he remains sceptical about the longevity of such desire. He rationalises that if he is married quickly by the dubious priest Sir Oliver Martext, he will have grounds to 'leave' his wife should his physical attraction to her wear thin (94).

To Jaques Touchstone justifies his need to marry as the human urge to mate, since 'man hath his desires, and as pigeons bill, so wedlock would be nibbling' (80–2). Like the clown Lavatch in *All's Well that Ends Well* who, 'driven on by the flesh', is honest about marrying to satisfy his sexual needs (1. 3. 27–9), or Parolles, who derides virginity as 'too cold a companion' (1. 1. 132), Touchstone insists on the universality of desire. By including the courtly couples in the group of 'country copulatives' about to be wed, he implies that all lovers, whatever their social rank, marry for sexual fulfilment (*As You Like It*, 5. 4. 55–6). Jaques, too, considers animal instinct rather than high-flown romanticism the basis of matrimony. Scathingly he refers to all those flocking to wed as animals 'coming to the ark', Touchstone and Audrey being just the most prominent of the 'very strange beasts' (36–7).

Touchstone is anti-romantic in the extreme; he provides a counterweight to Orlando's heady idealism and the Petrarchan worship of 'most faithful' Silvius (5. 4. 14). This doting young shepherd describes the romantic lover's passion for his mistress as

> All adoration, duty, and observance,
> All humbleness, all patience, and impatience (5. 2. 96–7)

Only the word 'impatience' is a reminder of the sexual desire that cannot always be contained within the 'humbleness' of the Petrarchan lover. Even Silvius, notes Jaques, will go to a 'long and well-deserved bed' when he finally wins Phoebe, shocked out of her infatuation with a male impersonator when Rosalind/Ganymede is unmasked as a woman (5. 4. 190). The green world of the forest, after all, is full of reminders of fertility. The huntsmen's song pays tribute to the 'lusty horn' as a phallic symbol (4. 2. 17). Later the page boys' ditty to Touchstone and Audrey, 'It was lover and his lass', celebrates how 'pretty country folk' lie 'between the acres of the rye', making love in the 'present time' because youth, like life, is short (5. 3. 22–30). Unlike the pining Petrarchan male, these country lovers refuse to defer sexual fulfilment. All too soon the literary lover that Jaques describes in the Seven Ages of Man speech as 'Sighing like a furnace' will become an old man, shuffling from ardour to 'mere oblivion' (2. 7. 148, 165). Touchstone's commitment to seizing the moment with Audrey is echoed higher up the social scale in the swift pairing of Celia and Oliver near the end of the play, lovers who cannot wait to 'enjoy' each other. As Rosalind remarks, they will climb the 'stairs to marriage ... incontinent [immediately], or else be [sexually] incontinent before marriage' (5. 2. 4, 38–9). In the final marriage ceremony the uniting of all the couples by the pagan god Hymen[38] is a reminder of the physical consummation that follows a successful courtship.

Gratiano, who weds the maid Nerissa when Bassanio marries her mistress Portia in *The Merchant of Venice*, also counters his master's romantic aspirations with a more grounded approach to love. Gratiano is a sceptic when it comes to romance; he would rather 'play the fool' and 'heat' his liver with wine than act the part of a Petrarchan lover who cools his heart with 'mortifying groans' (1. 1. 79–82). Like the jester Touchstone, he emphasises how quickly desire fades, noting, when Lorenzo is late for his planned elopement with Jessica, that all things 'Are with more spirit chased than enjoy'd' (2. 6. 13). As Bassanio's foil, Gratiano offsets his master's courtly wooing with frank sensuality. Bassanio may start as a debt-ridden opportunist, adventuring for 'richly left' Portia (1. 1. 161) and valuing her 'sunny locks' as a lucrative 'golden fleece' to be won (169–70), but by the time he chooses the lead casket, discarding the world's love of 'ornament' (3. 2. 74), he has transformed into an adoring Petrarchan lover. Finding Portia's picture inside the casket, Bassanio embarks on a traditional *blason* of his lady's physical beauty; he praises the depiction of her lips 'Parted with sugar-breath' and the 'golden mesh' of her hair before turning to her amazing eyes (3. 2. 119–22). Like Berowne stunned by Rosaline's ocular power ('O but her eye!' (*Love's Labour's Lost*, 4. 3. 9)), Bassanio wonders how the painter, presumably struck blind by the beauty of just one of Portia's eyes, could 'see to do them' both (124). His love, though, is spiritual as well as physical. Chastened by Portia in the final scene, Bassanio swears by his 'soul' – no longer by his lady's 'fair eyes' – that he will always be true to her (5. 1. 242, 247).

It is his servant who stays on the level of appearance. Gratiano manifests the superficial 'fancy' that is defined in song as 'engendered in the eyes' (3. 2. 63–7) when he recounts his sudden passion for Nerissa: 'My eyes, my lord, could look as swift as yours: / You saw the mistress, I beheld the maid' (197–8). And whereas Bassanio recognises the serious implications of giving away his betrothal ring, even as a reward to the young lawyer (Portia-Balthazar) who saved Antonio's life, Gratiano fails to respect the significance of Nerissa's equivalent token. Blind to the fact that the 'little scrubbed boy' to whom he delivered the token was his own wife in disguise, he calls it a 'paltry ring' (5. 1. 162, 147). When the women briefly trick their new husbands into believing that they have just slept with the lawyer and his clerk, it is Gratiano who focuses on the sexual indignity of the situation, threatening to 'mar the young clerk's pen', expressing male outrage when he demands to know 'are we cuckolds ere we have deserv'd it?' (265). His very last words in the play focus on the physical side of marriage. Waiving the reverential attitude of the Petrarchan lover, Gratiano hopes that Nerissa will agree to 'go to bed now, being two hours to day'. Then, with a pun on 'ring' as vagina, he swears that he will henceforth dedicate himself to 'keeping safe Nerissa's ring' (303–7).

As a tragicomic romance, *The Winter's Tale* returns to the strategy of the earlier comedies, balancing aristocratic wooing, Florizel's reverential courtship of Perdita, with the more urgent quest for physical gratification lower down the social scale. The rogue Autolycus is the first to introduce the idea of sexual freedom. A demoted courtier, now a Bohemian vagrant making a living by picking pockets and selling trinkets, Autolycus is not tied to one class or to one woman. While Touchstone, who also segues from court to country, chooses to satisfy the sexual imperative by marrying rustic Audrey, Autolycus remains happily promiscuous. Celebrating 'tumbling in the hay' with his whores, he reminds the audience in his opening song that 'the red blood reigns in the winter's pale' and not just in the 'sweet o' the year' (*The Winter's Tale*, 4. 3. 12, 3–4). Later, at the sheep-shearing fair, he bawdily offers to sell maids what they 'lack from head to heel', dildo-like 'Pins and poking-sticks of steel' (4. 4. 226–7). One of the ribald ballads he touts, the tale of a woman 'turn'd into a cold fish' when she 'would not exchange flesh with one that lov'd her' (279–80), warns about the penalties of sexual abstinence – the strict chastity expected of the Petrarchan mistress.

Autolycus's peddling of his wares and ballads at the festival is interrupted by a version of the mating game that is anything but courtly. The Young Shepherd (the Clown) is caught between two rustic females, Mopsa and Dorcas, who both lay claim to him. Nearly sixteen years after the arrival of the infant Perdita the Clown is still unmarried. Now the shepherdesses wrangle spitefully about what he has 'promis'd' them, Mopsa implying that the Clown has favoured Dorcas, perhaps even made her pregnant if (as she claims) 'he has paid you more, which will shame you to give him again' (4. 4. 239–41). Whereas Florizel is chastely committed to the one woman he loves with 'reason' as well as 'affection' (481–2), the Young Shepherd has clearly spread around his sexual favours. Soon after Autolycus encourages Mopsa and Dorcas to vent their frustration by joining him in the song 'Two maids wooing a man', there's a fresh eruption of sexuality into the pastoral scene. Twelve shepherds who have made themselves into 'men of hair' perform the dance of the satyrs.

These three strands of action – Autolycus selling his knick-knacks and lewd ballads, rival shepherdesses quarrelling over the Clown, and the dance of the satyrs (342) – all emphasise sexual desire above romance. Embellished with song and dance, this part of the sheep-shearing scene (about 160 lines of text) might take up twenty minutes of stage time before the action returns to what frames it: Prince Florizel's heightened courtship of Perdita as he moves toward a formal betrothal. Certainly the prince emulates a Petrarchan lover in wooing his chaste mistress. Sensing Princess Perdita's inborn gentility despite her upbringing as a rustic, Florizel praises her in elaborate hyperbole; he compares Perdita's dazzlingly 'white' hand to an 'Ethiopian's tooth, or the fann'd snow' (363–4). But the authenticity of Florizel's passion, the sense that the two chaste lovers are soul-mates, is expressed more convincingly in his unvarnished declaration to Perdita when they are alone: 'I cannot be / Mine own, nor any thing to any if / I be not thine' (43–5). His tribute to his beloved's natural grace, beginning 'What you do / Still betters what is done' (135–46), trades on superlatives, causing the realist Perdita to remark that his 'praises' are 'too large' (147). Still, Florizel's allusions to

Perdita's singular grace in performing her everyday activities – buying and selling or giving alms – take his speech far beyond any conventional *blason* or catalogue of praise. Because this couple anticipates the 'nuptial' that they 'have sworn will come' (50–1), their love is already infused with realism; they are not just playing courtly games, nor do they crave gaudy love-tokens, the 'trifles' sold by Autolycus. Whether it is Florizel disguised as a shepherd, comparing himself to gods in sexual pursuit of mortals – he notes that even Jupiter 'Became a bull and bellow'd' (28) – or Perdita candidly imagining her beloved on 'a bank, for love to lie and play on' (130), it's clear that romantic idealisation has not effaced sexual desire. The rustic entertainment that surrounds the couple foregrounds libido. But just as Mercutio's bawdy insistence on sex becomes irrelevant once Romeo and Juliet prepare to consummate their 'true-love passion' (*Romeo and Juliet*, 2. 2. 104), so Florizel and Perdita do not need constant reminders of the sexual nature of love. Their wooing shows how erotic love, expressed as rapturous adoration, fully acknowledges the essential nature of the loved one, so 'singular in each particular' (144). Thus Florizel celebrates not only Perdita's 'bodily presence' but 'a moral life that is entirely hers'.[39]

Offering a contrast to heightened expressions of romantic love, several of Shakespeare's comedies show courtly males and females engaging in witty banter that is ripe with sexual innuendo. These bawdy exchanges are decidedly anti-Petrarchan, a further reminder of the realities that underlie courtship. Clever wordplay among aristocrats constitutes a kind of verbal fencing match in which erotic energy is channelled into language games. Such double entendre also permits what William C. Carroll calls 'the eruption of female sexuality into ordinary utterance';[40] it acknowledges that women are not the ethereal creatures envisaged by male Petrarchan lovers but are as sexually aware as their suitors – an awareness they can express through witty repartee while protecting themselves against any threat of sexual aggression.

When Hamlet jests lewdly with Ophelia before the performance of 'The Mousetrap', his intention is to be cruel. Their love affair over, he has abandoned romantic courtship (the 'never doubt I love' of his letter to her (*Hamlet*, 2. 2. 119)) in favour of punishing crudeness. This is not a contest between intellectual equals. Ophelia is mortified when he asks 'Lady, shall I lie in your lap . . . I mean, my head upon your lap' (3. 2. 112–14), echoing the coarse-mannered but more jovial Hotspur, who urges his wife Kate to 'Come, quick, quick, that I may lay my head in thy lap' (*Henry IV, Part 1*, 3. 1. 227). Hamlet taunts Ophelia for interpreting his words in a bawdy sense: 'Did you think I meant country [cunt-ry] matters?' And when she replies 'I think nothing, my lord', he plays on the sense of nothing as 'no thing' or vagina with his biting retort 'that's a fair thought to lie between maid's legs' (3. 2. 116–19).

Something of the same crudeness, wilfully destroying any worshipful attitude toward the female or the civility of romance, operates in the opening exchange between 'mad-cap ruffian' Petruchio and 'curst' Kate in *The Taming of the Shrew* (2. 1. 292, 128). Petruchio's 'peremptory', unrefined manner (2. 1. 131) counters that of Lucentio, the stereotypical Petrarchan lover who falls in love with Kate's sister Bianca the moment his 'wounded eye' sees her 'coral lips' and senses her 'breath . . . perfume the air' (1. 1. 220, 174–5). In traditional fashion Lucentio laments 'I burn, I pine, I perish, . . . / If I achieve not this young modest girl' (155–6); in his first encounter with Kate, Petruchio trades barbs with her instead of romantic compliments. When Kate disparagingly refers to her suitor as a stool, an ass and a jade, Petruchio turns these insults into ribaldry. If he is a 'join'd-stool' then he feels free to invite Kate to 'sit on' him. To her rejoinder 'Asses are made to bear, and so are you' he reminds her that 'Women are made to bear, and so are you'. Playing on the secondary meaning of 'light' as wanton, Petruchio facetiously promises not to 'burden' Kate because she is young and 'light' (2. 1. 198–203). When Petruchio calls Kate a 'wasp' she warns him to 'beware [her] sting', which allows him bawdily to retort that a wasp's tongue is in its 'tail'. And although she tries to turn this around by referring to his sharp, waspish tongue, urging him to stop telling tales and leave, he is the one who caps the conversation with insulting coarseness: 'What, with my tongue in your tail?' (209–18).

Briefly Kate gains the upper hand by taunting Petruchio that his heraldic device ('crest') should be the picture of a foolish 'coxcomb'. She triumphs by branding Petruchio as a timid rooster after he offers to be 'a combless cock, so Kate will be my hen'. Still, she makes it clear that she doesn't want a sexless male – or to shun the physical side of a successful marriage – by calling him 'no cock of mine, you crow too like a craven' (225–7). This 'cock' nevertheless regains the conversational momentum with his fifteen-line speech claiming to admire her as 'passing gentle' (242); once she concedes that he has only enough 'wit' to keep himself 'warm', Petruchio again plays the anti-Petrarchan lover by turning her quip into sexual repartee:

Pet. Am I not wise?
Kath Yes, keep you warm.
Pet. Marry, so I mean, sweet Katherine, in thy bed. (265–7)

Petruchio's linguistic opportunism, taking up signifiers and turning them to his own advantage, is used with more deadly effect in Richard of Gloucester's wooing of Anne in *Richard III*. Richard's rhetorical challenge, skilfully developed through the alternating lines of stichomythia, is to convert Anne from viewing him as a 'dreadful minister of hell' to accepting him as a romantic partner in marriage (1. 2. 46). The odds are heavily against him. He has, after all, just participated in killing Anne's father-in-law (Henry VI) and her young husband Edward. At first Anne succeeds in countering his courtly accolades with insults that balance his phrases with exact antithesis. When Richard calls her 'Sweet saint' she brands him 'Foul devil' (49–50), and rather than accepting his compliment 'divine perfection of woman', she insists, in a reversal that precisely keeps the syllabic score, that he is the 'defus'd infection of a man' (75, 78). Like Petruchio, except that he avoids crude ribaldry, Richard wins the upper hand by turning the conversation to the business of lovemaking. After Anne deems him unfit for any place but a 'dungeon', his rejoinder, within the same line, is that he is more fit to lodge in her 'bedchamber' (111). Boldly he seizes on the sexual potential of the verb 'to lie':

Anne. Ill rest betide the chamber where thou liest!
Glou. So will it, madam, till I lie with you. (112–13)

As Petruchio never does, Richard goes on to refine the role of Petrarchan lover, daringly citing Anne's 'beauty' as the reason he murdered her loved ones (121). With standard hyperbole he asserts that 'Thine eyes, sweet lady, have infected mine' and now they 'kill [him] with a living death' (149, 152). Clearly much more is at stake here than taming a shrew – Richard needs to justify two murders and quickly forge a political alliance through marriage – but his technique, as 'villain' masquerading as 'lover' (1. 1. 28–30), is to use clever repartee to win his lady over sexually. In playing the game opportunistically, reproducing a rhetoric that, as Catherine Belsey notes, is 'already familiar' and 'derivative', Richard's 'impersonation'[41] of the Petrarchan lover nevertheless works; Anne proves susceptible to his hollow declaration of romantic love.

Despite being set at court and preoccupied with rhetorical decorum, *Love's Labour's Lost* is, surprisingly, bawdier than *The Taming of the Shrew*. A streak of ribaldry, even obscenity, is never far from the play's surface, reminding the audience of the physical desire that roils beneath the Petrarchan lover's exaggerated idealisation of his lady. When the King meets the Princess for the first time and declares that he does not intend to break his oath to be celibate, the Princess replies, 'will shall break it, will, and nothing else' (2. 1. 100). By inviting the secondary meaning of 'will' as sexual impulse her wordplay reveals the truth – that determination to fulfil sexual desire is what drives the males to renege on their original vow.

The ladies adeptly sharpen their wits through risqué badinage. Their repartee among themselves resembles a tennis match, or what the Princess calls 'a set of wit well play'd' (5. 2. 29). Rosaline's ribald admonition 'Look what you do, you do it still i' th' dark' leads smoothly into Katherine's 'do not you, for you are a light wench', riffing on the meaning of 'light' as sexually wanton. Rosaline deflects the insult by retorting that she is indeed 'light' – in the sense of unencumbered, not wanton – because Katherine possesses no gravity or value that might weigh down her companion (24–6). Later Maria and Rosaline engage in conversation with Boyet and Costard that rapidly turns to double entendre. Since they are hunting deer, Boyet jokes about horns, cuckoldry and marksmanship. Before he ramps up the repartee with 'Let the mark have a prick in't' (4. 1. 132), he indecently suggests that he may have 'hit' Rosaline 'lower' (118). Answering in kind, Rosaline mirrors Mercutio's ribald comment that 'If love be blind, love cannot hit the mark' (*Romeo and Juliet*, 2. 1. 33) when she quips back in song: 'Thou canst not hit it, hit it, hit it . . . my good man' (4. 1. 125–6). While she may be warding off Boyet's inappropriate advances rather than indulging in sexual innuendo for its own sake, Rosaline proves adept at this kind of parrying to defend against her suitor's romantic overtures.

Bantering with her at the opening of Act 2, Berowne complains that she is too hasty in her answer: 'You must not be so quick' (2. 1. 117). 'Quick' carries the innuendo of being pregnant, having conceived a child. It could also mean being too sexually responsive (like Mistress Quickly, the receptive bawd in the *Henry IV* plays), especially since Rosaline replies that Berowne should not 'spur' her with questions. 'Spur' is a loaded word; pregnant Hermione in *The Winter's Tale* arouses Leontes's suspicions that she is sexually loose when she innocently remarks how men may 'ride' their mates a 'thousand acres' with 'one soft kiss' before women 'with spur' will 'heat an acre' (1. 2. 94–6). Continuing the racy metaphor of riding, Berowne complains 'Your wit's too hot, it speeds too fast, 'twill tire'.[42] This allows Rosaline, now wishing to deflect his desire, to complete the rhyming couplet by hoping that he, as would-be rider, will be left 'in the mire' (*Love's Labour's Lost*, 2. 1. 119–20). Berowne further exposes the sexual layer of the conversation when he hopes that luck will 'send' Rosaline 'many lovers' (125). Soon after, claiming that his 'sick' heart needs to be bled, he manages to deflate the grandiose Petrarchan notion of being wounded by the mistress's eye by alluding to male anatomy when he asks 'Will you prick't with your eye?'. Rosaline stays grounded, giving him no encouragement when she offers to use a 'knife', not her eye, to lance his heart (185–90).

In Act 5, feeling crushed by Rosaline's biting scorn – the ladies have mocked the lords' failed masquerade as Russians – Berowne rejects verbal ostentation. Bluntly he declares, 'Peace, for I will not have to do with you' (5. 2. 428). Perhaps inadvertently, however, he lays himself open to the meaning of 'do' as to perform sexually, suggested in Rosaline's earlier 'do it still in the dark' and even more blatantly in *Troilus and Cressida*, when Cressida chides Pandarus for his post-coital mockery with 'You bring me to do – and then you flout me too' (4. 2. 26). Rosaline counters Berowne's threat to have nothing to 'do' with her with 'Nor shall not, if I do as I intend', implying that she plans to find a suitor or sexual partner elsewhere (5. 2. 429). Their sophisticated word games, skirting around the edges of sexual desire, contrast sharply with the passionate exchanges between Romeo and Juliet – young lovers who avoid any bawdiness as they move toward erotic fulfilment. One can only imagine how Rosaline would have responded to the innocent anguish of Romeo's 'O, wilt thou leave me so unsatisfied?' when Juliet bids him 'good night' in the balcony scene (*Romeo and Juliet*, 2. 2. 123–5).

Because *Much Ado about Nothing* is also a comedy about finding a suitable marriage partner, we might expect to find plenty of sexual wordplay in the 'merry war' and 'skirmish of wit' between Beatrice and Benedict (1. 1. 62–3). The scenes in which they are tricked into thinking that each has fallen madly in love with the other certainly emphasise passion rather than simply mental rapport. In Act 2, scene 3, where Benedict overhears his friends commiserating over Beatrice's 'ecstasy' (madness) of love, the men make it clear that the 'enrag'd affection' they have supposedly observed in Beatrice (100–1) is sexual in nature; they emphasise too that Beatrice's 'blood' (passion) is vying against her 'wisdom' (163). Similarly, the women tricking Beatrice into love insist that Benedict must 'wrestle' with his strong 'affection' while criticising Beatrice for being too proud to manifest such sexual 'affection' (3. 1. 42, 55).

Early in the play, however, the couple don't engage in risqué banter; they openly spurn 'enraged affection' and the demands of a committed love relationship. While Benedict fears marriage as a 'yoke' that invites a cuckold's 'horns' (1. 1. 261–3), Beatrice vows that she will never be 'overmaster'd' by a 'piece of valiant dust', a mere man (2. 1. 61). Yet both appear more vulnerable to falling in love than they will admit. Since they remain sensitive to each other's barbs, their skirmishes of wit carry a defensive edge. Benedict complains 'She speaks poniards, and every word stabs' after he overhears Beatrice calling him 'a very dull fool' (2. 1. 247–8, 137–8). Beatrice herself seems unduly angry when Benedict abruptly terminates their first witty exchange with 'But keep your way, a' God's name, I have done'. Comparing herself to a rider suddenly stalled by a skittish or tired (jaded) horse, she retorts 'You always end with a jade's trick, I know you of old' (1. 1. 142–5).

Whereas Berowne and Rosaline develop a horse-riding innuendo that ends with the rider thrown 'in the mire', it's not clear that Beatrice is making a sexual gibe here. The mutual ribbing of Beatrice and Benedict mainly avoids racy badinage;[43] instead their verbal sparring is a game of intellectual one-upmanship. Only after the intensity of Beatrice's frank confession 'I love you with so much of my heart that none is left to protest' (4. 1. 286–7), which leads to Benedict's pledge to challenge Claudio to a duel, does their banter turn more sexual in its wit. Being engaged to be married frees Benedict to jest about how the couple have transformed from sparring partners into lovers. His teasing Beatrice with 'I love thee against my will' (5. 2. 67) echoes his racy interpretation of Beatrice's 'Against my will I am sent to bid you come in to dinner' at the end of the garden scene (2. 3. 247–8). Freshly tricked into thinking that Beatrice is in love with him, Benedict chooses to find a 'double meaning' favourable to him. He interprets 'will' as sexual appetite and 'against' not in the sense of opposed to, but in its secondary meaning of anticipating something – as when Old Capulet plans to 'prepare' Juliet 'against' her 'wedding-day' with Paris (*Romeo and Juliet*, 3. 4. 32).

Since he doesn't need to court Beatrice for any length of time, Benedict never wholeheartedly assumes the role of devoted Petrarchan lover. Wittily he continues to emphasise sexual desire over ethereal romance.[44] His promise to Beatrice near the end of the play, 'I will live in thy heart, die in thy lap, and be buried in thy eyes; and moreover I will go with thee to thy uncle's' (5. 2. 102–4), builds to comic anticlimax while turning Petrarchan sentiment into sexual suggestiveness. 'Die [achieve orgasm] in thy lap' is fairly blatant, 'buried in thy eyes' less so. When Perdita in *The Winter's Tale* tells Florizel that she would like him to be 'buried' – not as a corpse but 'quick' and in her 'arms' (4. 4. 131–2) – she is expressing frank sexual desire. The intimacy of Benedict's 'buried in thy eyes' instead parodies the stock Petrarchan notion that the mistress's amazing eyes, capable of smiting down a lover, should be worshipped from a distance.

On the whole Benedict appears more comfortable trading bawdy wordplay with a social inferior than playing the Petrarchan lover with Beatrice, his dear 'lady Disdain' (1. 1. 118). He deflects some of his sexual wit on to the servant Margaret, who willingly indulges Benedict's flair for double entendre. Despite affirming she would 'have no man come over [her]', she saucily requests 'swords' to accompany the 'bucklers' (shields) with which women are endowed by nature

(5. 2. 9, 18–19). Benedict responds with more suggestive wordplay about genitalia, advising her to screw 'pikes' (spikes) firmly into these bucklers (21). Ready to sing 'Light a' love' while Hero solemnly prepares for her wedding, Margaret has privileged the physical realities of marriage above romance, jesting that Hero's heart will soon be 'heavier' by the 'weight of a man' (3. 4. 44, 26–7). And when love-sick Beatrice claims that her nose is stuffed up because of a head cold, Margaret takes up the word in its sexual sense, pretending to be shocked that Beatrice is 'a maid, and stuff'd!' (65).

Predictably, in the hierarchical society of Shakespeare's plays it is the servants who transmit much of the ribaldry – whether it's the phallic puns exchanged by Capulet's servants at the opening of *Romeo and Juliet* (1. 1. 15–29), Dromio in *A Comedy of Errors* obsessed with finding 'countries' in kitchen maid Luce's body (3. 2. 114–39), or Curtis taunting Petruchio's serving-man Grumio with being a 'three-inch fool' in *The Taming of the Shrew* (4. 1. 26). More directly than the aristocratic lovers, who dance around the end result of courtship with witty double entendres, characters from the underclass are frank about the realities of sexual desire. Like the bawdy Nurse in *Romeo and Juliet* or the wise Fool Touchstone in *As You Like It*, they counter any Petrarchan tendency to glorify human desire as a purely spiritual quest or a heightened aesthetic response to the beauty of the loved one. The body, they are quick to recognise, makes its demands even while a lover's soul may yearn toward a higher ideal.

All of Shakespeare's comedies offer some challenge to romantic idealism. The healthy scepticism projected in these plays, the insistence that sexual desire, the animal urge to mate, be recognised as part of love, doesn't necessarily cancel out the possibility of a more ideal, lasting devotion. Yet it continues to test it. Despite the happy endings (deferred only in *Love's Labour's Lost*), the audience is left to wonder whether each couple will be able to negotiate the different facets of love and transform the ideals of romance – in particular, the reverence for the mistress required by the Petrarchan convention – into a marriage between equals. For after romantic courtship, the challenge of matrimony is to move into a more grounded 'companionate love', to achieve the 'intimacy and commitment'[45] that can sustain a successful long-term bonding.

Notes

1. Phyllis Rackin, 'The Lady's Reeking Breath', in *Shakespeare and Women*, notes how freely the poet celebrates this female whose imperfect body defies

being 'sanitized by Petrarchan abstraction' (p. 106), whereas objectifying the female as 'an aggregate of impossibly idealized features ... dehumanizes her' (p. 5). William Slights, 'Bodies of Texts and Textualized Bodies in *Sejanus* and *Coriolanus*', also comments that 'By *dis*membering the beloved in order to remember her, Petrarch set the pattern for subsequent lyric poets' enumeration of idealized but often scattered female body parts – eyes, arms, hair, feet' (182).
2. In *The Body Emblazoned: Dissection and the Human Body in Renaissance Culture*, Jonathan Sawday discusses how sixteenth-century male poets competed with one another, dissecting the 'female form' through their *blasons* (p. 192). Ironically, when Olivia falls in love with Viola in the guise of Cesario she celebrates the youth likewise: 'Thy tongue, thy face, thy limbs, actions, and spirit / Do give thee fivefold blazon' (*Twelfth Night*, 1. 5. 292–3).
3. Shakespeare may be alluding to an actual competition that awarded a prize for the best *blason* elaborating on the mistress's body parts. The winner of such a competition in 1536 was the French poet Maurice Scève, who wrote a tribute to his lady's eyebrow ('blason du sourcil').
4. Maurice Charney, *Shakespeare on Love and Lust*, also finds that Shakespeare is 'both a follower and a satirist' of Petrarchan conventions (p. 9).
5. Juliet Dusinberre, Preface to the Second Edition of *Shakespeare and the Nature of Women*, p. xx.
6. George Watson, *The English Petrarchans*, p. 1.
7. There's significant overlap between the poet's symptoms and what Robert Burton, in *The Anatomy of Melancholy* (1621), cites as symptoms of 'Love-Melancholy'. Burton writes that lovers may suffer from 'want of sleep, sighing, sobbing, and lamenting' or they may 'burn and freeze' (vol. 3, pp. 135–6). Burton also envisages love in paradoxical terms, as 'a sweet bitterness, a delightful grief, a cheerful torment' (p. 141).
8. Irving Singer, 'Love in Three Italian Poets', in *The Nature of Love, Vol. 2: Courtly and Romantic*, contends that in the *Canzoniere* Petrarch remains torn between 'the sentiments of a troubadour and those of a devout Christian' (p. 131).
9. Richard B. Young, 'English Petrarke: A Study of Sidney's *Astrophil and Stella*', also notes that in this convention the lady, idealised 'both spiritually and physically', is 'always unobtainable', and that Petrarchan poetry explores 'the attitude of the lover in this static situation' (p. 10).
10. John Lyly, *Endimion*, p. 98.
11. Watson, *The English Petrarchans*, points out that only fifty of the *Canzoniere* had been translated by 1625 (p. 2).
12. In *Posthumous Love: Eros and the Afterlife in Renaissance England*, Ramie Targoff analyses how Wyatt (in the English tradition) restricts Petrarch's 'narrative of heavenly transcendence through love', instead presenting love as 'earthly and transient' (pp. 74, 77).
13. 'I find no peace and all my war is done', no. 26 in the Egerton MS 2711, in *Collected Poems of Sir Thomas Wyatt*, ed. Kenneth Muir, p. 21 (spelling modernised in all citations).
14. 'Petrarch: *The Canzoniere*', no. 3 (sonnet), in Stephen Minta, *Petrarch and*

Petrarchism: The English and French Traditions, p. 27. All quotations from Petrarch's *Canzoniere* are from this study and are likewise italicised.

15. Baldassare Castiglione, *The Book of the Courtier*, trans. Thomas Hoby (1561), bk. 4, pp. 312–13.
16. William C. Carroll, *The Great Feast of Language in Love's Labour's Lost*, discusses how the men in this play are 'primarily narcissistic, projecting their own desires and images' on to the women around them (p. 161). In a Lacanian analysis, Carolyn Asp, '*Love's Labour's Lost*: Language and the Deferral of Desire', finds the men trapped in what Lacan calls the Imaginary Order, which is 'basically narcissistic and sees only its own image in "others"' (5). C. L. Barber, *Shakespeare's Festive Comedy*, likewise indicts Berowne for being focused on 'what happens within the lover' rather than on the experience of love 'between two people' (p. 106).
17. M. C. Bradbrook, 'Courtier and Courtesy: Castiglione, Lyly and Shakespeare's *Two Gentlemen of Verona*', p. 173.
18. In *Desire and its Interpretation*, Lacan writes that 'distance' is necessary 'to maintain, sustain, and even preserve the dimension of desire' (p. 439) and that 'human desire is fixed ... not to an object, but always essentially to a fantasy' (p. 19).
19. Mark Breitenberg, 'Introduction', in *Anxious Masculinity in Early Modern England*, p. 30. Breitenberg analyses how Petrarchism is based on a '"necessary" contradiction' – that 'the frustration of desire impels desire itself' (p. 134).
20. Petrarch's 23rd canzone employs the same myth; after the lover Actaeon is transformed into a stag for spying on the goddess Diana, he is killed by his own hounds. Nancy J. Vickers, 'Diana Described: Scattered Woman and Scattered Rhyme', discusses how in Petrarch's poem 'the lady is corporeally scattered; the lover is emotionally scattered' (p. 104).
21. This echoes and perhaps gives a nod of recognition to Samuel Daniel's early sonnet sequence *Delia* (1592), where Daniel admits that his poetry cannot rival that of Petrarch but claims that he is just as devoted to his lady:

    He never had more faith, although more rime.
    I love as well, though he could better show it. (Sonnet 35)

22. As Heather Dubrow comments in *Echoes of Desire: English Petrarchism and its Counterdiscourses*, Romeo and Juliet's love discourse is not defiantly anti-Petrarchan in that it 'recycle[s] some images associated with Petrarchism' (p. 266).
23. Gayle Whittier, 'The Sonnet's Body and the Body Sonnetized in *Romeo and Juliet*', p. 48.
24. In *Collected Poems*, ed. Muir, no. 4, p. 4.
25. In 'Love that liveth and reigneth in my thought', Sonnet VI in Gerald Bullett (ed.), *Silver Poets of the Sixteenth Century*, Surrey offers a franker translation of Petrarch's lines; the mistress teaches the lover to suffer 'pain' rather than pursue his 'hot desire' (p. 118).
26. Roger Stilling, '*Romeo and Juliet*', in *Love and Death in Renaissance Tragedy*, p. 78.
27. Evelyn Gajowski, *The Art of Loving: Female Subjectivity and Male Discursive Traditions in Shakespeare's Tragedies*, finds that Juliet 'tutors

Romeo in love ... making possible his metamorphosis from stereotypical Petrarchan lover to true lover' (p. 23).
28. Mary Bly, 'The Legacy of Juliet's Desire in Comedies of the Early 1600s', comments that Juliet breaks the norm by being both 'chaste and desirous' and as such is 'unsuited to the role of Romeo's Petrarchan mistress' (pp. 52, 55).
29. Juliet's imagining Romeo's death here is an example of what Jonathan Dollimore posits in *Death, Desire and Loss in Western Culture*: that death is desired because it 'arrests beauty' and pre-empts 'inevitable transience', including that of desire itself (p. 112).
30. In *Posthumous Love*, Ramie Targoff points out that whereas the play's sources project union in the next life for the lovers (just as Petrarch hopes eventually to be with Laura for eternity), Shakespeare's *Romeo and Juliet* offers no hope of an afterlife. In line with this, Juliet's elaborate conceit envisages Romeo's remains 'scattered' throughout the cosmos and not the 'resurrection' of his body (p. 114).
31. Rosalie Colie, *Shakespeare's 'Living Art'*, p. 145. G. K. Hunter, in *English Drama 1586–1642: The Age of Shakespeare*, also notes how Romeo and Juliet 'discover that Petrarchan tropes can become real experiences' (p. 444).
32. Jean E. Howard, 'Power and Eros', in *The Stage and Social Struggle in Early Modern England*, points out how Rosalind/Ganymede, by manipulating patriarchal 'representations of the feminine', is able to help her future mate, Orlando, to move beyond constricting 'ideologies of gender' (p. 119).
33. This is the view of Juliet Stevenson, who played Rosalind in a 1985 Royal Shakespeare Company production of *As You Like It*, quoted in Carol Rutter, *Clamorous Voices: Shakespeare's Women Today*, p. 105.
34. Alexander Leggatt, *Shakespeare's Comedy of Love*, p. 206. Marianne Novy, 'Mutuality in Shakespearean Comedy', in *Love's Argument: Gender Relations in Shakespeare*, also notes that Rosalind is encouraging 'mutuality' in any love relationship that will endure (p. 31).
35. E. A. M. Colman, 'Combination and Contrast', in *The Dramatic Use of Bawdy in Shakespeare*, also finds that Mercutio offers 'perspective' on love in *Romeo and Juliet* rather than replacing idealism with 'reductive realism' (p. 68).
36. The Folio simply reads 'open'; Quarto 1 gives the euphemism 'open *Et cetera*'.
37. The effect is similar to that of the 'double plots' that William Empson, *Some Versions of Pastoral*, discusses (pp. 27–74). Empson finds that the comic plot 'provides a sort of parody or parallel in low life to the serious part' (p. 31).
38. Ann Jenalie Cook, *Making a Match: Courtship in Shakespeare and his Society*, notes how *As You Like It* deliberately departs from orthodox forms of betrothal when pagan Hymen, representing 'the liberty' that 'commoners enjoyed in courtship', officiates instead of a priest (pp. 233, 103). In other words, sexual desire appears to triumph over romantic idealism.
39. This is how Roger Scruton, *Sexual Desire: A Moral Philosophy of the Erotic*, differentiates between 'love' and sexual desire (p. 236).
40. William C. Carroll, 'Language and Sexuality in Shakespeare', p. 15.
41. Catherine Belsey, 'Desire in the Golden World: *Love's Labour's Lost* and *As*

You Like It', in *Shakespeare and the Loss of Eden*, discusses the 'inevitable citationality of desire' (p. 30).

42. There may be a 'tantalizing coded subtext' in this line, but Pauline Kiernan, *Filthy Shakespeare*, replaces subtext with overt crudeness when she glosses the line as 'Your cunt's too hot, it climaxes too fast, it'll tire'. She arrives at this by asserting that 'The word "wit" is spoken more often in *Love's Labour's Lost* than in any other Shakespearean work, and almost always carries with it the primary meaning of "cunt," "vagina" or "genitals"' (pp. 28, 44). In fact thirty-eight of the forty instances of 'wit' in *Love's Labour's Lost* denote only wittiness, or the 'civil war of wits' (2. 1. 225) played between the lords and ladies. Colman, *The Dramatic Use of Bawdy in Shakespeare*, reminds readers that despite some obscene wordplay in Shakespeare, his bawdy is more often 'indirect, metaphorical, or allusive' (p. 3).

43. John Russell Brown, 'Representing Sexuality in Shakespeare's Plays', finds that in *Much Ado about Nothing*, 'sexual allusion' in the sparring of Benedict and Beatrice 'gallops ahead as if both speakers are willing riders of their most libidinous desires even while they are pretending to be at crossed purposes with each other' (p. 173). I argue that this effect is more evident in *Love's Labour's Lost*.

44. Margaret Loftus Ranald, '*Much Ado about Nothing*: From Legalism to Love', in *Shakespeare and his Social Context*, notes that Beatrice and Benedict both 'mock romantic pretensions' and 'excessive passion' rather than viewing love as a 'mystical neoplatonic union with the ultimate being' (pp. 31–2).

45. These are the terms used by Robert J. Sternberg in *Cupid's Arrow: The Course of Love through Time*, in which he convincingly defines '*companionate love*' as '*intimacy plus commitment*' (p. 20). While Sternberg defines '*romantic love*' as '*intimacy plus passion*', I contend that the Petrarchan love convention encourages worship and idealisation – spiritual adoration rather than the 'intimacy' of sexual passion.

Chapter 6

Sex, Love and Paradigms of Marriage

'Let me not to the marriage of true minds, / Admit impediments,' writes Shakespeare at the opening of Sonnet 116. Without any obvious irony, this sonnet celebrates love as an 'ever-fixed mark' that is not 'Time's fool', even though 'rosy lips and cheeks' – prompts for sexual desire – are inevitably destroyed by Time's 'bending sickle'. The poem stresses constant love, the union of minds rather than bodies. As such the sonnet's theme, an affirmation of unconditional, even spiritual love (*agape*) founded in deep romantic passion (*Eros*),[1] is the polar opposite of that expressed in Sonnet 129, 'The expense of spirit in a waste of shame', which projects instead the speaker's disgust at the 'hell' of 'lust in action' when it is devoid of tenderness.

The poet's refusal to 'admit impediments' to true love echoes part of the marriage service of 1559: the request, which tries to forestall any future legal problems, that anyone who knows 'impediments' to the couple's 'being joined together in matrimony' should declare them before the service begins. But can the sonneteer's firm intention to stay bonded, springing from the deepest form of romantic love, survive the mundane challenges of being married? Aristocrats and upper-class gentry in Shakespeare's society often viewed marriage more as a contract to solidify family and property interests – the 'cementing of alliances and the production of children'[2] – than as a bond forged in romantic attraction and emotional compatibility. Accordingly, such alliances were often arranged by parents. Old Capulet, by insisting that his daughter (a minor not yet fourteen) marry Paris, helps to accelerate the tragedy when Juliet is forced to hide her consummated union with Romeo. True, as historians Sarah Mendelson and Patricia Crawford indicate in their study *Women in Early Modern England*, conditions for marrying were more flexible lower down the social scale.[3] Shakespeare's city comedy, *The Merry Wives of Windsor*, promotes the idea that a middle-class daughter should be able to choose her own husband. Anne Page outwits her parents by marrying her chosen suitor Fenton, who then lectures the Pages on how 'forced marriage' – in a society where divorce was rarely an option and was never condoned by the church – would have inflicted on Anne 'a thousand irreligious cursed hours' (5. 5. 229).

But even such a marriage, based on mutual affection (fondness and passion), is bound to develop very differently from how it begins in romantic courtship. Whereas the Petrarchan and courtly love conventions place the lover at the mercy of his mistress, paradigms of early modern marriage, by and large, are still founded on the patriarchal assumption that wives should remain subservient to their husbands. As Cressida tersely points out, the ardent, pleading wooer is far removed from the complacent male who, having won his mate, expects to control her: 'Achievement is command; ungain'd, beseech' (*Troilus and Cressida*, 1. 2. 293). In *Of Wisdom* (published in English in 1627), Pierre Charron recognises a husband's need to mediate between these two extremes; he should neither 'hold' a wife under, as if she were 'a servant', nor 'make her mistress' by subjecting himself unto her.[4]

In fact Shakespeare's society never envisaged romantic passion as the keynote of a workable marriage. A couple's 'contract of eternal bond of love', as the Priest defines betrothal in *Twelfth Night* (5. 1. 156), would most likely entail a more sober union than the giddy newly-weds Olivia and Sebastian anticipate. Early modern discourses on the subject usually drive a wedge between intense sexual love – what the 'Solemnization of Matrimony' (in the Prayer Book of 1599) calls 'carnal lusts and appetites' associated with 'brute beasts' – and the committed companionship of marriage. Rather than a union in which a couple could fulfil their love for one another sexually, marriage is viewed as a 'remedy against sin'. Similarly the *Homily of the State of Matrimony* (1563), read in churches and printed twenty-two times by 1640, considers marriage a containment strategy, a means of 'bridling the corrupt inclinations of the flesh within the limits of honesty'.[5]

Earlier literature on courtly love had never associated marriage with passion. Moreover medieval theologians considered excessive 'carnal desire' to be an 'evil', even in sexual acts between spouses that might result in conceiving a child.[6] In *The Instruction of a Christian Woman* (1523) Juan Luis Vives gives a stern warning against marrying in the throes of sexual passion, because 'great hate' often ensues once the 'heat of love' is over.[7] Neither is love foregrounded in the wedding service outlined in the 'Solemnization of Matrimony'. After offering two prime justifications for marrying – to procreate children and to guard against 'fornication' – the ceremony goes on to emphasise the 'mutual society, help, and comfort' that husband and wife 'ought to have of the other'.

Rather than recognising that a couple's desire to marry might be based on romantic attraction, the *Homily of the State of Matrimony* reiterates this idea of partnership. 'Perpetual friendly fellowship' and 'sweet amity' are seen as the cornerstones of a successful marriage.[8] It's clear that sixteenth-century treatises on marriage do not allow for what has now become so important in contemporary Western society: a high degree of emotional and sexual intimacy for married couples as 'a continuation' of what the sociologist David R. Shumway calls 'the romantic state'.[9] Instead the *Homily* focuses on how to deal with domestic difficulties, disruptions likely to occur after the wedding that could threaten the couple's bond of 'friendly fellowship'.

Beyond homiletic texts, other sixteenth-century writers tend to decentre sex and romantic love in marriage in favour of 'amity'. 'A good marriage', writes Montaigne in the 1603 Florio translation of his *Essais*, 'refuseth the company and conditions of love; it endevoureth to present those of amity'.[10] He finds dangerously unstable those unions based on sensual attraction, averring '*I see no mariages faile sooner, or more troubled, th[a]n such as are concluded for beauties sake, and hudled up for amorous desires*'.[11] Likewise Pierre de La Primaudaye's popular *French Academie* (1586) carefully distinguishes 'true and good love' – a 'fountain of friendship' that is 'always grounded upon virtue and tendeth to that end' – from 'slippery and loose love' and 'carnal concupiscence'.[12] No wonder that Edmund Tilney capped his 1571 treatise, *A Brief and Pleasant Discourse of Duties in Mariage*, with the explanatory subtitle *Called the Flower of Friendshippe*.

The idea that wedlock is strong friendship or 'constant enduring fellowship'[13] – a bond for life in which husband and wife work together as loving partners – formed the basis of the post-Reformation model of 'companionate' marriage. As this paradigm gained ground in the early seventeenth century it also, as Catherine Belsey has argued convincingly, encouraged the expression of 'desire' (for all its potential unruliness) 'within the legality of marriage'.[14] Unlike medieval theologians, Erasmus and Calvin did not consider sex in marriage to be tainted by original sin.[15] These Reformation thinkers, no longer promoting celibacy or the monastic life above the married state, envisaged companionate marriage as a contract between loving equals, a spiritual union sealed by sexual intimacy. Thomas Gataker's sermon *A Good Wife Gods Gift* (1623) stresses the 'secret links of affection' (passion) that bind spouses in marriage.[16]

While Puritans still abhorred carnal delight for its own sake,[17] by 1622 William Gouge's *Of Domesticall Duties* approves the 'earnest . . . and ardent affection' of a husband, as long as it doesn't exceed the bounds of 'Christian modesty and decency'. What's more, Gouge finds reciprocity rather than imbalance between partners expressing sexual 'affection' in the bedroom. He claims that a wife, though expected to be 'a servant to yield her body' to her husband, is also a 'mistress' who has 'power over' her husband's sexuality,[18] which implies the kind of erotic power a mistress wields over her Petrarchan lover. Robert Burton's *Anatomy of Melancholy* (1621) also finds this balance of power in marriage; he writes that 'The husband rules [his wife] as head, but she again commands his heart, he is her servant, she his only joy and content'.[19]

Do Shakespeare's plays present the kind of marriage that encourages sexual fulfilment within a strong partnership? The endings of most of the comedies offer no real insight into how the lovers' marriages will progress, and whether spouses can turn romantic courtship into the intimate friendship of companionate love.[20] In Shakespeare's tragedies marriages almost always end badly. As Belsey points out in *Shakespeare and the Loss of Eden*, the playwright remains sceptical about 'the stability' of this 'institution' in a 'fallen world'.[21] Ironically, the union of Claudius and Gertrude in *Hamlet* – a marriage that Hamlet reviles as lustful and that the Ghost considers both adulterous and incestuous – has some claim to be a companionate marriage. It appears to combine passion with loving partnership when Claudius claims that Gertrude is 'so conjunctive' to his 'life and soul' that he cannot function without her (*Hamlet*, 4. 7. 14). Even this intimate second marriage turns out to be flawed, however. In the mayhem of the play's final scene the King seems more concerned with saving face than strenuously preventing his wife from drinking from the 'pois'ned cup' he has prepared for Hamlet (5. 2. 292). At the beginning of *Macbeth* the hero and his 'dearest chuck' are close companions, bonded sexually as they share their ambition to gain the throne of Scotland. When Macbeth's murder spree escalates, however, their partnership disintegrates; they are estranged by the time Lady Macbeth dies in Act 5. Ironically it is Desdemona, reuniting with Othello in Cyprus, who anticipates a future of happy married intimacy, assuring him that 'our loves and comforts should increase / Even as our days do grow!' (*Othello*, 2. 1. 194–5). Within a day or two, though, this optimistic bride will be murdered by her jealous husband.

In Shakespeare's history plays, political marriages calculated to solidify the monarchy[22] tend to founder. One such alliance is the marriage of King John's niece Blanch to Lewis the Dauphin, hastily arranged to shore up peace between England and France. Initially the match is framed as a union that could lead to domestic happiness. Blanch, claims the matchmaker Hubert, possesses beauty and virtue as well as high rank; Hubert even emphasises her sexual attractiveness as a wife: 'If lusty love should go in quest of beauty, / Where should he find it fairer than in Blanch?' (*King John*, 2. 1. 426–7). But on the wedding day itself the Dauphin eagerly renews hostilities against England, leaving Blanch, with no opportunity to forge a companionate marriage, simply to fade out of the action. Meanwhile Queen Margaret in the *Henry VI* trilogy appears to enjoy more conjugal intimacy with her adulterous partner Suffolk than in her arranged marriage to the doting King Henry. In *Richard III* we hear from the 'wretched' Ghost of Queen Anne that she never 'slept a quiet hour' after she married the unloving Richard (5. 3. 159–60). In sharp contrast, at the end of *Richard II* the deposed king movingly bids farewell to his wife, Anne, bitterly lamenting that he has been 'doubly divorc'd', both from his 'crown' and from his 'married wife' (*Richard II*, 5. 1. 71–3). But because this is the only scene in the play where the two appear together, we have little sense of a close marital relationship.

The only husband and wife couple in the history plays whose marriage might pass for companionate is Hotspur and Kate in *Henry IV, Part 1*. At least it seems so initially. We see the two interact with rough affection; Kate threatens to break Hotspur's 'little finger' if he won't tell her his campaign plans (2. 3. 87). But like the soldier Henry V, who admits to Princess Katherine that he would much rather 'leap into a wife' than be a romantic companion (*Henry V*, 5. 2. 139), Hotspur is more committed to being a warrior than a husband. Maddeningly Hotspur goes so far as to swear that he loves Kate only when he is in the saddle, on horseback (2. 3. 101–2). He will use his wife sexually, even treat her as a 'domesticated sex object',[23] but will not trust her as a companion with whom he can share his political aspirations. In Shakespeare's Roman plays, too, women must give place to their husbands' military rivalries or alliances with other men. Octavia in *Antony and Cleopatra* becomes a pawn, her arranged marriage to Antony an unsuccessful effort to 'cement' the partnership between Antony and her brother, Octavius Caesar (3. 2. 29). In *Coriolanus* the hero's marriage to Virgilia is marginalised; clearly, as Lisa Hopkins points out, the warrior's 'emotional energies' are 'invested elsewhere',[24] in humouring his mother and pursuing a love-hate relationship with his Volscian military rival, Aufidius.

Shakespeare presents one possible exception – marriage as a loving partnership – in *Julius Caesar*. Brutus's wife Portia challenges her husband for his failure to honour her as his life partner, keeping her in the 'suburbs' of his 'good pleasure' while he remains preoccupied with the future of Rome and its leader (2. 1. 285–6). Since she boasts mental 'constancy' equal to a man's (299), she is determined to be Brutus's trusted confidante. Claiming to be co-equal within the marital 'bond', she envisages herself as 'incorporate' and 'one' with her husband, 'half' of his very self (280, 273–4). Anachronistically Portia is appropriating St Paul's template on Christian marriage: the Apostle's affirmation, in the Epistle to the Ephesians (5: 32), that husband and wife 'shall become one flesh'.[25] When she insists on her right to conjugal intimacy, Portia also draws on Paul's words about the mutual sexual debt incurred in marriage. To prevent 'fornication', writes St Paul, 'Let the husband render unto the wife due benevolence; and likewise also the wife unto the husband' (1 Corinthians 7: 2–3).

Like the Church Fathers, Paul favours celibacy over marriage. But because he believes it 'is better to marry than to burn' (1 Corinthians 7: 8–9) he justifies marriage, in the words of the 'Solemnization of Matrimony', as equivalent to the 'mystical union . . . betwixt Christ and his Church'. By the same token, just as Christ is the head of the Church, so must the husband be 'the head of the wife' (Ephesians 5: 3). Endorsed by Paul's words in the New Testament, the patriarchal paradigm of marriage is still part of the dominant ideology in Shakespeare's time, only to some extent contested by the Protestant ideal of a 'companionate' marriage.[26] This more recent model, which, as outlined by Mary Beth Rose, valued both 'spiritual equality' and sexual intimacy as part of the marital relationship, also promoted a practical sharing of duties between husband and wife.[27] In such a partnership the wife might expect, at least, to be treated more as an equal than as subordinate to her husband.

In *The Comedy of Errors*, Shakespeare presents a fascinating clash between the newer and older paradigms of marriage. Adriana, wife to Antipholus of Ephesus, argues the case for equal rights with her husband while her sister Luciana subscribes to the patriarchal view – that a wife should obey her husband as her lord and master. Through the sisters Shakespeare presents two opposed views of the role of women in marriage. Adriana endorses the 'Protestant idealization of marriage',[28] the belief that a loving relationship that approves of sexual intimacy can also be based on equality. In contrast to Adriana's position, defined by Valerie Wayne as the 'emergent view' in Shakespeare's time,[29] Luciana represents the residual dominant ideology; she believes the male should be both the head of the household and, in St Paul's words, the 'head of the wife'. Therefore a wife's duty is to obey her husband.

Early in the play Adriana is dissatisfied (and jealous) because her merchant husband enjoys freedom while she remains a house-bound wife. When she accuses her husband, the Ephesian Antipholus, of cheating with 'some other mistress' (2. 2. 111) – she doesn't realise she's addressing the wrong twin – she expands fully on the argument that St Paul made centuries before. Appropriately it is part of Paul's address to the Ephesians: that because 'a man . . . shall be joined to his wife, and they two shall be one flesh', husbands ought to 'love their wives as their own bodies' (Ephesians 5: 31, 28). Like Roman Portia insisting on her conjugal rights, Adriana claims to be 'incorporate' in her husband, his 'dear self's better part'. If he is unfaithful then she, as his intimate partner, will be 'possess'd with an adulterate blot' (2. 2. 122–3, 140). Skilfully she twists St Paul's 'one flesh' dictum, which supports an authoritarian model of marriage, into a defence of sexual parity between husband and wife. In rejecting the double standard for men and women, Adriana anticipates Emilia's argument in *Othello*: that if a husband is liberal in his sexual favours, then a wife has the right to behave in the same way. Emilia puts her case strongly:

> And have not we affections,
> Desires for sport, and frailty, as men have?
> Then let them use us well ... (4. 3. 100–2)

It is Adriana's traditional sister Luciana who becomes, instead, an advocate for female obedience and patience in marriage. Voicing the orthodox position on gender roles, Luciana urges Adriana not to be disturbed by her husband's absence because 'A man is master of his liberty' (*The Comedy of Errors*, 2. 1. 7).[30] When spirited Adriana, unwilling to accept 'servitude' in marriage (26), counters with 'Why should [men's] liberty than ours be more?' (10), Luciana uses an analogy from the natural world. Just as 'beasts' and 'fishes' submit to male authority, so men, occupying a higher position in the cosmos, are entitled to be 'masters to their females, and their lords' (18–24). She also recommends that a husband be dominant sexually. Since women are naturally subservient, a husband should be the 'bridle' of his wife's 'will', controlling her sexuality as well as her other desires (13). When Adriana speculates that if her sister were married she would seek a more equitable arrangement, Luciana still embraces female subordination as a condition of marriage; she pledges ''Ere I learn love, I'll practice to obey' (29). Even when she believes she's being pursued by her sister's husband – in fact Antipholus of Syracuse is the one courting her – Luciana advises him to pursue marital harmony at all costs, even to the point of deceiving his wife: 'Look sweet, speak fair, become disloyalty' (3. 2. 11). Again her assumption is that because women, inferior to men, are destined to move within the male orbit – 'We in your motion turn, and you may move us' (24) – wives are naturally disposed to trust their spouses. Females are credulous, easily deceived and readily placated: 'Alas, poor women! Make us [but] believe / ... that you love us' (21–2). With supreme irony, while Luciana demeans her own sex Antipholus of Syracuse is elevating her to the status of a 'divine' creature. While she insists that men are masters, he adopts the role of the worshipful Petrarchan lover, happy to 'yield' any male privilege to this woman who is a 'god' to him (32, 39–40).

The Abbess to whom Adriana appeals for help straddles the debate. At first she seems to endorse the companionate view of marriage. When Adriana explains what has led to marital discord, the Abbess agrees that it's appropriate for a wife to rebuke her husband if she thinks 'his eye / Stray'd his affection in unlawful love' (5. 1. 50–1). Then she does a surprising about-turn. Reverting to the traditional view, promoting wifely submission, she criticises Adriana for behaving like a scold or a jealous shrew by berating Antipholus, apparently driving him to madness. To preserve the status quo in marriage, implies the Abbess, the wife should be conciliatory at all costs, restraining her 'jealous fits' (85) even if she believes her husband is breaking his vows.

The play reflects competing paradigms that cannot easily be reconciled. Indeed, during the age of Shakespeare the ideal of companionate marriage offered a challenge to but never completely replaced the traditional patriarchal model. Most tracts on marriage, including the *Homily of the State of Matrimony*, still assumed that the husband would be governor of the household. Writing about the duties of both wives and husbands in *Of Domesticall Duties* (1622), the Puritan Gouge concedes some 'equality' in marriage because 'man and wife are after a sort even fellows, and partners'. He nevertheless prefaces this by repeating the orthodox position – that a wife's place is one of 'inferiority' and 'subjection' to her husband.[31] By knowing their place, married women can avoid domestic strife: 'If wives would learn . . . to be subject, many jars' between spouses 'would be allayed if not prevented'.[32]

In his study *The Family, Sex and Marriage in England 1500–1800*, the social historian Lawrence Stone also finds no clear distinction between old and new models of marriage. The words of St Paul in the New Testament – 'Wives, submit yourselves unto your own husbands' (Ephesians 5: 22) – still held firm, authorising the male's right to rule. And because a woman's 'sacred duty' to love her husband could best be demonstrated by accepting his 'authority', Stone argues that the 'Protestant sanctification of marriage and the demand for married love' paradoxically encouraged 'the subordination of wives'.[33] Common law in the early modern period facilitated this. While married women might have some control over what was called 'household stuff',[34] in most cases the husband was entitled to his wife's material goods and property. Through the legal principle of the 'feme covert',[35] husband and wife were considered as one person under the law, which meant that wives usually lost the right to represent themselves. Certainly cultural expectations, bolstered by the law, encouraged dependency in a married woman; she was constrained to rely on the good will of her husband.

Although the *Homily of the State of Matrimony* advises tolerance and understanding on both sides, urging the husband who seeks 'concord' with his wife to treat her with moderation and not 'tyranny', the onus remains on the wife's duty to obey. She has the right to command her children and manage the day-to-day household affairs. But she should always 'apply herself' to her husband's 'will' and 'eschew all things that might offend him', to the point of learning 'patiently' to 'bear' his physical abuse if necessary. This suggests that even a husband's conciliatory gestures ultimately enable the hegemony of patriarchal rule. By tolerating his spouse's frailties and not being 'too stiff' in correcting her, a husband can more insidiously establish his authority over her. This is perfectly captured in the homilist's reassurance that 'By this means thou shalt not only nourish concord, but shalt have her heart in thy power and will'.[36] 'Power and will' sound an ominous note. The husband, it's assumed, can find subtle ways in which to dominate his wife and control her sexually, imposing his 'will' in all senses of that word. Edmund Tilney makes this even more explicit in *The Flower of Friendship* (1571), when his spokesman Pedro explains how 'the wise man . . . little by little must gently procure that he may also steale away [his wife's] private will, and appetite', so that their 'two bodies' become 'one . . . heart'.[37]

Certainly not every wife in late Renaissance England happily conformed to social expectations that she should be patient and submissive. But the basic question of how far a woman might assert her 'private will', striving toward equal 'fellowship' in marriage without being branded as too bold or shrewish, continues to preoccupy Shakespeare. It is explored in most detail in *The Taming of the Shrew* (1594), composed not long after Adriana in *The Comedy of Errors* voices her dissatisfaction with the confinements of patriarchal marriage.

Before examining Kate's controversial final speech – is it a genuine endorsement of Petruchio as her 'lord' and 'governor' (*The Taming of the Shrew*, 5. 2. 138) or a set piece that conveys a subtext of resistance? – it is important to consider what Kate is seeking in marriage. As a fiercely independent woman she seems suited neither to companionate marriage (a loving partnership between equals) nor to wifely submission under the patriarchal Petruchio. Certainly Kate's reputation as 'curst' and wilful or 'froward' (1. 2. 89–90) has preceded her; indeed *A Homily of the State of Matrimony* warns that a husband will 'flee' from a 'stubborn, froward, and malapert' wife.[38] On her first appearance Kate strongly objects to being paraded around as a commodity or a 'stale', a sexually available woman or a laughing-stock (1. 1. 58). Yet for all her playing up to the stereotype of a shrew, a woman who fights back with her hands and especially her tongue, we find that Kate is not averse to marriage. In fact she seeks it.

Early in the play Kate resents how her father Baptista favours his younger daughter Bianca in the marriage stakes. That would leave Kate, the older sister, with the humiliating prospect of dancing 'barefoot' on Bianca's wedding day and eventually 'lead[ing] apes in hell', the traditional punishment for old maids (2. 1. 33–4). As Marianne Novy emphasises, Kate needs to be married in order to be socially accepted and to 'live in relative comfort' in her patriarchal culture.[39] Being single in Shakespeare's day remained a stigma; in *Henry IV, Part 2* Mistress Quickly would rather tie herself to the debauched scrounger Falstaff than run the Boar's Head tavern on her own as a single, widowed woman (2. 1. 86–92).[40] Although social historians such as Amy M. Froide estimate that as many as a third of urban women remained unmarried in the early modern era,[41] single females had limited options for financial independence. Without family connections to wealth they might scrape a living on their own – apprenticed to a trade such as the textile industry, perhaps working as midwives or nurses or, lower down the social scale, as domestic servants or agrarian labourers.[42] Usually, though, it was more economically advantageous, as well as socially prestigious, for a woman to be supported by a husband, performing domestic duties in a shared household. In *The Taming of the Shrew* the father Baptista and his future son-in-law carefully work out marriage details for Kate, ensuring that she will be well provided for if she marries Petruchio. But for all these practical arrangements – in return for bringing a substantial dowry as a rich merchant's daughter she will receive a generous jointure of 'land and leases' if she is widowed (2. 1. 125) – Baptista tells her suitor that winning his daughter's love is 'all in all' (129).

Can a union with Petruchio be a romantic love match for Kate? Petruchio, who claims not to feel 'affection's edge' except when it comes to wealth (1. 2. 73), is actually the one who mentions love in connection with Kate, not the other way round. After he hears that Kate has attacked Hortensio by breaking a lute over his head, Petruchio is so impressed by the feistiness of the 'lusty wench' that he declares 'I love her ten times more than e'er I did' (2. 1. 160–1). There is no sign that Kate reciprocates these feelings, however.[43] Petruchio is the aggressor, determined to override her wishes: 'And will you, nill you, I will marry you' (271). And despite Baptista's taking their hands and declaring ''tis a match' (319), Kate doesn't formally give her consent as was expected in a betrothal. Instead she remains passionate in her rejection of this suitor. Following his coarse wooing – a travesty of romantic courtship

– and his arrogant declaration 'I am he am born to tame you, Kate', she rebukes her father for planning to marry her to such a 'madcap ruffian'. She would rather see Petruchio 'hang'd' than return to wed her (276, 288, 299). Even more fiercely, when the bridegroom fails to arrive on time Kate expresses anger at being coerced into marrying without love, 'forc'd / To give [her] hand oppos'd against [her] heart' (3. 2. 8–9). Once married, and suffering through Petruchio's taming tactics of depriving her of food and sleep at his house, what she most resents is his claim to be doing this 'under name of perfect love' (4. 3. 12). Certainly we find no signs, leading up to the play's conclusion, that Kate has fallen in love with her tamer.

It also seems unlikely that Petruchio wants to forge a reciprocal partnership, a marriage of mutual respect. His shrew-taming tactics are likely to strike a modern audience (and quite possibly an early modern one too) as too cruel to savour of love. Several male critics have defended him as a 'skillful psychologist' who adopts an outrageous role to bring out the 'best in Kate',[44] showing her the dark side of being shrewish and the importance of mutual cooperation within a workable marriage (2. 1. 137, 4. 1. 180). But Petruchio's strategies during his politic 'reign' (4. 1. 188) seem more designed to 'master' the female as a possession ('what is mine own') than to respect her as an equal (3. 2. 229). True, Petruchio does not resort to violent physical abuse of his wife, as happens in the cruder shrew-taming ballads and jests such as *A Merry Jest of a Shrewd and Curst Wife Lapped in Morel's Skin, for her Good Behavior* (c. 1550) that were circulating in Shakespeare's time. Instead of beating Kate into submission, Petruchio uses the stratagem of denial or contradiction; he simply refuses to admit that Kate is difficult to handle. After their first rough encounter he infuriatingly calls her 'pleasant' and 'sweet as springtime flowers' rather than an angry scold (2. 1. 245–6), explaining to Baptista that Kate is playing the shrew in public to disguise her true nature, which he terms modest, temperate and patient (293–5). This is tantamount to ignoring Kate's refusal to be 'conformable' (278) and thereby defusing her power as a subversive woman.

Petruchio goes on to win almost all their confrontations. Every time Kate shows a spirit of resistance, he manages to crush it. Determined to make a strong stand at the wedding feast, Kate twice repeats that she won't leave with Petruchio ''til I please myself' (3. 2. 209, 212). Yet despite a protest that is physical as well as verbal – we gather from the text that she stamps her foot and looks daggers at him – Petruchio imposes his will on her. Drawing on the prerogative of a husband whose bride is now his 'goods' and 'chattels', he pledges 'I will be master of what is mine own' before flamboyantly abducting her at sword-point

(229–30). After their marriage, even though Kate resolves 'I will be free, / Even to the uttermost, as I please, in words' (4. 3. 79–80), Petruchio continues to silence her. When Kate is angry because Petruchio refuses to let her keep the fashionable cap she likes, he again neutralises her by pretending she hasn't contradicted him; he claims instead that she's agreed the cap is a 'paltry . . . bauble' (81–2).

Petruchio's perverted quest to 'kill a wife with kindness', as he describes it (4. 1. 208), means taking Kate in hand, pretending to act in her best interests. But his strategy seems less like a form of 'kindness', or a way of encouraging cooperation between partners in a viable marriage, than it resembles taming a wild falcon (190–1) or curbing an unruly horse.[45] By taming Kate, Petruchio is confident that he will indeed achieve a traditional patriarchal marriage predicated on his wife's submission. This is the message of John Dod and Robert Cleaver's popular conduct book *A Godly Form of Household Government* (1621), which underlines how 'the husband, without any exception, is master over all the house', and how accepting this hierarchy will result in 'quietness' in the home, a 'mutual concord and love of man and wife'.[46] Near the end of the play Petruchio similarly praises wifely obedience with 'Marry, peace it bodes, and love, and quiet life' (5. 2. 108), a line in which married 'love' is de-emphasised, sandwiched between 'peace' and 'quiet'. Petruchio's recipe for a viable, harmonious marriage is unequivocal. A wife's refusal to show her 'duty', demonstrated by the Widow and Bianca (123–5), would prove a grave impediment to achieving his version of domestic bliss – that 'sweet and happy' state in which a husband maintains 'An awful rule and right supremacy' (108–10).

Much depends on whether the audience is convinced by the play's end that Kate can be of one mind with Petruchio, subscribing to his recipe and thereby forging a mutually satisfying union. Act 4, scene 5 may signal a crucial turning point in their relationship. This is the scene where 'gamesome' Kate (2. 1. 245) decides to collaborate with Petruchio's strategy of contrariness and scores points by doing so. If Kate's 'sporting nature is not crushed but redirected', as Alexander Leggatt suggests,[47] this would indeed offer hope that her marriage could be a mutual enterprise, not a battle of wills or complete submission to her husband. When Petruchio insists, in broad daylight, that the moon and not the sun is shining brightly, Kate allows that it can be 'moon, or sun, or what you please' (4. 5. 13). Joining in the absurd game, pushing comic delusion even further by addressing the Pedant they meet on the road as 'young budding virgin' (37), she just as adroitly reverses direction to concede her 'mad mistaking' as soon as Petruchio points out that the Pedant is actually a 'wrinkled' old man (43). Much will depend on how the actress delivers the lines here – with bold panache or weary resignation.⁴⁸ True, there's ironic bite in Kate's remark to Petruchio that 'the moon changes even as your mind' (a complaint traditionally levelled at women) and that she has been 'bedazzled with the sun', which, since the sun is usually associated with the dominant male, could be a gibe at her bamboozling husband (20, 46). As Petruchio's equal or even superior in wit, she need not be demonstrating subservience. Nevertheless Hortensio believes that Petruchio is the one who has scored a decisive victory – 'the field is won' (23) – once Kate agrees to speed things along by conforming to whatever switch in perception her husband decrees. Certainly Petruchio still appears to be controlling her performance when they next appear in public. Demanding a kiss, he wins from Kate the entreaty 'now pray thee, love, stay' (5. 1. 148).

Unless the scene on the road convinces the audience that Kate has become a willing 'partner' in the linguistic game,⁴⁹ a shrewd player who can wittily hold her own with Petruchio during their married life, Kate's final oration will strike the audience as shockingly compliant with the older patriarchal model of marriage:

> I am asham'd that women are so simple
> To offer war where they should kneel for peace,
> Or seek for rule, supremacy, and sway,
> When they are bound to serve, love, and obey.
> Why are our bodies soft, and weak, and smooth,
> Unapt to toil and trouble in the world,
> But that our soft conditions, and our hearts,
> Should well agree with our external parts?
> Come, come, you forward and unable worms! (5. 2. 161–9)

Feminist critics in particular have been loath to accept the speech at face value. One way to explain Kate's apparent capitulation is to agree with Coppélia Kahn that Kate is being disingenuous, framing the whole speech as a parade of irony.⁵⁰ Perhaps Kate and Petruchio have arranged in advance that she can have her way at home but must play the dutiful wife outside. There's no evidence, though, that the couple have forged the kind of mutually agreeable arrangement that Chaucer promotes in *The Franklin's Tale*, where Dorigen's husband Averagus promises never to exert 'mastery' against his wife's 'will' in private as long as he can keep 'the name of sovereignty' in public.⁵¹

It is more plausible that Shakespeare could be using the convention of all-male actors in his theatre – the fact that Kate is played by a boy – to deconstruct the overt message of the speech. The Induction to *The Taming of the Shrew* also features a boy actor, the page Bartholomew, who plays the role of an upper-class woman. He is being instructed to do so in order to trick the tinker Christopher Sly into thinking that he is a lord, married to a lady who is nevertheless a submissive wife. The character Kate could be pulling off the same sleight of hand. Just as Bartholomew impersonates a gentlewoman who will 'show her duty' and 'obedience' by doing everything in her power to please her husband (Induction, 1. 116–17, 2. 107), so the boy actor playing Kate could be consciously role-playing wifely obedience at the end of the play. Patriarchs in the audience, witnessing a 'male performance of female compliance',[52] might nod approvingly as this message about female submission resonates with them. Meanwhile those females in the audience who, like Emilia in *Othello*, favour equal rights for married women would more likely smile or scoff at Kate's speech as representing a male fantasy of the perfect marital partner.

This interpretation, though, depends on the audience's heightened awareness that the speech is being delivered by a cross-dressed male. If the convention is effaced and spectators are fully immersed in the dramatic illusion, they are more likely to register Kate as a credible female (a character who has moved far beyond the farcical stock figure of the shrew) and will thus take her words straight. Hers is a persuasive speech that commands attention by its sheer length.[53] And in an uncanny parallel to Gouge's question when he is discussing appropriate behaviour for wives in *Of Domesticall Duties* – 'Is not obedience to be yielded to an *Head*, *Lord*, and *Master*?'[54] – the ideological import of Kate's speech remains clear:

> Thy husband is thy lord, thy life, thy keeper,
> Thy head, thy sovereign; one that cares for thee,
> And for thy maintenance, commits his body
> To painful labor, both by sea and land;
> To watch the night in storms, the day in cold,
> Whilst thou li'st warm at home, secure and safe;
> And craves no other tribute at thy hands
> But love, fair looks, and true obedience. (5. 2. 146–53)

Never mind that Petruchio has failed to show he is capable of 'painful labor' to ensure Kate's security. In fact marrying her will allow him, as Frances E. Dolan points out, to remain a wealthy member of the landed gentry who need not work for a living.[55] Nor, judged by the bleak homecoming he provides for Kate in Act 3, has Petruchio proved to be a responsible husband who will keep his wife 'secure and safe' in their marital home. It's difficult to argue that the play was designed to promote the kind of compromise in marriage offered by some Protestant conduct books of the time, through which, as Margaret Lael Mikesell puts it, 'a man's authority is vested through his love and a woman's love through her obedience': a vision of 'mutuality within hierarchy'[56] that still seems to favour the male in a companionate marriage. In fact Kate's speech endorses the traditional patriarchal model. She underscores Petruchio's contention that love in a harmonious marriage depends on each partner assuming a particular role, 'supremacy' for the husband and 'duty' for the wife (163, 178). Kate seems to have sold out, becoming what she previously resisted: a 'puppet' of the patriarchal system (4. 3. 103) rather than a woman who boldly opposes it.

What's more, the vision of harmony in marriage, once all female resistance is contained, may prove illusory at the end of *The Taming of the Shrew*. The play's traditional romantic lover, Lucentio, discovers that Bianca is not the sweet, compliant wife he expected; she refuses to come at his bidding. The audience might feel as queasy about the future of these couples as they do at the conclusion of *Measure for Measure*, where the three marriages hastily arranged by Duke Vincentio (Angelo to Mariana, Lucio to Kate Keepdown, and the Duke himself to Isabella) promise neither lasting peace nor mutual commitment. Certainly *The Taming of the Shrew*, which raises so many questions about the treatment of wives and the viability of a truly companionate relationship in this era, let alone the continuation of romantic love into marriage, doesn't offer a tidy comic solution.[57]

At first it seems odd that when Portia, the resourceful heroine of *The Merchant of Venice*, is betrothed to Bassanio she uses words almost identical to those of Kate. While Kate urges every woman to accept her husband as her 'lord', 'king' and 'governor', Portia is eager to be 'directed' by Bassanio as 'her lord, her governor, her king' (*The Merchant of Venice*, 3. 2. 165). So why does the audience feel that Portia, rather than Kate, is able to negotiate a companionate marriage that will accommodate erotic desire and mature romantic love? In fact Portia, expressing the breadth of her love for Bassanio – 'for you, / I would be trebled twenty times myself' – also emphasises the mutuality of their married relationship. She reminds Bassanio 'I am half yourself', requesting that just as she generously enables him to use her wealth, so he will 'freely' share with her the bad news he receives about Antonio (3. 2. 152–3, 248–9). Above all, Portia makes a binding contract with her husband by giving him her ring. Flouting convention,[58] she reverses the marriage ceremony by taking the initiative, making the ring a pledge to deliver herself and all she owns to Bassanio. If he parts with the ring, however, she will call him out, 'exclaim' on him (3. 2. 174). When she discovers that he has given away this sacred token to the lawyer who saved Antonio's life (Portia herself in disguise), she uses his apparent betrayal to gain the upper hand; she manoeuvres Bassanio into reaffirming his constancy as a husband within an equal, companionate partnership. It is difficult to imagine Portia offering to place her hand 'below' her 'husband's foot' to signify service to him, as Kate does to endorse old-style marriage in *The Taming of the Shrew* (5. 2. 177).

Surprisingly, the one love affair in Shakespeare's plays that does eventually prove to be a lasting, mutually inspiring union is that between Antony and Cleopatra. It also triumphantly dissolves the dichotomy between love and strong physical desire that underpins so much moral discourse in Shakespeare's era, from the wedding ceremony's assumption that marriage will guard against 'carnal lusts' to the firm distinction between lust and love that the youthful hero draws in Shakespeare's *Venus and Adonis*.[59] As a couple Antony and Cleopatra forge a passionate bond in which sexual desire and romantic love are not in conflict. They embody what modern culture, following Freud, sees as an ideal married relationship, in which 'two currents of feeling ... the tender, affectionate feelings and the sensual feelings' can be united.[60] True, the relationship of the Roman and the Egyptian is hardly a traditional paradigm of fidelity or the marriage of two minds that have determined to be 'true' to one another. Nevertheless the fickle chameleon Cleopatra, lambasted as a 'Triple-turn'd whore' (4. 12. 13) because her previous lovers include the elder Pompey and Julius Caesar, makes claim at the play's end to be the wife of Antony. By the time she confidently declares 'Husband, I come!' as she prepares to join him in death (5. 2. 287), the audience can assess how far they have achieved such a union.

In many ways Cleopatra has been presented throughout as the quintessential courtesan. To the Romans this colonised queen is a 'cunning' quean (slut), as in the pun when Antony resolves 'I must from this enchanting queen break off' (1. 2. 145, 128) and Caesar, failing to recognise the monarch among her women, asks 'Which is the Queen of Egypt?' (5. 2. 112). Like the loved one of Sonnet 40, 'Lascivious grace, in whom all ill well shows' (13), Cleopatra presents herself as a blend of comeliness (grace) and bold sexuality. Enobarbus, praising her mixture of artifice and natural beauty, compares it to the art of the prostitute when he declares that 'custom' cannot 'stale' (with a pun on 'stale' as a woman who sells herself) Cleopatra's 'infinite variety' (2. 2. 234–5). When he is angry with her, Antony resents not only that she slept with former political leaders, but that she almost certainly enjoyed 'hotter hours' of pleasure with her commoners. This 'boggler', he rages, has never known 'temperance' (3. 13. 118, 110, 121).

On stage the queen enacts another negative feminine stereotype: the shrew or scold. Cleopatra seems the very opposite of what is traditionally desired in a good wife. In Robert Snawsel's *A Looking Glass for Married*

Folks (1610), Eulalie, representing the temperate, obedient wife, reminds the 'malapert' Margery that 'it becomes an honest wife to frame herself to her husband's affection, and not be merry when he is melancholy, nor jocund when he is sad'.[61] Cleopatra, however, is always contrary in the extreme. She deliberately crosses Antony to keep his passion simmering, advising Charmian, 'If you find him sad, / Say I am dancing; if in mirth, report / That I am sudden sick' (1. 3. 3–5). She scolds him for being at his wife Fulvia's beck and call ('What, says the married woman you may go?' (20)) and displaces her own shrewishness on to this wife when she accuses Antony of running back to Rome 'when shrill-tongu'd Fulvia scolds' (1. 1. 32). More violently than Kate in *The Taming of the Shrew*, Cleopatra vents her spleen in physical abuse. Hearing that Antony has married Octavia, the queen 'hales' the Messenger 'up and down' and threatens to kill him with a knife (2. 5. 64, 73).

Her behaviour contrasts sharply with that of the modest Roman matron Octavia. Embodying all the 'virtue' and 'general graces' that characterise the ideal Roman or Renaissance wife (2. 2. 129), Octavia is described as having 'wisdom' and 'modesty' (240), looking on with 'sober' and 'modest' eyes (5. 2. 54, 4. 15. 27). She is 'a piece of virtue' (3. 2. 28) and not, like Cleopatra, a 'wonderful piece of work' (1. 2. 153–4). While Octavia is reticent, shrewish Cleopatra holds court as the loquacious, 'wrangling' queen (1. 1. 48), goading Antony into a Herculean 'chafe' with her verbal taunts (1. 3. 84–5). After Enobarbus affirms that Octavia is of a 'holy, cold, and still conversation' and Menas asks 'who would not have his wife so?', Enobarbus sagely replies, 'Not he that himself is not so' (2. 6. 122–5). Antony's 'affection' (130), his sexual 'pleasure' (2. 3. 41), indeed resides in Egypt and not in a Roman marriage made for political purposes.

In Shakespeare's theatre Cleopatra, emblem of erotic female power, was of course played by a boy. Portrayed by a cross-dressed male, Cleopatra the character envisages how she may be cruelly travestied in Rome – 'I shall see / Some squeaking Cleopatra boy my greatness / In th' posture of a whore' (5. 2. 219–21) – while also acknowledging to the audience at the Globe Theatre that the boy's performance may be woefully inadequate in capturing the Queen of Egypt's multifaceted persona. By drawing attention to the boy actor convention, Shakespeare invites us to think beyond the actor's limitations, to respond with imagination to help create the character. Just as importantly, the audience will be reminded that gender is not a fixed set of feminine or masculine traits but is fluid in its representation, amenable to theatrical construction. The presence on stage of a boy playing the woman Cleopatra suggests other dimensions of cross-gendering too. In particular, it points to something important about the relationship of Antony and Cleopatra – the lovers' achievement of a vibrant androgyny, the blending of male and female that joins them in a marriage quite different from the orthodox paradigms promoted in Shakespeare's society.

The term 'androgyny', defined as the 'union of two sexes in one individual' (*OED*), was not current in Shakespeare's time; the first recorded use of the noun came in 1651. When the adjective 'androgynous' occurs earlier it is used pejoratively, as when the Puritan William Prynne, a staunch opponent of the theatre, refers to 'men-women', effeminate men, as 'androgynous'.[62] The Romans' sense of harmful cross-over, an unwelcome transvestite gender-bending, is captured in Caesar's contemptuous description of Antony in Egypt as 'not more manlike / Than Cleopatra, nor the queen of Ptolomy / More womanly than he' (1. 4. 5–7). For the lovers, though, the ability to transcend distinct genders is a source of pride. Cleopatra exuberantly recalls the time that she drank Antony to his bed and wore his 'sword Philippan' after dressing him in her woman's 'tires and mantles' (2. 5. 21–3).

The idea that androgyny was part of the original (and superior) state of being human appears in Plato's *Symposium*, later recounted by the fifteenth-century Neo-Platonist Ficino in the 'Myth of Plato on the Ancient Nature of Man'. There Aristophanes envisages a primordial splitting of the third sex of human beings, who were 'bi-sexuals' with 'two faces, completely identical, and joined on a round neck'.[63] After being forced apart, each of these individuals was destined to seek out a complementary half with which to unite – male to female in the original androgynous model. *Antony and Cleopatra* echoes this in the lovers' quest for a more complete union, Roman male joined with Egyptian female in a 'heavenly mingle' (1. 5. 59). Antony aspires to be Cleopatra's 'soldier, servant' (1. 3. 70), blending aggression with submission, while Cleopatra becomes the 'captain's heart' (1. 1. 6), riding in triumph at the very centre of Antony's military might while simultaneously prized as his supreme sexual partner (4. 8. 15–16). Through the lovers' androgynous blending their partnership, as Peter Erickson points out, gains strength.[64]

Sylvester's English translation of Du Bartas's poem 'The First Week' of the Creation, published in 1605 and 1608 (close in date to *Antony and Cleopatra*), depicts the union of Adam and Eve as an androgynous one. The couple in the Garden of Eden joyfully becomes the 'sweet *Hee-Shee*-Coupled One' when God makes 'Two of One, and One of Two againe'.[65] While the 'Solemnization of Matrimony' service in the Prayer Book of 1559 also draws on this biblical story, it more soberly reminds the audience that marriage was 'instituted of God in Paradise' in 'the time of man's innocency'.[66] Certainly the androgynous union of Antony and Cleopatra defies the norms of a traditional Christian marriage. The lovers attain what St Paul called the 'one flesh' of marriage by passionate sexual coupling rather than through the analogy of Christ's mystical union with his church.[67] Nevertheless the Roman and the Egyptian appear to achieve the mythical blending of the two individual 'distincts', the 'Co-supremes and stars of love' that Shakespeare celebrates in *The Phoenix and the Turtle* (27, 51). This poem from 1601 presents 'married chastity' (without offspring) as grounded in 'Love and Constancy' (61, 22) – hardly the model for Antony and Cleopatra, who welcome sexual pleasure and produce several children together.[68] For all their sensuality, though, the lovers also define themselves in mythological terms. Theirs is a union in which, as Cleopatra boasts, 'none our parts so poor / But was a race of heaven' (*Antony and Cleopatra*, 1. 3. 36–7). At their best the lovers attain, like the mythical birds, unity in diversity: not an asexual 'concordant one' but rather a bisexual union in which 'To themselves yet either neither, / Simple were so well compounded' (*The Phoenix and the Turtle*, 41–4).[69]

At the same time, though, we never lose sight of Cleopatra as a volatile woman whose fickleness may sometimes turn treacherous, as Antony suspects (3. 13. 110). Unlike the phoenix, she does not accompany her mate in death. She may even hope to reconcile with Octavius Caesar by seducing him as her next lover; ironically she demonstrates a wifely obedience to this conquering hero (as she never does to the living Antony) when she kneels and twice addresses him as 'my master and my lord' (5. 1. 116, 190). It is Cleopatra's suicide that finally confirms her as 'marble-constant' in her devotion to Antony (5. 2. 240). She tests herself to discover whether she can finally transform into Antony's wife. Desiring him to 'praise' her 'noble act' (5. 2. 285), she exclaims:

> Husband, I come!
> Now to that name my courage prove my title!
> I am fire and air, my other elements
> I give to baser life. (5. 2. 287–90)

Despite moving toward the ethereal, Cleopatra retains her image as a sensual, vital woman whose 'fire and air' are counterpointed by the 'baser' element of 'dungy earth' (1. 1. 35). Indeed the whole ceremony of her suicide is infused with sexuality. The 'rural fellow' bringing in a basket of figs containing asps jokes with Cleopatra that the 'falliable' (phallic) worm provides a mortal bite from which, unlike dying in orgasm, women almost 'never recover' (5. 2. 233, 257, 247–8). Caesar sees her staged death as yet another act of seduction in which the comely Cleopatra 'looks like sleep, / As she would catch another Antony / In her strong toil of grace' (346–8). Cleopatra, it's true, envisages an eternity of sensuality spent with her 'husband' Antony, enjoying the 'heaven' of his betrothal kiss (302–3). Dying Antony, too, plans to share the Underworld not with any previous lover or married partner but with the queen, anticipating that 'Where souls do couch on flowers we'll hand in hand'. Just as they have proudly displayed themselves in life, the lovers will make other shades 'gaze' at them in awe (4. 14. 51–2).

What is Shakespeare portraying here? This play, which offers such multiple perspectives on human existence, does not over-romanticise the lovers' union. It suggests that such an intensely passionate relationship cannot easily conform to the steady comradeship of a traditional marriage; it may need absence to rekindle desire. Cleopatra appreciates Antony most, celebrating him as 'demi-Atlas of this earth', when he has departed for Rome (1. 5. 23), and she mythologises him as a Colossus whose 'legs bestrid the ocean' once he is dead (5. 2. 82). Antony, too, after the death of his first wife Fulvia, exemplifies the old adage that absence makes the heart grow fonder; he acknowledges that his wife is 'good, being gone' (1. 2. 126).

The playwright's contemporaries would also be mindful that Antony and Cleopatra are pagans yearning for a sensual afterlife, not Christians aspiring to spend eternity in heaven with God.[70] Nor would the audience necessarily approve of their committing suicide, choosing a *Liebestod* (love fulfilled in death) instead of making a good Christian end. It could be hubris that makes the 'peerless' pair (1. 1. 40) expect to prolong the 'play' of their lovemaking after death. Arguably they focus too exclusively on *Eros* rather than *agape* (spiritual love) or *philia* – what the *Homily of the State of Matrimony* recommends as the 'perpetual friendly fellowship' in which a harmonious marriage is grounded. Audiences may nevertheless grasp something different: that the mature relationship of Antony and Cleopatra, while triumphantly sexual, is not incompatible with *agape* or *philia*, for it cannot simply be branded as lust at odds with love. It constitutes a vibrant partnership that rivals, even exceeds, conventional marriage. To some extent the lovers' androgynous union also succeeds in erasing gender boundaries, as well as the standard expectation that a husband will be lord and master to a submissive wife: those confining roles that can form impediments to a loving and enduring marriage.

As he expires, Antony no longer images himself as a military leader but as an eager 'bridegroom' running into death 'As to a lover's bed' (4. 14. 100–1). Meanwhile death holds in check Cleopatra's volatile, protean nature. Through 'resolution' and 'courage', as she transforms a histrionic ritual into a nuptial rite, the Queen of Egypt wins the right to call Antony her 'husband' (5. 2. 238, 287–8). Whereas death ends the marriage of Romeo and Juliet, for Antony and Cleopatra death offers 'a new beginning in marriage'.[71] Echoing the Anglican marriage service, in which the woman pledges to 'take' in perpetuity the man as her 'wedded' husband, Cleopatra declares 'O Antony! – Nay, I will take thee too' (312).[72] The irony is that the lovers achieve this only at the end of their lives. But they gesture toward marriage as a passionate and romantic commitment, a union that might, through the creativity of their imaginations, have continually renewed itself on earth. Together this 'mutual pair' (1. 1. 37) has embodied not simply the 'one flesh' of lovers and lawfully married couples,[73] but a marriage of two minds or souls that can finally remain 'true' to one another without worldly impediments.[74]

Notes

1. This fits the category of '*consummate love*' that Robert J. Sternberg, *Cupid's Arrow: The Course of Love through Time*, defines as '*intimacy plus passion plus commitment*' (p. 22).
2. Lisa Hopkins, *The Shakespearean Marriage*, p. 9.
3. Sarah Mendelson and Patricia Crawford, *Women in Early Modern England, 1550–1720*, cite evidence that for the English lower and middle classes courtship might also be prolonged for some time, as the average age of marriage for women at this socio-economic level was twenty-five, and a little older for men (p. 108).
4. Pierre Charron, *Of Wisdom*, p. 487.
5. *A Homily of the State of Matrimony* (1563), in Gerald Bray (ed.), *The Book of Homilies: A Critical Edition*, p. 472. All citations from the homily are from this source.
6. C. S. Lewis, *The Allegory of Love*, notes the medieval theological view that although the act of intercourse might be 'innocent', sexual desire, even within marriage, remains 'morally evil'. Meanwhile courtly love's 'idealization of sexual love' entails an 'idealization of adultery' (pp. 14, 13). Jean H. Hagstrum, *Esteem Enlivened by Desire: The Couple from Homer to Shakespeare*, offers a balanced view: while medieval romance often celebrates illicit love, this genre (including some of Chaucer's tales) also honours the 'consensual marriage based on sexual attraction and free choice' promoted by a 'churchly settlement' from the twelfth century on (p. 247).
7. Juan Luis Vives, *The Instruction of a Christian Woman*, bk. 1, ch. 16, p. 83 (spelling modernised).
8. *A Homily of the State of Matrimony*, pp. 472, 474.
9. David R. Shumway, *Modern Love: Romance, Intimacy, and the Marriage Crisis*, p. 3. Shumway finds that romantic love gradually became a 'dominant discourse' following the rise of capitalism and the 'dawning of individualism among the bourgeoisie'. He contends that whereas marriage

in the early modern period (Shakespeare's era) was still 'understood mainly as a social institution and a property relation rather than a personal commitment and an emotional relation' (p. 12), the 'discourse of intimacy' – the promotion of sexual and emotional closeness in marriage – became widely current during the last third of the twentieth century (pp. 24–5).
10. 'Upon Some Verses of *Virgil*', in *Essays*, trans. John Florio, vol. 3, ch. 5, pp. 74, 77.
11. Ibid. pp. 73–4.
12. Pierre de La Primaudaye, 'Of Voluptuousness and Lechery', in *The French Academie*, pp. 239–40, 238 (spelling modernised).
13. Irving Singer, 'Puritans and the Rationalists', in *The Nature of Love, Vol. 2: Courtly and Romantic*, analyses the maturing relationship of Adam and Eve in Milton's *Paradise Lost* to demonstrate how Puritans thought of 'married love' as enduring fellowship rather than 'a passionate or extravagantly emotional oneness' (p. 242).
14. Catherine Belsey, 'Love as Trompe-l'oeil: Taxonomies of Desire in *Venus and Adonis*', 271.
15. Juliet Dusinberre, 'The Puritans and the Playwrights', in *Shakespeare and the Nature of Women*, pp. 43–4. Dusinberre quotes from Erasmus's *A Mery Dialogue, declaringe the Propertyes of Shrowde Shrewes, and Honest Wyves* (trans. Antony Kytson, 1557), where the speaker maintains that a wife lying with her husband should 'shew him all the pleasure that she can' (p. 74).
16. Thomas Gataker, *A Good Wife Gods Gift*, p. 11 (spelling modernised). By 1658, the physician Lemnius warns that marriages without regular sexual intercourse 'shall see the house turn'd upside down'. Cited in Laura Gowing, 'Consent and Desire', in *Common Bodies: Women, Touch and Power in Seventeenth-Century England*, p. 82.
17. Dusinberre, 'The Problem of Equality', in *Shakespeare and the Nature of Women*, notes that for Puritans, marriage without that 'union of like minds ... can only be a legalized fornication' (p. 127).
18. William Gouge, 'Duties of Husbands', in *Of Domesticall Duties*, p. 361. Committed to moderation, the Puritan Gouge rebukes 'intemperate' husbands who practise 'wantonness, lightness and uncleanness' with their wives (p. 416). Spelling is modernised in all quotations from this source.
19. Robert Burton, *The Anatomy of Melancholy*, vol. 3, sec. 2, p. 53.
20. The 'love triangle' that Sternberg describes in *Cupid's Arrow*, which consists of 'intimacy, passion, and commitment' (p. 5), helps to define basic differences between 'romantic' and 'companionate' love in Western culture. In this model romantic love accentuates 'passion' (desire for union with the beloved) as it moves toward 'intimacy', whereas the companionate love of marriage privileges 'intimacy plus commitment' over passion (pp. 20–1). Marcus Nordlund, *Shakespeare and the Nature of Love*, also draws on Sternberg's 'love triangle' to discuss how companionate love emphasises 'maintenance of the relationship over a period of time' (p. 24).
21. Catherine Belsey, 'Marriage: Imogen's Bedchamber', in *Shakespeare and the Loss of Eden*, p. 60.

22. Ann Jenalie Cook, 'Courtship and Politics', in *Making a Match: Courtship in Shakespeare and his Society*, also discusses the 'use of marriage as an instrument of state' throughout Shakespeare's plays (p. 241), noting that marriage to cement 'political alliances . . . fails more often than it succeeds in Shakespeare' (p. 246).
23. Jonathan Goldberg, 'Desiring Hal', in *Sodomotries: Renaissance Texts, Modern Sexualities*, p. 168. Goldberg finds Hotspur misogynistic, which seems borne out in the scene set in Wales, where Hotspur tries to bully Kate into singing and taunts her with his desire to go to 'the Welsh lady's bed' (*Henry IV, Part 1*, 3. 1. 242).
24. Hopkins, 'Roman Marriage', in *The Shakespearean Marriage*, p. 111.
25. All biblical citations are from the King James Bible (1611).
26. See 'The Companionate Marriage' in Lawrence Stone, *The Family, Sex and Marriage in England 1500–1800*, pp. 325–404.
27. Mary Beth Rose, *The Expense of Spirit: Love and Sexuality in English Renaissance Drama*, p. 126. Margo Todd, *Christian Humanism and the Puritan Social Order*, finds continuity and 'consensus' between humanist and Puritan views of marriage, as both emphasise mutuality and shared duties (p. 238).
28. Rose, *The Expense of Spirit*, p. 6.
29. In her edition of Edmund Tilney, *The Flower of Friendship: A Renaissance Dialogue Contesting Marriage*, Valerie Wayne contends that while the idea of completely 'egalitarian relations' between husband and wife was an 'emergent' view in Shakespeare's time (p. 3), the dominant ideology promoted companionate marriage – but only as long as the husband still had ultimate authority over his wife.
30. Margaret Loftus Ranald, 'Society's Conventions and *The Comedy of Errors*', in *Shakespeare and his Social Context*, notes that the audience might have recognised in this debate the pattern of one of Erasmus's colloquies, 'Conjugium', in which Eulalia speaks well of marriage while Xantippe takes the part of the shrewish wife (p. 112).
31. Gouge, 'Duties of Husbands', in *Of Domesticall Duties*, p. 356.
32. Gouge, 'Duties of Wives', in *Of Domesticall Duties*, p. 322.
33. Stone, *The Family, Sex and Marriage in England 1500–1800*, pp. 141–2. Lisa Jardine, *Still Harping on Daughters: Women and Drama in the Age of Shakespeare*, finds that despite 'sophisticated mutual consent theories . . . the actuality of a woman's role in the household remained, as far as one can discover, unchanged' (p. 43). Phyllis Rackin, *Shakespeare and Women*, also considers companionate marriage 'an innovation by no means universally celebrated in Shakespeare's time' (p. 136). Keith Wrightson, *English Society 1580–1680*, concludes that 'patriarchal' and 'companionate' marriages were 'poles of an enduring continuum in marital relations in a society which accepted both the primacy of male authority and the ideal of marriage as a practical and emotional partnership' (p. 112).
34. See John Dod and Robert Cleaver, *A Godly Form of Household Government* (1621). The authors state that while the husband is 'master over all the house', he may give his wife the right to oversee the 'household stuff' (p. 206). Natasha Korda, *Shakespeare's Domestic Economies: Gender and Property in Early Modern England*, discusses how these 'moveables

[household stuff] were the form of property most often owned and inherited by women in early modern England' (p. 11).
35. Outlined in Frances E. Dolan (ed.), *The Taming of the Shrew: Texts and Contexts*, pp. 193–5.
36. *A Homily of the State of Matrimony*, pp. 474, 475, 477, 474.
37. Tilney, *The Flower of Friendship*, p. 112, ll. 440–4.
38. *A Homily of the State of Matrimony*, p. 475.
39. Marianne Novy, 'The Taming of the Shrew', in *Love's Argument: Gender Relations in Shakespeare*, p. 55. Mendelson and Crawford, *Women in Early Modern England, 1550–1720*, also note that women of this period might feel 'impelled to make marriage work as a social and economic partnership, even when it was not viable as an emotional and sexual bond' (p. 131).
40. Apparently in some cities single women were legally discouraged from running a tavern, which might explain Mistress Quickly's need to find another husband. Mendelson and Crawford report that in 1589 a Manchester court decreed that no single woman was allowed 'to keep any house or chamber, or sell ale or bread' (*Women in Early Modern England*, p. 172).
41. Amy M. Froide, *Never Married: Single Women in Early Modern England*, pp. 2–3. Amy Louise Erickson, 'Portions and Marriage', in *Women and Property in Early Modern England*, conjectures that women might remain unmarried because they lacked 'sufficient capital to set up housekeeping' (p. 83). Marriage, certainly lower down the social scale, was a joint venture.
42. See Mendelson and Crawford, 'Occupational Identities and Social Roles', in *Women in Early Modern England*, p. 329.
43. Sometimes Kate and Petruchio are played as having 'fallen headlong in love with each other' from the very start, as in the Royal Shakespeare Company's Stratford-upon-Avon production of 1961, starring Vanessa Redgrave and Derek Godfrey. See Penny Gay, 'The Taming of the Shrew', in *As She Likes It: Shakespeare's Unruly Women*, p. 98.
44. Most notably Robert B. Heilman (ed.), *The Taming of the Shrew*, Introduction, pp. xxviii–xxix.
45. See Lynda E. Boose, 'Scolding Brides and Bridling Scolds: Taming the Woman's Unruly Member'. Boose discusses the shaming devices, including the bridle, inflicted on unruly women in Shakespeare's time and relates them to *The Taming of the Shrew*. Ranald, 'The Manning of the Haggard: or *The Taming of the Shrew*', in *Shakespeare and his Social Context*, justifies Petruchio's training of Kate as if she were a falcon by arguing that 'mutual respect between bird and keeper' equates to 'respect and consideration on the part of the man, and obedience and respect on the part of the woman' in marriage. Any move toward 'mutuality, trust and love' is surely undercut, though, by the need for the bird or the wife to be 'obedient' to her master (pp. 117–19).
46. Dod and Cleaver, *A Godly Form of Household Government*, pp. 205–6.
47. Alexander Leggatt, 'The Taming of the Shrew', in *Shakespeare's Comedy of Love*, p. 58.
48. Sarah Werner, 'The Taming of the Shrew: A Case Study in Performance Criticism', in *Shakespeare and Feminist Performance: Ideology on Stage*, comments that in Gale Edwards's 1995 Royal Shakespeare Company

production the couple at this point projected a relationship of 'mutual appreciation and loving flirtation' (p. 83).
49. Novy, '*The Taming of the Shrew*', in *Love's Argument*, p. 54. More recently, in ' "'My hand is ready, may it do him ease"': Shakespeare and the Theatre of Display', in Evelyn Gajowski (ed.), *Presentism, Gender, and Sexuality in Shakespeare*, pp. 143–56, Michael Mangan argues that Kate finds a 'paradoxical liberty in the submissive role-playing of a consensual sadomasochistic relationship with Petruchio' (p. 151).
50. Coppélia Kahn, *Man's Estate: Masculine Identity in Shakespeare*, emphasises game-playing here, and that Kate's long final speech most likely 'apes' Petruchio's 'verbal dominance and moralistic stance for satirical effect' (pp. 114–15).
51. 'The Canterbury Tales', in *The Works of Geoffrey Chaucer*, p. 136 (spelling modernised).
52. Rackin, 'Our Canon, Ourselves', in *Shakespeare and Women*, p. 55. Barbara Hodgson, 'Katherina Bound: Or, Play(K)ating the Strictures of Everyday Life', also finds that the speech works as a 'realization of male desire' (541).
53. Karen Newman, 'Renaissance Family Politics and Shakespeare's *Taming of the Shrew*', in *Fashioning Femininity and English Renaissance Drama*, pp. 33–50, points out the 'conflict between the explicitly repressive content of Kate's speech and the implicit message of independence' when a 'powerful female' delivers the longest speech in the play (p. 48).
54. Gouge, 'Duties of Wives', in *Of Domesticall Duties*, p. 286.
55. Dolan (ed.), *The Taming of the Shrew: Texts and Contexts*, p. 34.
56. Margaret Lael Mikesell, ' "Love Wrought these Miracles": Marriage and Genre in *The Taming of the Shrew*', 156, 143. John C. Bean, 'Comic Structure and the Humanizing of Kate in *The Taming of the Shrew*', also finds that Kate's speech 'reflects a number of humanist assumptions' on the 'reciprocity of duties in marriage' rather than the idea of male tyranny (68–9). Ranald, 'The Manning of the Haggard: or *The Taming of the Shrew*', in *Shakespeare and his Social Context*, similarly argues that the speech celebrates a 'mutual agreement, a bargain in terms of separation of powers'; Petruchio will fulfil his 'duties' as head of the household, and as his wife Kate will love him and 'not rebel against his reasonable demands' (p. 131).
57. Richard A. Burt, 'Charisma, Coercion and Comic Form in *The Taming of the Shrew*', comments on how the play's comic form is being used to 'coerce solutions to what in fact are unresolvable conflicts in the family and in the social structure in Renaissance England' (296).
58. Marjorie Garber, *Coming of Age in Shakespeare*, comments on Portia's 'deliberate reversal of the traditional marriage ceremony' (p. 40).
59. Stanley Wells, *Shakespeare, Sex, and Love*, also finds in this play 'Shakespeare's most complex exploration of the intricate entanglements of lust and love' and notes that it ends 'like a romantic comedy, with the expectation of marriage' (p. 216).
60. In 'The Most Prevalent Form of Degradation in Erotic Life' (1912), Freud explains how a male may fail to fuse tenderness and sensuality, so that his libidinal interest focuses on a 'lower type of sexual object' (p. 64).
61. Robert Snawsell, *A Looking Glass for Married Folks*, p. 190.

62. As in Prynne's 1628 reference to 'all androgynous and effeminate persons' (Prynne, *Love-Lockes*, 49, cited in *OED* under sense 2 of 'androgynous').
63. See *Marsilio Ficino's Commentary on Plato's Symposium*, bk. 4, ch. 1, p. 154. While Ficino's *De Amore* (1484) was available in Tuscan Italian and Latin, Robert Kimbrough, *Shakespeare and the Art of Humankindness: The Essay toward Androgyny*, p. 212, n. 11, suggests that Shakespeare's contemporaries could have found this treatment of love, stemming from *The Symposium*, in Geoffrey Fenton's *Monophylo* (1572).
64. Peter Erickson, *Patriarchal Structures in Shakespeare's Drama*, argues that this 'gender role exchange' enlarges the 'primal sexual identity' of both Antony and Cleopatra (p. 133).
65. 'The Sixth Day of the First Week', in *The Divine Weeks and Works of Guillaume de Saluste, Sieur du Bartas*, vol. 1, p. 291, ll. 1051–4.
66. In *The City of God*, trans. Marcus Dods, bk. 14, chs. 23–4, St Augustine speculates on possible sexual innocence for Adam and Eve in Eden. He conjectures that had the Fall into sin not occurred, the male's 'members [sex organs] might have served his will for the propagation of offspring without lust'. Now procreation can only take place through involuntary arousal, or 'shameful' sexual desire (pp. 471, 473).
67. The Epistle of Paul the Apostle to the Ephesians, 5: 31–2.
68. In the play Antony is compared to Mars, god of war (2. 5. 117) while Cleopatra personifies Venus, goddess of love, at Cydnus (2. 2. 200–1). Appropriately, their analogues in classical myth unite adulterously to conceive, among other offspring, Eros (Cupid) and the child Harmony.
69. Murray M. Schwartz, 'Shakespeare through Contemporary Psychoanalysis', in Schwartz and Kahn (eds), *Representing Shakespeare: New Psychoanalytic Essays*, also finds that this 'interplay' of male and female enables 'metamorphosis, active transformation of self' while allowing for 'differentiation' (p. 30).
70. Along these lines, Arthur Kirsch, *Shakespeare and the Experience of Love*, suggests that the lovers' quest would be seen as 'inescapably regressive and self-destructive' (p. 179). In contrast Maurice Charney, *Shakespeare on Love and Lust*, finds that dying for love 'is made to seem a triumphant end' in this play (p. 88).
71. Singer, 'William Shakespeare: Philosopher of Love', in *The Nature of Love, Vol. 2: Courtly and Romantic*, p. 226.
72. Usually this line is linked to Cleopatra's applying another asp to her arm, but Cook, *Making a Match*, points out that no such stage direction is given in the Folio, and thus Cleopatra seems to echo 'the *de futuro* pledges in the prayer book' (p. 225).
73. In the First Epistle to the Corinthians, St Paul concedes that if a man is joined to a 'harlot', the 'twain' shall 'become one flesh' (6: 16–17).
74. Hopkins, *The Shakespearean Marriage*, also considers that in their unconventional union Antony and Cleopatra 'already share the affective dimension' of the 'married state' (p. 126), even though their passion 'can defeat worldly customs only after life, not during it' (p. 131).

Chapter 7

Homoerotic Desire and Same-Sex Bonding: Challenges to Heterosexual Partnership?

Since the 1990s, when the 'new sexuality criticism' became fully established,[1] critics have analysed how Shakespeare's work draws on homoeroticism or same-sex attraction. Our current views on the issue are informed by Western society's legalisation of same-sex marriage – implemented in the UK by 2014 and in the US one year later, after the Supreme Court ruled that a ban on same-sex marriage was unconstitutional. While early modern society never publicly sanctioned such unions, same-sex desire nevertheless circulates within Shakespeare's comedies (especially in performance) and his sonnets. Most postmodern readers now agree that the sonneteer's expressions of love for his 'fair friend' go beyond Platonic admiration into full-blown sexual desire, a passionate relationship that the poet prizes above his affair with a 'dark' woman. And since the early modern period often privileges the ideal of male friendship, with or without homoerotic undertones, above male-female unions, how far does that complicate the progress towards heterosexual marriage in several of Shakespeare's romantic comedies?

It's now a given that the Elizabethan theatrical convention in which female characters were played by boy actors foregrounded gender as a social construct. As the feminist critic Catherine Belsey argued more than three decades ago, this theatrical practice, by disrupting 'the system of differences on which sexual stereotyping depends',[2] challenged 'essentialized' versions of what it means to be male or female.[3] By the same token, cross-dressing in the theatre surely generated 'polymorphous desires',[4] blurring the distinction between same-sex and mixed-sex desire.[5] Queer studies have continued to emphasise, as Stephen Guy-Bray puts it, that 'If masculinity is not inherent but . . . can be put on like a garment, then heterosexuality and homosexuality themselves cannot be stable categories'.[6] Certainly the fear that theatrical performance could provoke illicit desire fuelled the Puritan argument for closing down these 'goodly pageants', after which, Philip Stubbes fantasised, the male members of the audience would go to their 'secret conclaves' and 'play *the Sodomits*'.[7] And John Rainolds in *Th'Overthrow of Stage-Plays* (1599) warned that cross-dressing was likely to 'kindle' lust and 'uncleane affections'.[8] While crosscurrents of same-sex and mixed-sex desire are more subtle in Shakespeare's comedies, when a male character responds to the androgynous figure of a female character dressed as a boy – Orsino in *Twelfth Night* erotically drawn to Viola/Cesario, for instance – the effect may be to destabilise what is assumed to be the sexual norm: heterosexual love leading to marriage.

To be sure, Shakespeare's society, in which men made a 'striking political and emotional investment' in one another,[9] often to the exclusion of women, fostered male camaraderie. This male bonding, which Eve Kosofsky Sedgwick helpfully distinguishes as 'homosocial' rather than homoerotic or homosexual,[10] informs Shakespearean drama. It is cemented by the men's jokes on cuckoldry in *Much Ado about Nothing*.[11] And it's idealised in *As You Like It*'s Forest of Arden, where the exiled Duke and his comrades philosophise away their hardships and hunt for food in a 'golden world' from which female partners are noticeably absent (1. 1. 118–19).[12] Male camaraderie, especially pronounced in wartime, can even override class distinctions; Henry V on St Crispin's Day promises his outnumbered 'band of brothers' that 'he today that sheds his blood with me / Shall be my brother, be he ne'er so vile' (*Henry V*, 4. 3. 60–2).

Such male bonding easily slides into the homoerotic. In *Henry V* we are told that the soldier York 'threw his wounded arm' over Suffolk's neck 'and kiss'd his lips' and bleeding gashes, with both men sealing their 'noble-ending love' (4. 6. 24–7) as they die. Coriolanus, moving to embrace his comrade Cominius in 'arms as sound as when [he] woo'd', claims as much passion as when he moved 'bedward' with his bride (1. 6. 29–32). In turn he is 'hotly and nobly' embraced by the Volscian leader Aufidius, whose heart races faster than when he first saw his 'wedded mistress' step over his 'threshold' (4. 5. 111, 116–18). Aufidius 'makes a mistress' of Coriolanus in public (194–5) and even develops a fantasy of male intercourse: 'We have been down together in my sleep / . . . fisting each other's throat, / And wak'd half dead with nothing' (124–6). Yet we do not deduce that these two military rivals turned allies are practising homosexuals, and Coriolanus shares a 'long' kiss with his wife when they meet outside the gates of Rome (5. 3. 44–5).

At least within Shakespeare's classical Roman context, erotically charged same-sex relationships remain compatible with heterosexual ones. Achilles's love for Patroclus in *Troilus and Cressida* is a case in point. Even if Patroclus is what Thersites brands him, the warrior's 'masculine whore' (5. 1. 17), no one appears surprised that Achilles is also 'in love' with Priam's daughter Polyxena; in fact this affair is blamed for Achilles's refusal to fight (3. 3. 193, 207–8; 5. 1. 41–4). When Patroclus reminds his friend that in 'time of action' an 'effeminate man' is despised (218–21), he is not using the term 'effeminate' to refer to a passive homosexual. Rather, he is subscribing to the idea, expressed in Plutarch's *Moralia*, that a male is weakened by 'effeminate' lust for a woman.[13] And while Achilles's commitment to Patroclus eventually proves stronger than his love for Polyxena – it is only when his beloved friend is killed that Achilles is 'roused' to arms to avenge his death (5. 5. 32) – one kind of love doesn't necessarily displace the other. *Richard II* goes further in showing how homoerotic, even homosexual, activities may co-exist with marriage. Bolingbroke explicitly accuses the king of 'sinful hours' with Bushy and Green, favourites who 'broke the possession of a royal bed' and made the queen weep (3. 1. 11–14). Yet when Richard kisses his wife farewell in Act 5 the couple shows mutual affection, severed 'heart from heart' (5. 1. 82). The king rebukes Northumberland for causing him to be 'doubly divorc'd' (71), from his queen as well as his throne.

It has long been established that the noun 'homosexual', identifying an individual who prefers male-male sex, did not become current until the nineteenth century. Instead early modern satires used disparaging labels such as 'catamite', 'ganymede' and 'ingle'[14] to refer to a male sexual partner, often a boy. The act of sodomy itself, described by moralists as the depraved and 'filthy' end product of debauchery,[15] theoretically carried a death sentence in sixteenth- and seventeenth-century England.[16] Yet we know from contemporary records that anal intercourse did take place – sometimes between masters and servants, or in all-male enclaves such as universities or apprentice housing.[17] This almost schizoid attitude within Shakespeare's society, defined by Alan Bray as 'deep horror' at the deed itself co-existing with 'reluctance to recognize homosexual behavior' among individual males,[18] is confirmed at the very top. King James I's treatise *Basilikon Doron* (1599), written for his son, denounced sodomy as a 'horrible' crime, as bad as murder, but in a private letter the king addressed his favourite Villiers (later the Duke of Buckingham) as his 'wife', implying that they engaged in all the rites that go with marriage.[19]

In Shakespeare's male-dominated society, homoeroticism (harder to pin down than homosexual acts) apparently escaped censure. Alan Sinfield convincingly argues that the sparking of erotic energy between persons of the same sex didn't disturb Shakespeare's contemporaries because the 'proper signs of friendship', as 'supported by legitimate institutions of friendship, patronage, and service', closely resembled those of 'same-sex passion'.[20] Unlike the Greek endorsement of male-male sex (reflected in Achilles's love for Patroclus), the classical ideal of friendship current in the Renaissance – Cicero's *amicitia*[21] or Aristotle's notion of two close male friends as twinned souls of equal virtue[22] – did not presuppose sexual intimacy. But it might still be tinged with strong eroticism. In his essay 'Of Friendship', Montaigne, taking a Christian Renaissance stance, censures the Greek 'licence' of men sharing their bodies as well as their minds. Yet the feelings Montaigne expresses for his friend La Boite are nothing if not passionate. Florio's translation uses the sexually loaded signifier 'will', in combination with 'plunge' and 'greedinessse', to convey the erotic force of this unique bond of friendship, which (writes Montaigne) 'having seized all my will, induced the same to plunge and lose it selfe in his, which likewise having seized all his will, brought it to lose and plunge it selfe in mine, with a mutuall greedinesse'.[23] And the same essay privileges the 'settled heat' of male friendship not only above what Montaigne calls the 'rash and wavering fire' of 'affection toward women' but even over the covenant of marriage, which is full of 'knots' that can 'break the web' of a satisfying union.[24] John Lyly's play *Endimion* (c. 1590) also debates the rival claims of heterosexual romantic love and friendship between men. Endimion's friend Eumenides is passionately in love with Semele, whom he eventually marries; nevertheless he declares that whereas 'the love of men to women is a thing common', the 'friendship of man to man' is 'infinite and immortal'.[25]

Lyly, whose play was performed by boy actors in the 1590s, frames love between males in ideal classical, even Neo-Platonic terms. The homoeroticism in two prime instances of aristocratic friendship in Shakespeare, indicated by the plays' titles – *The Two Gentlemen of Verona* and *The Two Noble Kinsmen* – I single out for discussion later. But Shakespeare's presentation of close male friendship almost always seems tinged with erotic interest. One possible exception is Hamlet's relationship with Horatio. While Horatio calls his close friend 'sweet lord' and 'sweet prince', Jeffrey Masten has pointed out that in the early modern period the epithet 'sweet', while indicating strong feeling – even the 'interchangeability of selves' that Montaigne celebrates in 'Of Friendship' – can signify asexual 'affection between men, between men and women, and between women'.[26] True, Hamlet wears Horatio in his 'heart of heart' (*Hamlet*, 3. 2. 73). But this strong bond, while it counterbalances Hamlet's tortured ties with Gertrude and Ophelia, appears not to rival them in eroticism.

Falstaff's friendship with Prince Hal indicates more sexual affection.[27]

The elderly man feels as if he has taken an aphrodisiac: 'If the rascal hath not given me medicines to make me love him, I'll be hang'd' (*Henry IV, Part 1*, 2. 2. 18–19). And the Hostess, who uses the unusual verb 'foin' to denote fornication rather than fencing,[28] suggests his bisexuality when she complains that 'If his [Falstaff's] weapon be out', he 'will foin like any devil, he will spare neither man, woman, nor child' (*Henry IV, Part 2*, 2. 1. 15–17). Falstaff's homoerotic attraction to the prince appears to be one-sided, however. Although Hal enjoys the fellowship of their escapades, he remains cool and anticipates casting off his companion ('I do, I will') when he plays the part of the king (*Henry IV, Part 1*, 2. 4. 481). By *Henry V*, the Hostess bluntly comments that the new king has 'kill'd' Falstaff's 'heart' (2. 1. 88).

Enobarbus in *Antony and Cleopatra* provides another instance of heartbreak over the rupture of male friendship. Initially his devotion to Antony seems part of the soldier's homosocial camaraderie. Enobarbus never tries to rival Antony's love for Cleopatra; his appreciation for this female's sexual power comes through in his admiring 'Age cannot wither her' speech (2. 2. 234–9). Ultimately though, driven to desertion by the doting Antony's failures in military judgement, and then filled with remorse after Antony generously returns his treasure, Enobarbus simply dies of a broken heart. His last words – 'O, Antony! O Antony!' – suggest, on his side at least, intense same-sex feelings (4. 9. 23).

Unlike Antony and Enobarbus, the co-generals Brutus and Cassius in *Julius Caesar* share a friendship based on equal rank. They consider themselves kin; Cassius, the less reserved of the two, addresses Brutus as 'most noble brother' (4. 2. 37) and 'my dear brother' (4. 3. 233). But whereas Brutus stays within the bounds of 'good friends' (1. 2. 43) – aspiring to the Stoic ideal of chaste *amicitia* between men alike in virtue – Cassius manifests deep, erotically charged affection. Early in the play, working to convince his 'noble' friend to join the conspiracy to kill Caesar (1. 2. 308), Cassius complains to Brutus, as a lover might to his mistress, 'I have not from your eyes that gentleness / And show of love as I was wont to have' (33–4). It is in the quarrel scene of Act 4, scene 3 that Cassius's passionate feelings for his friend emerge more fully. When high-minded Brutus reminds Cassius of his faults (avarice and a quick temper), Cassius is hurt: 'Brutus hath rived my heart' (85–6). Moving from anger to masochism, feeling 'Hated by one he loves', Cassius, like Richard III playing the spurned Petrarchan lover with Anne, offers his dagger to allow his beloved friend to take his very 'heart' (96, 104). When he thinks that Brutus is about to be captured Cassius commits suicide, unable to bear the sight of his 'best friend ta'en' (5. 3. 35).

The case of Othello's ensign Iago is more complicated. Unlike

Enobarbus, who accepts Antony's love for Cleopatra, Iago wants to destroy Othello's marriage to Desdemona. To do so he exploits military comradeship – what Jonathan Dollimore calls the 'primacy and tenacity of the homosocial bond'[29] – to gain Othello's trust. Iago cleverly responds to Othello's urgent plea for more information, 'If thou dost love me, / Show me thy thought', with 'My lord, you know I love you' (*Othello*, 3. 3. 115–16). Yet because he has earlier stated in soliloquy 'I hate the Moor' (1. 3. 386), other critics have discerned latent homosexuality in the ensign's love-hate struggle with his master.[30] Certainly Iago inflames Othello's suspicions by offering 'superimposed images of heterosexual and homosexual lovemaking'[31] when he salaciously conjures up the image of how Cassio, sharing a bed with him, dreamed of making love to Desdemona. Seeming to 'pluck up kisses by the root', Cassio (according to Iago) even mounted his bedmate by laying 'his leg' over Iago's 'thigh' (*Othello*, 3. 3. 424–5). Iago's solemn pronouncement to Othello at the end of this scene – 'I am your own forever' (480) – could signify a wish for sexual surrender rather than simply a commitment to avenge sexual infidelity. While many stage actors, most notably Laurence Olivier in Tyrone Guthrie's Freudian production of 1937, have found it difficult to project an undertow of homosexual desire, Kenneth Branagh, playing Iago in Oliver Parker's film of *Othello* (1995), succeeded in conveying it.[32]

In *Romeo and Juliet*, which traces Romeo's progress from adolescent infatuation and male alliances to deep passion for Juliet, the bond between Romeo and Mercutio appears for the most part homosocial. It is based on male camaraderie. Mercutio encourages Romeo to view women as sex objects, deriding Rosaline in a mock Petrarchan *blason* on her 'quivering thigh' and genitalia (2. 1. 19),[33] and urging his friend to be aggressively phallic in combating romantic love: 'Prick love for pricking, and you prick love down' (1. 3. 28). Jonathan Goldberg nevertheless contends that Shakespeare's Verona – a place where the 'homosocial order' cannot simply 'be reduced to a compulsive and prescriptive heterosexuality'[34] – accommodates both cross-sex and same-sex desire. This plays out in Baz Luhrmann's gender-bending 1996 film, in which Mercutio attends the Capulets' fancy dress ball as a transvestite drag queen clad in a silver-sequined garter belt and bra, and pointedly addresses the song 'Young hearts, run free' to Romeo.[35] It's true that in the text bawdy repartee between men, rather than actual encounters with women, is what turns Mercutio on. Delighted by Romeo's jest on 'goose' (as prostitute), Mercutio offers to bite Romeo 'by the ear' (2. 4. 76–7). And Mercutio's heated reaction to Tybalt's taunt 'Thou consortest with Romeo' (3. 1. 45) could also suggest erotic interest. On the face of it his reply – 'And thou make minstrels of us, look to hear nothing but discords' (47–8) – takes the verb 'consort' in the sense of its cognate noun, 'a company or set of musicians' (*OED*, *sb.* 4). He is offended by a slur on his masculinity: the idea that he would engage in music rather than a manly pursuit like street brawling. Alternatively, though, he could be taking the verb 'consort' in its now obsolete meaning of 'to have sexual commerce with' (*OED*, *v.* I. 2). In this reading Tybalt has touched on a sore point, and Mercutio (who is certainly not openly gay) seems overly concerned to maintain his macho image. Shocked at Romeo's refusal to respond aggressively to Tybalt's insults, he takes up the challenge, acting as Romeo's surrogate. Romeo himself later regrets, in Plutarchan vein, that the 'beauty' of 'sweet Juliet' has made him 'effeminate' (113–14).

It is in Shakespeare's *Sonnets* (1609), remarkably frank about the narrator's desire for a male loved one, that a 'specifically homosexual subjectivity'[36] fully emerges. The poet's personal declaration in Sonnet 121, 'I am that I am', boldly owns what outsiders may condemn as the aberrant 'frailties' of his 'sportive blood' (6–9). So while W. H. Auden finds the poet's experience in loving the young man primarily 'mystical',[37] Michael Keevak, writing from the perspective of twenty-first-century queer studies, makes a more blunt assessment: 'Shakespeare's Sonnets are unquestionably queer or sodomitical poems.'[38] Homosexual passion had already been titillatingly delineated in at least one contemporary set of poems in the pastoral genre. Richard Barnfield's line from *The Affectionate Shepherd* (1594) – 'I came, I saw, I view'd, I slipp'd in' – seems shockingly explicit as a description of Daphnis's dealings with the young shepherd Ganymede.[39] What makes Shakespeare's sonnet sequence unique is that it is unapologetically bisexual;[40] the second half of the sequence (after Sonnet 126) dramatises the speaker's heterosexual affair with a dark-haired, dark-eyed woman, conducted at the same time that he remains intensely in love with the fair youth. What stayed as a subtext in *Troilus and Cressida* – how Achilles's deep affection for Patroclus trumps his 'love' for Polyxena – is pushed to the fore in the *Sonnets*, which privilege male-male love above lustful male-female relations. In the painful sexual triangle that ensues, the poet's feelings range from abject romantic adoration of the youth to the 'arousal' and self-loathing' induced by the mistress.[41]

The narrator's romance with the youth blossoms slowly. In a tone of respectful admiration, suitable for addressing an aristocratic patron, the poet initially urges the young man to perpetuate his beauty by marrying and begetting children. It is Sonnet 20, 'A woman's face, with Nature's own hand painted', that first acknowledges the fair youth as the 'master-mistress' of the poet's 'passion' (1–2). Like the transvestite boy actor who appeals to both genders, this androgynous young man 'steals men's hearts and women's souls amazeth' (8). He is gifted with both a lovely 'woman's face' *and* a penis, the 'one thing' that has 'prick'd' him out for women and not for men to enjoy (13). But while conceding that he may never possess the youth sexually, the sonneteer consoles himself in the clinching couplet with having attained something more valuable – the friend's romantic 'love' as opposed to women's sexual 'use' of him:

> But since she [Nature] prick'd thee out for women's pleasure,
> Mine be thy love, and thy love's use their treasure. (13–14)

Subsequent poems, however, indicate that the speaker moves beyond Platonic friendship with this male. By Sonnet 22 we assume that the friends, who have exchanged hearts, have become lovers. Echoing Philip Sidney's well-known sonnet 'My true love hath my heart, and I have his',[42] the poet reminds the youth that 'my heart / ... in thy breast doth lie, as thine in me'; what's more, he is not about to 'give' it 'back' (7–8, 14). Sonnet 25 ends with the satisfaction of mutual passion and commitment: 'Then happy I that love and am beloved / Where I may not remove, nor be removed' (13–14). More openly celebrating sexual consummation, Sonnet 52 uses the metaphor of a locked treasure chest to emphasise that the poet holds the 'key' to his lover's rich sexuality ('treasure'), valued all the more because it is opened only rarely:

> So am I as the rich whose blessed key
> Can bring him to his sweet up-locked treasure,
> The which he will not ev'ry hour display,
> For blunting the fine point of seldom pleasure. (1–4)

'Fine point of seldom pleasure' seals the sexual nature of what the poet is experiencing, as does the 'unfolding' of his 'imprison'd pride' (12), where 'pride', like 'will', carries the secondary meaning of sexual arousal. The sonnet ends with the poet's hope that he will find more opportunities to enjoy his exceptional lover: 'Blessed are you whose worthiness gives scope, / Being had, to triumph, being lack'd, to hope' (13–14). The verb 'to have' again points to sexual possession – a meaning accentuated in Sonnet 129, where the object of 'lust in action' is 'no sooner had' than 'hated' (2, 6–7).

This love affair is rarely secure, however. It never conforms to the classical ideal of steady friendship uniting men of equal virtue; rather, the sequence is shot through with suspicion over the cooling of homoerotic desire and sadness over separation. The disillusioned Sonnet 133, 'Full many a glorious morning have I seen', strongly implies the 'stain' of sexual infidelity (14), since the young man, like the sun being blotted out, has allowed 'basest clouds' to 'ride' on his 'celestial face' (5–6). The clinching couplet of Sonnet 87, 'Farewell, thou art too dear for my possessing', laments how the speaker 'had' the young man only 'as a dream doth flatter' (13). What undoubtedly causes the poet the most chagrin is the discovery that his male lover, now apparently bisexual, has been seduced by the poet's own mistress. Once the capricious youth has developed a 'wilful taste' for the gender he previously 'refuse[d]' (Sonnet 40, 8), this heterosexual attraction threatens the bond between the two males.

Yet the sonnets invariably prioritise the poet's romantic love for the youth above desire for the mistress. Sonnet 144, dramatising the sexual triangle, bristles with misogyny. Disgusted by the erotic power of the female, the poet literally demonises her while idealising the youth, in conventional Petrarchan fashion, as an angel or saint:

> Two loves I have of comfort and despair,
> Which like two spirits do suggest [urge] me still;
> The better angel is a man right fair
> The worser spirit a woman color'd ill. (1–4)

The dark woman is positioned as a devilish temptress who creates hell for both her lovers. She is eager to corrupt the 'purity' of the young man with her sexual wiles ('foul pride'), to transform him from 'saint' to 'devil' (7–8). At the same time, she makes sure that her older lover will suffer the torments of jealousy. Guessing that her seduction of the youth has been successful, the spurned sonneteer imagines 'one angel in another's hell' – the youth in the mistress's vagina (12). Although this treacherous woman is almost bound to infect her new lover with the 'fire' of venereal disease, the poet must meanwhile 'live in doubt, / Till my bad angel fire my good one out' (13–14).

Despite the torments of the bisexual love triangle, the poet continues to cherish his male friend. Sonnet 40, 'Take all my loves, my love, yea take them all', acknowledges, with some exasperation, that his overriding love for the youth mitigates the pain of having to share the mistress with him. The poet's reluctant admission 'I cannot blame thee for my love thou usest' (6) plays on the two meanings of 'love' – as lover and as loving – to exonerate his 'lascivious' friend from guilt. Because the youth is expected to capitalise on (use) the great 'love' of his devoted partner, for 'All mine was thine before thou hadst this more' (4), he is entitled to 'use' the poet's female lover sexually. Again it becomes clear from Sonnet 42, 'That thou hast her, it is not all my grief', that the poet is more jealous over the youth than the mistress; he admits his friend's infidelity 'touches [him] more nearly' (4). But since, after all, 'my friend and I are one' – as lovers they have exchanged hearts, and as friends they aspire, at least, to Aristotle's standard for perfect male friendship, two bodies sharing one soul – the poet can console himself that in loving the fair youth the dark lady 'loves but me alone' (12–14). What is more, as Eve Kosofsky Sedgwick comments, a female may be used 'as exchangeable ... property for the primary purpose of cementing the bonds of men with men'.[43]

Meanwhile the woman herself is usually depicted as a degrading object, a deceiver who is 'black' in 'deeds' as well as looks (Sonnet 131, 13). The poet resents how passion for her overrides his better judgement: the 'simple truth' that such an amoral woman is unworthy of his attentions (Sonnet 138, 8). Indeed, his heterosexual liaison with her suggests Sonnet 129's 'lust in action' more than mature love. And the darkly humorous Sonnet 135, 'Whoever has her wish, thou hast thy *Will*', is frankly derogatory about the mistress's insatiable lust: a 'large and spacious' sex drive/vagina that can accommodate many lovers (5). To this fellowship of other men[44] who enjoy her she is encouraged to add the desire of the poet William ('one will of mine'). Her promiscuity will increase the couple's mutual lust, making 'large *Will* more' (12).

In contrast, the poet's idealisation of his 'fair friend' follows the Plutarchan idea that same-sex love is worthier than a man's 'effeminate' desire for a woman. There is no mockery or sense of shame here. Several sonnets even daringly apply the imagery of Christian marriage to this homosexual relationship. Sonnet 116, 'Let me not to the marriage of true minds / Admit impediments', for instance, appears among the poems that focus on the young man (1–126), while Sonnet 97 notes the irony of how, during the loved one's absence, the poet experienced the fecundity of 'teeming' autumn, just as 'widow'd wombs' may bear the fruit of spring after 'their lords' decease' (6–8). Sonnet 93, 'So shall I live, supposing thou art true', compares the poet to a 'deceived husband' (2). If the narrator considers that he has become, in St Paul's words on marriage, 'one flesh' with his male partner, it is logical that he would fear any threat to that marriage – especially from a female.

If same-sex love triumphing over heterosexual lust is the hallmark of the sonnets, Shakespeare's romantic comedies progress toward a different end; there are no queer marriages at the conclusion of these plays. The hetero-normative direction of the drama – mixed-sex couples being paired off in the resolution of marriage – is dictated by the comic genre itself. Nevertheless, the sparking of homoerotic and bisexual desire by the cross-dressed boy actor heroines in *As You Like It* and *Twelfth Night* complicates the expected outcome. Even more, the presence of a devoted male friend (Antonio) in both *Twelfth Night* and *The Merchant* of *Venice* briefly threatens to subvert orthodox romantic love. The challenge remains. Must sexual 'will' always be directed toward the goal of heterosexual union? Should queer ties be waived or, if accepted as compatible with mixed-sex ones, are they always relegated to second place?

In *As You Like It* erotic desire is channelled into conventional marriage by the end of the play, but only after some interesting diversions. Since Rosalind describes herself as 'more than common tall' for a woman (1. 3. 115), the boy actor playing her can flaunt his masculine side in the 'swashing' and 'martial' exterior (120) of Rosalind's disguise. The very name she chooses to call herself – Ganymede, Jupiter's favoured young cup-bearer – would prime the audience to expect homoerotic attraction between her and Orlando. Marlowe's play *Dido, Queen of Carthage* (1587) opens with Jupiter fondling and offering to 'play' with Ganymede (1. 1. 1),[45] while Marston's *Certaine Satyres* (1598) uses the term in its early modern sense to signify a young homosexual partner, depicting a '*Ganimede*' hired by a 'gallant' for two days of secret pleasure (3. 31–2).[46] In offering to be wooed by Orlando in lieu of his beloved Rosalind, Shakespeare's 'Ganymede' virtually equates 'boys and women'; both are 'effeminate, changeable ... proud, fantastical, apish, shallow, inconstant, full of tears, full of smiles' (3. 2. 410–15). More to the point, as Stephen Orgel and other scholars have argued, women and boys were both 'acknowledged objects of sexual attraction for men' in early modern England.[47]

This breakdown of fixed gender through the Ganymede persona enables a 'marvellously fluid sexuality'[48] to circulate throughout the Forest of Arden, a form of desiring that can easily shift from mixed-sex to same-sex. Having fallen in love with female Rosalind, Orlando – played with more than a 'hint of bisexuality'[49] by Ian Bannen in the Royal Shakespeare Company's renowned 1961 production – happily continues his courtship with male Ganymede. When he warmly responds 'With all my heart, good youth' to Rosalind's offer (as Ganymede) to lead him to her sheep-cote, she has to remind him to call her 'Rosalind' (3. 2. 433–4). Later Rosalind suggests to Celia that she and her suitor have kissed, albeit chastely – she describes his 'kissing' as 'full of sanctity' (3. 4. 13) – and indeed her masculine role allows her to be a more aggressive agent in the courtship than would be expected of a woman. In a 'more coming-on disposition' she urges Orlando, 'Come, woo me, woo me, for now I am in a holiday humor and like enough to consent' (4. 1. 68–9). Her swain responds in kind: 'And wilt thou have me?' (118). In fact the game may heat up too much once Rosalind/Ganymede asks Celia to play the 'priest, and marry us' (124–5). When Orlando answers on cue with 'I take thee, Rosalind, for wife' (137), what Shakespeare's audience briefly observes is a form of queer marriage: not just a man and boy flirting but, as Bruce R. Smith notes, a 'licensed way of arousing and satisfying homosexual desire'.[50]

Polymorphous desires in the Forest of Arden also include a degree of same-sex attraction between females; Phoebe the shepherdess becomes besotted with double-gendered Rosalind/Ganymede. True, she believes she has fallen in love with an adolescent male. But while she is riveted by Ganymede's rudely masculine dismissal of her 'beauty' (3. 5. 37), Phoebe also responds to his feminine appearance, noting his damask complexion and the 'pretty redness' of 'his lip' (113, 120). Meanwhile Rosalind appears to enjoy becoming what Valerie Traub calls the '"masculine" object of Phoebe's desire'[51] when she stridently commands Phoebe 'down on your knees' (57), cultivating a 'despiteful and ungentle' attitude toward her (5. 2. 80). Of course the effect is to enslave Phoebe all the more, complicating her progress toward heterosexual union with the devoted shepherd Silvius.

We are not shown Orlando's shock – perhaps surprise laced with slight disappointment – when Rosalind resumes her female attire and identity in Act 5. She now restores the traditional, patriarchal model of early modern marriage when she gives herself, as Rosalind, first to her father ('for I am yours') and then, using the same words, to Orlando as his wife (5. 4. 116–17). It is the epilogue, spoken by the actor of Rosalind, that coyly returns to having it both ways. Unmasked as a boy, the young player can appeal to both genders because he has represented both – 'a woman in supposition and a man in actuality', as Jean E. Howard puts it.[52] Teasingly he promises the male onlookers, 'If I were a woman I would kiss as many of you as had beards that pleas'd me . . . and breaths that I defied not', which allows the men, at least, to think about kissing a she-male. The actor placates the females on more heterosexual grounds, enjoining them 'for the love you bear to men . . . to like as much of this play as please you' (Epilogue, 12–20). The invitation to kiss, as well as the repetition of 'please' (suggesting sexual pleasure), is a reminder that erotic interest defies gender boundaries.[53] While the play ends with three couples joined in conventional marriage, the transvestite actor delivering the epilogue evokes what Janet Adelman calls the 'fantasy' of simultaneously forging 'homosexual and heterosexual bonds',[54] allowing the fulfilment of bisexual desires.

As You Like It embraces these nuanced cross-gender games more fully than does *Twelfth Night*. At any moment Rosalind could end her prolonged masquerade as Ganymede and reveal her identity as a woman. Viola, a stranger shipwrecked in Illyria, must adopt a protective male disguise as Cesario in order to survive, yet she doesn't welcome the subversive gender-bending potential of cross-dressing. Like the Puritans who abhorred transvestism for blurring gender distinctions and exciting queer passions – Philip Stubbes called women who wear men's clothes 'Hermaphrodites: that is, Monsters of bothe kindes, half women, half men'[55] – Viola ponders the 'wickedness' of 'disguise' in causing gender confusion (2. 2. 27–8). She derides herself as a 'poor monster' (34) for exciting sexual desire in Olivia.

Rosalind, who relishes the androgyny of her role as Ganymede, can take the initiative in the wooing game. Not so Viola. While she finds opportunities to hint at her romantic feelings for Orsino, she must maintain some distance. Otherwise, because she is so favoured as his male page, she risks encouraging a homoerotic or even a homosexual relationship between master and servant – making herself, as Lisa Jardine puts it, 'available' for the duke's own 'sexual pleasure' as a 'desired dependant'.[56] Certainly she is happy to forge a homosocial tie with Orsino when she reminds him that 'We men may say more, swear more', even as she covertly defends her own sex as more 'true of heart' (2. 4. 116, 206). Her claim to have loved an older woman who resembles Orsino in 'complexion' might be interpreted as a sexual come-on (2. 4. 26–8). And by inventing a surrogate sister who passively submitted to melancholy and 'grief', Cesario could appear to be offering to play the woman's part for her master:

> My father had a daughter lov'd a man –
> As it might be perhaps, were I a woman
> I should your lordship. (107–9)

In the play's finale, too, Orsino claims that Viola/ Cesario has told him a 'thousand' times that she would 'never ... / love woman' as much as she loves him (5. 1. 267–8). Hyperbole, perhaps. But Viola has had to play a dangerous game, hinting at her sexual identity as a nubile female while evading any desire Orsino might have for a homosexual affair.[57]

In performance Orsino could be played, like Orlando, as bisexual, showing erotic affection for Cesario by calling him 'boy' (2. 4. 15, 25, 32, 119) rather than the more gender-neutral 'youth'.[58] But whereas Orlando responds to the male Ganymede released within the female character Rosalind, Orsino seems just as strongly attracted to the femininity underlying the Cesario persona. He compares Cesario's 'smooth' red ('rubious') lips to those of the goddess Diana, noting that because his voice is as high-pitched as a girl's he cannot yet be classified as 'a man' (1. 4. 30–3). What attracts the narcissistic Orsino to the Viola character is not just her androgynous appearance but her mirroring of his own love-sick melancholy. Her self-effacing compassion is a traditionally feminine attribute. So while her disguise almost certainly generates some homoerotic desire in Orsino, it also enables Viola/Cesario to forge a cross-sex friendship – what David Schalkwyk calls the conjunction of '*phila* and *eros*' – when Orsino confides in a sympathetic female posing as a male.[59]

This bond should make it relatively easy for Orsino, whose mind is described as a 'very opal' (2. 4. 75), to segue from desiring the 'marble-breasted tyrant' Olivia to accepting Viola/Cesario – 'the lamb that I do love' – as his wife (5. 1. 124, 130). Unless, that is, he prefers to worship the mere 'image of the creature / That is belov'd' (2. 4. 19–20), locked into a perpetual state of desire that fails to satisfy his sexual 'will'. When Viola reveals her gender, Orsino points out that the 'service' she rendered him as a page boy went 'much against the mettle of [her] sex' (5. 1. 322). Presumably he is not using 'service' in its sexual sense. Rather he is suggesting that he prefers, like a Petrarchan lover, to serve his lady from afar instead of letting his new 'belov'd' serve him as devoted wife. And the fact that he cannot fully accept Viola as his mistress, and not a 'man', until he sees her attired in woman's 'habits' (386–7) suggests that he might prefer the homosocial/homoerotic bond they have formed as master and servant. If so, he is not, as W. Thomas MacCary argues, ready to move beyond the narcissistic phase in which he seeks a 'mirror image of himself', towards the 'mature object-choice'[60] of a committed heterosexual union. Alternatively, the audience might conclude that 'changeable' Orsino, whose 'intent' (according to wise fool Feste) wanders 'every where' (2. 4. 77), will remain happily bisexual. Finding his own version of what Sonnet 20 calls the 'master-mistress', he can enjoy both worlds, cross-sex and same-sex, in the company of his 'fancy's queen' (5. 1. 388).[61]

Viola is the only member of the triangle who doesn't appear susceptible to same-sex desire. To be sure, she admires Olivia's 'fair' exterior (1. 5. 251). Like the sonneteer conventionally urging his 'sweet' friend to make a 'copy' of his 'loveliness' for posterity (Sonnet 4, 1, 10), Viola chides her rival for shunning marriage and thus leaving 'the world no copy' of her beauty (1. 5. 243). But while an actor playing Viola might project some erotic 'intrigue and excitement' as she woos the lady by proxy, there's little textual evidence to support Valerie Traub's view that a 'mutual exchange' of desire takes place between the women.[62] It's surely more a case of female bonding; Viola recognises that both of them are in love with someone whose sexual interest is focused elsewhere. In emphasising 'I am not what I am' (3. 1. 141), she tries to give Olivia fair warning about her gender. And although she courteously offers the lady her hand in 'humble service' (95), her dominant emotion is 'pity' for the deluded Olivia (123) – the womanly compassion that Rosalind as Ganymede never shows toward Phoebe. Viola is not toying with Olivia's affections.

As for Olivia, her feelings for Cesario resemble Orsino's complicated attraction to the youth – a blend of same-sex and heterosexual. Malvolio describes the youth as an unripe adolescent, barely out of puberty, like the boy actor who resembles a 'squash' or 'codling' (lacking mature 'cods', slang for testicles) before it becomes a 'peascod' or an apple (1. 5. 157–8). Rather than falling in love with ruggedly masculine traits, Olivia, in her 'fivefold blazon' of Cesario (292–3), praises the youth's 'tongue' (speaking voice), 'face' and 'limbs', which Orsino has already characterised as decidedly feminine. Only the youth's final two attributes, 'actions' and 'spirit' (292–3), have male associations ('spirit' can connote semen, as in Sonnet 129's 'Th'expense of spirit in a waste of shame / Is lust in action'). It is not male assertiveness but rather gentleness – sensitivity, as well as gentility – that she responds to most fully, addressing Cesario as 'gentle friend'.[63] The play's message, projected in Feste's final song, is that a man in search of a wife is unlikely to 'thrive' by 'swaggering' (5. 1. 399).

In this play subtitled 'What You Will' (what you determine to achieve as well as what you desire), Olivia's desperate appeal to Cesario, 'I would you were as I would have you be' (3. 1. 141), is happily fulfilled through the arrival of Sebastian. In him Olivia finds a romantic and sexual partner, a heterosexual male version of her androgynous beloved. Sebastian has already shown some delicacy of feeling – a traditionally feminine trait – with Antonio, while (as I argue below) he appears to resist a homosexual relationship with this friend. In the madness of her 'passion' as she aggressively pursues Cesario (3. 1. 152), Olivia has risked becoming betrothed to a woman, creating an image, at least, of how 'queer desire' might turn into 'queer marriage'.[64] When Sebastian remarks that Olivia 'would have been contracted to a maid' (5. 1. 261), the ambiguity of 'would', signifying futurity as well as the wishing (or willing) of sexual desire, suggests that Olivia may be somewhat susceptible to same-sex love. Granted, she responds erotically without knowing Viola's true sex. And after the twelfth-night epiphany, the revelation not only that Viola's male twin is alive, a 'spirit' clad in flesh (5. 1. 236), but that Viola herself is female, the play rapidly progresses from a series of mistakings into two orthodox marriages. But if Olivia shows even a hint of homoerotic attraction to the female Viola character, that would support Janet Adelman's contention that, like Orsino, Olivia doesn't have to 'choose between a homosexual and a heterosexual bond';[65] she can continue to enjoy both.

The play challenges heterosexual bonding more significantly through the character of Antonio, who, unlike the Platonic friend or dispassionate mentor of Shakespeare's source,[66] clearly desires Sebastian. In his first words to Sebastian, the reiterated verb 'will' conveys intensity of desire rather than simple futurity: 'Will you stay no longer? ... will you not that I go with you?' (2. 1. 1–2). Once Sebastian insists on breaking away, Antonio acts like a spurned Petrarchan lover desperately offering devoted service: 'If you will not murder me for my love, let me be your servant' (35–6). Later he reveals strong erotic attraction in a phallic image: 'My desire / (More sharp than filed steel), did spur me forth' (3. 3. 4–5). Twenty-first-century audiences and critics are likely to identify Antonio as a gay man; Stephen Orgel even claims that Shakespeare presents the two men as an 'overtly homosexual couple'.[67] But Shakespeare's audience could well have viewed Antonio differently – as a devoted friend or, more judgementally, as a would-be sodomite whose love is equated with 'idolatry'.

Certainly Antonio's devoted reverence for Sebastian might strike Christian audiences as blasphemous. Through Antonio's unabashed use of the words 'adore' and 'idol' Shakespeare represents intense same-sex love as a form of passionate worship, without 'retention or restraint' (5. 1. 81). Determined to follow Sebastian to the court of Orsino, Antonio confesses (in soliloquy) 'I do adore thee so / That danger shall seem sport and I will go' (2. 1. 47–8). Indicating the sheer excess of desire in *Twelfth Night*, the verb 'adore' appears three times apart from Antonio's use of it – the most occurrences in any Shakespeare play. Sir Toby calls Maria 'one that adores me', while Sir Andrew Aguecheek sadly reminisces 'I was adored once too' (2. 3. 179–81). The punchline of Maria's forged letter, calculated to convince Malvolio that his mistress loves him, is ' "I may command where I adore" ' (2. 5. 115). In Shakespeare's work as a whole, however, 'adore' usually applies to worship of the gods – as when Albany in *King Lear* invokes 'gods that we adore' (1. 4. 289) – while 'idol' indicates (as it still does) a blindly romantic misapplication of worship to a human love object. The speaker of Sonnet 105 strongly protests 'Let not my love be called idolatry'. But the conventional romantic lover in Shakespeare often tilts towards 'mad idolatry', as Hector puts it in *Troilus and Cressida* (2. 2. 56); Helena in *A Midsummer Night's Dream* 'dotes in idolatry' on inconstant Demetrius (1. 1. 109), while Proteus finds Silvia worshipped as an 'idol' in *The Two Gentlemen of Verona* (2. 4. 144). Deeply hurt when Viola/Cesario, mistaken for Sebastian, seems to 'deny' him help, Antonio complains to the bystanders how he 'did ... devotion' to the 'image' of this youth after rescuing him. His sense of betrayal is acute: 'Oh how vile an idol proves this god!' (3. 4. 362–5). To

Shakespeare's mainly Protestant audience, his language would imply a breaking not only of the first commandment, 'Thou shalt have no other gods before me', but also of the second, which prohibits worship of any 'graven image'.

Yet in the same passage that calls Sebastian an 'idol', Antonio claims to have treated him with all the 'sanctity of love' (3. 4. 361). This 'sanctity' might seem to conform to the medieval model of 'exalting and ennobling' love between men that C. Stephen Jaeger considers a residual part of Shakespeare's culture. Such publicly conducted relationships, based on the classical idea of *amicitia* and infused with spiritual passion, were, according to Jaeger, nevertheless asexual, shunning the 'male-male sexuality'[68] that informs Antonio's conversation with Sebastian. It seems more likely, then, that Antonio is modelled on Plutarch's description of the manly man who loves boys rather than desiring women, but who doesn't necessarily consummate that love.

Steering Shakespeare's audience away from the idea that Antonio practises sodomy is the sense that Sebastian does not cooperate; he has no wish to play the Ganymede role. Rather than the two friends being presented as an 'overtly homosexual couple' (Orgel's term), in which case Olivia's marriage to Sebastian could be problematic, homoerotic feeling appears to be generated on Antonio's side only. Asked about his family history, Sebastian wards off intimacy (2. 1. 14), and once tracked down, he deflects sexual interest with the courteous apology 'I would not by my will have troubled you' (3. 3. 1). It is true that Sebastian greets Antonio with more than casual affection after a brief absence when they meet at Olivia's house: 'O my dear Antonio! / How have the hours rack'd and tortur'd me / Since I have lost thee!' (5. 1. 218–20). Ironically his 'dear' Antonio has just heard a person he thinks is Sebastian assure Orsino that s/he loves him 'More by all mores than e'er I shall love wife' (5. 1. 136) – on its face, a sudden revelation that an aristocratic male rival has won his friend's affections.

Because the play toys so much with same-sex attraction among Orsino, Viola and Olivia, a modern audience may wonder whether, like Orsino, Sebastian represents a bisexual youth who, as Joseph Pequigney sees it, is 'willing sexually to enjoy . . . both a man and a woman'.[69] Symmetrical as this would be, a pansexual Sebastian hardly fits with the play-text. Only Antonio is left wondering 'Which is Sebastian?' (5. 1. 224) – the male twin or the female – while also struggling to reconcile the dear friend with whom he has kept company without a 'minute's vacancy' for three months (95) with the Sebastian who is now the husband of Olivia. Since Antonio remains under arrest, there is no guarantee he will be reunited with his friend. Olivia's reaction when Cesario affirms his devotion to Orsino – she cries out 'Ah me, detested! How am I beguil'd!' (139), shocked to discover that her bridegroom apparently prefers men – surely confirms how reluctant Olivia would be to integrate an intense male friendship into her marriage. It's therefore highly unlikely that Antonio, as Pequigney imagines, would leave the stage 'arm in arm' with Olivia and Sebastian.[70] Rather, Antonio's apparent exclusion from the final festivities removes him as a threat, positioning him as a scapegoat for the potentially disruptive 'homoerotic energy'[71] generated by the other principal characters.

Antonio in *The Merchant of Venice*, who privileges love for Bassanio above his worldly wealth, also shows no romantic interest in women. While the two men are confidants, their relationship fails to fit the classical ideal of friendship, for they are equals neither in social rank (Bassanio is an aristocrat, Antonio a merchant) nor in love of virtue; Bassanio admits that he has been a spendthrift who 'owe[s] the most in money' as well as 'love' to his friend (1. 1. 131). Like Antonio in *Twelfth Night*, Antonio the merchant is likely to strike modern audiences, in Marianne Novy's words, as a 'man who loves men in a society in which "gay" or homosexual is not yet a recognized identity category'.[72] But whereas *Twelfth Night*'s Antonio is frank about his passion for his friend, Antonio of Venice at first veils any homoerotic desire for Bassanio. In the opening scene, admitting 'I have much ado to know myself', he claims not to realise why he is 'so sad' (1. 1. 7, 1). It is Solanio, who later observes about Antonio's feelings for Bassanio 'I think he only loves the world for him' (2. 8. 50), who tries to account for this melancholy: 'Why then, you are in love.' Antonio's response, 'Fie, fie' (1. 1. 46), evades the question of erotic interest. If he does indeed desire what the Old Testament calls the 'abomination' of male-male sexual intercourse (Leviticus 18: 22), this would explain why, in the trial scene, he refers to himself as a 'tainted wether of the flock / Meetest for death' (4. 1. 114–15).

Successful in the commercial world of Venice, Antonio tends to express his love in terms of money. Like *Twelfth Night*'s Antonio, who impulsively gives his entire 'purse' to the youth he believes is his beloved Sebastian, Antonio assures Bassanio that 'My purse, my person, my extremest means, / Lie all unlock'd to your occasions' (1. 1. 138–9). 'Purse' and 'person', linked by sound, are virtually equated in meaning. In effect Antonio is not only handing his money and his very being to Bassanio but, through the submerged pun on 'purse' as genitalia (either vagina or scrotum), he appears to be offering himself sexually too. His promise that his 'person' will stay 'unlock'd' to his friend's 'occasions' echoes the sonneteer's erotic anticipation of enjoying his beloved's 'sweet, up-locked treasure' (Sonnet 52, 2).

Antonio's passionate feelings toward Bassanio become more explicit as the action progresses. Solanio notes that Antonio not only shed tears at parting from his friend but 'wrung Bassanio's hand' with 'affection wondrous sensible' (2. 8. 48–9), manifesting sexual feeling rather than simple fondness. Later, when his bond with Shylock 'is "forfeit"' (3. 2. 17) and he requests a final visit from his friend, Antonio pressures Bassanio emotionally by reminding him of their own bond: 'if your love do not persuade you to come, let not my letter' (321–2). And in the trial scene he sets himself up as a rival to Portia:

> Say how I lov'd you, speak me fair in death;
> And when the tale is told, bid her be judge
> Whether Bassanio had not once a love. (4. 1. 275–7)

Is Antonio's devotion reciprocated? When he learns that his friend's ventures have foundered, Bassanio describes Antonio to Portia as 'The dearest friend to me, the kindest man' (3. 2. 292). In the courtroom he goes further, asserting that although he loves his wife dearly, he would gladly sacrifice 'life itself, [his] wife, and all the world' to save Antonio (4. 1. 284). This confirms the rivalry among the three – a competition in love that the disguised Portia wryly underscores with 'Your wife would give you little thanks for that / If she were by to hear you make the offer' (288–9). Portia has earlier accepted Antonio as her lord's 'bosom lover' (close friend, even soul-mate), reasoning that because such 'companions' bear an 'equal yoke of love' they must mirror one another in 'manners' and 'spirit' (3. 4. 11–17). In offering to rescue Antonio with her own wealth she presumably views their relationship as 'amicable love' rather than 'amorous reciprocal love'.[73] But once Antonio stakes his claim and Bassanio talks of sacrificing her, Portia demands the ring to test her husband's loyalty: will he honour his marriage above any homoerotic tie? She has some cause for concern. After Antonio urges that the lawyer's 'deservings, and my love withal / Be valued 'gainst your wife's commandment' (4. 1. 450–1), Bassanio is persuaded to give up the ring. Back in Belmont Portia concedes that Bassanio is 'infinitely bound' to his friend Antonio (5. 1. 135). Nevertheless, by shaming Bassanio over the missing ring, she pushes him to recognise that marriage overrides male friendship. As Catherine Belsey points out, 'the new model' of companionate marriage in this period, which 'identified wives precisely as friends', enables Portia to establish her priority: she is now Bassanio's partner in friendship as well as in (licensed) sexual love.[74] So when Antonio offers to be 'bound again' that Portia's husband will 'never more break faith advisedly' – this time with his 'soul upon the forfeit' rather than the previous, erotically charged mortgage of his body – he is graciously accepting a shift from 'bosom lover' to trusted friend of the family. He can be welcomed to Belmont on Portia's terms.[75]

Alan Sinfield points out how the comedy's generic ending (in marriage) also reinforces the economic reality, in this period, that 'same-sex love is allowed a certain scope' even while it 'has to be set aside' in the interests of upper-class marriage, with all this entails in the 'transmission of property' and the production of heirs to continue the family line.[76] As the play ends, two couples exit to consummate their marriages: Gratiano with Nerissa and Bassanio with Portia. It is up to the director to decide whether Antonio remains on stage alone, excluded from the upcoming festivities, or, alternatively, whether he exits as part of a friendly threesome.

In *Twelfth Night* and *The Merchant of Venice* male-male desire is concentrated in one individual, Antonio. But at the beginning and end of his dramatic career, in his early play *The Two Gentlemen of Verona* (1592) and his late play written in collaboration with John Fletcher, *The Two Noble Kinsmen* (1613), Shakespeare experiments with a different paradigm: homoerotic desire generated within aristocratic friendship. The endings of these plays to some extent reverse the dynamic of the romantic comedies. Rather than being compromised or superseded by traditional marriage, the friendships between Valentine and Proteus in *Two Gentlemen of Verona* and between Palamon and Arcite in *The Two Noble Kinsmen* remain strong to the end. And by returning to the pattern of the sonnets – men's rivalry over a woman, which doesn't permanently destroy their relationship – Shakespeare again suggests that male-male love sometimes wins out over heterosexual desire. The competition between the males confirms Sedgwick's point that 'the bond that links the two rivals' may be as 'intense and potent' (or more so) than either man's tie to the desired female.[77]

Valentine and Proteus, close 'companions' like Bassanio and Antonio, have 'convers'd and spent [their] hours together' since childhood (*The Two Gentlemen of Verona*, 2. 4. 63). Mirroring one another almost to the point of fused identities – Valentine says of Proteus, 'I knew him as myself' (62) – they seem the very model of classical friendship, Aristotle's twinned souls or, as in Cicero's *amicitia*, equals who are striving for 'virtuous perfection'.[78] Emulating aristocrats like those in Castiglione's *The Courtier*, each aspires to become a 'complete' Renaissance 'gentleman' (74). Perhaps without consciously recognising what he is doing, Valentine fosters an erotic triangle by asking Silvia to 'entertain' Proteus as his 'fellow-servant' to her 'ladyship' (105); in other words, the men will partner as devoted Petrarchan lovers serving one mistress. In a classic case of mimetic or mirroring desire, Proteus becomes his best friend's rival. Even though his 'too too much' love for the lady has cooled his 'zeal' for Valentine (203–5), he is unsure whether his conviction of Silvia's 'true perfection' comes from his own 'eye' or from Valentine's 'praise' of her (196–7).

In other words, as in the sonnets, where a homoerotic relationship launches heterosexual competition, Proteus's very closeness to Valentine is what drives him to compete for Silvia. Caught in binary thinking as he veers between love and hate, friendship and enmity, Proteus rationalises that he must reject his best friend as an 'enemy' if he is to win Silvia as a 'sweeter friend' (2. 6. 29–30). At the end of the play it is Valentine who proves the truer friend. Even after Proteus aggressively threatens to take Silvia by force in the final scene, Valentine prioritises male affection over mixed-sex romantic love. In a sequence that has baffled modern audiences, he offers to sacrifice his mistress to gratify his friend, declaring, 'And that my love may appear plain and free, / All that was mine in Silvia I give to thee' (5. 4. 82–3). Jolted out of lust for Silvia, Proteus then quickly returns to his first love, Julia, his affections rekindled when he discovers she has devotedly followed him in the guise of a boy. When Valentine enthusiastically proposes a double wedding, he aims not just to celebrate the male-female couples, but to unite the two male friends in one 'day of marriage ... / One feast, one house, one mutual happiness' (172–3). Rather than a romantic-comedy 'progression' from 'male friendship to mixed-sexed love', the play works to integrate the two, refusing, as Stephen Guy-Bray points out, to subordinate 'homosociality to marriage'.[79] Janet Adelman calls this a 'magical' wishing away of problems[80] – the young man's fantasy of maintaining a same-sex fusion with his own mirror image, even while he moves toward a heterosexual union that is likely, at the very least, to recalibrate the ideal of male bonding.

The Two Noble Kinsmen offers no such 'magical' resolution. In Act 1 Shakespeare sets up the main theme, that intense same-sex relationships prove more resilient than heterosexual partnerships;[81] his contribution to Act 5 of the play goes further in questioning whether traditional marriage can be sexually and romantically fulfilling. The cousins' exceptionally close tie, 'dearer in love than blood' (1. 2. 1), is not the only challenge to cross-sex love that Shakespeare presents in Act 1. The deep friendship between Theseus and his general Pirithous, described as 'half' of Theseus's own 'heart' (4. 1. 14), competes with Duke Theseus's marriage to Hippolita. The new bride evokes the two fellow warriors as so bonded that

> Their knot of love
> Tied, weav'd, entangled, with so true, so long,
> And with a finger of so deep a cunning,
> May be outworn, never undone. (1. 3. 41–4)

When she confesses to her sister Emilia that Theseus cannot decide which of the two, wife or intimate male friend, he 'loves best' (47), Emilia can reply only cautiously. Her tactful double negative, 'There is a best, and reason has no manners / To say it is not you' (48–9), inspires little confidence that Hippolita is the one most loved.

It is when Palamon and Arcite are imprisoned together in Athens that Fletcher (responsible for most of Act 2) develops, often with comic exaggeration, the passionate nature of their friendship. It far exceeds the male bonding explored in *The Two Gentlemen of Verona*. Arcite consoles his cousin that 'We are one another's wife' (2. 2. 79–80). No sooner has Palamon concurred – 'Is there a record of any two that lov'd / Better than we do, Arcite?' (112–13) – than they both see Emilia. Predictably and almost absurdly, their loyalty to one another collapses into rivalry, and Palamon calls out Arcite as a 'traitor' for usurping his new 'affections' (171). More patently than in *Two Gentlemen of Verona*, the drama enacts the classic erotic triangle. Still, the kinsmen's rivalry seems increasingly forced, as Emilia, who has already stated her lack of interest in men, becomes a remote, almost incidental figure.[82] Even when they plan to fight to the death at the opening of Act 3, Arcite brings sustenance and weapons to his 'sweet' Palamon (3. 1. 92), while Palamon, a reluctant adversary, would prefer 'embraces' with his friend to 'blows' (3. 6. 22–3). Again expressing the depth of his same-sex feelings, Arcite assures Palamon, 'Defy me in these fair terms, and you show / More than a mistress to me' (25–6).

After Palamon admits to Theseus that he wishes the two friends could 'die together, at one instant' (177), the duke envisages no easy solution for what he calls the pair's 'agony of love' (219–20) – for Emilia, or possibly for one another? Once Theseus steers them toward traditional marriage by insisting that Emilia must wed the winner of the joust, the two friends are deeply conflicted; Palamon uses the image of 'one eye' set 'Against another' to convey the unnaturalness of their fighting to the death (5. 1. 21–2). Significantly, Palamon's chaste prayer to the goddess Venus, composed by Shakespeare, depicts heterosexual love 'from eleven to ninety' (130) as frankly distasteful. The graphic description of a gout-ridden old man, a tortured 'anatomy' who manages to beget a child with a 'lass of fourteen' (107–18), is particularly grotesque. Palamon's depiction of traditional marriage as sexually humiliating betrays his deep reluctance to embrace a mixed-sex union.

To the end the play privileges male-male love over male-female romance. When Arcite wins the contest but is crushed to death by his stumbling horse, Palamon complains

> That we should things desire which do cost us
> The loss of our desire! that nought could buy
> Dear love but loss of dear love! (110–12)

The final line's blocking of cherished same-sex 'dear love' by the 'dear love' of heterosexual desire highlights 'loss' rather than any joyful anticipation of sexual consummation in marriage.

In a dramatic passage attributed to Shakespeare, Emilia offers an even clearer case of prioritising same-sex affection over heterosexual love. Emilia is the only female in all of Shakespeare's work who fully defies a nubile woman's expected trajectory toward marriage. After Hippolita discloses her husband's affection for Pirithous, Emilia tops this by recounting the intimate friendship that she 'enjoy'd' at age eleven with her 'playfellow' Flavina (1. 3. 50). In contrast to the men's 'maturely season'd' love, based on 'strong judgment' (56–7), Emilia characterises her prepubescent love for Flavina as a spontaneous, intuitive bonding. Like Valentine and Proteus, the girls mirrored one another completely; Emilia invariably 'lik'd' what Flavina liked, while Flavina would place in her own bosom a flower matching the one between Emilia's breasts, which were just 'beginning / To swell about the blossom' (64, 67–8). The feelings between the two girls are nevertheless presented as spiritual and romantic rather than explicitly erotic. Placed in such 'innocent cradle[s]', the matching flowers became 'phoenix-like' when they 'died in perfume' (70–1), recalling the 'mutual flame' and 'division none' of Shakespeare's chaste phoenix married to the turtle dove (*The Phoenix and the Turtle*, 24–7). Since Flavina died at age eleven full consummation was never achieved, but Emilia remains convinced that 'the true love 'tween maid and maid may be / More than in sex [dividual]' (1. 3. 81–2). While Hippolita is sceptical that her sister will never 'Love any that's called man', Emilia retains her 'faith' in true romantic love between women (85, 97). We infer that she plans to remain unmarried.[83]

Although Flavina is long dead, Emilia's preference for her own gender persists. Early in the play Emilia responds 'ardently' to the grief of the Third Theban Queen, calling her a 'natural sister of our sex' (1. 1. 125–6). And the sequence where she walks in the garden with her servant (simply called the Woman) generates a strong sense of female intimacy. In teasing that has a definite sexual edge, Emilia calls her 'wanton', and when the Woman, alluding to the popular game 'laugh and lie down', jests 'I could lie down, I'm sure', Emilia asks whether she will 'take one with' her (2. 2. 146, 150–1). Ironically, it is during this erotic badinage that Emilia, spied by the two kinsmen, becomes an object of their desires. When she's pushed by patriarchal Theseus into marriage Emilia finds it difficult to prefer either man; initially she's attracted to Arcite's androgynous looks, describing his brow as 'Arch'd like the great-ey'd Juno' and comparing him to 'wanton Ganymede' who 'set' Jove 'afire' (4. 2. 7, 20, 15–16). Still, in praying to 'cold' Diana, goddess of chastity (5. 1. 137), Emilia would clearly prefer to remain a 'virgin flow'r', growing 'alone, unpluck'd' (167–8). Her idealisation of deceased Flavina, together with Palamon's commitment to the dead Arcite, offers little promise that Emilia's heterosexual union will prove romantically or sexually fulfilling.

Shakespeare also presents erotically charged female friendships in two of his romantic comedies, *A Midsummer Night's Dream* and *As You Like It*. Neither pair of friends is as exclusively devoted to same-sex friendship as is the reluctant bride Emilia. But just as Shakespeare presents homoerotic male-male friendship most fully in his final play (co-authored with Fletcher), so he presents female-female love as progressing in intensity from *A Midsummer Night's Dream* through *As You Like It* to culminate in the Emilia-Flavina bond in *The Two Noble Kinsmen*. While in the early comedy Helena and Hermia are shown to have been closely bonded in the past before they turn to heterosexual love, the romantic friendship between Rosalind and Celia remains strong at the opening of *As You Like It*. Celia's passionate commitment to her friend is particularly pronounced, and only near the end of the play does she, like Rosalind, enthusiastically embrace heterosexual marriage.

In *A Midsummer Night's Dream* female friendships are forged despite, or perhaps as a release from, the strict patriarchal control that operates in Athens. At the opening of the play Hippolita has capitulated to Theseus, surprisingly agreeing to marry him because of the 'injuries' he inflicted on her when he 'woo'd [her] with his sword' (1. 1. 16–17). Her counterpart in the forest, the fairy queen Titania, is also treated harshly by her 'lord' Oberon when she refuses to give him the boy she adopted after his Indian mother died in childbirth. Initially Titania counters Oberon's homoerotic attraction to the 'lovely boy' (2. 1. 22) by celebrating strong fellowship between the two women, queen and mortal 'vot'ress', who 'gossip'd' and 'laugh'd' together on the sands (125–8). But Oberon responds by punishing her sexually for her insubordination. Sadistically he plans to drive her into shameful bestiality with some 'vile thing' – ape, lion and bull are some of the bedmates he fantasises for her (180–1). Just as Hippolita prefers marriage with Theseus to being queen of the female Amazons, so Titania, who initially would not hand over the changeling for 'all' of Oberon's 'fairy kingdom' (144), forfeits loyalty to her female friend; she surrenders the boy to Oberon as soon as he offers to release her 'charmed eye' from humiliating sexual infatuation with Bottom the ass (3. 2. 376).

In the main plot Hermia faces an even more severe punishment if she refuses to conform to her father's will and marry Demetrius. Reinforcing the sovereign power of the father, Theseus warns Hermia that if she defies Egeus she must be executed or enter a convent. Becoming a nun who 'Grows, lives, and dies in single blessedness' (1. 1. 78) is not a welcome prospect in the context of romantic comedy. Unlike Emilia in *The Two Noble Kinsmen*, who would prefer to remain a 'virgin flow'r', Hermia's future 'withering on the virgin thorn' is envisaged as 'barren' (72, 77) – a female's regression into an outdated monastic ideal of celibacy rather than her embrace of the Reformation drive toward marriage.

Against this background we learn of Hermia's close early friendship with Helena. Confiding her plan to elope with Lysander, Hermia reminds Helena of how as adolescents the 'sweet playfellow[s]' lay on 'primrose beds' in the wood, 'Emptying [their] bosoms of their counsels sweet' (1. 1. 215–20). Now, however, they have transferred their affections to men; two scenes later it is Lysander who proposes sharing 'one bed' with Hermia on the forest floor, claiming 'One heart ... two bosoms, and one troth' with his beloved (2. 2. 42). While Helena still wishes to model herself on Hermia, even to be 'translated' into her friend and 'catch' exactly the trick of her friend's 'voice', 'eye' and 'tongue' (1. 1. 188–91), this is only to regain the love of Demetrius after his defection to Hermia. And when Demetrius (anointed by the magic juice) swears eternal love for her in Act 3, Helena is quick to believe that her trusted female companion has joined the men in playing a cruel trick on her. To shame Hermia she conjures up the memory of their intense 'schooldays friendship', when they shared 'sisters' vows' and sewed matching samplers together (3. 2. 199–202). Bonded 'As if [their] hands', their 'sides, voices, and minds / Had been incorporate' (207–8), Hermia and Helena are envisaged as 'one flesh', the term St Paul uses to define heterosexual marriage. Shakespeare further develops the erotic image of the two girls as a 'double cherry', enjoying 'union in partition' and growing 'together' as

> Two lovely berries molded on one stem;
> ... two seeming bodies, but one heart. (208–12)

Here Helena equates female-female love with the ideal of male-male spiritual union, the 'one soule in two bodies' that Montaigne cites as

Aristotle's definition of perfect male friendship,[84] as well as the 'conjugal love' that Robert Burton describes as 'one heart in two bodies'.[85] But their 'ancient love' (215) now lies in the past. Even more than Emilia lamenting the loss of Flavina, Helena can offer only what Valerie Traub calls a 'requiem for female affection'.[86]

While Helena strongly rebukes Hermia for tearing apart this love, betraying their bond of friendship by seeming to 'join with men' in attacking her (3. 2. 215–16), Hermia is more focused on the idea that her friend has stolen her lover. Helena has apparently disrupted what now matters most to Hermia: her heterosexual relationship with Lysander. Bosom friends transform into rivals, hurling insults at one another – 'puppet' and 'vixen' for short Hermia (288, 324), 'painted maypole' for tall Helena (296). As the more loyal of the two, Helena insists, before running off, 'I evermore did love you, Hermia' (307). Whereas rivalry between the male suitors never seems grounded in homoeroticism (they pursue the same woman only briefly), the animosity generated between the females seems all the fiercer because they were previously inseparable.

Once the two couples are restored to their original partners, they move quickly into traditional marriage. The conclusion of *A Midsummer Night's Dream*, with Theseus and Oberon in charge of the festivities, reaffirms 'patriarchal order and hierarchy', and returning to this order may well depend, as Shirley Nelson Garner contends, on 'the breaking of woman's bonds with each other'.[87] While the lovers can dismiss the nightmarish events of the night as the 'fierce vexation of a dream' (4. 1. 69), Helena and Hermia never speak to one another after their confused awakening in Act 4, scene 1. It is left to the men to comment wittily on the 'Pyramus and Thisbe' performance in Act 5; apart from Hippolita, the females say not a word throughout. This leaves open the question of whether Helena and Hermia demonstrate (by their body language on stage) renewed fondness for one another, or whether female friendship has been permanently ruptured, sacrificed to comedy's relentless progress toward heterosexual union.

Rosalind and Celia in *As You Like It* are cousins, but as with Palamon and Arcite in *The Two Noble Kinsmen*, their feelings for one another go beyond familial affection. Charles the Wrestler declares that 'never two ladies lov'd' as Rosalind and Celia do (1. 1. 112) – a judgement reinforced by Le Beau, who describes their love as 'dearer than the natural bond of sisters' (1. 2. 276). Feelings are certainly intense on Celia's side. Trying to rally the melancholy Rosalind, she accuses Rosalind of caring more about her absent father than about her present cousin: 'Herein I see thou lov'st me not with the full weight that I love thee' (1. 2. 8–9).

She also uses the sexually loaded word 'affection' when she promises to repay Rosalind 'in affection' what her own father, Duke Frederick, has taken away by banishing Rosalind's father (21). If she breaks that promise she will turn 'monster' (22) – a signifier that Viola also uses to critique her androgynous boy/girl role (*Twelfth Night*, 2. 2. 34). Medical treatises of the time used the adjective 'monstrous' to refer to both hermaphrodites and tribades (women who have sex with other women),[88] and Shakespeare's audience might well have registered the implications of that term. Once Duke Frederick decides to banish Rosalind, Celia speaks out passionately about their intimacy:

> We still have slept together,
> Rose at an instant, learn'd, play'd, eat together,
> And wheresoe'er we went, like Juno's swans,
> Still we went coupled and inseparable. (1. 3. 73–6)

When Rosalind envisages the punishment of exile as hers alone, Celia again chides her for apparently lacking 'the love / Which teacheth thee that thou and I are one', shaming Rosalind with 'Shall we be sund'red? Shall we part, sweet girl?' (96–8). Like Antonio in *Twelfth Night*, desperate to follow Sebastian at any cost, Celia tells her father she 'cannot live out of' Rosalind's 'company' and insists to her cousin, 'Say what thou canst, I'll go along with thee' (86, 105).

In matters of heterosexual desire – Rosalind's sudden attraction to Orlando – Celia plays the sceptic. Early on she sagely advises, 'love no man in earnest' (1. 2. 127). Amazed that her companion would fall into 'so strong a liking' (she avoids the signifier 'love') with this young stranger, she urges her cousin to 'wrestle with [her] affections' for Orlando (1. 3. 27–8, 21). Only her devotion to Rosalind allows her to do what her cousin requests: to 'love [Orlando] because I do' (38–9). While Rosalind readily appropriates a masculine disguise in their escape to the Forest of Arden, Celia is content to play Ganymede's sister. Her chosen name Aliena registers her sense of being an outsider; in Arden she must often simply tag along, witnessing the heated courtship between Rosalind/Ganymede and Orlando. Mocking mixed-sex romantic love, she characterises, perhaps jealously, the kisses that Orlando gives to her beloved friend as having 'the very ice of chastity in them'. The oath of a lover, she advises, is not to be trusted, for while Orlando may be 'true in love' when he is actually in love, she opines that 'he is not in' (3. 4. 17, 26–8). Later Celia baulks at playing the preacher in a mock marriage ceremony for the lovers – her response 'I cannot say the words' (4. 1. 128) could be played with deep reluctance – until, being a good sport, she rises to the occasion. Afterwards, standing up for her gender, she rebukes Rosalind for having 'simply misused our sex' in 'love prate', disloyally portraying women as fickle and cunning (201–2).

Conveniently for the closure of this comedy, Celia makes a quick shift into heterosexual desire. When Rosalind declares that her 'affection' for Orlando has 'an unknown bottom, like the bay of Portugal', Celia ruefully replies, 'Or rather bottomless, that as fast as you pour affection in, it runs out' (4. 1. 207–10). Emotions are transferable, after all. Like Nerissa, Portia's maid in *The Merchant of Venice* who readily seeks marriage once her mistress is betrothed, Celia mirrors Rosalind by falling in love with Orlando's brother, Oliver. As soon as he arrives in the forest and announces his 'conversion' to goodness, Celia is eager to invite him to their sheepcote, urging, 'Good sir, go with us' (4. 3. 178). These are the last words Celia utters in the play. In Act 5 the swift progress of her love affair is reported, not enacted, as the 'giddiness' of Oliver's 'sudden wooing' is followed by Celia's 'sudden consenting' (5. 2. 5–7). Rosalind confirms that 'they no sooner look'd but they lov'd', and now they are in 'the very wrath of love' (33, 40).

Rosalind's comment that 'they will together. Clubs cannot part them' (40–1) recalls how Celia described the two females, before they left for Arden, as 'coupled and inseparable'. In the play's action Celia's strong attraction to Rosalind – female-to-female love – is displaced on to the shepherdess Phoebe, infatuated with Rosalind-as-Ganymede. The timing of Celia's switch to heterosexual desire is significant. Almost immediately after she empathises with the 'poor shepherd' Silvius, rejected by Phoebe (4. 3. 65), Oliver enters, and Celia finds a new object for her affections. Rosalind looks 'paler and paler' to her – literally, since her cousin has just fainted at the sight of Orlando's blood on the napkin (177), but perhaps not only literally. While Celia's 'passionate friendship'[89] with Rosalind parallels, though in a less overtly sexual way, that of Antonio with Sebastian in *Twelfth Night*, it never threatens the two women's anticipated progress toward marriage.

In *As You Like It* and *A Midsummer Night's Dream*, female-female affection, authentic in its intensity, is ultimately presented as a mirroring phase on the route to adulthood.[90] The case is different with male-male sexual desire in Shakespeare's sonnets and romantic comedies. At the end of *The Merchant of Venice* and *Twelfth Night*, the two Antonios are not pushed into the circle of marriage. They remain outsiders, privileging male intimacy over heterosexual partnership. The male couples in *The Two Gentlemen of Verona* and *The Two Noble Kinsmen* also refuse to relinquish same-sex bonding, nor do they behave as if it's simply a 'phase on the way to marriage' (as Alan Sinfield puts it),[91] even when they enter into male-female unions. But in the early modern period nubile women – even Emilia in *The Two Noble Kinsmen*, who would prefer to stay single – were expected to marry. Choosing a single life, or cohabiting with other females, was regarded by Shakespeare's patriarchal society as anomalous. Except for financially independent upper-class women, it would also be a difficult choice to sustain economically.[92] No wonder, then, that close, even passionate friendships between females in Shakespeare's romantic comedies ultimately present no significant threat to conventional marriage.

Notes

1. See Jean E. Howard, 'The Early Modern and the Homoerotic Turn in Political Criticism'.
2. Catherine Belsey, 'Disrupting Sexual Difference', p. 190.
3. Jean E. Howard, 'Power and Eros', in *The Stage and Social Struggle in Early Modern England*, p. 94.
4. This is the term Valerie Traub uses in 'The Homoerotics of Shakespearean Comedy', in *Desire and Anxiety: Circulations of Sexuality in Shakespearean Drama*, p. 131.
5. Lisa Jardine, ' "As boys and women are for the most part cattle of this colour": Female Roles and Elizabethan Eroticism', in *Still Harping on Daughters: Women and Drama in the Age of Shakespeare*, finds the androgynous figure of the boy actor a powerful combination of 'effeminacy, dependence and desirability', with an erotic appeal designed for 'a male audience's appreciation' (p. 31). While Traub, 'Desire and the Differences It Makes', in *Desire and Anxiety*, argues that the male-female composite could also elicit desire in 'female audience members' (p. 122), Stephen Greenblatt, 'Fiction and Friction', in *Shakespearean Negotiations* (pp. 66–93), considers that the all-male cast makes the circulation of erotic energy ultimately an all-male affair (p. 93).
6. Stephen Guy-Bray, 'Shakespeare and the Invention of the Heterosexual', 19.
7. Philip Stubbes, *The Anatomie of Abuses* (1583), p. 145.
8. John Rainolds, *Th'Overthrow of Stage-Playes*, pp. 10–11.
9. Peter Erickson, *Patriarchal Structures in Shakespeare's Drama*, p. 6.
10. Eve Kosofsky Sedgwick, *Between Men: English Literature and Male Homosocial Desire*, p. 1.
11. Lisa Hopkins, *The Shakespearean Marriage*, also argues that the 'cuckold topos' serves as a 'mechanism for the production' of strong 'male-male bonds' (p. 14).
12. Laurie Shannon, *Sovereign Amity: Figures of Friendship in Shakespearean Contexts*, discusses the 'repeated privileging of (erotic and non-erotic) same-sex bonds over (presumptively erotic) heterosexual relations' in this period (p. 1).
13. Outlined in 'Of Love' in Plutarch's *Moralia*, fol. 1132.

14. Paul Hammond, *Figuring Sex between Men from Shakespeare to Rochester*, p. 8.
15. Alan Bray, *Homosexuality in Renaissance England*, p. 16, quotes this condemnation from George Tuberville, *Tragical Tales*, p. 373. Often the term 'sodomy' was used more loosely to excoriate politically suspect activities such as heresy or sorcery. See Jonathan Goldberg's exploration of '"That Utterly Confused Category"' in his introduction to *Sodometries: Renaissance Texts, Modern Sexualities*, pp. 1–26.
16. In fact the only execution for sodomy recorded during the reigns of Elizabeth and James, in 1569, identified the victim as a five-year-old boy. See Bruce R. Smith, *Homosexual Desire in Shakespeare's England*, p. 48.
17. In 'The Passionate Shepherd', in *Homosexual Desire in Shakespeare's England*, pp. 82–8, Smith analyses in detail these subcultures in which homosexual acts were likely to take place.
18. Bray, *Homosexuality in Renaissance England*, pp. 7, 76.
19. G. P. V. Akrigg (ed.), *Letters of King James VI and I*, p. 431.
20. Alan Sinfield, 'How to Read *The Merchant of Venice* without Being Heterosexist', pp. 135, 129. Valerie Traub, *The Renaissance of Lesbianism in Early Modern England*, notes that 'no strict boundary separates friendship from eroticism in Renaissance versions of *amicitia*' (p. 18), while James M. Bromley, *Intimacy and Sexuality in the Age of Shakespeare*, also finds that 'intimate' friendship in this period 'straddled the erotic and non erotic' (p. 7).
21. John S. Garrison, *Friendship and Queer Theory in the Renaissance*, notes how Cicero's *De Amicitia* (44 BC), popular in grammar schools in Shakespeare's time, presented the idealised classical model of friendship between 'two souls linked by parity' (p. xiii).
22. See *Aristotle: Eudemian Ethics*, which discusses the amicable bond of *philia* (rather than erotic love) and promotes the idea of the 'one soul' in friendship based on virtue (bk. VII, 1240b 1–2, p. 137).
23. Montaigne, 'Of Friendship', in *Essays*, vol. 1, ch. 27, p. 202.
24. Ibid. pp. 198–9.
25. John Lyly, *Endimion* (3. 4), p. 99.
26. Jeffrey Masten, *Queer Philologies: Sex, Language, and Affect in Shakespeare's Time*, p. 75.
27. Goldberg, *Sodometries*, finds a parallel between Falstaff's 'desire' for Hal and 'the desire of the sonneteer' for the narcissistic young man of Shakespeare's sonnets (p. 153).
28. Stanley Wells, 'Whores and Saints', in *Shakespeare, Sex, and Love*, speculates that Mistress Quickly's speech 'implies both sodomy and pederasty' (p. 219).
29. Jonathan Dollimore, 'Forget Iago's Homosexuality', in *Sexual Dissidence*, p. 159. Rather than repressed homosexual desire in Iago, Dollimore finds 'homosocial bonding' through the men's envy of the 'usurping male' Cassio (p. 158).
30. Stanley Edgar Hyman theorises this in *Iago: Some Approaches to the Illusion of his Motivation*, p. 139.
31. Erickson, 'Maternal Images and Male Bonds', in *Patriarchal Structures in Shakespeare's Drama*, p. 97.

32. In '"Through the Eye of the Present": Screening the Male Homoerotics of Shakespearean Drama', Anthony Guy Patricia describes how Branagh's Iago projects homoeroticism, holding back tears of relief when he pledges to Othello, 'I am your own forever' (p. 175).
33. In '*Romeo and Juliet*'s Open Rs', Jonathan Goldberg deduces that the crux at 2. 1. 38, where Mercutio wishes that for Romeo's sake Rosaline 'were / An open-arse, and thou a poperin pear', figures the 'utterly unspeakable/ absolutely commonplace nature of anal sex' (p. 95, n. 11). While modern editors, such as Brian Gibbons in the Arden edition of *Romeo and Juliet* (1980), provide the explicit 'open-arse' reading, Goldberg contends that Q2's 'an open, or' (followed by the Folio) and Q1's 'open *Et caetera*' both imply the same thing – anal sex. He concludes that 'this is how Mercutio voices – through Rosaline – his desire for Romeo' (p. 92).
34. Goldberg, '*Romeo and Juliet*'s Open Rs', p. 84.
35. Barbara Hodgson, '*William Shakespeare's Romeo + Juliet*: Everything's Nice in America?', notes how the 'close-up of Romeo embracing the dead Mercutio', which 'dissolves to a shot of Juliet on her bed', emphasises the 'widening circle of homoerotic and homosocial relations', 95.
36. Smith, *Homosexual Desire in Shakespeare's England*, p. 23.
37. W. H. Auden, Introduction to William Shakespeare, *The Sonnets*, p. xxix.
38. Michael Keevak, *Sexual Shakespeare*, p. 36.
39. Richard Barnfield, *The Complete Poems*, p. 116. Barnfield himself, perhaps disingenuously, disavowed the poems as 'nothing else, but an imitation of *Virgill*'.
40. Joseph Pequigney, *Such Is My Love: A Study of Shakespeare Sonnets*, notes the mainly 'bipartite' structure that reflects the 'bisexual subject matter' of the sonnets; the first 126 focus primarily on the poet's love for his 'fair' male 'friend' before he turns to explore his heterosexual affair (p. 180). In what follows I am especially indebted to Pequigney's plausible tracing of the developing sexual relationship between the poet and the young man.
41. Helen Vendler, *The Art of Shakespeare's Sonnets*, p. 17.
42. Sir Philip Sidney, *The Countess of Pembroke's Arcadia*, bk. 3, p. 643. The sentiment of line 5 of Sidney's sonnet, 'His heart in me keeps me and him in one', is echoed in Shakespeare's Sonnet 42, 'my friend and I are one' (13).
43. Sedgwick, 'Gender Asymmetry and Erotic Triangles', in *Between Men*, pp. 25–6.
44. Sedgwick, 'Swan in Love: The Example of Shakespeare's Sonnets', in *Between Men*, discusses how a homosocial bond is forged through the poet's imagined 'amalgamation ... with the other men received' by the mistress (p. 38).
45. Christopher Marlowe, *The Complete Plays*, p. 45.
46. *The Poems of John Marston*, p. 112. Alan Sinfield, 'Near Misses: Ganymedes and Page Boys', contends that the page boy, associated with Ganymede in the early modern period, was 'available as a sexual object choice' (p. 125).
47. Stephen Orgel, *Impersonations: The Performance of Gender in Shakespeare's England*, p. 70. The same equation between boys and women is made in *Cymbeline* by Roman Lucio, who, bitter when Imogen disguised as Fidele seems to betray him, declares 'Briefly die their joys / That place them on the truth of girls and boys' (5. 5. 106–7). Jean E. Howard, 'Sex and Social

Conflict: The Erotics of *The Roaring Girl*', notes that the biological model promoted by Galen and still current in Shakespeare's time, which depicted 'both boys and women as unfinished men', may to some extent 'have enabled adult males ... to treat boys and women as interchangeable sexual objects' (p. 171).
48. Penny Gay, *As She Likes It: Shakespeare's Unruly Women*, p. 48.
49. Ibid. p. 58.
50. Smith, *Homosexual Desire in Shakespeare's England*, pp. 146–7.
51. Traub, 'The Homoeroticism of Shakespearean Comedy', in *Desire and Anxiety*, p. 126.
52. Howard, 'Power and Eros', in *The Stage and Social Struggle*, p. 120.
53. Phyllis Rackin, 'Boys Will Be Girls', in *Shakespeare and Women*, notes that the 'doubly gendered figure' is the 'embodiment' of 'erotic excitement' (p. 82).
54. Janet Adelman, 'Male Bonding in Shakespeare's Comedies', p. 86.
55. Stubbes, *The Anatomie of Abuses*, p. 73.
56. Lisa Jardine, in 'Twins and Travesties: Gender, Dependency and Sexual Availability in *Twelfth Night*', views this relationship as more openly sexual. She argues that when Orsino claims Viola as a 'sexual partner', he is simply making good on the services expected from a male servant (a 'dependant') and transferring them to a wife (p. 33).
57. The film *Shakespeare in Love*, winner of Best Picture at the 1999 Academy Awards, reproduces this male-male attraction by showing how Will is first drawn to Viola when she is cross-dressed as a male actor. The difference is that Will is relieved to discover that the young actor is female, while in *Twelfth Night* Orsino appears to welcome same-sex attraction. As James Shapiro notes in *Shakespeare in a Divided America*, whereas 'intimations of same sex love' are 'hard-wired into the circuitry of many of Shakespeare's comedies', in 1999 many American audiences were still 'uncomfortable with same-sex relationships' (p. 194).
58. Masten, 'Reading "Boys": Performance and Print', in *Queer Philologies*, notes this, together with Olivia's choice of 'youth' to refer to Cesario, as part of the 'multiplicity' the early modern audience might register 'when it saw boy actors playing women, sometimes playing boys and men' (pp. 113, 111).
59. David Schalkwyk, *Shakespeare: Love and Language*, p. 59.
60. W. Thomas MacCary, *Friends and Lovers: The Phenomenology of Desire in Shakespearean Comedy*, makes this argument (p. 5). This is also the Freudian thesis of Helene Moglen, in 'Disguise and Development: The Self and Society in *Twelfth Night*', who notes that confronting himself in a homoerotic relationship (with Cesario) allows Orsino to transition into 'mature, heterosexual love' (15).
61. Joseph Pequigney, 'The Two Antonios and Same-Sex Love in *Twelfth Night* and *The Merchant of Venice*', considers that the 'love that commences as homoerotic and conducts Orsino into nuptial heterosexuality is an unbroken wave, a bisexual continuity' (207). Mario DiGangi, *The Homoerotics of Early Modern Drama*, speculates that because Orsino 'imagines not Viola in her female clothes but a transvestite *Cesario*', his sexual preference is still for a 'submissive' boy (p. 42).

62. Traub, *Desire and Anxiety*, pp. 131, 108.
63. Alexander Schmidt, *Shakespeare Lexicon and Quotation Dictionary*, defines sense 4 of 'gentle' in Shakespearean contexts as 'soft, tender, meek ... as opposed to wild, rough, and harsh' (vol. 1, p. 470).
64. Arthur L. Little, Jr, '"A Local Habitation and a Name": Presence, Witnessing, and Queer Marriage in Shakespeare's Romantic Comedies', p. 210. Commenting on this proposed marriage – Olivia to Cesario in *Twelfth Night* as well as Orlando to Ganymede in *As You Like It* – Little finds that Shakespeare 'insists upon marking out a space for the possibility of queer matrimony', even while these comedies stage 'compulsory heterosexual marriage' (pp. 210–11). In *Coming of Age in Shakespeare*, published nearly thirty years earlier, Marjorie Garber more harshly judges 'misdirection of sexual desire, doting on a disguised member of one's own sex', as an 'indication of self-indulgence and consequent immaturity in love' (p. 141).
65. Adelman, 'Male Bonding in Shakespeare's Comedies', p. 91. Adelman contends that the twin who mirrors Viola but differs in gender supplies the image of a 'fragile androgyny that alone can satisfy all our desires' (p. 91).
66. Hammond, *Figuring Sex between Men*, points out that Antonio's equivalent in Shakespeare's source, *Gl'Ingannati*, is presented as a tutor, not as an adoring friend (p. 97).
67. Stephen Orgel, 'Nobody's Perfect: or Why Did the English Stage Take Boys for Women?', 29, 27.
68. C. Stephen Jaeger, *Ennobling Love*, p. 25.
69. Pequigney, 'The Two Antonios', 209.
70. Pequigney, 'The Two Antonios', reads the text against the grain by asserting that the play sets up an expectation that in 'taking a wife' Sebastian is unlikely to lose his male lover (206) and that the threesome of Olivia, Sebastian and Antonio could leave the stage together (p. 206, n. 5).
71. Traub, 'The Homoerotics of Shakespearean Comedy', in *Desire and Anxiety*, p. 133.
72. Marianne Novy, *Shakespeare and Outsiders*, p. 12. In Venice at that time, as in England, sodomy was legally punishable by death. In *The Unfortunate Traveller* (1594), Thomas Nashe lambasts Italy as an 'Epicures heaven' that specialises in 'the art of Sodomitrie' (p. 336).
73. Pequigney, 'The Two Antonios', 220.
74. Catherine Belsey, 'Love in Venice', p. 86. Portia needs to assert her superiority as Bassanio's 'partner and friend' (p. 82) over Antonio's claim to those roles within the ideal of male friendship.
75. Linda Charnes, 'Uncivil Unions', argues that rather than pushing Antonio (and same-sex desire) into second place, Portia recognises that 'the *only* way to secure her marriage to Bassanio is to make accommodation within it for Antonio'; when Antonio hands Portia's ring to Bassanio, he is included in 'the ceremonial "loop" of desire' (p. 204). More traditionally, Margaret Loftus Ranald, '*The Merchant of Venice* – Portia the Friendly Adversary', in *Shakespeare and his Social Context*, finds that while Portia accepts 'the obligations of Bassanio's friendship as compatible with and complementary to those of marriage', she teaches both men the 'relative values of matrimonial love and masculine friendship' (pp. 68, 71).

76. Sinfield, 'How to Read *The Merchant of Venice* without Being Heterosexist', p. 139.
77. Sedgwick, 'Gender Asymmetry and Erotic Triangles', in *Between Men*, p. 21. This Freudian theory was first applied to literary contexts by René Girard in *'Triangular' Desire*.
78. John D. Cox, 'Shakespeare and the Ethics of Friendship', 23.
79. Guy-Bray, 'Shakespeare and the Invention of the Heterosexual', 9, 6.
80. Adelman, 'Male Bonding in Shakespeare's Comedies', p. 79.
81. Maurice Charney, *Shakespeare on Love and Lust*, uses *The Two Noble Kinsmen* as evidence that in Shakespeare's plays 'various sexualities' often 'exist comfortably side by side' (p. 160). But Hopkins, *The Shakespearean Marriage*, finds that although 'homosocial bonds' can successfully 'negotiate the marriage tie' in most of Shakespeare's comedies (p. 13), one notable exception is *The Two Noble Kinsmen*, where marriage disrupts rather than promotes 'homosocial relationships' (p. 183). Jean H. Hagstrum, *Esteem Enlivened by Desire*, also argues that same-sex friendship is privileged in the play, while romantic love is 'degraded' (p. 386).
82. Alan Sinfield, 'Intertextuality and the Limits of Queer Reading in *A Midsummer Night's Dream* and *The Two Noble Kinsmen*', makes this point. Richard Mallette, 'Same-Sex Erotic Friendship in *The Two Noble Kinsmen*', also finds that the two men are 'interested overwhelmingly in each other' (42), a clear case of the 'bonds between the rivals' being elevated over 'those with the beloved' (39).
83. Emilia doesn't conform to the pattern discerned by John R. Gillis in *For Better, for Worse: British Marriages, 1600 to the Present* – that adolescents in Shakespeare's England 'initially experienced love as a form of polygamous play', investing same-sex friendship with an 'emotional intensity' that can later transfer to heterosexual relationships (p. 37).
84. Montaigne, 'Of Friendship', in *Essays*, vol. 1, ch. 27, p. 203.
85. Robert Burton, *The Anatomy of Melancholy* (1621), vol. 3, sec. 2, p. 54.
86. Traub, 'The (In)significance of Lesbian Desire', in *The Renaissance of Lesbianism in Early Modern England*, p. 172.
87. Shirley Nelson Garner, '*A Midsummer Night's Dream*: "Jack shall have Jill; / Nought shall go ill"', 47, 59.
88. Traub, 'Setting the Stage behind the Seen: Performing Lesbian History', in *The Renaissance of Lesbianism*, discusses how the 'line between the hermaphrodite and the tribade' (used to refer to a woman with an enlarged clitoris) is often blurred (p. 45). She cites Helkiah Crooke, *Microcosmographia* (1618), on 'monstrous' stories of 'unnatural lusts' among tribades (p. 195). Shakespeare never uses the term but, as cited by the *OED*, 'tribade trine' appears in a lyric in Ben Jonson's *Forest* (1601).
89. Sarah Mendelson and Patricia Crawford, in *Women in Early Modern England, 1550–1720*, point out how 'romantic' or 'passionate friendship' between women need not be sexual (p. 240). Traub, 'Introduction: "Practicing Impossibilities"', in *The Renaissance of Lesbianism*, discusses in detail the period's representation of 'chaste yet passionate eroticism' among women (p. 29).
90. Thus Garber, *Coming of Age in Shakespeare*, finds the dissolving bonds between Hermia and Helena a necessary part of the 'separation and dif-

ferentiation' that signals the 'advent of sexual maturity' (p. 34). Adelman, in 'Male Bonding in Shakespeare's Comedies', also takes as her premise that we move 'from family bonds to marriage' through 'an intervening period in which our friendships with same-sex friends help us to establish our independent identities' (p. 75). Gay critics have challenged such assumptions, however. Traub, 'Desire and the Difference It Makes', in *Desire and Anxiety*, objects to the 'elision of erotic difference' when 'same gender love between women' in Shakespeare is not treated as valid in its own right (pp. 92–3).

91. Sinfield, 'How to Read *The Merchant of Venice* without Being Heterosexist', finds Adelman's premise demeaning to adult same-sex relationships; he contends it is a 'slap in the face' to a gay individual to be told that 'such passions are simply a phase on the way to marriage' (p. 128).
92. See the discussion of this in Chapter 6.

Chapter 8

'The Buildings of My Fancy': Family Ties and Sexual Desire

Many of Shakespeare's plays are grounded in what Richard Wheeler calls the 'interdependence of identity, family, and sexuality'.[1] The comedies enact a life-changing transition, 'freeing sexuality from the ties of family'[2] as young men and women make a bid for independence, fulfilling erotic needs within the union of marriage. Daughters must try to break away from controlling fathers; sons, resolving any lingering maternal influence that may lead to their over-idealising or distrusting females, seek out wives with whom to bond in a reciprocal love relationship. Likewise fathers and mothers, within the conventions of the comedies and romances, eventually accept the individuation of their children and allow them to marry their chosen partners. In several of Shakespeare's tragedies, however, the process is blocked. Desire may be short-circuited back into the primary source: the love that children feel for their parents and parents for children.

Montaigne (in Florio's 1603 translation) probably shocked Renaissance readers by citing, among unfamiliar social customs, countries 'where men may lawfully get their mothers with childe: where fathers may lie with their daughters, and with their sons'.[3] More often Shakespeare's contemporaries warned sternly against breaking the incest taboo. In *Of Domesticall Duties* (1622), William Gouge condemns parents whose abnormal love, turning to 'dotage', can make them so 'hellishly enamoured with their children as to commit incest or buggery with them'.[4] Love between blood relatives was supposed never to turn sexual. Lyly's play *Mother Bombie* confirms that 'the nearer we are in blood, the further we must be from love', for 'the greater the kindred is, the lesse the kindness must be'.[5]

Freud's writings in the early twentieth century, especially his formulation of the Oedipus complex, offer a different perspective on incest. Freud postulated the universal nature of incestuous desire – normally repressed by the individual and certainly suppressed in most societies

– within family relationships.⁶ It's nevertheless risky to infer hidden psychological motives in Shakespeare's characters before examining how dramatic conventions of the time shape character and action. Both Egeus in *A Midsummer Night's Dream* and Old Capulet in *Romeo and Juliet* fall within the tradition of the *senex iratus* of Roman New Comedy – the bullying, blocking father who tries to prevent his daughter from marrying the man she loves – rather than manifesting as overly possessive fathers who are jealous of their daughters' new-found independence.⁷ Bertram in *All's Well that Ends Well* and Angelo in *Measure for Measure* are presented as lustful males who treat women badly. Yet their behaviour has been partly excused by assuming that deep-seated pre-Oedipal and Oedipal anxieties affect both men.⁸ In this reading, Angelo's effort to seduce Isabella, his sudden desire for what is pure but forbidden, arises from his rediscovery of 'shaming and exciting ... maternal sexuality',⁹ so that 'the return of repressed desire' takes the form of 'debased sexuality'.¹⁰ This post-Freudian approach also concludes that Macbeth can affirm his manhood by murdering Duncan only after he makes himself 'a child to the demonic motherhood of Lady Macbeth'.¹¹ For critics who seek them, the residual effects of maternal influence crop up everywhere in Shakespeare's plays.

This psychoanalytic approach can never fully account for the behaviour of Shakespeare's male characters; nevertheless, several of his plays show how passionately family members often act toward one another. The romance *Pericles* comes closest to dramatising the actual 'sin', the breaking of the incest taboo, when it reports that the King of Antioch has been coupling with his own daughter (Gower's Prologue, 30). But Shakespeare avoids the prurient fascination with forbidden fruit that fuels several Jacobean plays, as when Vindice in *The Revenger's Tragedy* (1606) relishes the 'hour of incest', the ultimate moral decadence when 'uncles are adulterous with their nieces, / Brothers with brothers' wives' (1. 3. 62–3).¹² With more nuance *Hamlet*, *Coriolanus* and *King Lear* all explore how one member of the dyad – whether brother for sister, son for mother, mother for son, or father for daughter – shows an erotic interest that goes beyond what is usual in family bonding.

Among taboo unions sibling incest has been regarded as the 'least reprehensible of the three variations',¹³ presumably because it's not based on parents' exertion of power and authority. It also entails no generational barrier. A brother, close to his sister in age, might see himself as a surrogate husband,¹⁴ or a sister might view her male sibling in a romantic light. In Sophocles's tragedy *Antigone*, the heroine suggests this when she makes a point of privileging her blood tie with her brother Polynices above any bond between husband and wife. Defying

Theban law in order to give him burial rites, Antigone rationalises that while husbands are replaceable, 'no brother', if lost, 'could ever spring to light again' (1000–3).[15] Choosing death with her brother over life with her fiancé Haemon, she even refers to her tomb as a 'bridal-bed' (978) where she can fulfil her desire to 'lie with the one I love [Polynices] and loved by him' (87). In the Renaissance, despite some infamous aristocratic sibling couplings such as that of Lucretia Borgia, brother-sister unions were firmly prohibited by biblical, social and natural law.[16] The Old Testament reinforces this in Leviticus 18: 9, which decrees that 'the nakedness of thy sister ... whether born at home or abroad ... thou shalt not uncover [possess sexually]'.

Notwithstanding the taboo, several Jacobean dramatists depicted in detail incestuous desire or incest between cross-gender siblings. Nothing in Shakespeare rivals the lubricious fantasies of Duke Ferdinand in Webster's *The Duchess of Malfi* (1613), who vicariously imagines himself as the sexual partner of his twin sister, the widowed duchess – a 'strong-thigh'd bargeman' or 'some lovely squire / That carries coals up to her privy lodgings' (2. 5. 42–5).[17] John Ford's tragedy *'Tis Pity She's a Whore* (c. 1630) more boldly dramatises the consummated love affair of Giovanni and his sister Annabella. Justifying his incestuous desire as no 'sin', Giovanni rationalises that because 'Nearness in birth and blood doth but persuade / A nearer nearness in affection' a brother shouldn't be 'banished' from his sister's 'bed' (1. 2. 251–2, 1. 1. 43, 37–8).[18] Shakespeare, in contrast, outlines the norm for sibling behaviour in *Much Ado about Nothing*. Claudio is adamant that during his courtship he never behaved in a sexually inappropriate way to Hero, but 'as a brother to his sister, show'd / Bashful sincerity and comely love' (4. 1. 53–4).

Not all brother-sister relationships in Shakespeare's plays cross this line and border on sexual 'affection'. At the opening of *Twelfth Night*, Olivia's claim to keep 'fresh' a 'brother's dead love' by retreating into mourning for seven years (1. 1. 30–1) turns out to be less an intense attachment to her deceased sibling than a strategy to keep unwanted suitors at bay; it breaks down quickly when she falls in love with Viola in the guise of Cesario. For her part Viola is deeply distressed by the likelihood that her twin brother Sebastian has drowned. Once Antonio mistakes her for Sebastian, she is ecstatic that 'salt waves' may prove 'fresh in love' (3. 4. 384) if her twin is indeed still alive. Again, though, this 'love' represents a strong bond of kinship that doesn't impede Viola's growing passion for Orsino – a man unrelated to her family.[19] In *Cymbeline* sibling attraction, which happens unknowingly, also poses no immediate threat. Enchanted by Imogen when she is disguised as the page boy Fidele, Guiderus confesses that he would 'woo' Fidele in earnest were the 'youth' a woman (3. 6. 68–9). Since he was abducted from the court as an infant, Guiderus cannot know that he is actually desiring his own sister, Imogen. The implication here is clear, however. If kinship ties are hidden, siblings may become more strongly attracted to one another than to strangers.[20]

The love between Imogen and Posthumus in *Cymbeline* offers a mirror image of this. Being raised together from infancy as if they were siblings has sparked sexual desire between them; Imogen explains to her father that she fell in love with Posthumus because he was 'bred' as her 'playfellow' (1. 1. 145). And since Posthumus is not her blood brother, she remains free to marry him.[21] Helena in *All's Well that Ends Well*, brought up with the Countess's biological son Bertram as her stepbrother, finds herself in a similar situation. Uneasy when the Countess refers to herself as Helena's 'mother', Helena dismisses any suggestion of incest. She reiterates that Bertram 'cannot be my brother'; indeed he 'must not' be her 'brother' if she is to marry him (1. 3. 155, 160). Since the step-siblings are not related, the Countess welcomes the prospect of Helena becoming her 'daughter-in-law' (167). Meanwhile Beatrice in *Much Ado about Nothing* mocks the tendency to be over-anxious about the incest taboo. Wittily she claims that since all human beings are ultimately related – 'Adam's sons are my brethren' – that will be her excuse to avoid marriage; she asserts, 'truly I hold it a sin to match in my kindred' (2. 1. 63–5).

Among the three cross-gender sibling pairings to be discussed – Laertes and Ophelia in *Hamlet*, Octavius and Octavia in *Antony and Cleopatra*, and Claudio and Isabella in *Measure for Measure* – the least erotic relationship is that between Claudio and Isabella. Isabella pleads her brother's case to Angelo after the stern deputy has sentenced Claudio to death for pre-marital intercourse. Still, she remains reluctant to press her suit. As a novitiate nun in the process of renouncing the flesh, she 'abhor[s]' the 'vice' of fornication (2. 2. 29). Without much resistance she accepts Angelo's argument that it is illogical to 'Condemn the fault, and not the actor of it', conceding that her brother deserves to die: 'O just but severe law! / I had a brother then' (37, 41–2). She is understandably horrified when Angelo tries to strike a bargain with her; he is prepared to save Claudio's life if she submits to his sexual will. And since chaste Isabella prefers death to giving up the 'treasures' of her virginal body (2. 4. 96), she cannot comprehend why Claudio, once she reveals Angelo's bargain to him, would ponder it as a 'remedy' (3. 1. 60). When he begs 'Sweet sister, let me live' (132), Isabella is outraged. Her excoriation of her brother as 'beast', 'coward' and 'wretch' culminates in her accusing him, by proxy, of incest – the most abhorrent sin she can imagine: 'Is't not a kind of incest, to take life / From thine own sister's shame?' (135–9). Her accusation is harsh, even though in a strict sense it rings true. To save Claudio's life, Angelo has demanded that Isabella, as Marc Shell notes, 'exchange her maidenhead for the head of her brother';[22] if Claudio goes along with that ransom, in effect he makes himself part of the sexual bargain. To Isabella that constitutes 'a kind of incest'.

It is consistent with her spiritual goals that Isabella prizes her virginity so highly. She identifies her brother with her father, the traditional protector of her chastity, when she praises Claudio for his initial welcoming of death: 'There spake my brother; there my father's grave / Did utter forth a voice' (3. 1. 85–6). Still, it remains troubling, particularly to a modern audience, that Isabella's fierce adherence to her ideal of chastity trumps any sisterly compassion; as soon as Claudio begs Isabella to let him 'live', she harshly dismisses him with ''Tis best that thou diest quickly' (150). Even in the denouement of Act 5 she remains cold toward him. Isabella is prepared to pardon the deputy's 'intent' to violate her because he did not actually carry out his plan. But in arguing that Claudio, unlike Angelo, 'had but justice, / In that he did the thing for which he died' (5. 1. 448–9), she is, in effect, condoning Angelo's duplicity and sexual coercion while still branding her brother as a sinner who deserves death. This means ignoring that Claudio's pre-marital sex, far from being sinful, was a mutually loving act with his fiancée Juliet. Isabella's downgrading of any erotic relationship perhaps accounts for her apparent lack of affection toward her brother. By privileging Angelo's life above Claudio's, she coldly waives any stronger tie of loyalty to her sibling.

Hamlet, with its three instances of the words 'incest' or 'incestuous', lays the groundwork for sexual desire between family members. The widow Gertrude has married her brother-in-law, Claudius, which counts as incest under Old Testament Levitical law; Leviticus 20: 21 calls it an act of 'impurity'.[23] Certainly the Ghost of Hamlet's father concurs, urging Hamlet not to let the 'royal bed of Denmark' be polluted by 'damned incest' (1. 5. 82–3). Forcing poison down Claudius's throat in the play's finale, Hamlet underlines the epithet 'incestuous' when he contemptuously dismisses Claudius as 'incestuous, [murd'rous], damned Dane' (5. 2. 325). In Shakespeare's late play *Henry VIII*, co-authored with John Fletcher, the king calls on Levitical law when he claims that his conscience is troubled by his marriage to Catherine of Aragon, his brother Arthur's widow. Wanting to obtain a divorce so that he can remarry, Henry defines Queen Catherine bluntly as 'Sometime[s] our brother's wife' (*Henry VIII*, 2. 4. 182). Claudius more glibly glosses over the incest question by introducing Gertrude as 'our sometime sister, now our queen' (*Hamlet*, 1. 2. 8).

By presenting a strongly bonded brother and sister in the play, Laertes and Ophelia, Shakespeare adds another layer to the question of what constitutes incestuous desire. From the beginning, the relationship of this duo is depicted as much warmer than that between brother and sister in *Measure for Measure*. Whereas Claudio would allow the sacrifice of Isabella's virginity to help his own cause, Laertes is fiercely protective of his 'dear' sister's purity. Leaving for France, he warns Ophelia to keep her 'affection' in check, 'Out of the shot and danger of desire' (1. 3. 33–5). Nothing could be more damaging, he feels, than were she to open her 'chaste treasure' to the 'unmaster'd importunity' of Hamlet's persistent wooing (31–2). Cynically he assumes that even the purest individuals are susceptible to sexual corruption – 'Virtue itself scapes not calumnious strokes' (38) – just as Ophelia's father Polonius pessimistically assumes a universal 'savageness in unreclaimed blood' (2. 1. 34).

A brother may, of course, take on a paternal role to protect his sister's honour. Isabella commends Claudio for taking over her dead father's 'voice' when he initially rejects Angelo's 'devilish' bargain (*Measure for Measure*, 3. 1. 86, 64). But Laertes's interest in Ophelia's chastity surely exceeds any paternal concern that would make it 'indistinguishable'[24] from that of her father Polonius. Dismissing the prince's courtship as sexual 'trifling', Laertes virtually positions himself as a rival suitor,[25] offering the specious rationalisation that Hamlet, as future king, cannot choose ('carve') for himself (1. 3. 5, 20). His concession 'Perhaps he loves you now' quickly turns into a warning to Ophelia not to 'believe' the prince 'if he says he loves' her (14, 24–5). Polonius also cautions his daughter that a would-be seducer offers false 'vows' when 'the blood burns' (127, 116). But unlike Laertes, Polonius is mainly concerned with family honour and patriarchal privilege. He prefers to block the possible union of his daughter with Hamlet (despite the social 'gain' to his family if Ophelia marries the prince[26]) because the courtship has not been arranged or controlled by him. He fears, too, that sexual dalliance without marriage would leave his daughter as damaged goods. Tetchy about his own reputation, Polonius worries that Ophelia's 'free' behaviour with Hamlet may 'tender' (offer up[27]) the patriarch as a 'fool', one who will be ridiculed and disgraced (93, 109).

In Act 4, when Laertes furiously accuses Claudius of being complicit in the killing of his father Polonius, his determination to avenge his father's death is compounded by the horror of witnessing Ophelia's decline into madness. To him she remains the acme of purity, the 'rose of

May! / Dear maid, kind sister, sweet Ophelia!' (4. 5. 158–9). Traditional epithets used to describe a female loved one ('dear' and 'sweet') become more intense when joined to 'kind', an epithet that denotes blood relationship as well as the quality of being compassionate; Ophelia seems all the sweeter to Laertes because she is his kinswoman. Acting more like a Petrarchan suitor than a brother, Laertes over-idealises Ophelia, elevating her 'worth' by declaring how it 'Stood challenger on mount of all the age / For her perfections' (4. 7. 28–9). Once she is dead he views her as a sacred 'minist'ring angel' (5. 1. 241). Shocked that the priest offers such scant ritual at Ophelia's funeral (twice Laertes questions 'What ceremony else?' (223, 225)), he remains fiercely protective of his sister's purity, anticipating 'violets' will grow 'from her fair and unpolluted flesh' (239–40).

His sexual rivalry with Hamlet surfaces most fully in this graveyard scene. Even before the prince suddenly appears, Laertes venomously prays that 'treble woe' may 'Fall ten times [treble] on that cursed head / Whose wicked deed' has deprived Ophelia of her senses (246–8). The nature of the 'deed', the murder of Polonius, goes unremarked in his intense preoccupation with what has happened to his sibling. When Laertes leaps into his sister's grave to embrace her, to hold her 'once more' in his 'arms', he urges the gravediggers to bury them both in a mountain of dust higher than Olympus (250–4). It is as though, like Romeo seeking Juliet in the tomb, he wishes to join his beloved Ophelia in death. When Hamlet joins him to grapple in Ophelia's grave, the two resemble rival suitors, not mourners. Gertrude has already linked this site of death with sexual consummation when she wishes she could have 'deck'd' Ophelia's 'bride-bed' and not her 'grave' with flowers (245–6). Defying Laertes, Hamlet backs up his counter-claim 'I lov'd Ophelia' by matching hyperbole with hyperbole, sneering at sibling love when he insists that 'Forty thousand brothers / Could not with all their quantity of love / Make up my sum' (269–71). Hamlet continues to taunt Laertes for his showy bravado, sarcastically outdoing him in 'rant' when he calls for 'millions of acres' to be thrown on both him and Ophelia, making Mount Ossa appear no bigger than a 'wart' (281–3). Yet until the prince reasserts his claim to be the one most moved by Ophelia's death, it is Laertes who positions himself as the grief-stricken romantic lover.

In *Antony and Cleopatra* Octavius Caesar seems cool towards all women other than his sister Octavia. His wife Livia is briefly mentioned when Cleopatra claims near the play's end that she has saved some trinkets 'For Livia and Octavia' (5. 2. 169), but we never see Livia on stage, and it is telling that Cleopatra's one reference yokes the wife's name with that of her sister-in-law. Octavius first reveals his devotion to Octavia when questioning whether she should marry the widower Antony. On one level the marriage is a political manoeuvre, a plan to tie together the two world leaders in an 'unslipping knot' (2. 2. 126), but Octavius evidently regards his sister as much more than a female pawn who can cement a homosocial bond. For him the agreement is a solemn bargain, the giving of a 'great part' of himself' (3. 2. 24) to his rival. He has made clear how much he cares for Octavia by reminding Antony 'A sister I bequeath you, whom no brother / Did ever love so dearly' (2. 2. 149–50). When Octavia leaves Rome with her new husband, her stoical brother is moved to tears; 'Will Caesar weep?' asks the incredulous Enobarbus (3. 2. 50). Octavius is unusually lyrical in parting from his 'dearest' sister, his sadness expressed through the rhythmic repetition of 'Farewell' expanded twice into the poignant 'Fare thee well':

> Farewell my dearest sister, fare thee well,
> The elements be kind to thee, and make
> Thy spirits all of comfort! Fare thee well. (39–41)

Like a lover taking leave of his mistress, he pledges to correspond with Octavia continuously ('You shall hear from me still') and to think of her constantly (60–1). As the Folio's stage direction indicates, Octavius seals this promise with a kiss and another emotionally charged 'Farewell, farewell' (66).

When his sister returns to Rome unexpectedly, without a large retinue, the Roman leader's pride is hurt by this insult to his family's honour. But he has also been deprived of the chance to demonstrate his devotion to Octavia, the 'ostentation' of an impressive show of public reverence for her (3. 6. 52). His grandiose idea of a wished-for welcome for her, which he can now conjure up only verbally, far surpasses decorum. He projects his own covert desire on to the 'longing' of those male bystanders anticipating Octavia's arrival:

> the trees by th' way
> Should have borne men, and expectation fainted,
> Longing for what it had not. (46–8)

Rivalling the bravura vision of the 'ceremony' Laertes thinks is due to the dead Ophelia – the mountains of dust out-topping Olympus – Octavius imagines how the dust raised by 'populous troops' honouring Octavia's return should have ascended to 'the roof of heaven' (49–50). Even though he was already preparing for war against Antony, witnessing his 'most wronged' sister (65) is the decisive factor for him; Octavius resolves to administer the gods' 'justice' in avenging Antony's abandonment of Octavia (88). The 'augmented greeting' that Octavius planned for his sibling, promising to meet her in person by 'sea and land' (54–5), even outshines the display that Antony and Cleopatra put on in Egypt, where the two lovers are described by envious Octavius as 'publicly enthron'd' in 'chairs of gold' (4–5). Antony and Octavius are positioned not simply as military rivals but as suitors vying for Octavia's affections. Now that Antony has abandoned her, Octavia remains her brother's 'best of comfort'. 'Nothing' is 'more dear' to him as he welcomes her back to Rome (89, 86).

True, Octavius is ostensibly a brother taking on a protective, paternal role. But he also becomes part of the 'triangular father/daughter/suitor configuration' in Shakespeare's plays, a situation in which, as Jane M. Ford notes, a father may either reluctantly relinquish his daughter to a suitor (conquering any latent incestuous feelings) or try to keep her for himself.[28] Although Octavius allows his 'dear'st sister' (3. 6. 98) to be married to Antony to cement the Roman alliance, he never loses his sense of having a prior claim on her. Like a surrogate father he welcomes Octavia, as Antony's 'castaway', back into the family fold (40). Shades of the rival lover remain, however. While Antony returns to his mistress Cleopatra, calling her his 'sweet' when they venture into battle together (3. 7. 23), Octavius is content to reclaim his beloved sister, his 'sweet Octavia' (3. 2. 59), from her delinquent husband.

While erotic desire informs the brother-sister relationship in *Hamlet*, the play has notoriously offered much more scope for analysing incestuous feelings between son and mother. Hamlet has many reasons to delay avenging his father's murder – the difficulty of publicly exposing the crime of the new king of Denmark and his own moral reluctance to assume the corrupt, bloodthirsty role of avenger are two significant ones. But unquestionably part of Hamlet's inertia stems from being preoccupied with his mother's remarriage; he is sickened by what he envisages as her uncontrolled lust with Claudius. Since Ernest Jones expanded the idea, in *Hamlet and Oedipus* (1954), that Hamlet is suffering from an Oedipus complex, Freudian critics have conjectured that unresolved infantile conflicts buried deep within Hamlet's unconscious – the desire to kill his father and sleep with his mother – are what 'puzzles' Hamlet's 'will' (3. 1. 79). Feminist critics have delved further into Hamlet's psyche, arguing that he is suffering from pre-Oedipal ambivalence, or the infant's sense of betrayal when he finds himself unable to merge with his all-powerful mother. Accordingly, Janet Adelman theorises that Hamlet's primal revulsion from the 'sexualized maternal body' must be resolved before he can reclaim his 'masculine identity' and pursue his quest for revenge.[29]

Certainly up until the end of Act 3 Hamlet seems more crippled by his mother's sexual betrayal than energised by the moral task of avenging his father's murder. Rebuking Gertrude in the closet scene, he insists on her sexual fall from grace with Claudius, a union that makes even 'Heaven's face' blush (3. 4. 48). Lamenting his stalled mission en route to England, Hamlet reviews his justification for taking action to kill Claudius:

> I then,
> That have a father kill'd, a mother stain'd,
> Excitements of my reason and my blood (4. 4. 56–8)

Leaving aside the possible Freudian slip of the phrasing – the faint suggestion of Oedipal patricide in 'I . . . / That have a father kill'd' beneath the overt meaning of 'I am a man whose father has been murdered' – the parallelism between the noun phrases in lines 57–8 is telling; it pairs 'father kill'd' with 'excitements of my reason', and 'mother stain'd' with 'excitements' of 'my blood'. We deduce that while the murder of Hamlet's father has activated his son's intellect ('reason'), convincing him that revenge is a reasonable course of action, it's the sexual disgrace of his mother that now stirs up Hamlet's 'blood' or passion. Indeed the play-within-a-play not only re-enacts the murder of the old king but communicates Hamlet's deep animus toward a widow who declares undying love for her first husband but then callously takes a second one. Planning to visit his mother after the disrupted performance, Hamlet resolves to curb passionate anger that may lead to violence: to 'speak [daggers] to her, but use none' (3. 2. 396).

Even by the time he more calmly leaves for England, Hamlet is still brooding over a 'mother stain'd'. But is his inertia the result of a full-blown Oedipus complex? Ernest Jones pursues that premise to explain why Hamlet is reluctant to kill Claudius. If Hamlet, in a case of arrested development, desires to kill his father and marry his mother, then he will intuit in Claudius a sexual rival who has fulfilled Hamlet's primal fantasy of doing just that. And if Hamlet's uncle 'incorporates the deepest and most buried part of his personality', then the prince 'cannot kill him without also killing himself'.[30]

Audiences in the theatre, though, are less likely to delve into this character's unconscious drives than to judge him by his words and actions. And Hamlet shows no overt sign of resenting, let alone hating, his father. While Hamlet finds the Ghost deeply ambivalent – he's unsure whether the apparition is a 'spirit of health, or goblin damn'd' (1. 4. 40) – he expresses no such reservations about the father he knew.[31] Rather, he remembers the former king with admiration. As well as mythologising his dead father as the sun-god Hyperion who boasted the 'front of Jove himself' (3. 4. 56), he soberly praises him to Horatio as a complete 'man' whose equal he 'shall not look upon ... again' (1. 2. 187–8). What disgusts Hamlet in his opening soliloquy is not simply his mother's hasty remarriage but that she has betrayed his father's memory through her union with an inferior man. He recalls his parents as a deeply loving couple. Nostalgically he notes how deeply protective ('loving') King Hamlet was toward his wife, satisfying in her the 'appetite' that then grew 'By what it fed on' – a sexual craving that her son can condone because it was sanctified by marriage (140–5). Rather than exhibiting a desire to displace his father, Hamlet longs to return to the era in which this ideal patriarch ruled. It is kinship with Gertrude, a shameful 'husband's brother's wife', that he wishes he could renounce, harshly reminding her in the closet scene, 'And would it were not so, you are my mother' (3. 4. 15–16).

Freud, in any case, emphasises that such conflicts – in this case, Hamlet's pre-Oedipal feelings toward his mother rather than an Oedipal wish to supplant his father – remain repressed. But several twentieth-century film versions of *Hamlet* have not kept the prince's sexual fascination with his mother in check; rather they have played up for viewers the subtext of Hamlet's incestuous desire for his mother as well as her attraction to him. Certainly Hamlet's language and actions in the closet scene are highly charged. The text confirms his anger at the untamed 'heyday' in Gertrude's 'blood' and her wallowing in the 'rank sweat of an enseamed bed' (3. 4. 69, 92). And twice in the play-script Hamlet forcefully urges his mother 'Sit you down' (18, 34), calling for at least a chair in the original staging. But instead of a chair, the marriage bed itself – the object that most fuels Hamlet's disgust – has often, since the 1930s, become a mandatory prop on stage[32] and then on screen. In many productions Hamlet pushes Gertrude on to this bed before forcing her to look at contrasting portraits of her two husbands.

Laurence Olivier's 1948 film, in which Olivier plays the prince, begins this tradition on screen. The royal bed is not only visually prominent; it frames the action. Early in the film the camera pans around the castle and through archways, coming to rest (accompanied by ominous music) on the curtained bed. A penultimate shot, before silhouetted figures carry Hamlet's body up to the battlements, foregrounds the bed again. Influenced by Ernest Jones's Oedipal theories,[33] Olivier eroticises the mother-son relationship; Gertrude, played by Eileen Herlie, injects incestuous desire into their first court scene together when she ostentatiously kisses her son on the mouth to seal his promise not to return to Wittenberg. Terrified in the closet scene, she tries to deflect her son's anger by moving to embrace him and stroking his face.

In that scene Olivier's Hamlet counters his mother's affection with sexual aggression. Demanding 'Sit you down', he throws his mother on to her bed, towering over Gertrude in close-up as he threatens her with a phallic sword. He then kneels on the royal bed to lecture her on the portrait medallions and lambast her for 'honeying and making love / Over the nasty sty' with Claudius. Only towards the end of the scene, after the exit of the Ghost, does Hamlet reciprocate his mother's loving tenderness. But when he confides, with his head on her lap, 'I must to England', he behaves more as a lover than an adult son with his parent. Gertrude kisses him on the lips when he speaks of wanting her 'blessing' and, more strikingly, they share an embrace and a fairly prolonged kiss on the mouth before he leaves to 'lug' away Polonius's corpse.

The 1980 BBC/Time Life production of *Hamlet*, featuring Derek Jacobi as Hamlet and Claire Bloom as Gertrude, builds on Hamlet's aggression towards his mother. Bitterly angry, Jacobi's Hamlet forcefully straddles her on the bed to simulate coupling when he derides her 'compulsive ardour'. Crudely he jabs at the weeping Gertrude to emphasise how 'stew'd in corruption' she is with Claudius. Yet because this Hamlet has enacted something similar with Ophelia – in the 'nunnery' scene he pushes Ophelia down, briefly imitating copulation as he verbally assaults her with 'You jig, you amble' – he conveys the impression of being furious with women in general. Rather than indulging any Oedipal fantasy with Gertrude, he is lashing out against one more 'pernicious' woman. Sardonically he warns her not to continue sleeping with the 'bloat king'.

It is Franco Zeffirelli's 1990 Hollywood production, starring Mel Gibson as Hamlet and Glenn Close as an enticingly blonde and very youthful Gertrude, that most fully turns the closet scene into an incestuous encounter. Building on Olivier's presentation of Gertrude as a sensual woman who shows considerable erotic interest in her son, this production also projects Hamlet as a troubled young man who loves but simultaneously wants to punish his mother. Entering her bedroom, Gibson's Hamlet pursues Gertrude with a bestial roar and a drawn sword. After killing Polonius he backs the terrified woman on to her bed. Forcing her to look at contrasting medallions of her two husbands, almost strangling her with the chain of the one she is wearing around her neck, he mounts Gertrude, roughly assaulting her as he imitates the action of 'honeying and making love'. It is almost a rape, certainly more pronounced than the simulated thrusts of Jacobi's Hamlet. Gertrude protests until, stunningly, she silences his verbal tirade on Claudius as a 'king of shreds and patches' by passionately kissing her son on the mouth. It is a long, reciprocated kiss, interrupted only when Hamlet observes the Ghost entering. Gertrude is clearly the sexual aggressor here. But Gibson's Hamlet perpetuates the physical intimacy; after the Ghost's exit he holds his mother's face in his hands, kissing the side of her head to plead with her to 'confess' herself to 'heaven'. This Hamlet, whose approach to his mother is an ambivalent mixture of attraction and repulsion, conveys intense disgust when he kneels to implore Gertrude not to resume relations with Claudius – the 'bloat king' whom, judged by his partial acceptance of his mother's erotic overtures, Hamlet may well regard as his sexual rival.

More recent screened versions of *Hamlet* have avoided such decidedly erotic emphasis in the mother-son encounter. The bed remains a central part of the closet scene, but not the kissing or sexual rough-housing. In the 1996 film directed by and starring Kenneth Branagh, Branagh's mercurial Hamlet appears deeply troubled both by his father's death and by his mother's remarriage. He does not, however, show any Oedipal tendencies.[34] Entering the bedroom, he angrily reminds Gertrude (played by Julie Christie) of her blind lust in marrying Claudius. When he pushes her down on the bed at 'Sense, sure you have', it is to emphasise the gravity of her licentious behaviour; he wants to reclaim her morally, not engage with her sexually. Apart from gripping Gertrude's shoulders and kneeling behind her to make her look at the dual portraits, he doesn't stay on the bed to deliver his diatribe on her 'compulsive ardour'. Incensed by her suggestion that he is mad (suffering from 'ecstasy'), he pulls her on to a sofa – at a firm distance from the bed – to convince her he is sane. Later mother and son, shown in alternating close-ups, communicate quietly with one another. Although Gertrude initiates a hug that Hamlet reciprocates, they share no lingering embraces or kisses. Branagh's film makes it clear that Hamlet's sexual interest has centred exclusively on Ophelia; earlier flashbacks show the couple passionately making love, and he kisses Ophelia warmly at the opening of the nunnery scene.

The BBC's version of the Royal Shakespeare Company's modern-dress *Hamlet*, directed by Paul Symonds and starring David Tennant, was televised in 2010. In this production the closet scene becomes an extraordinarily intense confrontation between mother and son; again, though, it is not an erotically charged one. Tennant's Hamlet enters in antic fashion, wearing the player's crown, but quickly turns serious. Following convention, he throws Gertrude down on the bed at the first 'Sit you down' and kneels there to rivet her attention on newspaper photographs of the two husbands. Mother and son remain physically close, Hamlet locking eyes with Gertrude and gripping her face to impress on her the horror of 'honeying and making love' with her second husband. Rather than getting astride his mother, as Hamlet does in both Jacobi's and Gibson's performances, he flings aside the covers to expose his view of the royal bed as a 'nasty sty'. Later he breaks into tears when his mother promises not to reveal any of this encounter to Claudius and sprawls across her lap after a fierce embrace. Even here, though, he strikes the viewer more as a troubled adolescent than a would-be lover. What's more, this Gertrude, played by Penny Downie as attractive but definitely middle-aged, is more comforting and maternal than sexually responsive to her son. She does not appear to be Hamlet's contemporary, as does Eileen Herlie (who was actually thirteen years younger than Olivier in that production) or Glenn Close in Zeffirelli's film. When Tennant's Hamlet leaves, giving his mother a quick peck on the lips, Gertrude looks surprised.

While vestiges of the convention established by Olivier – Hamlet's erotic bedroom encounter with his mother – have remained in twenty-first-century productions, the provocative rendering of incestuous passion is no longer in vogue. As Philip Weller comments when he denounces exaggeratedly Freudian performances, a man with an Oedipus complex 'almost certainly would not act it out in simulated sex with his mother, for then the problem would not be unconscious, but terrifyingly conscious'.[35] No critic denies Hamlet's anger at Gertrude, his disillusionment with females, and his revulsion towards sexuality in general. But it limits the scope of the play to focus exclusively on unresolved Oedipal or pre-Oedipal obsessions as the cause of Hamlet's delay in avenging his father's death.

If Hamlet's attitude toward his mother veers between residual love and horrified disgust, that of Coriolanus is consistent: he reveres his mother Volumnia unequivocally. Shakespeare's source for the play, 'The Life of Coriolanus' in North's translation of Plutarch's *Lives of the Noble Grecians and Romans* (1579), sets the tone for a strong mother-son bond by noting that Caius Martius, later Coriolanus, 'left an orphan by his father, was brought up by his mother'.[36] While Shakespeare presents Menenius as a loving male mentor – Coriolanus affirms that the elderly man 'Lov'd me above the measure of a father' (5. 3. 10) – it is Coriolanus's stalwart mother Volumnia, called 'mankind' (masculine) by the Tribunes (4. 2. 16), who serves as his role model. It is she who inspires her son to march into battle. Lauding her for her 'ancient courage' (4. 1. 3), Coriolanus elevates Volumnia to 'most noble mother of the world' (5. 3. 49).

Early in the play the dramatist alerts us to what becomes a key factor in the play: Coriolanus's need for his mother's approval. Shakespeare folds Plutarch's remark that 'the only thing that made him to love honor was the joy he saw his mother did take of him'[37] into the First Citizen's explanation that the warrior's achievements spring from two sources – his being 'proud' and his eagerness to 'please his mother' (1. 1. 39). After Coriolanus has scorned the commoners as 'mutable' and 'rank-scented' (3. 1. 66), he is surprised that the patrician Volumnia fails to come forward to 'approve' his action (3. 2. 7–8). When he further riles up the people instead of placating them, Menenius chides him with 'Is this the promise that you made your mother?' (3. 3. 86). His reputation for being a loving, obedient son continues unchanged. In Act 5, fearing that Coriolanus will sack Rome in revenge, the Tribune Sicinius desperately hopes that the warrior will relent at Volumnia's urging because he always 'lov'd his mother dearly' (5. 4. 15).

Freudian feminist critics, Janet Adelman in particular, have argued that Coriolanus's need for his mother's approval stems from the infant's pre-Oedipal hunger for maternal affection – a craving that can never fully be satisfied.[38] Yet it's surprising to learn that Volumnia has defied the convention, followed both in the ancient world and in Shakespeare's time, for aristocratic mothers to hand out their babies to wet nurses – a practice that historian Lawrence Stone argues decreased 'close emotional ties' between biological mother and infant.[39] Instead Volumnia has chosen to breastfeed her son herself. Rather than forging a warm, nurturing bond through suckling him, however, she takes credit instead for endowing Coriolanus with her own bold nature: 'Thy valiantness was mine, thou suck'st it from me' (3. 2. 129). Volumnia boasts of having sent him to a 'cruel war' (1. 3. 13) at an age when most young children would stay protected at home. She admits to more 'joy' at 'seeing [Marcius] had prov'd himself a man' in battle than when she first heard she had given birth to a male (16–17). Even in her final appeal to his filial duty in Act 5, she again reminds him of her legacy, how she moulded him to become a military hero: 'Thou art my warrior, / I [helped] to frame thee' (5. 3. 62–3).

Mother's milk, it seems, is less important to Volumnia than blood spilled in battle. She proudly tells her daughter-in-law, Virgilia, that the breasts of Hecuba, when she suckled the infant Hector, 'look'd not lovelier / Than Hector's forehead when it spit forth blood' (1. 3. 40–2). And whereas gentle Virgilia fervently rejects the idea of bodily harm to her husband, crying out 'O Jupiter, no blood' (38), Volumnia doesn't shun it; instead she gives 'thanks' to the gods when she hears her son has been wounded (2. 1. 121). Cherishing his wounds as part of his 'pursuit of heroic masculinity', Volumnia eroticises her warrior-son's violence.[40] She treats his triumphant return from Corioli as a peak experience that has fulfilled her 'very wishes' and the 'buildings of [her] fancy' (199–200). While 'fancy' here refers primarily to the glorious edifice of victory she has imagined for her son, the word (as discussed in Chapter 4) often denotes deep infatuation, as when Helena in *All's Well that Ends Well* confesses her 'idolatrous fancy' for Bertram (1. 1. 97).

From her first appearance in the play, Volumnia, as the warrior's mother, takes precedence over Coriolanus's wife Virgilia. Plutarch observes that Coriolanus was actually following his mother's 'desire' when he 'took a wife'.[41] Shakespeare goes further, showing Volumnia proudly instructing Virgilia on the requirements of the conjugal role. Were she in her daughter-in-law's place, she insists, she would privilege her spouse's military quest above her own sexual needs: 'If my son were my husband, I should freelier rejoice in that absence wherein he won honor than in the embracements of his bed where he should show most love' (1. 3. 2–5). After his victory at Corioli, Volumnia stands first in line to greet her son in Rome and savour his triumph; Coriolanus kneels to receive her praise as her 'good soldier' before he acknowledges Virgilia. It is his mother, recalling 'But O, thy wife!', who draws his attention to the spouse silently waiting in second place (2. 1. 171, 175).[42] Volumnia's way of taking precedence, insinuating her superiority over her son's wedded wife, is most pronounced when she addresses Coriolanus at the gates of Rome in Act 5. She, and not Virgilia or the matron Valeria, is the one who takes charge and 'speak[s]' out to persuade her son not to attack the city (5. 3. 155).

Does Volumnia view herself, subliminally, as wedded to her son?[43] *All's Well that Ends Well* opens with the widowed Countess, whose son Bertram is leaving for the army, lamenting that 'In delivering my son from me, I bury a second husband' (1. 1. 1). The widow Constance in *King John* likewise shows deep attachment to her son Arthur.[44] But widowed Volumnia, eager for her son Coriolanus to be a god-like warrior, elevates her bond with him to a much grander level when she compares herself to Juno, the sister/wife of Jove. Several times in the play Coriolanus is linked to the supreme Roman god. We learn how the nobles 'bended' to him 'As to Jove's statue' (2. 1. 265–6) on his victorious return from Corioli. Later Aufidius asserts that he would trust the word of Coriolanus above that of Jupiter himself (4. 5. 103–6). So when Volumnia says that she will 'lament' her son's exile 'in anger, Juno-like' (4. 2. 53), it's as though she is setting herself up as the wife of the thunder-bearer – the god she later associates with her son because Coriolanus too can 'tear' the air with 'thunder' (5. 3. 151).

But while the text suggests that the widowed Volumnia's devotion to her son is at least latently sexual, it never shows Coriolanus sharing those feelings. In fact Shakespeare changes the account in North's Plutarch of how, when his family arrives, Coriolanus first 'kissed his mother, and embraced her a pretty while, then his wife'.[45] Reversing the order, Shakespeare's hero instead savours from his wife Virgilia a 'kiss' – 'Long as my exile, sweet as my revenge!' – before apologising for failing to salute and kneel to his 'most noble' mother (44–5, 49–50). Coriolanus, it appears, continues to desire his wife sexually. But Volumnia owns, and can play, the card that Virgilia lacks; she is able to make her son feel guilty for disobeying her. By exploiting his need for her approval she exposes Coriolanus's fatal error: his conviction that he can sever all family ties, acting as autonomously as a 'lonely dragon' (4. 1. 30) or an 'author of himself' who knows 'no other kin' (5. 3. 35–7). Although he resolves 'out, affection, / All bond and privilege of nature, break!' (24–5), he cannot fulfil his earlier boast that 'Wife, mother, child, I know not' (5. 2. 82). Seeing Volumnia again at the gates of Rome, he acknowledges that his own 'trunk' (body) was once part of his mother's (5. 3. 22–3). For her part, Volumnia exploits their interdependence. She suggests that by forcing his 'mother' (other family members come second) to witness the destruction of Rome – 'Making the mother, wife, and child, to see / The son, the husband, and the father tearing / His country's bowels out' (101–3) – he will inflict violent bodily harm on her. By association, disembowelling Rome is equivalent to treading on the 'womb' of the mother who 'brought' him 'to this world' (123–5).

When her rational arguments (that brokering a peace would be more honourable than destroying the homeland) leave Coriolanus silent, Volumnia continues her emotionally charged appeals. She reminds her son of what they both know is true: that 'no man in the world' is 'more bound to 's mother' (5. 3. 158–9). In North's Plutarch, rather than the mother-son bond, Volumnia stresses the 'duty and reverence' that honourable men owe their 'parents', and how Coriolanus should be 'bound' to be 'thankful' to them.[46] In contrast, Shakespeare's Volumnia shames her son not only for failing to be 'bound' (obliged) to his mother, but for degrading her by allowing her to 'prate / Like one i' th' stocks'. Self-pityingly she resorts to another falsehood – that he has never shown his 'dear' mother any 'courtesy'. A superb rhetorician, Volumnia makes a further appeal to pathos through the homely image of herself as a 'poor' mother hen guarding a single chick. 'Fond of no second brood', she boasts of how she protected the military honour of her only son when she clocked or 'cluck'd'[47] him into battle and brought him 'safely home / Loaden with honor' (159–64).

When he 'turns away', Volumnia instructs the women to kneel and 'shame him' with their 'knees' (5. 3. 168–9). Like Cordelia in *King Lear*, shocked when her father kneels to her in contrition (4. 7. 58), Coriolanus has already shown distress at the sight of Volumnia going down on her knees when she first greets him. This reversal of the usual pattern, the child showing obedience to the parent, he finds as unnatural as if the 'pebbles on the hungry beach' should strike the 'stars' (5. 3. 58–9). But Volumnia continues to exert pressure on him. Her subsequent resolve, 'So, we will home to Rome / And die among our neighbors' (172–3), subtly implies that her son will be guilty of matricide if he doesn't relent.[48] Inflicting a final wound, she equates his unpatriotic handing over of Rome to the Volscians to a total severing of cherished family ties. Her contemptuous accusation, 'This fellow had a Volscian for his mother' (178), is deeply insulting.[49] She vows to speak again only when the city is burning – the result of her son's failure to show the 'affection' due to his mother.

Volumnia's emotional blackmail works. Coriolanus's vengeful desire to destroy Rome disintegrates into his need to please his mother; he cannot bear her scorn. The Folio stage direction reads 'holds her by the hand, silent'. This gesture suggests the dependency of a child, holding on to his mother's hand so that she can lead and guide him. But it might also signify, to Shakespeare's audience, a sacred pledge between those being married; the 'Solemnization of Matrimony' in the *Book of Common Prayer* (1559) requires the '*man to take the woman by the right hand*' so that the couple can '*give their troth*' to each other. This church ceremony is often preceded by the couple's 'spousal', a promise of marriage that also included clasping hands to signify a solemn contract.[50] Coriolanus immediately acknowledges the gravity of what Volumnia has accomplished when he breaks the silence with 'O mother, mother! / What have you done?' (182–3). Less a question than a resigned statement – contrast the accusatory 'Oh, Mother, what have you done to me?' in North's Plutarch[51] – his words gain poignancy through the dying fall on the repeated word 'mother'. Coriolanus instinctively knows that although Volumnia has won a victory for Rome, she has sealed his own fate with the Volscians.

Indeed Aufidius, his military rival briefly turned comrade, now views Coriolanus as a child dependent on his mother. The strong warrior has turned into a 'boy of tears', all too susceptible to his 'nurse's tears' (5. 6. 100, 92–6). It is Aufidius's derogatory word 'boy', even more than 'traitor' (86), that touches a nerve in Coriolanus. Despite his boast of conquering Corioli 'alone' (116), he has failed to separate himself from his mother. And although she exerts a more powerful influence over him than does his wife, Volumnia lacks the means to keep her beloved son alive. After she returns to her city in triumph, Coriolanus is butchered at the instigation of Aufidius. Having capitulated to his mother, this 'boy' warrior seems to welcome death; he dares the Volscians to 'cut' him 'to pieces' (111).

Hamlet and *Coriolanus* explore mother-son relationships; Shakespeare's *King Lear* and his romances (1608–11) focus on how fathers relate to their nubile daughters. Freud emphasised that incestuous desire, though usually repressed, is likely to be present on both sides of father-daughter relationships. But whereas Golding's influential translation of Ovid's *Metamorphoses* includes the story of Myrrha's passionate attraction to her father Cinyras, Shakespeare's plays never explicitly touch on a daughter's incestuous desire. Rather it is the patriarch's authority over his female child that may morph into jealousy and sexual possessiveness.[52]

Early modern England expected a daughter to show unquestioning obedience to her father – an assumption Theseus demonstrates forcefully in *A Midsummer Night's Dream* when he instructs Hermia that her father Egeus should be as a 'god' to her (1. 1. 47). Portia in *The Merchant of Venice* must reluctantly accept that her 'will' – her sexual choice of a mate – is 'curb'd' by 'the will of a dead father' who has imposed the casket test on her suitors (1. 2. 24–5). Each of these fathers exerts firm control over his daughter's chastity and decrees which man she can marry. The feminist critic Phyllis Chester suggests a further consequence of this: that 'while most women do not commit incest with their biological father', patriarchal marriage is 'psychologically predicated on sexual union between Daughter and Father figures'.[53] A bold post-Freudian generalisation, perhaps, but in his Renaissance *Instruction of a Christian Woman* (1523), Juan Luis Vives also links the female's role as daughter with her persona as wife. Despite emphasising that marriage makes man and wife 'one person', he comments that the woman, being weaker by 'nature', also acts 'as a daughter unto her husband'.[54]

King Lear begins with Lear's abdication from his throne but combines it with the long-standing ritual of relinquishing a daughter to a husband. The early modern wedding ceremony, as Lynda E. Boose makes clear, accentuates a father's 'possessive love' at the same time as his 'overwhelming fear of loss'.[55] Apparently Lear has postponed his separation from Cordelia, putting off her suitors, France and Burgundy, for as long as possible, and even delaying settling his other daughters' dowries until Cordelia's future is decided. His determination to keep his daughter for himself becomes evident in the absurd love test. By demanding that she comply publicly with his request 'Which of you shall we say doth love us most' (1. 1. 51), Lear makes it virtually impossible for reticent Cordelia to claim a third of the kingdom 'more opulent' than those of her sisters (86). In such a game of hollow flattery, he sets her up for failure. By angrily disinheriting her when she fails the test, he also makes it difficult for her to marry well.

As a jealous father,[56] Lear demonstrates extreme possessiveness by furiously turning on Cordelia when she fails to offer him unconditional love. Is there also evidence in the text that he has transgressed the boundaries of appropriate behaviour, engaging in a relationship that is at least 'bordering on the incestuous' and 'deeply disquieting in nature'?[57] This play is not *Pericles*, in which the daughter of Antiochus has found sexual 'kindness' in her father and has served as both his 'wife' and 'child' (*Pericles*, 1. 1. 67, 69). We assume that Cordelia has not known Lear as a wife would. The issue of incestuous desire is handled only indirectly in this play. But the opening scene provides some evidence that Cordelia, while refusing an exclusive relationship with her father, is also acknowledging and deflecting his erotic feelings toward her.

Several of Cordelia's speeches are ambiguous in this respect. On one level her statement 'I love your majesty / According to my bond, no more nor less' (1. 1. 92–3) is a coolly rational, almost legal definition of what a daughter owes her father, yet the word 'bond' also signifies a deep connection with him. And despite reminding Lear that her future husband will take 'half' her love with him, her promise to 'Obey you, love you, and most honor you' (98) echoes the wedding ceremony in the Prayer Book of 1559 – a ceremony in which the priest asks the bride, 'Wilt thou have this man to thy wedded husband . . . wilt thou obey hym and serve him, love, honour and kepe him, in sycknes and in health?' Cordelia's 'most' (in 'most honor you') even seems to provide an answer to Lear's loaded question: 'Which of you shall we say doth love us most?' When Desdemona faces a similar 'divided duty' between her father Brabantio and her husband Othello, she doesn't guarantee that 'half' her love will stay with her father. Her acknowledgement of indebtedness to him – 'To you am I bound for life and education' (*Othello*, 1. 3. 181–2) – is restrained, much less open to sexual innuendo (through 'bred me') than is Cordelia's blunt 'You have begot me, bred me, lov'd me' (*King Lear*, 1. 1. 96).

When France debates marrying Cordelia, his perplexity over the king's rejection of his favourite child hints at darker possibilities within the father-daughter relationship. He finds it strange that Cordelia, the '[best] object' of Lear, should 'Commit a thing so monstrous, to dismantle / So many folds of favor' (217–18). He reasons to Lear that Cordelia's 'offense'

> Must be of such unnatural degree
> That monsters it, or your fore-vouch'd affection
> Fall into taint; which to believe of her
> Must be a faith that reason without miracle
> Should never plant in me. (219–23)

Within four lines France uses both the adjective 'monstrous' and the verb 'monsters' to characterise any 'offense' of Cordelia's grotesque enough to forfeit her father's regard. 'Monstrous' in Shakespeare's work can point to sexual transgression, as when Othello finds 'monstrous! monstrous!' the lubricious 'dream' of Cassio that Iago conjures up for him (*Othello*, 3. 3. 427), or when King Antiochus in *Pericles* is finally struck down for 'monstrous lust' in making his daughter serve as his wife (5. 3. 86). Refusing to believe that Cordelia would be guilty of such an 'unnatural' act, France feels compelled to put the blame on Lear. It must be the father's love that is impure – an 'affection' (the noun signifying sexual passion) that, as France puts it, 'Fall[s] into taint'.

Curiously, Cordelia does not respond directly to France's consternation; instead she continues to defend herself to her father. Over a hundred lines have elapsed since she confirmed herself to Lear as 'So young, my lord, and true', precipitating his terrible vow to sever all his 'paternal care' (1. 1. 107, 113). Now she breaks her silence to remind him that it is her reticence, and not any 'foulness' or 'unchaste action' – in other words, not a sexual sin – that has forfeited his 'grace and favor' (227–9). Why would she need to do so? Coming straight after France's speech speculating on 'unnatural' offence, Cordelia's words should be addressed to her suitor, the 'Majesty' of France, rather than to her father. This would be her way of defending herself from any 'vicious blot' on her honour (227) and assuring France that it is 'lawful' for him to take her as his wife. Indeed her speech inspires France's full commitment – 'Thee and thy virtues here I seize upon' – and his confidence that marriage to such a 'precious' and chaste woman is indeed legitimate (252–3, 259).

Rather than inferring any oblique denials of incest on Cordelia's part, commentators usually focus on the limits she sets on her filial 'duties' (97) and her refusal to indulge in the 'glib and oily art' of flattering rhetoric (224). Ironically it is Regan who more ostentatiously speaks to her father as a lover might do. Her oration is calculated to trump Goneril's hyperbolic assertion that her love for Lear goes 'Beyond what can be valued, rich or rare' (57). Exploiting the sexual implications of 'deed' in 'I find she names my very deed of love' (71), Regan goes on to claim that she can experience complete sensual pleasure, all 'joys / Which the most precious square of sense [possesses]' (73–4), only in her father's loving presence. The sisters' sexual flattery sounds particularly odd, if not downright disingenuous, because it is spoken in the presence of their husbands, Cornwall and Albany. Cordelia succinctly makes this point to her father: 'Why have my sisters husbands, if they say / They love you all?' (99–100).

When Lear asks Cordelia what she can add to Regan's words to earn a richer parcel of land, she simply reiterates 'Nothing' (87–9). While we can never be sure what innuendo the Jacobean audience might register, it is a stretch to infer a crude sexual reference here, as when Hamlet taunts Ophelia by reminding her that 'nothing' or no-thing (female genitals) 'lie[s] between maids' legs' (*Hamlet*, 3. 1. 118–19). Most of Cordelia's speeches convey a different subtext: not that she is complicit with desires bordering on incest, but that being aware of them she is setting limits, letting Lear know that 'a daughter cannot be a substitute wife'[58] even as she confirms her strong bond with her father.

Pericles, which begins with flagrant sexual 'sin' in Antioch, not surprisingly uses the word 'incest' five times. But *King Lear* is the only play in the canon apart from *Hamlet* that contains the epithet 'incestuous'. After the opening scene, the theme of incestuous attraction doesn't impede the ongoing momentum of the play – Lear's breach with his daughters, his journey through madness, and his eventual loving reconciliation with Cordelia – but it remains a subtext. When the king, battling the storm, addresses an imaginary offender as 'thou similar of virtue / That art incestuous' (3. 2. 54–5), he is praying that cosmic upheaval will help to expose 'undivulged crimes' in his society (52). Notwithstanding, Lear may also be obliquely acknowledging his own guilt, his hidden desire for his daughter. Similarly, when Kent in Act 4 mentions the 'sovereign' and 'burning shame' that prevents Lear from confronting Cordelia, he is overtly referring to Lear's 'unkindness' in having banished his youngest daughter (4. 3. 42, 46). Yet Lear's 'burning shame' could indicate his sense of violating sexual boundaries by having fantasised the 'unkindness' of committing incest with his next of kin.

The Fool, who often speaks in riddles, uncovers parts of Lear's psyche that the old king cannot fully confront. A few of his gibes, voiced before Lear's humbling experience in the storm, seem to tap into the king's incestuous desire. Early in the play, the Fool remarks that by banishing Cordelia, Lear did her a 'blessing against his will' (1. 4. 103) – a favour Lear did not intend but also, calling on the secondary meaning of 'will', an act that ran counter to his deeper sexual needs. Exposing Lear's hidden desire with his parable about the Cockney's phallic 'eels', the Fool imagines subduing the king's 'rising heart' – overtly his passionate rage at being unable to control his daughters – in the same way that the female Cockney, crying 'Down wantons, down', beat down the phallic eels with a stick (2. 4. 121–5). In the storm, the fragment of a ballad that Edgar sings as Poor Tom, 'Come o'er the [bourn], Bessy to me', speaks to Lear's subconscious wish that Cordelia will return from France to end their separation. But the Fool's cryptic rejoinder, 'Her boat hath a leak, / And she must not speak / Why she dares not come over to thee' (3. 6.

26–8), implies a darker reason for Cordelia's continued absence – the undercurrents of incest, the taboo practice that 'dares not' speak its name but which has urged her separation from her father. When the Gentleman arrives in Act 4 with news of Lear's 'most dear daughter' (4. 6. 189) this prompts the mad king's escape because of 'burning shame'; his thoughts turn sexual with the simile 'I will die bravely, like a smug bridegroom' (198).

All this remains on the level of suggestion. The other more explicit family dynamic explored in the play is the one the Fool pointedly insists on – how Lear has turned his 'daughters' into his 'mothers'. Like a masochistic infant, Lear is almost begging to be punished by these harsh parental figures by handing them 'the rod' and pulling down his own 'breeches' (1. 4. 173–4). This has led some feminist commentators to posit in the old king a regression into the infant's pre-Oedipal phase. Rather than desiring Cordelia as an 'incestuous object', Lear has a deep 'need for Cordelia as a daughter-mother', concludes Coppélia Kahn.[59] In Lynda E. Boose's reading Lear deflects his 'original incestuous passions into Oedipal ones', hoping to keep his daughter close to him by placing her in a maternal role.[60]

Such an interpretation is compelling. Because Lear has no wife, he might well regard his daughters as nurturing mother figures who can fulfil his emotional needs; when they fail to comply he flies into infantile rage. Thus he lashes out at Cordelia after she declines to provide a 'kind nursery' for him in his old age (1. 1. 124), a shelter from which he can, like an infant, 'crawl toward death' (41). Comparing her to the 'barbarous Scythian' who devours his own children, Lear implies that she is a cruel mother as well as a hard-hearted daughter (116–20). It is in his two other daughters, however, that Lear discovers real maternal malevolence. Goneril's derisory 'Old fools are babes again' comments coldly on Lear's increasing senility (1. 3. 19). Indeed both daughters capitalise on their father's childish weakness (2. 4. 201), chastising him for his 'unsightly tricks' (157) and 'new pranks' (1. 4. 238) while cutting down on the retinue of knights that serves as Lear's security blanket. 'What need one?' asks Regan callously (2. 4. 263). In the storm Lear indicts Goneril and Regan as 'pelican daughters' (3. 4. 75). By doing so he replaces the traditional image of the pelican who feeds her offspring with her own blood – an emblem of the self-sacrificing mother that he craves – with a vision of daughters who have drained his very life-blood. Instead of supporting him through the second childhood of old age, these females have robbed him of everything that sustains him.

This strand of the play, Lear's yearning to be taken care of by a nurturing female, is not, after all, incompatible with a father's latent incestuous desire for his adult daughter.[61] In Freudian terms, Lear's need to possess Cordelia signals a return to the male infant's pre-Oedipal desire to merge completely with his mother.[62] Indeed Lear's final fantasy of spending the rest of his life blissfully 'alone' with Cordelia in prison, where they will 'pray, and sing, and tell old tales' (5. 3. 12), represents just this need for 'undifferentiated union'[63] with the family member who is now closest to him. By the time he and his daughter are led off to prison, King Lear has moved far beyond the figure of the authoritarian, controlling father. But even though he now treats Cordelia as an equal – he promises humbly to 'kneel down' to her when she asks his 'blessing' (10) – he still yearns for an exclusive relationship with the beloved daughter he has finally 'caught' (21). There is no suggestion that Cordelia's husband, France, will intervene to prevent this. Instead the king envisages father and daughter as mutually loving partners, as sufficient to one another as a devoted husband and wife would be. Plaintively beautiful though Lear's vision of the couple in prison singing 'like birds i' th' cage' (9) may be, it remains a regressive fantasy. As Montaigne emphasises in his comparison of marriage to a bird-cage in which the birds outside 'despaire to get in' but those inside 'despaire to get out',[64] such an exclusive relationship, were it to be fulfilled, would surely signal an unnaturally claustrophobic relationship, too cloying for a father and daughter to sustain.

But since Lear unconditionally offers himself to Cordelia, a clear divergence from his selfish demands in the opening scene, it seems misguided to over-analyse his devotion as latently incestuous. What matters in the play's tragic ending, when Lear experiences the horror of losing the one person he loves completely and who loves him in return, is that his 'whole being' is now 'launched toward another'.[65] If Cordelia were miraculously to come back to life, that would 'redeem all sorrows' that Lear has ever 'felt' (5. 3. 267–8). The philosopher-critic Stanley Cavell puts it well. As spectators and auditors empathising with King Lear's heartbreak over losing Cordelia, we are not concerned with 'the *nature* of that love'. We do not care 'whether the *kind* of love felt between these two is forbidden according to humanity's lights'.[66] Rather, we care deeply about our ability to register the scale of such devotion.

In 1607–8, just a year or two after *King Lear* was performed, Shakespeare composed *Pericles* in collaboration with George Wilkins. A dramatic foray into the older romance genre, *Pericles* is the first in the series of tragicomedies that focus on almost magical reunions, often mediated through a chaste daughter, among family members who have long been divided by personal quarrel or catastrophe. As such the romances provide an antidote to the ending of *King Lear* – a father's tragic loss of the daughter with whom he has been unusually close.

C. L. Barber aptly comments on how the symbolic action of the final plays 'works to restore family ties' by 'dissociating them from the threat of degradation by physical incest'.[67]

Counterbalancing mothers are either completely absent or excluded from much of the action in these late plays. In *Cymbeline* and *The Tempest* this increases the potential for an abuse of 'paternal' and 'sexual' power[68] as the father tries to control his daughter's choice of a husband. The fact that these dominating fathers are rulers – Cymbeline is a king, Prospero a duke – redoubles their protective power over their royal daughters. As Marilyn L. Williamson puts it, because 'the ruler's authority' is 'based in the family, incest is a terrifying specter'.[69] This spectre must be exorcised, incestuous desire waived or sublimated, if the father-daughter relationship is to remain uncompromised and the family is to move toward a fertile future. When a chaste daughter becomes a wife in an exogamous union, she cuts through the closed circle of incestuous attachment, ensuring the purity and continuation of the family line.

At the opening of *Pericles*, the prince of Tyre yearns to establish a family, seeking a wife with whom he will create royal 'issue' (1. 2. 73). But once he plans to win the princess of Antioch by solving the riddle, he's confronted with the dark reality that remains only latent in *King Lear*; King Antiochus is committing 'foul incest' with his own daughter (1. 1. 126). By accepting her father's 'kindness' sexually, the princess has collapsed essential distinctions among family members, turning herself into 'mother, wife – and yet his child' (67, 69). Before he discovers her unnatural 'sin' (121), Pericles is 'inflam'd' with 'desire' for her beautiful appearance (20); now he must escape to save his life and honour. At Pentapolis he finds a royal bride, but he marries princess Thaisa only to lose her (as he believes) in a 'terrible' childbirth at sea (3. 1. 56). Years later Pericles is falsely told that his daughter Marina has died in Tharsus.

The play's action, crisscrossing Asia Minor through many sea voyages, gradually moves toward the conclusion of romantic tragicomedy; Pericles fortunately recovers both wife and child. The scene where he discovers that Thaisa is still alive – after being washed ashore and revived, she has lived chastely at the temple of Diana in Ephesus – seems almost a dramatic afterthought, though. It is the extended father-daughter reunion at Mytilene that carries most weight, as Marina movingly rescues her father from his self-imposed isolation. In several ways this sequence recalls Lear's awakening to find that Cordelia has returned. Like Lear, who is dressed in 'fresh garments' as he sleeps (4. 7. 21), Pericles asks for 'fresh garments' to celebrate Marina's becoming his 'own' again (5. 1. 214). Just as the Doctor in *King Lear* orders 'Louder the music there!'

to restore the old king's sanity (4. 7. 24), so Marina in *Pericles* offers the 'sweet harmony' of 'music' when she sings to revive the unkempt, grief-stricken stranger who turns out to be her father (5. 1. 45, 80). After his ecstatic discovery that his only daughter is alive and 'no fairy', Pericles is privileged to hear the mystical 'music of the spheres' (153, 229); Lear too is amazed to find that Cordelia is no 'spirit' but his own flesh-and-blood child (4. 7. 48). But whereas the tragedy of *King Lear* plays out 'the destructive logic of Lear's possessiveness',[70] the romance *Pericles* opens into renewed family relations. Lear bypasses Cordelia's husband France to seek union with Cordelia 'alone' in prison; in contrast Pericles encourages the marriage of his only daughter to Lysimachus, the reformed governor of Mytilene.

No tinge of incestuous feelings shadows the asexual joy of Pericles's revival. Indeed in Shakespeare's earlier play *All's Well that Ends Well*, Helena's 'cure' of the King of France is much more erotically charged, since the king (old enough to be her father) responds to Helena's 'youth' and beauty' as much as to her 'physic' (2. 1. 181, 185); he becomes 'lustier' than a 'dolphin' once she has restored him to vigorous health (2. 3. 26). Instead Pericles experiences the surge of energy and happiness in his daughter's presence as a literal rebirth. Wonderingly, he addresses her as 'Thou that beget'st him that did thee beget' (5. 1. 195) – an exchange of roles in which daughter Marina is transformed into her father, miraculously conceiving Pericles so that he can be reborn into a state of grace. Rather than serving as a surrogate wife, as the princess of Antioch does – metaphorically feeding on her 'mother's flesh' by cohabiting with her father (1. 1. 65–6) – Marina becomes an incentive for Pericles to find the wife he has lost. Noting the family resemblance early in his encounter with Marina, Pericles laments that his 'dearest wife was like this maid, and such a one / My daughter might have been' (5. 1. 107–8). While Pericles seeks out his wife after he wakes from a dream-vision, his fullest epiphany nevertheless comes when he perceives himself as the newborn offspring of his own daughter. In that amazing moment, the rekindling of a lost family connection, he fears that a 'great sea of joys' may kill him, overwhelming the 'shores' of his 'mortality' (5. 1. 192–3).

Near the end of *Cymbeline* (1610), the king voices similar ecstasy mingled with trepidation when he wonders if 'the gods ... mean to strike [him] / To death with mortal joy' (5. 5. 234–5). He has finally recognised his missing daughter Imogen in her disguise as the page boy Fidele. Before this moment Cymbeline senses some hidden kinship with the youth who seems so 'familiar' to him that he confesses 'I love thee more and more' (93, 109). Immediately after Cymbeline's discovery, however, the focus shifts to Imogen and Posthumus, and any joyful renewal of the father-daughter bond must give place to the daughter's reconciliation with her estranged husband. Cymbeline begs to be part of the reunion:

> How now, my flesh, my child?
> What, mak'st thou me a dullard in this act?
> Wilt thou not speak to me? (264–6)

Being displaced from the centre of attention is a reminder that his daughter's chosen husband, the man Cymbeline banished from court, must take precedence over her father. And although the king has just lost his second wife, the wicked queen who dies in despair, there is no sign that he seeks in his daughter a surrogate wife. His rejoicing at the restoration of his family extends to the miraculous recovery of his abducted sons, Guiderus and Arviragus. While Pericles, overcome with joy at finding his sole offspring alive, imagines he is the newborn child of his daughter, Cymbeline re-establishes himself as a parent, albeit a female, nurturing one. Wonderingly he exclaims that he is 'A mother to the birth of three' restored children (369).

The Winter's Tale, like *Pericles*, centres on the restoration of a missing royal wife and daughter. Pericles chooses to wear sackcloth despite not being guilty of any sin; King Leontes, though, is criminally responsible for the disastrous breakdown of his family. He has caused both the long absence of Hermione, falsely accused of adultery sixteen years ago and assumed dead, and the disappearance of the baby he cast out as a 'bastard' (2. 3. 74). It is this daughter, Perdita, growing up as a shepherdess in Bohemia, who becomes an agent of restoration, transforming the play's action from sterile winter – Leontes locked in guilt over his past actions – to a springtime of renewed trust in female goodness. Perdita's elopement to Sicily with Florizel, Prince of Bohemia, comes at a fortunate moment; Leontes's penance for having (as he thinks) 'kill'd' Hermione has continued long enough (5. 1. 15–17). Eager for an advocate, Florizel begs Leontes to recall his own young 'affections' and persuade King Polixenes to accept his son's marriage (220), thereby sealing the reconciliation of the two 'brother' monarchs (142). Early in the play, Leontes's tortured speech, 'Affection, thy intention stabs the center' (1. 2. 138), expressed his jealous delusion that Hermione and Polixenes were committing adultery; now he can recognise tenderness as well as passion in the youthful affections of the 'gracious couple' who stand before him, 'begetting wonder' (5. 1. 134–5).

With supreme irony, Leontes is brought to acknowledge the 'wonder' of committed love through the daughter he rejected as a baby. He also becomes, though in a fleeting and unthreatening way, sexually attracted to her. Discovering that the Bohemian prince and Perdita are not yet married, Leontes wryly asks Florizel for a favour: 'I'd beg your precious mistress' (223). His mentor Paulina sternly intervenes with 'my liege, / Your eye hath too much youth in it', reminding Leontes that in her prime his own queen was even more beautiful than this young woman (224–6). Shakespeare's main source, Greene's *Pandosto* (1588), foregrounds the dangers of inadvertent incest when King Pandosto feels 'hot desire' – 'fresh affections and unfit fancies' – for Fawnia, whom he fails to recognise as his own daughter.[71] *The Winter's Tale*, though, introduces this hint of incestuous desire only to mitigate and gracefully dismiss it. Leontes reassures Paulina that when he first set eyes on Perdita he 'thought' of his queen (227).

Like Pericles mourning afresh his wife Thaisa when he sees Marina, Leontes still yearns for Hermione. In discovering his daughter Perdita, Leontes reportedly repeats 'O, thy mother, thy mother!', feeling the old 'loss' of his wife even in the new 'joy' of finding his child (5. 2. 50–2). Much stronger than any sexual attraction to her is his deep regret at being 'issueless' (5. 1. 174), his desire to be a parent again. Admiring the young couple, he reflects how blessed he would have been, 'Might I a son and daughter now have look'd on, / Such goodly things as you?' (177–8). Unlike in *Pericles*, the dramatic focus in *The Winter's Tale* shifts from the moment Leontes recognises his daughter – a scene narrated, not shown – to the climax of his discovery that his wife is still alive. Moving to 'awake' his 'faith' in womankind, watching the statue's magical metamorphosis into the 'warm' life of Hermione, Leontes responds as a loving husband (5. 3. 95, 109–10). After a gap of sixteen years it is questionable whether Leontes and Hermione could fully repair their marriage, and their son Mamillius is gone forever. But in the wonder of a theatrical finale that stresses the transformative power of forgiveness, Perdita as mediator not only heals the rift between the kingdoms of Bohemia and Sicilia but restores the sense of family. Leontes is given a second chance to show his devotion as both a husband and a father.

The Tempest, the finale to the romances, offers more resolution to the fraught father-daughter relationship; it revisits and redeems *King Lear*. Because Prospero ultimately abandons paternal possessiveness, focusing instead on guiding his daughter Miranda into a royal marriage based on romantic love, the play dispels the shadow of incestuous desire. Isolated with Miranda for twelve years on the island, with only the 'monster' Caliban and his spirits for occasional company, Prospero inevitably becomes a protective father. His 'cell' affords the unusually close contact with his daughter that King Lear yearns for with Cordelia in 'prison'. But in contrast to Lear, who is denied the chance to develop a mutually respectful relationship with his child, Prospero directs his energies, his magical powers, toward the future of his daughter by orchestrating her betrothal to Ferdinand, Prince of Naples.

Miranda has grown up without a mother. As a single parent, Prospero is responsible for her upbringing and education, serving as her 'schoolmaster' as well as her father (1. 2. 172). He assures her, with the stress falling on 'thee' at the end and beginning of adjacent lines, that she is his sole concern: 'I have done nothing, but in care of thee / Of thee my dear one, thee my daughter' (16–17). While Prospero punishes his 'slave' Caliban with 'cramps' if he disobeys (1. 2. 325) and threatens to 'peg' his servant Ariel in a 'knotty' oak tree for twelve years if the spirit rebels against his master (294–6), he refrains from bullying his daughter physically. Still, he insists on patriarchal privilege when he chastises Miranda as a lowly 'foot' that must not presume to 'tutor' the head of the family (470), and he roughly brushes her aside with 'Hence! Hang not upon my garments' when she tries to protect Ferdinand (475). More often, though, he exerts psychological control over her. He demands her complete attention when he recounts his history, twice insisting that she 'mark' what he's saying (67, 88) and accusing her of failing to listen attentively ('Thou attend'st not!' (87)), even when she is clearly riveted (78, 88).

When Prospero, with Ariel's help, manipulates Miranda's instant attraction to Ferdinand, inducing her to fall for the only 'brave' (splendidly handsome) young man she has ever seen (1. 2. 412), Miranda quickly obliges. As Boose comments, if a father chooses his daughter's husband her progression into marriage can remain, to some extent, 'a text defined by obedience to her father'.[72] As soon as she is in love, however, Miranda begins to defy the patriarch. Defending Ferdinand from Prospero's labelling him a 'traitor', she risks incurring her father's 'hate' (470, 477). In Act 3 she breaks her promise to Prospero when she tells the devoted prince her name. Her progress from an abnormally cloistered relationship with her father to total commitment to her suitor – she pledges either to marry Ferdinand or be his 'servant', whether he 'will or no' (3. 1. 83–6) – is refreshingly swift. It recalls Rosalind's privileging of her beloved suitor above her exiled father in the Forest of Arden when she exclaims to Celia, 'But what talk we of fathers, when there is such a man as Orlando?' (*As You Like It*, 3. 4. 38–9).

Once Ferdinand has passed the test of physical endurance (carrying logs for his future father-in-law), Prospero is prepared to bestow on him the daughter he knows 'will outstrip all praise' (4. 1. 10). Shakespeare does not bypass the emotional ambivalence of such a sacrifice, however. While 'rejoicing' at bringing Ferdinand and Miranda together, Prospero also confesses 'So glad of this as they I cannot be' (3. 1. 92). His words register the muted pain of a father about to lose a precious child who will become her husband's 'darling' and no longer just his own 'lov'd' one (3. 3. 93). In Act 5 Prospero confides to Alonso, who believes his son Ferdinand has drowned, that he too has 'lost' a child in the tempest (5. 1. 148). Forging a royal dynasty at some personal cost, Prospero conceals the reality that his only daughter has been lost not to death but to an upcoming marriage with Alonso's son. And whereas the King of Naples has coerced his unwilling daughter Claribel into marrying a distant African prince (2. 1. 131), Prospero more generously enables a love-match for his daughter.

He remains reluctant to relinquish all control over her, however. In Act 4 Prospero plays the controlling father when he insists that Miranda remain chaste until her marriage. Partly this answers to the romance convention, in which a virgin (Marina, Perdita and now Miranda) magically ensures the continuation and purity of the royal line. But in early modern culture nubile young women often served as commodities in a male system of exchange;[73] in such a system Prospero's daughter, the 'rich gift' that Ferdinand has 'worthily purchas'd', must pass unsullied from father to husband (4. 1. 8, 14). In his first encounter with Ferdinand, Prospero symbolically asserts his phallic power as Miranda's father when he puts a charm on the prince's sword, disabling him sexually by threatening to make his 'weapon drop' (1. 2. 474). Now he warns that if Ferdinand takes possession of Miranda too early, breaking her 'virgin-knot' before their wedding day, the couple's future will be cursed with 'barren hate' (4. 1. 15, 19). Despite Ferdinand's pledging prenuptial chastity, Prospero continues to fear that sexual 'dalliance' will defeat that vow. Accordingly he warns the couple attending the masque of spirits – a ceremony that by banishing lustful Venus and her fickle son Cupid augurs a chaste but fertile future – to be 'more abstemious!' (51–3).

Prospero, after all, is acutely aware of the disruptive nature of sexual desire. He has protected Miranda from Caliban's attempt to rape her ('violate' her 'honor') when the slave aimed, through a grotesque exogamous union, to have 'peopled' the 'isle with Calibans' (1. 2. 347–51). Symbolising what Leslie Fiedler calls the 'gross shadow of the father',[74] Caliban serves as a surrogate for Prospero's latent incestuous desire. Any sexual 'will', displaced on to the monster, is defused accordingly. For all his cultivation of reason and intellect, however, Prospero experiences 'passion / That works him strongly' after the visionary masque (4. 1. 143–4), perhaps as 'vex'd' by his chagrin at losing Miranda as by his slave's 'foul conspiracy' (158, 139). Near the end of the play he finally identifies himself with the earth-bound, bestial Caliban by publicly conceding 'this thing of darkness I / Acknowledge mine' (5. 1. 275–6), where 'I' (bound to 'darkness' and 'acknowledge') is strongly pointed by its position at the line's end.

Contrary to the endings of *Pericles* and *The Winter's Tale*, Prospero doesn't regain a wife. Instead he remains in 'sexual and social isolation'.[75] Having relinquished his magical 'art' at the same time he forfeits the daughter he calls 'that for which I live' (4. 1. 4), Prospero prepares to leave the island to witness the nuptials of the 'dear-belov'd' couple (5. 1. 310). His charmed existence, enabled by his skill as magus, is essentially over.[76] But Shakespeare's final romance, *The Tempest*, has succeeded in depicting what proved impossible in the tragedy of *King Lear* – a close but not cloyingly possessive father-daughter relationship. Even more than Leontes reacting to Perdita with Florizel, Prospero celebrates without envy the 'rare affections' between Miranda and Ferdinand (3. 1. 75) and thus renounces any exclusive, jealously guarded relationship with his daughter. As the magus graciously concludes his dramatic design by transferring power to the audience in the epilogue ('Gentle breath of yours my sails / Must fill' (11–12)), so Prospero the father generously bequeaths to Ferdinand any paternal rights to his daughter, trusting that the prince will prove a worthy and loving husband.

Notes

1. Richard P. Wheeler, *Shakespeare's Development and the Problem Comedies*, p. 33.
2. C. L. Barber, ' "Thou that beget'st him that did thee beget": Transformation in *Pericles* and *The Winter's Tale*', 61. Wheeler, *Shakespeare's Development and the Problem Comedies*, discusses how the 'bonds of family and friendship must yield to sexual passion and the bond of marriage' (p. 48).
3. Montaigne, 'Of a Custome, and How a Received Law Should Not Easily Be Changed', *Essays*, vol. 1, ch. 22, p. 112.
4. William Gouge, 'Duties of Parents', in *Of Domesticall Duties*, p. 500 (spelling modernised).
5. John Lyly, *Mother Bombie*, in *The Complete Works* (3. 1. 20–2).
6. In *Civilization and Its Discontents*, Freud finds that 'The love that instituted the family still retains its power'. Regretting that direct sexual expression within families is taboo, he concludes that 'prohibition against incestuous object-choice' is 'perhaps the most maiming wound ever inflicted throughout the ages on the erotic life of man' (pp. 42–4). Michel Foucault, *The History of Sexuality: An Introduction*, also notes that while every society must prohibit incest in the interests of becoming a civilised culture, 'sexual-

ity', at least from the eighteenth century on, 'has its privileged point of development in the family', which makes sexuality ' "incestuous" from the start' (vol. 1, pp. 108–9). C. L. Barber, 'The Family in Shakespeare's Development: Tragedy and Sacredness', concludes that the incest taboo is 'necessarily an urgent problem in such family-centered art' as Shakespeare's (p. 191).

7. Several critics have nevertheless concluded, as does Mark Taylor in *Shakespeare's Darker Purpose: A Question of Incest*, that 'a degree of incestuous desire is nearly always present in the mixture of concern, possessiveness, and love that Shakespeare's fathers feel for their daughters' (p. 72).
8. Wheeler, *Shakespeare's Development and the Problem Comedies*, speculates that Bertram has failed to separate from his mother, and therefore Helena arouses in him 'a son's fear of female domination and of his own oedipal wishes' (p. 42).
9. Janet Adelman, *Suffocating Mothers: Fantasies of Maternal Origin in Shakespeare's Plays, Hamlet to The Tempest*, p. 94.
10. Wheeler, *Shakespeare's Development and the Problem Comedies*, p. 139.
11. Ibid. p. 204. This argument is developed in more detail in Adelman, 'Escaping the Matrix: The Construction of Masculinity in *Macbeth* and *Coriolanus*', in *Suffocating Mothers*, pp. 130–46.
12. Thomas Middleton, *The Revenger's Tragedy*, in *The Collected Works*.
13. Jane M. Ford, *Patriarchy and Incest from Shakespeare to Joyce*, p. 3. Lawrence Stone, *The Family, Sex and Marriage in England 1500–1800*, notes that although 'brother-brother ties' were 'always threatened by the gulf of primogeniture' in Shakespeare's age, 'the brother-sister relationship was often the closest in the family' (pp. 115–16).
14. The Book of Genesis provides biblical precedent for marriage between brothers and sisters; to create the human race, the offspring of Adam were compelled to procreate with one another.
15. Sophocles, *Antigone*, in *The Three Theban Plays*.
16. 'Natural law' is open to interpretation. Mostly it is defined as an instinctive withdrawal from violating family boundaries, a 'reverence' for kin that Bishop Arthur Lake (*Sermons*, 1629) considers 'ingrained by nature'; cited by Richard McCabe, *Incest, Drama and Nature's Law 1550–1700*, p. 14. But the fact that animals, living in a state of nature, do not observe this barrier – an argument used by King Arbaces in Beaumont and Fletcher's *A King and No King* (1611) to justify his desire for Penthea, who he believes is his sister – suggests that social rather than 'natural' law underlies the incest taboo.
17. John Webster, *The Duchess of Malfi*. With his dying observation that men fall by '*lust*', and '*we are cut with our own dust*', Ferdinand acknowledges that he has been destroyed by sexual desire for his own family member, the female who shares his 'dust' (5. 3. 71–3).
18. John Ford, *'Tis Pity She's a Whore*, in *John Ford: Three Plays*.
19. Coppélia Kahn, 'The Providential Tempest and the Shakespearean Family', finds Viola at first protecting herself from love outside the family by in effect 'becoming ... another Sebastian' through her disguise as the male Cesario (p. 221).
20. Daniel Wilson, 'Science, Natural Law, and Unwitting Sibling Incest in

Eighteenth-Century Literature', calls 'the intuition which could attract siblings to each other' the 'voice of blood' (255).
21. In contrast, R. E. Gajdusek, 'Death, Incest, and the Triple Bond in the Later Plays of Shakespeare', considers Posthumus to be Imogen's brother by 'breeding' if not by 'blood' (130) and therefore Imogen's 'incestuous brother' (134).
22. Marc Shell, *The End of Kinship: Measure for Measure, Incest, and the Idea of Universal Siblinghood*, p. 97.
23. McCabe, 'Law and License', in *Incest, Drama and Nature's Law 1550–1700*, reports that 'Not until 1921 was marriage with a deceased husband's brother declared valid in England' (pp. 54–5).
24. Ernest Jones, *Hamlet and Oedipus*, p. 158. Jones links what he calls the 'brother-sister complex' to the 'father-daughter complex', arguing that both ultimately derive from the mother-son relationship (the Oedipus complex).
25. In the 1968 film production of *Hamlet*, directed by Tony Richardson, Laertes (played by Michael Pennington) and Ophelia (Marianne Faithfull) behave like lovers in their first appearance on stage. Delivering his advice about Hamlet, Laertes kisses his sister lingeringly on the lips after she assures him 'Do not doubt that'. His second long kiss after Ophelia's 'Fear me not' – definitely not a fraternal kiss – is interrupted only by the entrance of Polonius. In her madness this Ophelia embraces Laertes and addresses 'Pray you love, remember' to him. In the BBC/Time Life production directed by Rodney Bennett (1980), Ophelia also shocked the spectators (on stage and off) by going up to her brother at this point and kissing him lasciviously, as if releasing repressed incestuous desire.
26. Lynda E. Boose, 'The Father's House and the Daughter in It', p. 31. Boose argues that Polonius and Laertes forfeit any 'kinship benefits' by trying to preserve Ophelia's purity instead of encouraging her to accept Hamlet (p. 31); in marrying Prince Hamlet Ophelia would obviously advance socially.
27. This is surely the meaning of 'tender' here ('make me look like a fool') and not the third meaning suggested by the Riverside edition: 'present me with a (bastard) grandchild'.
28. Ford, *Patriarchy and Incest from Shakespeare to Joyce*, pp. 15, 33.
29. Adelman, *Suffocating Mothers*, p. 17.
30. Jones, *Hamlet and Oedipus*, p. 100.
31. Several critics, adopting a psychoanalytical approach, take a different view. Avi Erlich, *Hamlet's Absent Father*, argues that Hamlet fails to resolve his Oedipus complex because he cannot find in the old king a 'powerful father' with whom he can identify (p. 28). Harold C. Goddard, *The Meaning of Shakespeare*, posits that Hamlet 'unconsciously hates' his father because he recoils from the image of a leader who, by supporting a strong military in Denmark, 'dedicated' his life 'to violence' (p. 346).
32. James R. Simmons, Jr, ' "In the Rank Sweat of an Enseamed Bed": Sexual Aberration and the Paradigmatic Screen Hamlets', notes that J. Dover Wilson, in *What Happens in Hamlet* (1935), was the first critic to call the closet scene the 'bedroom scene' (118), while John Gielgud, in his 1936 performance of Hamlet, asked for a bed to be placed on stage during the scene.

33. In the earlier stage production of the play (1937), Olivier, on Tyrone Guthrie's advice, took to heart Jones's earlier essay on 'Hamlet and Oedipus' and then adopted this interpretation in his film of *Hamlet*.
34. Courtney Lehmann and Lisa D. Starks, in 'Making Mother Matter: Repression, Revision, and the Stakes of Reading Psychoanalysis into Kenneth Branagh's *Hamlet*', fault Branagh's production for 'avoiding any representation of non-normative sexual desire, repressing the sexualized maternal body with a vengeance' (1).
35. Philip Weller, 'Freud's Footprint in *Hamlet*', 124.
36. Plutarch's *Lives of the Noble Grecians and Romans*, trans. Sir Thomas North, p. 144 (spelling modernised in all citations).
37. Ibid. p. 147.
38. Adelman, 'Escaping the Matrix: The Construction of Masculinity in *Macbeth* and *Coriolanus*', in *Suffocating Mothers*, points out that by 'failing to feed him enough' Volumnia sets up an 'equation of starvation and masculinity' that moulds her son (p. 147).
39. Stone, *The Family, Sex and Marriage in England 1500–1800*, p. 99.
40. Madelon Sprengnether, 'Annihilating Intimacy in *Coriolanus*', p. 95. Sprengnether finds that 'eroticized violence' becomes 'the mark' of Volumnia's 'relationship with her son' (p. 99).
41. Plutarch's *Lives of the Noble Grecians and Romans*, p. 147.
42. Lisa Hopkins, *The Shakespearean Marriage*, notes the 'marginalization' of the 'marriage relationship' in *Coriolanus*, attributing that to an 'Oedipal fixation which binds Coriolanus to Volumnia' (pp. 111, 113).
43. In Ralph Fiennes's film production (2011), Volumnia, played by Vanessa Redgrave, lovingly bandages her son's wounds. Her appropriation of what should be the wife's duties is underlined when Virgilia (played by Jessica Chastain) retreats into her young son's bedroom upon seeing this.
44. Grieving the loss of her son, Constance calls Arthur 'My life, my joy, my food, my all the world! / My widow-comfort, and my sorrows' cure!' (*King John*, 3. 3. 104–5).
45. Plutarch's *Lives of the Noble Grecians and Romans*, p. 183.
46. Ibid. p. 185.
47. 'Clucked' is the Riverside Shakespeare's emendation. The Folio reading is 'clocked'; Shakespeare was presumably exploiting wordplay here.
48. Rufus Putney, 'Coriolanus and his Mother', argues that Coriolanus is forced to 'choose between his death' and that of his domineering mother (381). His 'inexorable maternal superego decrees that he sacrifices himself', triumphing over his latent 'matricidal impulses' (372).
49. In Ralph Fiennes's film of *Coriolanus*, Vanessa Redgrave's Volumnia builds her case to her son quietly until she finally wins him over by shouting this final insult.
50. Ann Jenalie Cook, 'Formal Proposals, Public Contracts, and Proper Weddings', in *Making a Match: Courtship in Shakespeare and his Society*, discusses the early modern tradition of spousal contracts sealed by the joining of hands, shown in several of Shakespeare's plays (pp. 151–84).
51. Plutarch's *Lives of the Noble Grecians and Romans*, p. 186.
52. Judith Herman and Lisa Hirschman, in 'Father-Daughter Incest', comment that 'the greater degree of male supremacy in any culture, the greater

the likelihood of father-daughter incest' (741). Arpad Paunez, 'The Lear Complex in World Literature', takes for granted 'the father's libidinous attachment to his daughter' in *King Lear* (p. 52) and goes on to extend this incest-motive, 'the Lear complex', to Balzac's novel *Père Goriot* and Henry James's *Washington Square*.
53. Phyllis Chester, *Women in Madness*, p. 43.
54. Juan Luis Vives, *The Instruction of a Christian Woman*, p. 94.
55. Boose, 'The Father's House and the Daughter in It', p. 37. In 'The Father and the Bride in Shakespeare', Lynda E. Boose points out how the wedding service, in which the father must hand over his daughter to her new husband, 'not only reaffirms the taboo against incest but implicitly levels the full weight of that taboo on the relationship between father and daughter' (327).
56. Diane Elizabeth Dreher, 'Lear: A Father in Turmoil', in *Domination and Defiance: Fathers and Daughters in Shakespeare*, finds that Lear combines 'all four types of the bad father': reactionary (refusal to accept that the daughter is now an adult); mercenary (prizing a daughter as a valuable possession); jealous (unable to accept a suitor who will marry his daughter); and egocentric (identifying too much with the child) (pp. 63–4).
57. Brian Crick, 'Lear and Cordelia's Tragic Love Revisited', 70. Crick emphasises that Lear 'cannot endure the thought of Cordelia's marriage, even when he has banished her from his life' (71). He suggests, but does not state outright, that the feelings between Lear and Cordelia may have been consummated. My argument is that Cordelia is presented as being aware of her father's intense, even sexual feelings for her, but she distances herself from them while maintaining her strong love for him.
58. McCabe, *Incest, Drama and Nature's Law 1550–1700*, p. 174.
59. Coppélia Kahn, 'The Absent Mother in *King Lear*', p. 40.
60. Boose, 'The Father and the Bride in Shakespeare', 334. Jeffrey Stern, '*King Lear*: The Transference of the Kingdom', also finds that because Lear craves 'maternal care' above all else (305) he tries to 'prevent' the 'departure' of Cordelia by dividing up the kingdom (299).
61. C. Hanley, 'Lear and his Daughters', notes that to demand 'all the love of a daughter' is a 'repetition of the child's possessive, incestuous love for his mother' (216).
62. In his essay 'The Theme of the Three Caskets' (1913), Sigmund Freud associates all three daughters with aspects of the maternal: the mother, the wife, and finally Mother Earth or death, as represented by Cordelia. In effect, Freud suggests, Lear's desire for maternal 'love' turns into a death wish, for the third of the three Fates, 'the silent Goddess of death, will take him into her arms' (p. 301).
63. Adelman, 'Suffocating Mothers in *King Lear*', in *Suffocating Mothers*, p. 121.
64. Montaigne, 'Upon Some Verses of *Virgil*', in *Essays*, vol. 3, ch. 5, p. 75.
65. Maynard Mack, *King Lear in Our Time*, p. 100.
66. Stanley Cavell, 'The Avoidance of Love: A Reading of *King Lear*', in *Disowning Knowledge in Seven Plays of Shakespeare*, pp. 70–1.
67. Barber, 'The Family in Shakespeare's Development', pp. 194–5. Leslie A. Fiedler, 'The New World Savage as Stranger: or, "'Tis new to thee"', in

The Stranger in Shakespeare, describes the pattern as 'the defeat of father-daughter incest, real or threatened' by a 'wished-for' marriage to 'someone else' (p. 175).
68. Carol Thomas Neely, 'Incest and Issue in *The Winter's Tale*', in *Broken Nuptials in Shakespeare's Plays*, p. 167. Taylor, *Shakespeare's Darker Purpose*, notes that one important way of asserting 'paternal dominance' is for the father to insist on 'his own candidate' as a husband for his daughter (p. 133).
69. Marilyn L. Williamson, 'The Romances: Patriarchy, Pure and Simple', in *The Patriarchy of Shakespeare's Comedies*, p. 113.
70. Barber, ' "Thou that beget'st him that did thee beget" ', 63.
71. Robert Greene, *Pandosto: The Triumph of Time*, p. 268.
72. Boose, 'The Father's House and the Daughter in It', p. 32.
73. The anthropologist Lévi-Strauss explores how the incest taboo – the triumph of culture over nature – facilitates 'the supreme rule of the gift', the process of giving away or exchanging females in marriage to ensure exogamous unions. (See Claude Lévi-Strauss, *The Elementary Structures of Kinship*, pp. 481–2.)
74. Fiedler, 'The New World Savage as Stranger', in *The Stranger in Shakespeare*, p. 187. Fiedler points out that Prospero, alone with his nubile daughter, seems 'an ultimate travesty of the endogamous family', just as Caliban, with his threats of rape and miscegenation, furnishes 'an ultimate travesty of the exogamous family' (pp. 194–5).
75. Kahn, 'The Providential Tempest and the Shakespearean Family', p. 239.
76. Dreher, *Domination and Defiance*, using a Jungian model, finds that Shakespeare 'resolves the father's conflict' in Prospero, so that by the play's end he achieves 'spiritual renewal, individuation, and integrity' and no longer needs to exert power over his daughter (p. 14).

Works Cited

Shakespeare Editions

Auden, W. H., 'Introduction' to *The Sonnets*, ed. William Burto, The Signet Classic Shakespeare (New York: New American Library, 1964).
Blakemore Evans, G. (ed.), *The Riverside Shakespeare* (Boston and New York: Houghton Mifflin, 1997).
Booth, Stephen (ed.), *Shakespeare's Sonnets* (New Haven and London: Yale University Press, 2000).
Cohen, Walter (ed.), *The Norton Shakespeare* (New York and London: W. W. Norton, 1997).
Dolan, Frances E. (ed.), *The Taming of the Shrew: Texts and Contexts* (Boston and New York: Bedford Books of St. Martin's Press, 1996).
Gibbons, Brian (ed.), *Measure for Measure*, The New Cambridge Shakespeare (Cambridge: Cambridge University Press, 1991).
Heilman, Robert B. (ed.), *The Taming of the Shrew*, The Signet Classic Shakespeare (New York: New American Library, 1966).
Muir, Kenneth (ed.), *King Lear*, The Arden Shakespeare (London: Methuen & Co. Ltd, 1964).
Orgel, Stephen (ed.), William Shakespeare, *The Winter's Tale*, The Oxford Shakespeare (Oxford: Clarendon Press, 1996).
Wilson, John Dover (ed.), *Titus Andronicus* (Cambridge: Cambridge University Press, 1948).

Primary Sources

Aristotle: Eudemian Ethics, trans. and ed. Brad Inwood and Raphael Woolf (Cambridge: Cambridge University Press, 2013).
Augustine, Saint, *The City of God*, trans. Marcus Dods (New York: Random House, Inc., 1950).
Bacon, Francis, *New Atlantis* (London, 1627), in *Three Early Modern Utopias*, ed. Susan Bruce (New York: Oxford University Press, 1999), pp. 149–86.
Barnfield, Richard, *The Complete Poems*, ed. George Klawitter (Selingrove: Susquehanna University Press, 1990).

Bray, Gerald (ed.), *The Book of Homilies: A Critical Edition* (Cambridge: James Clarke & Co., 2015).
Bullett, Gerald (ed.), *Silver Poets of the Sixteenth Century* (London: J. M. Dent & Sons Ltd, 1966).
Burton, Robert, *The Anatomy of Melancholy*, 3 vols (1621), ed. Holbrook Jackson (London: J. M. Dent & Sons Ltd, 1932).
Castiglione, Baldassare, *The Book of the Courtier*, trans. Thomas Hoby (1561), ed. W. B. Drayton Henderson (London: J. M. Dent & Sons Ltd, 1928).
Charron, Pierre, *Of Wisdom*, trans. Sam[p]son Lennard (London, 1627).
Chaucer, Geoffrey, *Works*, ed. F. N. Robinson (London: Oxford University Press, 1957).
Dod, John, and Robert Cleaver, *A Godly Form of Household Government* (1621), in Dolan (ed.), *The Taming of the Shrew: Texts and Contexts*, pp. 204–6.
Du Bartas, Guillaume de Saluste, *The Divine Weeks and Works of Guillaume de Saluste, Sieur du Bartas*, trans. Josuah Sylvester (1605), ed. Susan Snyder (Oxford: Clarendon Press, 1979).
Elyot, Sir Thomas, *The Defence of Good Women* (London, 1545).
Ferrand, Jacques, *Erotomania*, trans. Edmund Cilmead (Oxford, 1640).
Ficino, Marsilio, *Commentary on Plato's Symposium on Love*, trans. and ed. Sears Reynolds Jayne (Dallas: Spring Publications, Inc., 1985).
——, *Marsilio Ficino's Commentary on Plato's Symposium*, trans. and intro. Sears Reynolds Jayne, *The University of Missouri Studies*, 19.1 (1944): 154–63.
Ford, John, *'Tis Pity She's a Whore*, in *John Ford: Three Plays*, ed. Keith Sturgess (Harmondsworth: Penguin Books, 1970).
Gataker, Thomas, *A Good Wife Gods Gift* (London: John Haviland, 1623).
Gouge, William, *Of Domesticall Duties* (London, 1622).
Greene, Robert, *Pandosto: The Triumph of Time* (London, 1588), reprinted in Orgel (ed.), *The Winter's Tale*, pp. 234–74.
Hall, Edward, *The Union of the Two Noble and Illustre Families of Lancaster and York* (London, 1548), excerpted in Arthur Freeman (ed.), *Henry VI Part 3*, The Signet Classic Shakespeare (New York and London: New American Library, 1968), pp. 168–87.
Hooker, Richard, *Of the Laws of Ecclesiastical Polity* (London, 1593), intro. Christopher Morris (London: J. M. Dent & Sons Ltd, 1965).
Jonson, Ben, *Timber, or Discoveries*, in C. H. Herford and P. and E. Simpson (eds), *Ben Jonson* (Oxford: Clarendon Press, 1947), vol. 8, pp. 561–649.
Keats, John, *Letters*, selected by Frederick Page (London: Oxford University Press, 1965).
La Primaudaye, Pierre de, *The French Academie*, trans. T. B[owes] (London, 1586; New York: Verlag, 1972).
Lyly, John, *Endimion*, in *The Minor Elizabethan Drama (II): Pre-Shakespearean Comedies* (London: J. M. Dent & Sons Ltd, 1930).
——, *Mother Bombie*, in *The Complete Works of John Lyly*, ed. R. W. Bond (Oxford: Clarendon Press, 1902), vol. 3.
Marlowe, Christopher, *The Complete Plays*, ed. J. B. Steane (Harmondsworth: Penguin Books, 1962).

Marston, John, *The Poems of John Marston*, ed. Arnold Davenport (Liverpool: Liverpool University Press, 1961).

Middleton, Thomas, *The Revenger's Tragedy*, ed. Macdonald P. Jackson, in Gary Taylor and John Lavagnino (eds), *Thomas Middleton: The Collected Works* (Oxford: Clarendon Press, 2007).

Montaigne, Michel Eyquem de, *Essays*, trans. John Florio (1603), intro. L. C. Harmer (London: J. M. Dent & Sons Ltd, 1965).

Nashe, Thomas, *Christs Teares over Jerusalem* (London, 1593; Menston: Scholar Press, 1970).

——, *The Unfortunate Traveller* (1594), in George Saintsbury (intro.), *Shorter Novels: Elizabethan* (London: J. M. Dent & Sons Ltd, 1929).

Niccholes, Alexander, *A Discourse, of Marriage and Wiving* (London, 1615).

Pico della Mirandola, Giovanni, 'Oration on the Dignity of Man', trans. Elizabeth Livermore Forbes, in Ernst Cassirer, Paul Oskar Kristeller and John Herman Randall, Jr (eds), *The Renaissance Philosophy of Man* (Chicago: University of Chicago Press, 1967), pp. 225–43.

Plutarch, *Lives of the Noble Grecians and Romans*, trans. Sir Thomas North (London, 1579; New York: AMS Press, 1967).

——, *Moralia*, trans. Philemon Holland as *The Philosophie* (London, 1603).

Puttenham, George, *The Arte of English Poesie* (London, 1589).

Rainolds, John, *Th'Overthrow of Stage-Playes* (Middleburgh, 1599).

Rich[e], Barnabe, *The Excellencie of Good Women* (London, 1613).

——, *His Farewell to Military Profession* (1581), ed. Donald Beecher (Ottawa: Dovehouse Editions Inc., 1992).

Sidney, Sir Philip, *The Countess of Pembroke's Arcadia*, ed. Maurice Evans (New York: Penguin Books, 1977).

——, *The Defence of Poesy* (1595), in Robert Kimborough (ed.), *Sir Philip Sidney: Selected Prose and Poetry* (Wisconsin: University of Wisconsin Press, 1983).

Snawsell, Robert, *A Looking Glass for Married Folks*, in Dolan (ed.), *The Taming of the Shrew: Texts and Contexts*, pp. 187–93.

Sophocles, *The Three Theban Plays*, ed. Robert Fagles (New York: Viking Penguin Inc., 1984).

Stubbes, Philip, *The Anatomie of Abuses* (1583), ed. F. J. Furnivall (London: New Shakespeare Society, 1877–9).

Tilney, Edmund, *The Flower of Friendship* (1571), in Valerie Wayne (ed.), *The Flower of Friendship: A Renaissance Dialogue Contesting Marriage* (Ithaca and London: Cornell University Press, 1992).

Tuberville, George, *Tragical Tales* (London, 1587).

Vives, Juan Luis, *The Instruction of a Christian Woman* (1523), trans. Richard Hyrde (London, c. 1529), ed. Virginia Walcot Beauchamp, Elizabeth H. Hageman and Margaret Mikesell (Urbana and Chicago: University of Illinois Press, 2002).

Webster, John, *The Duchess of Malfi*, ed. John Russell Brown, The Revels Plays (London: Methuen & Co. Ltd, 1964).

Wright, Thomas, *The Passions of the Mind in General* (London, 1601), ed. William Webster Newbold (New York and London: Garland Publishing, 1986).

Wyatt, Thomas (Sir), *Collected Poems*, ed. Kenneth Muir (London: Routledge & Kegan Paul, 1963).

Secondary Sources

Adamson, Jane, *Othello as Tragedy: Some Problems of Judgment and Feeling* (Cambridge: Cambridge University Press, 1985).
Adelman, Janet, 'Male Bonding in Shakespeare's Comedies', in Peter Erickson and Coppelia Kahn (eds), *Shakespeare's 'Rough Magic': Renaissance Essays in Honor of C. L. Barber* (Newark: University of Delaware Press, 1985), pp. 73–103.
——, *Suffocating Mothers: Fantasies of Maternal Origin in Shakespeare's Plays, Hamlet to The Tempest* (New York and London: Routledge, 1992).
Akrigg, G. P. V. (ed.), *Letters of King James VI and I* (Berkeley: University of California Press, 1984).
Alexander, Catherine M. S., and Stanley Wells (eds), *Shakespeare and Sexuality* (Cambridge: Cambridge University Press, 2001).
Asp, Carolyn, '*Love's Labour's Lost*: Language and the Deferral of Desire', *Literature and Psychology*, 35.3 (1989): 1–21.
Baker, Aryn, 'War and Rape', *Time*, 18 April 2016, pp. 36–41.
Bakhtin, M., *Rabelais and His World*, trans. Helene Iswolsky (Cambridge, MA: MIT Press, 1968).
Baldini, Donatella, 'The Play of the Courtier: Correspondence between Castiglione's *Il libro del Cortegiano* and Shakespeare's *Love's Labour's Lost*', *Quaderni d'italianistica*, 18.1 (Primavera 1997): 6–22.
Barber, C. L., 'The Family in Shakespeare's Development: Tragedy and Sacredness', in Schwartz and Kahn (eds), *Representing Shakespeare: New Psychoanalytic Essays*, pp. 188–202.
——, *Shakespeare's Festive Comedy* (Princeton: Princeton University Press, 1959).
——, ' "Thou that beget'st him that did thee beget": Transformation in *Pericles* and *The Winter's Tale*', *Shakespeare Survey*, 22 (1969): 59–67.
—— and Richard P. Wheeler, *The Whole Journey: Shakespeare's Power of Development* (Berkeley: University of California Press, 1986).
Bean, John C., 'Comic Structure and the Humanizing of Kate in *The Taming of the Shrew*', in Lenz, Greene and Neely (eds), *The Woman's Part: Feminist Criticism of Shakespeare*, pp. 65–78.
Belsey, Catherine, 'Desire's Excess and the English Renaissance Theatre: *Edward II*, *Troilus and Cressida*, *Othello*', in Zimmerman (ed.), *Erotic Politics*, pp. 84–102.
——, 'Disrupting Sexual Difference', in John Drakakis (ed.), *Alternative Shakespeares* (London and New York: Methuen, 1985), pp. 166–90.
——, 'Love as Trompe-l'oeil: Taxonomies of Desire in *Venus and Adonis*', *Shakespeare Quarterly*, 46.3 (1995): 257–76.
——, 'Love in Venice', in Alexander and Wells (eds), *Shakespeare and Sexuality*, pp. 72–91.
——, *Shakespeare and the Loss of Eden* (Basingstoke and London: Macmillan, 1999).

Berggren, Paula S., 'The Woman's Part: Female Sexuality as Power in Shakespeare's Plays', in Lenz, Greene and Neely (eds), *The Woman's Part: Feminist Criticism of Shakespeare*, pp. 17–34.
Berry, Philippa, *Of Chastity and Power: Elizabethan Literature and the Unmarried Queen* (New York and London: Routledge, 1989).
Bloom, Allan, *Shakespeare on Love and Friendship* (Chicago and London: University of Chicago Press, 2000).
Bly, Mary, 'The Legacy of Juliet's Desire in Comedies of the Early 1600s', in Alexander and Wells (eds), *Shakespeare and Sexuality*, pp. 52–71.
Boose, Lynda E., 'The Father and the Bride in Shakespeare', *PMLA*, 97 (May 1982): 325–47.
——, 'The Father's House and the Daughter in It', in Lynda E. Boose and Betty S. Flowers (eds), *Daughters and Fathers* (Baltimore and London: Johns Hopkins University Press, 1989), pp. 19–74.
——, 'Scolding Brides and Bridling Scolds: Taming the Woman's Unruly Member', *Shakespeare Quarterly*, 42.2 (Summer 1991): 179–213.
Bradbrook, M. C., 'Courtier and Courtesy: Castiglione, Lyly and Shakespeare's *Two Gentlemen of Verona*', in J. R. Mulryne and Margaret Shewring (eds), *Theatre of the English and Italian Renaissance* (New York: St. Martin's Press, 1991), pp. 161–78.
Bray, Alan, *Homosexuality in Renaissance England* (New York: Columbia University Press, 1995).
Breitenberg, Mark, *Anxious Masculinity in Early Modern England* (Cambridge: Cambridge University Press, 1996).
Bromley, James M., *Intimacy and Sexuality in the Age of Shakespeare* (Cambridge: Cambridge University Press, 2012).
Bromley, Laura G., 'Lucrece's Re-Creation', *Shakespeare Quarterly*, 34.2 (1983): 200–11.
Brown, John Russell, 'Representing Sexuality in Shakespeare's Plays', in Alexander and Wells (eds), *Shakespeare and Sexuality*, pp. 168–82.
Brownmiller, Susan, *Against Our Will: Men, Women and Rape* (New York: Simon & Schuster, 1975).
Burt, Richard A., 'Charisma, Coercion and Comic Form in *The Taming of the Shrew*', *Criticism*, 26.4 (1984): 295–311.
Calderwood, James L., *If It Were Done: Macbeth and Tragic Action* (Amherst: University of Massachusetts Press, 1980).
Carroll, William C., *The Great Feast of Language in Love's Labour's Lost* (Princeton: Princeton University Press, 1976).
——, 'Language and Sexuality in Shakespeare', in Alexander and Wells (eds), *Shakespeare and Sexuality*, pp. 14–34.
Cavell, Stanley, *Disowning Knowledge in Seven Plays of Shakespeare* (Cambridge: Cambridge University Press, 2003).
Charlton, H. B., *The Dark Comedies* (Manchester: Manchester University Press, 1937).
Charnes, Linda, 'Uncivil Unions', in Gajowski (ed.), *Presentism, Gender, and Sexuality in Shakespeare*, pp. 195–206.
Charney, Maurice, *Shakespeare on Love and Lust* (New York: Columbia University Press, 2000).
Chester, Phyllis, *Women in Madness* (New York: Avon, 1973).

Clark, Anna, *Women's Silence, Men's Violence* (London: Pandora Press, 1987).
Colie, Rosalie, *Shakespeare's 'Living Art'* (Princeton: Princeton University Press, 1974).
Colman, E. A. M., *The Dramatic Use of Bawdy in Shakespeare* (London: Longman, 1974).
Cook, Ann Jenalie, *Making a Match: Courtship in Shakespeare and his Society* (Princeton: Princeton University Press, 1991).
Cook, Carol, '"The Sign and Semblance of Her Honor": Reading Gender Difference in *Much Ado about Nothing*', PMLA, 101.2 (March 1986): 186–202.
——, 'Unbodied Figures of Desire', *Theatre Journal*, 38 (March 1986): 34–52.
Cox, John D., ' "The Error of our Eye" in *Troilus and Cressida*', *Comparative Drama*, 10.2 (Summer 1976): 147–71.
——, 'Shakespeare and the Ethics of Friendship', *Religion and Literature*, 40.3 (2000): 1–29.
Crick, Brian, 'Lear and Cordelia's Tragic Love Revisited', *Critical Review*, 37.1 (1997): 61–80.
Daileader, Celia R., *Eroticism on the Renaissance Stage* (Cambridge: Cambridge University Press, 1998).
Davis, Natalie, 'Sexual Inversion and Political Disorder in Early Modern Europe', in Barbara A. Babcock (ed.), *The Reversible World* (Ithaca and London: Cornell University Press, 1978), pp. 147–89.
Desens, Marliss C., *The Bed-Trick in English Renaissance Drama* (London and Toronto: Associated University Presses, 1994).
DiGangi, Mario, *The Homoerotics of Early Modern Drama* (Cambridge: Cambridge University Press, 1997).
Dollimore, Jonathan, *Death, Desire and Loss in Western Culture* (Routledge: New York, 1998).
——, *Sexual Dissidence* (Oxford: Clarendon Press, 1991).
——, 'Transgression and Surveillance in *Measure for Measure*', in Dollimore and Sinfield (eds), *Political Shakespeare: New Essays in Cultural Materialism*, pp. 72–87.
—— and Alan Sinfield (eds), *Political Shakespeare: New Essays in Cultural Materialism* (Ithaca and London: Cornell University Press, 1985).
Dreher, Diane Elizabeth, *Domination and Defiance: Fathers and Daughters in Shakespeare* (Lexington: University Press of Kentucky, 1986).
Dubrow, Heather, *Echoes of Desire: English Petrarchism and its Counterdiscourses* (Ithaca: Cornell University Press, 1995).
Dundas, Judith, ' "To See Feelingly": The Language of the Senses and the Language of the Heart', *Comparative Drama*, 19.1 (Spring 1985): 49–57.
Dusinberre, Juliet, *Shakespeare and the Nature of Women* (New York: St. Martin's Press, 1996).
Elliott, Anthony, *Psychoanalytic Theory: An Introduction* (Durham, NC: Duke University Press, 2002).
Empson, William, *Some Versions of Pastoral* (Harmondsworth: Penguin Books, 1966).
Enterline, Lynn, *The Rhetoric of the Body from Ovid to Shakespeare* (Cambridge: Cambridge University Press, 2001).

Erickson, Amy Louise, *Women and Property in Early Modern England* (London and New York: Routledge, 1993).

Erickson, Peter, *Patriarchal Structures in Shakespeare's Drama* (Berkeley: University of California Press, 1985).

Erlich, Avi, *Hamlet's Absent Father* (Princeton: Princeton University Press, 1977).

Ferguson, Margaret W., Maureen Quilligan and Nancy J. Vickers (eds), *Rewriting the Renaissance: The Discourses of Difference in Early Modern Europe* (Chicago and London: University of Chicago Press, 1986).

Fernie, Ewan, *Shame in Shakespeare* (London and New York: Routledge, 2002).

Fiedler, Leslie A., *The Stranger in Shakespeare* (St Albans: Paladin, 1974).

Fineman, Joel, *Shakespeare's Perjured Eye: The Invention of Poetic Subjectivity in the Sonnets* (Berkeley: University of California Press, 1986).

Ford, Jane M., *Patriarchy and Incest from Shakespeare to Joyce* (Gainesville: University of Florida Press, 1998).

Foucault, Michel, *The History of Sexuality: An Introduction*, trans. Robert Hurley, vol. 1 (New York: Vintage Books, Random House, 1990).

Freud, Sigmund, *Civilization and Its Discontents* (Rough Draft Printing, 2013).

——, 'Group Psychology and the Analysis of the Ego' (1921), in James Strachey (trans. and ed.), *The Standard Edition of the Complete Psychological Works of Sigmund Freud*, vol. 18 (London: Hogarth Press, 1955), pp. 69–143.

——, 'The Most Prevalent Form of Degradation in Erotic Life' (1912), in Philip Rieff (ed.), *Sexuality and the Psychology of Love* (New York: Macmillan, 1963), pp. 58–70.

——, 'The Theme of the Three Caskets' (1913), in James Strachey (trans. and ed.), *The Standard Edition of the Complete Psychological Works of Sigmund Freud*, vol. 12 (London: Hogarth Press, 1974), pp. 289–302.

Froide, Amy M., *Never Married: Single Women in Early Modern England* (Oxford: Oxford University Press, 2005).

Gajdusek, R. E., 'Death, Incest, and the Triple Bond in the Later Plays of Shakespeare', *American Imago*, 31.2 (1974): 109–58.

Gajowski, Evelyn, *The Art of Loving: Female Subjectivity and Male Discursive Traditions in Shakespeare's Tragedies* (Newark: University of Delaware Press, 1992).

——, 'The Presence of the Past', in Gajowski (ed.), *Presentism, Gender, and Sexuality in Shakespeare*, pp. 1–22.

—— (ed.), *Presentism, Gender, and Sexuality in Shakespeare* (New York: Palgrave Macmillan, 2009).

Garber, Marjorie, *Coming of Age in Shakespeare* (London and New York: Methuen, 1981).

Garner, Shirley Nelson, '*A Midsummer Night's Dream*: "Jack shall have Jill; / Nought shall go ill"', *Women's Studies* 9 (1981): 47–63.

Garrison, John S., *Friendship and Queer Theory in the Renaissance* (Cambridge: Cambridge University Press, 2001).

Gay, Penny, *As She Likes It: Shakespeare's Unruly Women* (London and New York: Routledge, 1994).

Giddens, Anthony, *The Transformation of Intimacy: Sexuality, Love and Eroticism in Modern Societies* (Stanford: Stanford University Press, 1992).

Gillis, John R., *For Better, for Worse: British Marriages, 1600 to the Present* (Oxford: Oxford University Press, 1985).
Girard, René, 'The Politics of Desire in *Troilus and Cressida*', in Parker and Hartman (eds), *Shakespeare and the Question of Theory*, pp. 188–209.
Goddard, Harold C., *The Meaning of Shakespeare* (Chicago and London: University of Chicago Press, 1951).
Gohlke, Madelon (Sprengnether), ' "I wooed thee with my sword": Shakespeare's Tragic Paradigms', in Lenz, Greene and Neely (eds), *The Woman's Part: Feminist Criticism of Shakespeare*, pp. 150–70.
Goldberg, Jonathan, '*Romeo and Juliet*'s Open Rs', in Porter (ed.), *Critical Essays on Shakespeare's Romeo and Juliet*, pp. 82–96.
——, *Sodomotries: Renaissance Texts, Modern Sexualities* (Stanford: Stanford University Press, 1992).
Gowing, Laura, *Common Bodies: Women, Touch and Power in Seventeenth-Century England* (New Haven: Yale University Press, 2003).
Greenblatt, Stephen, *Renaissance Self-Fashioning: From More to Shakespeare* (Chicago and London: University of Chicago Press, 1980).
——, *Shakespearean Negotiations* (Berkeley: University of California Press, 1988).
Greene, Gayle, 'Shakespeare's Cressida: "A Kind of Self" ', in Lenz, Greene and Neely (eds), *The Woman's Part: Feminist Criticism of Shakespeare*, pp. 133–49.
Greer, Germaine, *The Female Eunuch* (New York: McGraw-Hill, 1971).
Guy-Bray, Stephen, 'Shakespeare and the Invention of the Heterosexual', *Early Modern Literary Studies*, Special Issue 16 (October 2007): 1–28.
Hagstrum, Jean H., *Esteem Enlivened by Desire: The Couple from Homer to Shakespeare* (Chicago: University of Chicago Press, 1992).
Hammond, Paul, *Figuring Sex between Men from Shakespeare to Rochester* (Oxford: Clarendon Press, 2002).
Hanley, C., 'Lear and his Daughters', *International Review of Psycho-Analysis*, 3.2 (1986): 211–20.
Hattaway, Michael, 'Male Sexuality and Misogyny', in Alexander and Wells (eds), *Shakespeare and Sexuality*, pp. 92–115.
Herman, Judith, and Lisa Hirschman, 'Father-Daughter Incest', *Signs*, 2 (1977): 735–56.
Higgins, Lynn A., and Brenda R. Silver (eds), *Rape and Representation* (New York: Columbia University Press, 1991).
Hodgson, Barbara, *The End Crowns All: Closure and Contradiction in Shakespeare's History* (Princeton: Princeton University Press, 1991).
——, 'Katherina Bound: Or, Play(K)ating the Strictures of Everyday Life', *PMLA*, 107.3 (May 1992): 538–53.
——, '*William Shakespeare's Romeo + Juliet*: Everything's Nice in America?', *Shakespeare Survey*, 52 (1999): 88–98.
Hopkins, Lisa, *The Shakespearean Marriage* (New York: St. Martin's Press, 1998).
Howard, Jean E., 'The Early Modern and the Homoerotic Turn in Political Criticism', *Shakespeare Studies*, 26 (1998): 105–20.
——, 'Sex and Social Conflict: The Erotics of *The Roaring Girl*', in Zimmerman (ed.), *Erotic Politics: Desire on the Renaissance Stage*, pp. 170–90.

———, *The Stage and Social Struggle in Early Modern England* (London and New York: Routledge, 1994).

——— and Phyllis Rackin, *Engendering a Nation: A Feminist Account of Shakespeare's English Histories* (London and New York: Routledge, 1997).

Hull, Suzanne W., *Chaste, Silent and Obedient: English Books for Women, 1475–1640* (San Marino: Huntington Library, 1982).

Hunter, G. K., *English Drama 1586–1642: The Age of Shakespeare* (Oxford: Clarendon Press, 1997).

Hyman, Stanley Edgar, *Iago: Some Approaches to the Illusion of his Motivation* (New York: Atheneum, 1970).

Jaeger, C. Stephen, *Ennobling Love* (Philadelphia: University of Pennsylvania Press, 1999).

Jardine, Lisa, *Still Harping on Daughters: Women and Drama in the Age of Shakespeare* (Brighton: Harvester, 1983).

———, 'Twins and Travesties: Gender, Dependency and Sexual Availability in *Twelfth Night*', in Zimmerman (ed.), *Erotic Politics: Desire on the Renaissance Stage*, pp. 27–38.

Jones, Ann Rosalind, 'Writing the Body: Toward an Understanding of *l'Écriture Féminine*', in Elaine Showalter (ed.), *The New Feminist Criticism: Essays on Women, Literature, and Theory* (New York: Pantheon, 1985), pp. 361–77.

Jones, Ernest, *Hamlet and Oedipus* (New York: Doubleday & Company, 1954).

Kahn, Coppélia, 'The Absent Mother in *King Lear*', in Ferguson, Quilligan and Vickers (eds), *Rewriting the Renaissance*, pp. 33–59.

———, '*Lucrece*: The Sexual Politics of Subjectivity', in Higgins and Silver (eds), *Rape and Representation*, pp. 141–59.

———, *Man's Estate: Masculine Identity in Shakespeare* (Berkeley: University of California Press, 1981).

———, 'The Providential Tempest and the Shakespearean Family', in Schwartz and Kahn (eds), *Representing Shakespeare: New Psychoanalytic Essays*, pp. 217–43.

———, 'The Rape in Shakespeare's *Lucrece*', *Shakespeare Studies*, 9 (1976): 45–72.

Kahn, Paul, *Law and Love: The Trials of King Lear* (New Haven and London: Yale University Press, 2000).

Keenan, Jillian, *Sex with Shakespeare* (New York: HarperCollins Publishers, 2016).

Keevak, Michael, *Sexual Shakespeare* (Detroit: Wayne State University Press, 2001).

Kiernan, Pauline, *Filthy Shakespeare* (New York: Gotham Books, 2006).

Kimbrough, Robert, *Shakespeare and the Art of Humankindness: The Essay toward Androgyny* (Atlantic Highlands and London: Humanities Press International, 1990).

Kirsch, Arthur, *Shakespeare and the Experience of Love* (Cambridge: Cambridge University Press, 1981).

Knoppers, Laura Lunger, '(En)gendering Shame: *Measure for Measure* and the Spectacles of Power', *English Literary Renaissance*, 23 (1993): 450–71.

Korda, Natasha, *Shakespeare's Domestic Economies: Gender and Property in Early Modern England* (Philadelphia: University of Pennsylvania Press, 2002).

Kott, Jan, *Shakespeare Our Contemporary* (London: Methuen & Co. Ltd, 1964).
Lacan, Jacques, *Desire and its Interpretation*, ed. Jacques-Alain Miller (Cambridge: Polity Press, 2019).
Laqueur, Thomas, *Making Sex: Body and Gender from the Greeks to Freud* (Cambridge, MA: Harvard University Press, 1990).
Leggatt, Alexander, *Shakespeare's Comedy of Love* (London: Methuen, 1973).
Lehmann, Courtney, and Lisa D. Starks, 'Making Mother Matter: Repression, Revision, and the Stakes of Reading Psychoanalysis into Kenneth Branagh's *Hamlet*', *Early Modern Literary Studies*, 6.2 (May 2000): 1–24.
Lenz, Carolyn Ruth Swift, Gayle Greene and Carol Thomas Neely (eds), *The Woman's Part: Feminist Criticism of Shakespeare* (Urbana: University of Illinois Press, 1980).
Lévi-Strauss, Claude, *The Elementary Structures of Kinship*, trans. James Harle Bell, John Richard von Sturmer and Rodney Needham (Boston: Beacon Press, 1969).
Levine, Laura, 'Rape, Repetition, and the Politics of Closure in *A Midsummer Night's Dream*', in Traub, Kaplan and Callaghan (eds), *Feminist Readings of Early Modern Culture*, pp. 210–28.
Lewis, C. S., *The Allegory of Love* (1936; New York: Oxford University Press, 1958).
Little, Jr, Arthur L., ' "A Local Habitation and a Name": Presence, Witnessing, and Queer Marriage in Shakespeare's Romantic Comedies', in Gajowski (ed.), *Presentism, Gender, and Sexuality in Shakespeare*, pp. 207–36.
Loughlin, Marie H. (ed.), *Same-Sex Desire in Early Modern England, 1550–1735* (Manchester and New York: Manchester University Press, 2014).
McCabe, Richard, *Incest, Drama and Nature's Law 1550–1700* (Cambridge: Cambridge University Press, 1993).
MacCary, W. Thomas, *Friends and Lovers: The Phenomenology of Desire in Shakespearean Comedy* (New York: Columbia University Press, 1985).
Mack, Maynard, *King Lear in Our Time* (Berkeley: University of California Press, 1965).
Maclean, Ian, *The Renaissance Notion of Woman* (Cambridge: Cambridge University Press, 1980).
McLuskie, Kathleen, ' "Lawless desires well tempered" ', in Zimmerman (ed.), *Erotic Politics: Desire on the Renaissance Stage*, pp. 103–26.
——, 'The Patriarchal Bard: Feminist Criticism and Shakespeare: *King Lear* and *Measure for Measure*', in Dollimore and Sinfield (eds), *Political Shakespeare: New Essays in Cultural Materialism*, pp. 88–128.
Mallette, Richard, 'Same-Sex Erotic Friendship in *The Two Noble Kinsmen*', *Renaissance Drama*, 26 (1995): 29–52.
Mangan, Michael, ' "My hand is ready, may it do him ease": Shakespeare and the Theatre of Display', in Gajowski (ed.), *Presentism, Gender, and Sexuality in Shakespeare*, pp. 143–56.
Masten, Jeffrey, *Queer Philologies: Sex, Language, and Affect in Shakespeare's Time* (Philadelphia: University of Pennsylvania Press, 2006).
Maus, Katharine Eisaman, 'Taking Tropes Seriously: Language and Violence in Shakespeare's *Rape of Lucrece*', *Shakespeare Quarterly*, 37.1 (1986): 66–82.

——, 'Transfer of Title in *Love's Labor's Lost*', in Ivo Kamps (ed.), *Shakespeare Left and Right* (New York and London: Routledge, 1991), pp. 205–23.

Meek, Richard, *Narrating the Visual in Shakespeare* (Farnham and Burlington: Ashgate Publishing, 2009).

Memmo, Jr, Paul E., 'The Poetry of the *Stilnovisti* and *Love's Labour's Lost*', *Comparative Literature*, 18.1 (Winter 1966): 1–14.

Mendelson, Sarah, and Patricia Crawford, *Women in Early Modern England, 1550–1720* (Oxford: Clarendon Press, 1998).

Menon, Madhavi, *Wanton Words: Rhetoric and Sexuality in English Renaissance Drama* (Toronto: University of Toronto Press, 2004).

Mikesell, Margaret Lael, ' "Love Wrought these Miracles": Marriage and Genre in *The Taming of the Shrew*', *Renaissance Drama*, N.S. 20 (January 1989): 141–67.

Minta, Stephen, *Petrarch and Petrarchism: The English and French Traditions* (Totowa, NJ: Barnes & Noble, 1980).

Moglen, Helene, 'Disguise and Development: The Self and Society in *Twelfth Night*', *Literature and Psychology*, 23 (1973): 13–20.

Mukherji, Subha, 'Consummation, Custom and Law in *All's Well that Ends Well*', in Alexander and Wells (eds), *Shakespeare and Sexuality*, pp. 116–45.

Nagel, Joane, *Race, Ethnicity, and Sexuality: Intimate Intersections, Forbidden Frontiers* (New York: Oxford University Press, 2003).

Neely, Carol Thomas, *Broken Nuptials in Shakespeare's Plays* (Urbana and Chicago: University of Illinois Press, 1985).

Newman, Karen, *Fashioning Femininity and English Renaissance Drama* (Chicago and London: University of Chicago Press, 1991).

Nordlund, Marcus, *Shakespeare and the Nature of Love* (Evanston: Northwestern University Press, 2007).

Novy, Marianne, *Love's Argument: Gender Relations in Shakespeare* (Chapel Hill: University of North Carolina Press, 1984).

——, *Shakespeare and Outsiders* (Oxford: Oxford University Press, 2013).

Orgel, Stephen, *Impersonations: The Performance of Gender in Shakespeare's England* (Cambridge: Cambridge University Press, 1996).

——, 'Nobody's Perfect: or Why Did the English Stage Take Boys for Women?', *South Atlantic Quarterly*, 88 (1989): 7–29.

Parker, Patricia, and Geoffrey Hartman (eds), *Shakespeare and the Question of Theory* (New York and London: Methuen, 1985).

Partridge, Eric, *Shakespeare's Bawdy* (New York: E. P. Dutton & Co., 1960).

Paster, Gail Kern, *The Body Embarrassed: Drama and the Disciplines of Shame in Early Modern England* (Ithaca: Cornell University Press, 1993).

Patricia, Anthony Guy, ' "Through the Eye of the Present": Screening the Male Homoerotics of Shakespearean Drama', in Gajowski (ed.), *Presentism, Gender, and Sexuality in Shakespeare*, pp. 157–78.

Paunez, Arpad, 'The Lear Complex in World Literature', *American Imago*, 11.1 (1954): 51–83.

Pequigney, Joseph, *Such Is My Love: A Study of Shakespeare Sonnets* (Chicago and London: University of Chicago Press, 1985).

——, 'The Two Antonios and Same-Sex Love in *Twelfth Night* and *The Merchant of Venice*', *English Literary History*, 22.2 (1992): 201–21.

Porter, Joseph A. (ed.), *Critical Essays on Shakespeare's Romeo and Juliet* (New York: G. K. Hall & Co., 1997).
Putney, Rufus, 'Coriolanus and his Mother', *Psychoanalytic Quarterly*, 31 (1962): 364–81.
Rackin, Phyllis, 'Dated and Outdated: The Present Tense of Feminist Criticism', in Gajowski (ed.), *Presentism, Gender, and Sexuality in Shakespeare*, pp. 49–60.
——, *Shakespeare and Women* (Oxford: Oxford University Press, 2005).
Ranald, Margaret Loftus, *Shakespeare and his Social Context* (New York: AMS Press, 1987).
Rose, Mary Beth, *The Expense of Spirit: Love and Sexuality in English Renaissance Drama* (Ithaca: Cornell University Press, 1988).
Rossiter, A. P., *Angel with Horns* (London: Longman Group Ltd, 1961).
Rougement, Denis de, *Love in the Western World* (Princeton: Princeton University Press, 1982).
Rutter, Carol, *Clamorous Voices: Shakespeare's Women Today* (New York: Routledge, 1985).
Sawday, Jonathan, *The Body Emblazoned: Dissection and the Human Body in Renaissance Culture* (London and New York: Routledge, 1995).
Schalkwyk, David, *Shakespeare: Love and Language* (Cambridge: Cambridge University Press, 2018).
Schmidt, Alexander, *Shakespeare Lexicon and Quotation Dictionary*, 2 vols (New York: Dover Publications, 1971).
Schwartz, Murray M., 'Leontes' Jealousy in *The Winter's Tale*', *American Imago*, 30.3 (1980): 250–73.
—— and Coppélia Kahn (eds), *Representing Shakespeare: New Psychoanalytic Essays* (Baltimore and London: Johns Hopkins University Press, 1980).
Scruton, Roger, *Sexual Desire: A Moral Philosophy of the Erotic* (New York: Free Press, 1986).
Sedgwick, Eve Kosofsky, *Between Men: English Literature and Male Homosocial Desire* (New York: Columbia University Press, 1985).
Shannon, Laurie, *Sovereign Amity: Figures of Friendship in Shakespearean Contexts* (Chicago: University of Chicago Press, 2002).
Shapiro, James, *Shakespeare in a Divided America* (New York: Penguin Press, 2020).
Shell, Marc, *The End of Kinship: Measure for Measure, Incest, and the Idea of Universal Siblinghood* (Stanford: Stanford University Press, 1988).
Shepherd, Simon, *Amazons and Warrior Women: Varieties of Feminism in Seventeenth-Century Drama* (Brighton: Harvester Press, 1981).
Shumway, David R., *Modern Love: Romance, Intimacy, and the Marriage Crisis* (New York and London: New York University Press, 2003).
Simmons, Jr, James R., ' "In the Rank Sweat of an Enseamed Bed": Sexual Aberration and the Paradigmatic Screen Hamlets', *Literature/Film Quarterly*, 25.2 (January 1997): 111–18.
Sinfield, Alan, 'How to Read *The Merchant of Venice* without Being Heterosexist', in Terence Hawkes (ed.), *Alternative Shakespeares*, vol. 2 (London and New York: Routledge, 1996), pp. 122–39.
——, 'Intertextuality and the Limits of Queer Reading in *A Midsummer Night's*

Dream and *The Two Noble Kinsmen*', in *Shakespeare, Authority, Sexuality*, pp. 68–85.

——, 'Near Misses: Ganymedes and Page Boys', in *Shakespeare, Authority, Sexuality*, pp. 112–33.

——, 'Rape and Rights: *Measure for Measure* and the Limits of Cultural Imperialism', in *Shakespeare, Authority, Sexuality*, pp. 181–96.

——, *Shakespeare, Authority, Sexuality: Unfinished Business in Cultural Materialism* (London and New York: Routledge, 2006).

Singer, Irving, *The Nature of Love, Vol. 2: Courtly and Romantic* (Cambridge, MA: MIT Press, 2009).

Slights, William, 'Bodies of Texts and Textualized Bodies in *Sejanus* and *Coriolanus*', *Medieval and Renaissance Drama in England*, 5 (1991): 181–93.

Smith, Bruce R., *Homosexual Desire in Shakespeare's England* (Chicago and London: University of Chicago Press, 1991).

Smith, Hilda L., *Reason's Disciples* (Urbana: University of Illinois Press, 1982).

Sokol, B. J., and Mary Sokol, *Shakespeare, Law, and Marriage* (Cambridge: Cambridge University Press, 2013).

Sprengnether, Madelon (Gohlke), 'Annihilating Intimacy in *Coriolanus*', in Mary Beth Rose (ed.), *Women in the Middle Ages and in the Renaissance* (Syracuse: Syracuse University Press, 1986), pp. 89–111.

Stallybrass, Peter, 'Patriarchal Territories: The Body Enclosed', in Ferguson, Quilligan and Vickers (eds), *Rewriting the Renaissance*, pp. 123–42.

Stanivukovic, Goran (ed.), *Queer Shakespeare: Desire and Sexuality* (London and New York: Bloomsbury Publishing, 2017).

Stern, Jeffrey, '*King Lear*: The Transference of the Kingdom', *Shakespeare Quarterly*, 41.3 (1990): 299–308.

Sternberg, Robert J., *Cupid's Arrow: The Course of Love through Time* (Cambridge: Cambridge University Press, 1998).

Stilling, Roger, *Love and Death in Renaissance Tragedy* (Baton Rouge: Louisiana State University Press, 1976).

Stimpson, Catherine R., 'Shakespeare and the Soil of Rape', in Lenz, Greene and Neely (eds), *The Woman's Part: Feminist Criticism of Shakespeare*, pp. 56–64.

Stone, Lawrence, *The Family, Sex and Marriage in England 1500–1800* (New York: Harper & Row, 1979).

Targoff, Ramie, *Posthumous Love: Eros and the Afterlife in Renaissance England* (Chicago: University of Chicago Press, 2014).

Taylor, Gary, 'Marlowe finally credited among cast of Bard's co-writers', *The Guardian*, 24 October 2016, p. 9.

Taylor, Mark, *Shakespeare's Darker Purpose: A Question of Incest* (New York: AMS Press, 1982).

Thomas, Keith, 'The Double Standard', *Journal of the History of Ideas*, 20 (1959): 195–216.

——, *Religion and the Decline of Magic* (London: Weidenfeld & Nicolson, 1971).

Thorne, Alison, *Vision and Rhetoric in Shakespeare: Looking through Language* (Basingstoke and London: Macmillan, 2000).

Todd, Margo, *Christian Humanism and the Puritan Social Order* (Cambridge: Cambridge University Press, 1987).

Traub, Valerie, *Desire and Anxiety: Circulations of Sexuality in Shakespearean Drama* (London and New York: Routledge, 1992).
——, *The Renaissance of Lesbianism in Early Modern England* (Cambridge: Cambridge University Press, 2002).
——, M. Lindsay Kaplan and Dympna Callaghan (eds), *Feminist Readings of Early Modern Culture* (Cambridge: Cambridge University Press, 1996).
Vendler, Helen, *The Art of Shakespeare's Sonnets* (Cambridge, MA, and London: Harvard University Press, 1997).
Vickers, Brian, *Shakespeare, Co-Author: A Historical Study of Five Collaborative Plays* (Oxford: Oxford University Press, 2002).
Vickers, Nancy J., ' "The blazon of sweet beauty's best": Shakespeare's *Lucrece*', in Parker and Hartman (eds), *Shakespeare and the Question of Theory*, pp. 95–115.
——, 'Diana Described: Scattered Woman and Scattered Rhyme', in Elizabeth Abel (ed.), *Writing and Sexual Difference* (Chicago and London: University of Chicago Press, 1980), pp. 95–109.
Watson, George, *The English Petrarchans* (London: Warburg Institute, 1967).
Weller, Philip, 'Freud's Footprint in *Hamlet*', *Literature/Film Quarterly*, 25.2 (1997): 119–24.
Wells, Stanley, *Looking for Sex in Shakespeare* (Cambridge: Cambridge University Press, 2004).
——, *Shakespeare, Sex, and Love* (Oxford: Oxford University Press, 2010).
Werner, Sarah, *Shakespeare and Feminist Performance: Ideology on Stage* (New York and London: Routledge, 2001).
Wheeler, Richard P., *Shakespeare's Development and the Problem Comedies* (Berkeley: University of California Press, 1981).
Whittier, Gayle, 'The Sonnet's Body and the Body Sonnetized in *Romeo and Juliet*', in Porter (ed.), *Critical Essays on Shakespeare's Romeo and Juliet*, pp. 47–63.
Willbern, David, 'Rape and Revenge in *Titus Andronicus*', *English Literary Renaissance*, 8.2 (March 1978): 159–82.
Williams, Gordon, *A Glossary of Shakespeare's Sexual Language* (London and Atlantic Highlands, NJ: Athlone Press, 1997).
Williamson, Marilyn L., *The Patriarchy of Shakespeare's Comedies* (Detroit: Wayne State University Press, 1986).
Wilson, Daniel, 'Science, Natural Law, and Unwitting Sibling Incest in Eighteenth-Century Literature', *Studies in Eighteenth-Century Culture*, 13 (1984): 249–70.
Wrightson, Keith, *English Society 1580–1680* (London and New York: Routledge, 2003).
Wynne-Davis, Marion, ' "The Swallowing Womb": Consumed and Consuming Women in *Titus Andronicus*', in Valerie Wayne (ed.), *The Matter of Difference: Feminist Criticism of Shakespeare* (Hemel Hempstead: Harvester Wheatsheaf, 1991), pp. 129–51.
Young, Richard B., 'English Petrarke: A Study of Sidney's *Astrophil and Stella*', in Benjamin Christie Nangle (ed.), *Three Studies in the Renaissance: Sidney, Jonson, Milton* (New Haven: Yale University Press, 1958), pp. 5–88.
Zimmerman, Susan (ed.), *Erotic Politics: Desire on the Renaissance Stage* (New York and London: Routledge, 1992).

Index

Adamson, Jane, 95n63
Adelman, Janet, 35n24, 79, 91nn2-3, 94n52, 192, 214-15n90, 224, 230, 247n11, 249n38
affection(s), affects (as sexual passion), 3-4, 13-16, 20, 22, 42, 47, 62n7, 68, 70, 82, 104-5, 111, 138, 143, 148, 157-8, 164, 182, 184, 187, 199, 202, 205-8, 218, 221, 236, 242, 243
agape see love: spiritual
amicitia (male friendship), 4, 184, 197, 200, 210nn20-1
androgynous / androgyny, 172-3, 180n62, 182, 188, 193, 195, 204, 207, 209n5, 213n65
appetite (sexual), 1, 3, 11n7, 14, 18-20, 24, 32-3, 44, 53, 55, 67-8, 78, 81, 85, 149, 156, 226
Aristotle, 67, 120n6, 184, 190, 200, 206, 210n22
Asp, Carolyn, 152n16
Auden, W. H., 187

Bacon, Francis, 26
Baker, Aryn, 65n50
Baldini, Donatella, 122n28
Barber, C. L., 152n16, 240, 246n2, 247n6, 251n70
Barnfield, Richard, 187, 211n39
Bean, John C., 179n56
Beaumont, Francis, and John Fletcher, 247n16
bed trick, 27-30, 33, 36n30
Belsey, Catherine, 27, 61n2, 71, 94n48, 146, 153-4n41, 157, 158, 181, 199, 213n74
Bembo, Pietro, 126
Berggren, Paula S., 94n39
Berry, Philippa, 122n23

blason, 44, 53, 64n39, 124, 135, 136, 142, 151nn2-3, 186, 195
blood (as sexual desire), 13, 18-20, 34n3, 36n27, 78, 81, 105, 120, 187, 221, 225, 226
Bloom, Allan, 35n21
Bloom, Claire, 227
Bly, Mary, 153n28
Boose, Lynda E., 178n45, 234, 244, 248n26, 250n55
Booth, Steven, 36n27
boy actor convention, 9, 134, 167-8, 171, 181, 187-8, 190-2, 195, 209n5, 212n58
Branagh, Kenneth, 49, 186, 211n32, 228, 249n34
Bray, Alan, 183, 210n15
Bray, Gerald, 61n3
Breitenberg, Mark, 42, 62n9, 128, 152n19
Bromley, James M., 210n20
Bromley, Laura G., 46
Brook, Peter, 109
Brown, John Russell, 154n43
buggery, 216; *see also* sodomy
Burt, Richard A., 179n57
Burton, Robert, 26, 151n7, 158, 206

Calderwood, James L., 62n8
Calvin, John, 157
Carroll, William C., 95n53, 144, 152n16
Castiglione, Baldassare, *Book of the Courtier*, 112, 116, 119-20, 122n34, 123n39, 126-7, 200
Charnes, Linda, 213n75
Charney, Maurice, 28, 36n28, 120n1, 151n4, 180n70, 214n81
Charron, Pierre, 156
Chaucer, Geoffrey, 38, 167
Chester, Phyllis, 234

Christie, Julie, 228
Cicero, 11n12, 184, 200, 210n21
Clark, Anna, 44
Close, Glenn, 227, 229
Cohen, Walter, 64n43
Colman, E. A. M., 153n35, 154n42
Cook, Ann Jenalie, 23, 35n18, 36–7n41, 153n38, 177n22, 180n72, 249n50
Cook, Carol, 28, 94n46
courtly love, 6, 20, 143, 156, 175n6
courtly lover, 118, 130
Cox, John, 121n13
Crick, Brian, 250n57
Crooke, Helkiah, 214n88
cross dressing *see* boy actor convention
cuckold / cuckoldry, 5, 53, 56, 78, 81–5, 94n41, 148, 182, 209n11

Daileader, Celia R., 63n33
Daniel, Samuel, 152n21
Dante, Alighieri, 112, 119, 123n44
Davis, Natalie, 92n16
desire
  bisexual, 185, 187, 189–94, 197, 211n40, 212n61
  heterosexual (mixed sex), 8, 10n5, 12nn20–1, 181–2, 184, 186–92, 194–5, 199, 200–1, 203–8, 209n12, 211n40, 212nn60–1, 214n83
  homoerotic, 2, 8–9, 181–5, 188, 190, 191, 193, 194, 197, 198–9, 200–1, 204, 206, 211n32, 212nn60–1
  homosexual, 10n5, 181–2, 183, 186, 187, 190, 191–3, 195–200, 208, 210n29, 211n33, 213n70
  incestuous, 9, 158, 216–19, 220–31, 233, 234–41, 243, 245, 246n6, 247n7, 247n20, 248n25, 250n57, 250n61
  same-sex, 8, 181, 184–6, 192, 194–5, 202, 212n57, 213n75, 214n82, 214–15nn90–1
  sexual / erotic, 1–9, 10n1, 11nn15–16, 13–26, 28–34, 35n24, 36n38, 39–44, 47, 55, 58–61, 62n10, 65n49, 66, 69–72, 74, 76–83, 87, 92n21, 97, 101–6, 108, 110–11, 116, 118–20, 123nn43–4, 124–5, 128–32, 134–44, 146–50, 152n25, 153nn38–9, 155–8, 169–70, 173–4, 175n6, 180n66, 181, 188, 190, 193, 210n22, 213n64, 219, 240, 249n34
Dessens, Marliss C., 36n30
DiGangi, Mario, 212n61

Dod, John, and Robert Cleaver, 166, 177n34
Dolan, Francis E., 168
Dollimore, Jonathan, 25, 153n29, 186
Downie, Penny, 229
Dreher, Diane Elizabeth, 250n56, 251n76
Du Bartas, Guillaume de Saluste, 172
Dubrow, Heather, 152
Dundas, Judith, 121n9
Dusinberre, Juliet, 11–12n18, 92n15, 176n15, 176n17

Elizabeth I (Queen), 68
Elliot, Anthony, 91n1
Elyot, Sir Thomas, 68
Empson, William, 153n37
Enterline, Lynn, 54, 64n39
Erasmus, Desiderius, 157
Erickson, Amy Louise, 178n41
Erickson, Peter, 96n64, 172, 180n64
Erlich, Avi, 248n31
Eros, 5, 6, 71–2, 123n42, 155, 174, 194
eyes (visual attraction), 6–7, 28, 43, 44, 47, 71, 80, 94n44, 97–120, 120n1, 120–1n8, 121nn9–10, 121nn13–14, 122n25, 126–7, 133, 142, 146, 147, 149, 201

fancy
  as fickle desire, 6, 62n10, 98–102, 104, 106–8, 110, 114, 116–20, 138, 230–1
  as imagination, 99, 108–10, 194
Fenton, Geoffrey, 120n2, 180n63
Fernie, Ewan, 25
Ferrand, Jacques 67
Ficino, Marsilio, 97, 110, 119–20, 120n2, 122n27, 172, 180n63
Fiedler, Lesley A., 51, 58, 64n37, 93n30, 245, 250–1n67, 251n74
Fiennes, Ralph, 249n43, 249n49
Fineman, Joel, 120–1n8, 34n5
Fletcher, John, 200, 202, 220
Ford, Jane M., 224
Ford, John, 218
Foucault, Michel, 10n4
Freud, Sigmund, 9, 36n38, 92n21, 110, 119, 170, 179n60, 216–17, 226, 246n6, 250n62
  Freudian, 25, 79, 212n60, 214n77, 224, 225, 229, 239
  post-Freudian, 10n6, 217, 234
friend (as lover), 4, 11n19, 82, 196, 200, 211n40

friendship (same-sex), 4, 11n12, 12n20, 181, 184, 188, 190, 198–9, 200–1, 202, 204–6, 208, 210nn21–2, 213nn74–5, 214n82, 214n89, 214–15n90
Froide, Amy M., 164, 178n41

Gajdusek, R. E., 248n21
Gajowski, Evelyn, 152–3n27
Galen, 34n2, 67, 91n12, 211–12n47
Garber, Marjorie, 92n22, 179n58, 213n64, 214–15n90
Garner, Shirley Nelson, 206
Garrison, John S., 210n21
Gataker, Thomas, 157
Gibbons, Brian, 35n19, 211n33
Gibson, Mel, 227–8
Giddens, Anthony, 10n3, 11n15
Gielgud, John, 248n32
Gillis, John R., 214n83
Giraud, René, 214n77
Globe Theatre, 7, 171
Goddard, Harold C., 248n31
Gohlke, Madelon (Sprengnether), 91n5
Goldberg, Jonathan, 177n23, 186, 210n15, 210n27, 211n33
Gouge, William, 45, 88, 157–8, 162, 168, 176n18
Greenblatt, Stephen, 40, 62n7, 91n4
Greene, Gayle, 94n45
Greene, Thomas, 243
Guthrie, Tyrone, 186
Guy-Bray, Stephen, 181, 201

Hagstrum, Jean H., 11n16, 12n20, 35n25, 123n42, 175n6, 214n81
Hammond, Paul, 11n10, 213n66
Hanley, C., 250n61
Hattaway, Michael, 63n24
Herlie, Eileen, 226, 229
Herman, Judith, and Lisa Hirschman, 249–50n52
Higgins, Lynn A., and Brenda R. Silver, 62n18
Hodgson, Barbara, 95n60
Homily of the State of Matrimony, 156, 157, 162, 163, 174
Hooker, Richard, 3, 34n8, 58, 64–5n46
Hopkins, Lisa, 34n12, 159, 180n74, 209n11, 214n81, 249n42
Howard Jean E., 9, 153n32, 192, 211–12n47
Howard, Jean E., and Phyllis Rackin, 49, 63n30, 93n30, 93n32, 94n50, 95n60
Hull Suzanne, 92n14
Hunter, G. K., 153n31

imagination (its role in love), 7, 108–9, 118
incest / incestuous, 216–21, 224, 227, 234–8, 240–1, 246–7n6, 247n16, 249–50n52, 250–1n67

Jacobi, Derek, 227, 228
Jaeger, C. Stephen, 122n22, 197
James I, King, 20, 183
  Bible, 13, 113
Jardine, Lisa, 177n33, 193, 209n5, 212n56
Jones, Ann Rosalind, 10n3
Jones, Ernest, 224–6, 248n24, 249n33
Jonson, Ben, 123n41, 214n88

Kahn, Coppélia, 45, 47, 62–3n21, 63n30, 73, 91n3, 93n28, 94n41, 167, 179n50, 247n19
Kahn, Paul, 93–4n38
Keats, John, 110
Keenan, Jillian, 121n12
Keevak, Michael, 92–3n25, 187
Kiernan, Pauline, 154n42
Kimbrough, Robert, 180n63
Kirsch, Arthur, 180n70
Knoppers, Laura Lunger, 36n40
Kott, Jan, 107

La Primaudaye, Pierre de, 59, 92n14, 119, 157
Lacan, Jacques, 91n4, 128, 152n16, 152n18
Lacanian (analysis), 152n16, 64n41
Laqueur, Thomas, 91–2n12
lechery *see* lust
Leggatt, Alexander, 166
Levi-Strauss, Claude, 251n73
Levine, Laura, 63n25
Levitical law, 218, 220
Lewis, C. S., 11n14, 175n6
Little, Arthur L. Jr., 213n64
love
  homosocial, 9, 182, 185, 186, 193–4, 201, 210n29, 214n81, 223
  romantic, 1–2, 4–9, 11n15, 17, 18, 20, 21, 55, 61n4, 70–2, 97–102, 104, 106, 108–19, 124, 127, 130, 132–4, 139, 140–4, 146, 149–50, 153n39, 154nn44–5, 155–8, 164, 169, 170, 175, 176n20, 184, 187, 190–1, 193, 201, 203, 207–8, 214n81, 217, 243, 247n19
  same-sex, 190, 196, 199–201, 203, 205, 206–8, 209nn11–12, 214n83, 214–15n90
  spiritual (*agape*), 71, 72, 98, 110–14,

119–20, 123n44, 136, 142, 143,
    153n30, 154n45, 155, 161–2,
    174–5, 197, 203
lover (romantic), 19, 24, 28, 53, 100–2,
    119, 132, 139, 169, 196, 222, 224
love's mind, 103–6, 109, 121n11,
    121n13
Luhrmann, Baz, 186
lust / lustful
  female, 5, 67, 69–70, 73–87, 90,
    93n35, 94n39, 124, 170, 190,
    214n88, 224, 236
  gender neutral, 1, 4, 12n20, 13, 16,
    19, 38, 61n2, 70–1, 155, 158,
    179n59
  male, 3, 16, 17–24, 26–8, 31, 33,
    39–44, 47–9, 50–3, 56–61, 82,
    87, 91n10, 100, 119, 130, 139,
    180n66, 182–3, 188, 201, 217,
    247n17
Lyly, John, 126, 184, 216

McCabe, Richard, 247n16, 248n23
MacCary, Thomas, 122n33
Maclean, Ian, 91n9
McLuskie, Kathleen, 35n19, 64n35,
    93n37
Mallette, Richard, 214n82
Mangan, Michael, 179n49
Marlowe, Christopher, 73, 78, 93n29,
    93n33
marriage
  companionate, 8, 11–12n18, 68, 71,
    92n18, 107, 156–63, 168–70, 174,
    176n13, 176n20, 177n27, 177n29,
    177n33, 179n56, 199–200,
    213n74
  heterosexual, 4–9, 12n20, 21,
    23–4, 26–7, 28–31, 33, 35n18,
    35nn20–1, 35n25, 36n31, 36n35,
    36–7n41, 39–40, 56, 61n4, 68,
    81–5, 90, 97, 107, 118–21, 134,
    150, 155–75, 175n3, 176n17,
    177n30, 178n39, 178n41, 178n45,
    179n59, 181, 182, 184, 190–1,
    192, 200–6, 208–9, 213n64,
    214n81, 214–15n90, 215n91, 216,
    221, 226, 231, 235–6, 239, 241–2,
    243–6, 247n14, 248n23
  intimate, 158–60, 170–5, 175n6,
    175–6n9, 176nn15–16, 176n18
  patriarchal, 8, 155–6, 160–70,
    173–4, 177n33, 221, 234–5, 245
  political, 158–9, 177n22, 223, 245
  queer, 191, 192, 213n64, 213n70
Marston, John, 191
Masten, Jeffrey, 11n10, 184

Maus, Katherine Eisaman, 62n11,
    62n20
Meek, Richard, 115
Memmo, Paul E. Jr., 122n23, 123n44
Mendelson, Sarah, and Patricia
    Crawford, 155, 175n3,
    178nn39–40, 214n89
Menon, Madhavi, 65n49, 122n30
Middleton, Thomas, 95n55, 95n61
Mikesell, Margaret Lael, 168–9
Moglen, Helene, 212n60
monster / monstrous, 235–6, 214n88
Montaigne, Michel Eyquem de, *Essays*
    (Florio's translation), 68, 157, 184,
    205–6, 216, 239
More, Sir Thomas, 92n15
Muir, Kenneth, 95n54
Mukherji, Subha, 28, 36n31

Nagel, Joane, 63n30
Nashe, Thomas, 20, 213n72
Neo-Platonic love / philosophy, 6–7,
    43, 72, 98, 107, 111, 119–20,
    122n23, 123n43
Neo-Platonism / Neo-Platonist, 58, 97,
    110
Newman, Karen, 179n53
Niccoles, Alexander, 40
Nordlund, Marcus, 176n20
Novy, Marianne, 153n34, 164, 198

Oedipal desire / Oedipus complex, 66,
    217, 224–9, 248n24, 248n31,
    249n42
  pre-Oedipal phase, 66, 79, 84,
    85, 91n1, 217, 224, 226, 229,
    238–9
Olivier, Laurence, 226–7, 229
Orgel, Stephen, 62n10, 191, 196,
    197
Ovid, 114
  Metamorphoses (Golding's
    translation), 53–4, 234

Parker, Oliver, 186
Partridge, Eric, 48
Paster, Gail Kern, 34n2, 91n8
Patricia, Anthony Guy, 211n53
Paunez, Arpad, 249
Peele, George, 50, 52, 63n32, 63–4n34,
    78
Pequigney, Joseph, 198, 211n40,
    212n61, 213n70
Petrarch, *Canzoniere*, 119, 123n44,
    125–7, 129–31, 137, 150–1n1,
    151n8, 151n12, 152nn20–1,
    152n25, 153n30

Petrarchan love convention, 6–7, 11–12n18, 43, 64n39, 97–8, 112, 122n23, 123–43, 149–50, 150–1n1, 151n4, 153n28, 156, 186, 189
Petrarchan lover, 19, 20, 43, 54, 55, 124, 127–30, 132–4, 138–46, 149, 158, 162, 185, 194, 196, 200, 222
Petrarchism, 125–6, 152n19, 152n22
philia (amicable bond), 174, 194, 210n22
Pico della Mirandola, Giovanni, 58
Plato, 58, 97, 103, 120n2, 172, 180n63
Platonic ideal, 104, 181, 196
Plutarch, *Lives of the Noble Grecians and Romans* (North's translation), 229, 231–2, 233
Moralia, 183, 187, 190, 197
Prynne, William, 172, 180n62
Putney, Rufus, 249n48
Puttenham, George, 117

Queer studies / theory, 2, 10n5, 187

Rackin, Phyllis, 67, 94n40, 150–1n1, 177n33, 212n53
Rainolds, John, 182
Ranald, Margaret Loftus, 30, 35n20, 63n22, 154n44, 177n30, 178n45, 179n56, 213n75
rape, 5, 28, 36n30, 40–57, 60–1, 62n14, 62n18, 63n25, 64nn35–6, 64n37, 65n50, 69, 70, 76, 90, 201, 245
Redgrave, Vanessa, 249n43, 249n49
rhetoric, 63n31, 114–18, 122n30
Rich[e], Barnabe, 67, 119, 123n36
Roman de la Rose, 10n1
Rose, Mary Beth, 92n18, 160
Rossiter, A. P., 17
Rougement, Denis de, 11n17

Saint Augustine, 3, 180n66
Saint Paul
 1 Corinthians, 39, 113, 180n73
 to the Ephesians, 160–1, 162, 173, 190, 205
 to the Romans, 1
Sawday, Jonathan, 152n2
Schalkwyk, David, 55, 64n41, 110, 121n19, 194
Schmidt, Alexander, 121n11, 213n63
Schumway, David R., 61–2n4, 157
Schwartz, Murray M., 180n69
Scruton, Roger, 123n43, 153n39

Sedgwick, Eva Kosofsky, 52, 190, 200, 211n44
'Sermon on Whoredom and Uncleanness' in *Book of Homilies*, 38–9
service (sexual), 23–4, 194
sex (as gender), 2, 13
sexuality
 female, 5, 10n3, 25, 59, 62n14, 67–87, 90, 92n17, 134, 138, 144, 161, 170–1, 173–4
 gender non-specific, 1, 2, 10n3, 10n5, 20, 34n1, 35n25, 39, 181, 217, 246–7n6
 male, 40, 56, 58, 60–1, 63n30, 143, 158, 188
Shakespeare, William
 PLAYS
 All's Well That Ends Well, 5, 16, 27–30, 33, 35n24, 36n30, 36n35, 48, 69, 100, 140, 217, 231, 241
 Antony and Cleopatra, 3, 4, 5–6, 8, 9, 16, 69, 70, 79, 99, 110, 121n17, 159, 170–5, 179n59, 180n64, 180nn68–9, 180n70, 180n72, 180n74, 185–6, 219, 222–4
 As You Like It, 7, 9, 68–9, 78, 97, 102, 124, 125, 133–4, 139–41, 150, 153nn32–3, 153n34, 153n38, 182, 190–3, 204, 206–8, 213n64, 244
 Comedy of Errors, 8, 58, 138, 150, 160–2, 163
 Coriolanus, 9, 50, 159, 182, 229–33, 249n38, 249n40, 249nn42–3, 249nn48–9
 Cymbeline, 35n15, 48, 52–4, 56, 57–8, 60, 64n37, 84–5, 90, 95–6n63, 97, 211–12n47, 219, 240, 241–2
 Hamlet, 3, 9, 47, 58, 66–7, 78–9, 144–5, 158, 184, 217, 219, 220–2, 223, 224–9, 234, 237, 248nn25–6, 248n27, 248nn31–2, 249nn33–4
 1 Henry IV, 55, 144, 159, 177n23, 184–5, 210n27
 2 Henry IV, 55–6, 64n42, 88–9, 95n60, 147, 164, 178n40, 185
 Henry V, 49–50, 61, 63n30, 76, 88–9, 95n59, 159, 182, 185
 1 Henry VI, 23, 49, 72–4, 76, 78, 93nn29–30, 93nn32–3, 93n35, 94n50
 2 Henry VI, 52, 74, 83, 159
 3 Henry VI, 74–5, 76, 77, 93n35
 Henry VIII, 220
 Julius Caesar, 4, 159–60, 161, 185

King John, 83, 133, 158–9, 231, 249n44
King Lear, 9, 69, 77, 85–7, 93n37, 93–4n38, 94n52, 94–5n53, 196, 217, 232, 234–9, 240, 243–4, 246, 250nn56–7, 250n60, 250n61–2
Love's Labour's Lost, 6–7, 15, 97, 102, 110–20, 122n28, 122n30, 122nn32–3, 123n42, 123n44, 126–7, 132, 134, 138–9, 142, 146–8, 152n16
Macbeth, 39, 41, 62n8, 158, 217
Measure for Measure, 4, 13, 15, 17, 20–8, 29, 30–2, 33–4, 35nn18–19, 35n21, 35n24, 35n25, 36n34, 36n40, 36–7n41, 38, 46, 89–90, 91n10, 94n49, 95n61, 217, 219–20, 221
Merchant of Venice, 98–9, 141–2, 169–70, 190–1, 198–200, 208, 213nn74–5, 234
Merry Wives of Windsor, 10n2, 31, 48, 55–6, 58, 85, 94n43, 155–6
Midsummer Night's Dream, 6, 34n4, 47, 63n25, 93n35, 97, 99, 102–4, 105, 106–10, 111, 112, 113, 114, 115, 118, 121n10, 121n12, 121n14, 121n16, 121n19, 196, 204–6, 208, 214–15n90, 217, 234
Much Ado About Nothing, 14, 81, 94n46, 100, 148–50, 154nn43–4, 182, 218, 219
Othello, 4, 10n20, 16–17, 23, 24, 48, 51, 69, 81–2, 83–4, 90, 95–6n63, 104, 158, 161, 168, 185–6, 210n29, 211n32, 235
Pericles, 9, 56–7, 64n43, 89–90, 95n62, 217, 236, 237, 240–1, 243, 246
Phoenix and the Turtle, 173, 203
Rape of Lucrece, 1, 5, 31, 40–7, 49, 50, 51, 53, 59, 61, 62nn9–10, 62n11, 62n14, 62n18, 62–3n21, 63n22, 63–4n34, 69, 70, 81, 113, 115
Richard II, 159, 183
Richard III, 46, 63n31, 75, 145–6, 159
Romeo and Juliet, 7, 15, 22, 31, 36n27, 48, 58, 67, 69, 88, 92n22, 97, 98, 100–1, 105–6, 125, 129–32, 135–7, 144, 147, 149, 150, 152n22, 152–3n27, 153nn28–9, 153nn30–1, 153n35, 175, 186–7
Taming of the Shrew, 8, 48, 145–6, 150, 163–70, 171, 178n43, 178n45, 178–9n48, 179nn49–50, 179nn52–3, 179nn56–7
The Tempest, 2, 9, 60–1, 64n37, 65n49, 69, 82–3, 97, 240, 243–6, 251n74, 251n76
Timon of Athens, 50, 87, 95nn55–6
Titus Andronicus, 50–2, 54–5, 60, 61, 63n32, 63–4n34, 64n39, 69, 75–6, 78, 90
Troilus and Cressida, 4, 14, 17–20, 28, 30, 31, 32–3, 42, 66, 68, 79–80, 88, 94n45, 104–5, 106, 121n13, 126, 135, 148, 156, 182–3, 196
Twelfth Night, 7, 9, 69, 97, 99, 103, 123n36, 124, 128–9, 151n2, 182, 190–1, 192–8, 200, 207, 208, 212nn56–7, 212n58, 212nn60–1, 213nn64–5, 213n66, 213n70, 218, 247n19
Two Gentlemen of Verona, 55, 64n41, 100, 127–8, 132, 138, 184, 200–1, 202, 208
Two Noble Kinsmen, 184, 201–4, 205, 206, 208–9, 214nn81–2, 214n83
Venus and Adonis, 1, 43, 69–72, 92–3n25, 93n28, 102, 112, 122n25
The Winter's Tale, 23–4, 36n27, 38, 59, 67, 82–4, 90, 94n51, 95–6n63, 96n64, 97, 99, 142–4, 147, 149, 242–3, 246

SONNETS
Sonnets, 8, 120–1n8, 187, 210n27
Sonnet 4, 194
Sonnet 14, 113
Sonnet 20, 101, 114, 187–8
Sonnet 21, 127
Sonnet 22, 188
Sonnet 25, 188
Sonnet 40, 170, 189
Sonnet 42, 189–90, 211n42
Sonnet 46, 101
Sonnet 52, 188
Sonnet 57, 15
Sonnet 87, 189
Sonnet 93, 190
Sonnet 97, 190
Sonnet 105, 196
Sonnet 113, 104
Sonnet 114, 101, 104, 116
Sonnet 116, 155, 190
Sonnet 121, 187
Sonnet 129, 19, 27, 31, 38, 40, 41–2, 61, 155, 188, 190
Sonnet 130, 124

Shakespeare, William (*cont.*)
  Sonnet 131, 190
  Sonnet 133, 188–9
  Sonnet 135, 3, 14–15, 34nn5–6, 190
  Sonnet 137, 101, 105
  Sonnet 141, 102
  Sonnet 144, 189
  Sonnet 146, 60–1
  Sonnet 147, 21, 101
  Sonnet 148, 101–2, 116
  Sonnet 151, 15–16, 59, 121n15
  Sonnet 152, 102
Shannon, Laurie, 209n12
Shapiro, James, 212n57
Shepherd, Simon, 93n35
Sidney, Sir Philip, 11n7, 126, 211n42
Simmons, James R. Jr., 248n32
Sinfield, Alan, 31, 35n16, 44, 200, 211n46, 214n82, 215n91
Singer, Irving, 11n13, 123n35, 151n8, 176n13, 180n71
Slights, William, 150–1n1
Smith, Bruce R., 192, 210n17
Smith, Hilda L., 92n16
Snaswell, Robert, 170–1
sodomy, 183, 210nn15–16, 210n17, 210n28, 211n33, 213n72
'Solemnization of Matrimony' (in *Book of Common Prayer*, 1559), 1, 4, 26, 33, 40, 172, 233
Sophocles, 217–18
Sowernam, Esther, 92n16
Spenser, Edmund, 123n44
spousal contracts, 23–4, 28–30, 35n18, 36n34, 60, 180n72, 233
Sprengnether, Madelon, 249n40
Stallybrass, Peter, 67, 91n8
Stanivukovic, Goran, 10n5
Stern, Jeffrey, 250n60
Sternberg, Robert J., 154n45, 175n1
Stilling, Roger, 130
Stimpson, Catherine R., 51, 62n14
Stone, Lawrence, 162, 230
Stubbes, Philip, 181–2, 193
Surrey, Earl of, 126, 152n25
Swetnam, Joseph, 92n16

Targoff, Ramie, 151n12, 153n30
Taylor, Gary, 93n33
Taylor, Mark, 247n7, 251n68
Tennant, David, 228–9

Thomas, Keith, 81, 93n31
Thorne, Alison, 116, 120n6, 121n17, 122n31
Tilney, Henry, 68, 157, 163
Todd, Margo, 177n27
Traub, Valerie, 92n17, 95n57, 121n14, 192, 194, 206, 209nn4–5, 210n20, 214nn88–9, 214–15n90

Vendler, Helen, 34n6, 101
venereal disease, 18–19, 87–90, 95n57, 95n59, 189
Vickers, Brian, 63–4n34, 95n55
Vickers, Nancy J., 43–4
Vives, Juan Luis, 68, 156, 234

Watson, George, 151n11
Wayne, Valerie, 160, 177n29
Webster, John, 218, 247n17
Weller, Philip, 229
Wells, Stanley, 8, 12n21, 15, 28, 34n5, 64n44, 179n59, 210n28
Werner, Sarah, 178–9n48
Wheeler, Richard P., 35n24, 246n2, 247n8, 247n10
Wilkins, George, 64nn43–4, 95n62, 239
will (as resolve, intention), 3, 18, 23, 42, 62n9
will (sexual desire), 3–6, 9, 11n7, 13–20, 22–3, 25, 26–7, 29–30, 32–4, 34n5, 34n8, 39–43, 50, 55, 56, 60, 61, 68, 70, 77, 79, 84, 97–9, 105–6, 109, 118, 120, 121n13, 135, 146, 149, 161, 163, 180n66, 184, 188, 190, 191, 194, 195, 196, 234, 237, 245
Willbern, David, 55
Williams, Gordon, 34n3, 94n44
Williamson, Marilyn L., 35n25, 36n35, 240
Wilson, Daniel, 247–8n20
Wilson, John Dover, 63n32, 248n32
Wright, Thomas, 15, 34n8
Wrightson, Keith, 177n33
Wyatt, Sir Thomas, 126, 130, 136, 151n12
Wynne-Davis, Marion, 64n36, 94n50

Young, Richard B., 151n9

Zefferelli, Franco, 227

EU representative:
Easy Access System Europe
Mustamäe tee 50, 10621 Tallinn, Estonia
Gpsr.requests@easproject.com

www.ingramcontent.com/pod-product-compliance
Lightning Source LLC
Chambersburg PA
CBHW052058300426
44117CB00013B/2180